PAST AND PROLOGUE

PAST AND PROLOGUE

POLITICS AND MEMORY IN THE AMERICAN REVOLUTION

Michael D. Hattem

Yale
UNIVERSITY PRESS
New Haven & London

Published with assistance from the Annie Burr Lewis Fund.
Published with assistance from the Mary Cady Tew Memorial Fund.

Yale University Press books may be purchased in quantity for educational, business, or promotional use. For information, please e-mail sales.press@yale.edu (U.S. office) or sales@yaleup.co.uk (U.K. office).

Designed by
Set in type by
Printed in the United States of America.

Library of Congress Control Number: 2020935118
ISBN 978-0-300-23496-1 (hardcover : alk. paper)

A catalogue record for this book is available from the British Library.

This paper meets the requirements of ANSI/NISO Z39.48-1992 (Permanence of Paper).

10 9 8 7 6 5 4 3 2 1

For Lucien, Tristan, and Lorelei,

and my parents, Sharon and Robert

CONTENTS

ACKNOWLEDGMENTS

Though the cover of this book suggests that I am the sole author, it could not have been written but for the indispensable contributions, support, and encouragement of many. First, I would like to thank my wife, Veronica, my two sons, Lucien and Tristan, and my daughter, Lorelei. My brothers, Sam, Dave, and Rich lent me more support and encouragement than any one person deserves, as did my mother who passed away in 1994 and my father who passed away a few months shy of the completion of the dissertation on which this book is based. I must also thank my graduate advisor, Joanne Freeman, who was willing to take a chance on a thirty-six-year-old graduate of the City College of New York. Along the way, she has repeatedly gone far above and beyond the advisor's call of duty, thereby teaching me a great deal about mentorship and professionalism. The opportunity to pay that forward is a real privilege. For her astute and timely guidance and wisdom and her unfailing support and friendship, I am forever grateful and eternally indebted. In addition, I would like to thank my other dissertation committee members: Steve Pincus, whose early and continued interest in and support for both this work and my career has been critically important and whose unmatched intellectual rigor as a historian will serve as a model for the rest of my life; and Benjamin H. Irvin, who early on helped broaden my perspective temporally, geographically, and thematically and later offered important, informed, and very timely professional advice and support.

I would also like to take this opportunity to acknowledge the immense impact that my undergraduate advisors—the late (and sorely missed) Edwin G. Burrows, Darren Staloff, and Carol Berkin—had (and continue to have) on both my professional and personal development. This book is the direct product of the encouragement they showed to a thirty-something community college student who had never graduated from high school yet had nevertheless developed an obscene obsession with early America and early American historiography. As a community-college student taking their classes at senior CUNY schools, it was a revelatory experience for me to talk with and be taken seriously by such eminent historians. Their support for me, from our first meetings to the present, has been unceasing and from them I have learned a great deal about what it means to be a good historian, scholar, teacher, and colleague. I should also acknowledge my gratitude to my professors and fellow students at the City College of New York, especially Gregory P. Downs, Joshua Clough, Will Hickox, and Fidel Tavarez. I would also like to thank everyone at the CUNY Baccalaureate for Interdisciplinary Studies—particularly Kim Hartswick, Rafal Szczurowski, Beth Kneller, Kate McPherson, and Jean Myers—for being especially supportive of me and for the amazing work they do in managing one of the best undergraduate programs in the country. I must also thank Jacob Kramer for giving me my first opportunity to do a research project at the Borough of Manhattan Community College, where I began this academic journey over ten years ago with only a dusty, fifteen-year-old GED.

Like the early national historians whom I write about in chapter 4, I, too, have been fortunate to be part of a supportive network of fellow historians. From the early American community at Yale University while I was a graduate student, I must thank Michael Blaakman, the contemporary epitome of "a scholar and a gentleman," as well as Zachary Conn, Alejandra Dubcovsky, Catherine Treesh, Emily Yankowitz, and the rest of the small but active Yale early American community. I count myself incredibly fortunate to call them friends and colleagues. My fellow members of *The Junto: A Group Blog on Early American History* have also been invaluable to me as both colleagues and friends. In particular, I must thank my fellow hosts of *The JuntoCast: A Podcast on Early American History*, Ken Owen and Roy Rogers. Ken has been a constant presence who offers both great historical insight and professional advice, and I am a better historian (and academic) thanks to his friendship over the last eight years. Roy, too, was an invaluable colleague and friend who, on more than one occasion, helped me keep both the past and present in perspective. I am especially grateful to those who were generous enough to offer feedback on the obscenely lengthy first drafts of chapters, including Mark Boonshoft, who tolerates far more of my online ranting (both about history and music) than he should, and Christopher F. Minty, who read more of and offered more crucial feedback on the dissertation this book came from than anyone outside of my committee, especially in its rough, early stages. Greg Brooking also offered valuable feedback on the prologue at a very inconvenient time for him, for which I am greatly appreciative. All three have been invaluable as periodic sounding boards. I am also grateful to the generous scholars at the CUNY Early American Republic Seminar—including John Blanton, Nora Slonimsky, Michael Crowder, and Laura Ping—for offering valuable feedback on a seminar paper based on my dissertation prospectus, inviting me to give my first presentation of this research at their 2015 conference. When workshopping my last chapter prior to final revisions there, I received important feedback and suggestions from David Waldstreicher, Michael Crowder, and Evan Turiano, for which I am highly grateful.

I must also thank my friend, and former Yale librarian, David J. Gary, for helping me in a number of ways, including tracking down sources, reading chapter drafts, listening to my periodic rantings, and generally offering invaluable support and encouragement. He made a really significant contribution to the early American community while he was at Yale, and I have been fortunate to continue to draw on his time and friendship now that he is at the American Philosophical Society. I should also thank my former boss and colleagues at the Papers of Benjamin Franklin for their support, particularly Ellen Cohn and Kate Ohno, from whom I learned a great deal about documentary editing, scholarly integrity, and historical research in general. Similarly, I would like to thank my colleagues in the history departments at both The New School and Knox College, where I taught while revising the manuscript, particularly Cate Denial, who has been an excellent model of thoughtful and inclusive pedagogy. I am also very grateful to the fellows of the Bright Institute for their important feedback on the final chapter. I must also thank James R. Vivian, Stephanie Reid, and Daniel Swann at the Yale National Initiative to strengthen teaching in public schools®, where I worked part time while completing my dissertation and afterward. Their dedication to bringing the intellectual and material resources of academia to bear on improving public school teaching has only reinforced my own belief in the importance of that work.

I would also like to thank a number of scholars who have engaged with or supported me or my work generally, including (but not limited to) Rosemarie Zagarri, R. B. Bernstein, John Demos, Karin Wulf, Annette Gordon-Reed, Douglas Bradburn, Jeffrey L. Pasley, Jon Butler, Jan Lewis, Pat Bonomi, and Benjamin Carp. I must also thank Andrew Shankman for the invaluable feedback in his reader report and Eric Nelson for a very helpful report on an article draft drawn from the dissertation.

The research and writing of this manuscript was supported financially by the American Philosophical Society, the Library Company of Philadelphia, the Historical Society of Pennsylvania, the Massachusetts Historical Society, the New-York Historical Society, the Omohundro Institute for Early American History and Culture, and the Smith National Library at Mount Vernon. I am indebted to the staff at those institutions, including Michael Ryan and Ted O'Reilly at the N-YHS; Jim Green and Connie King at the Library Company; Earle Spamer and Patrick Spero at the APS; and Douglas Bradburn, Michael Kane, and Stephen McLeod at the Smith National Library at Mount Vernon, where I was fortunate to receive two fellowships while working first on the dissertation and then the manuscript. My thanks go to the institutions at which I performed unfunded research as well.

Finally, I would like to thank my editor, Adina Berk, my three readers, including Andy Shankman, and everyone at Yale University Press who helped bring the publication of this book to fruition in any way, not least for their early and consistent confidence in the manuscript. This book would not exist without each and every individual and institution above. I am gratefully indebted to all those mentioned (and the many who have gone unmentioned), and I hope that one day I get the opportunity to pay their support forward.

PROLOGUE

Revolutions are often understood as decisive breaks with the past, both in the moment and by subsequent generations. For example, after the establishment of a republic in the late eighteenth century, French revolutionaries sought to erase their monarchical past by radically redefining their calendar and, in the process, their very sense of time. Following the Bolshevik Revolution in Russia, Stalin employed historians to craft an official version of its history with himself at the center and had historical documents that contradicted his own narrative destroyed. After a number of nineteenth-century colonial revolutions, many Latin American historians simply excluded their colonial pasts from their new national histories. For the United States, too, its revolution is often understood as a rejection of the past represented by the Old World of Europe, which was rendered irrelevant in the wake of the New World's first modern republic.

It is a long-held commonplace that Americans have traditionally been less interested in their past than in the present and future. This disregard for the past is supposed to have been at least partly a product of the revolutionary era. The eminent American cultural historian Michael Kammen summarized this idea: "As an attitudinal consequence of the Revolution,

Americans overwhelmingly believed that they had been liberated from the past: alike from the incubus of Old World history and from their own colonial heritage of nonage and oppression."[1] As a nation of Crèvecœur's "new men" forging a new republic through revolution, revolutionary Americans supposedly developed "a strong appreciation of the uniqueness of their political situation," which led to "a profound feeling that a radical break with the past was occurring."[2] Similarly, the historian Antonello Gerbi has argued, "America as a political concept came into being as anti-history."[3] Like Thomas Jefferson, Americans were supposed to have liked "the dreams of the future better than the history of the past."[4] The past then seems to have had little relevance to those revolutionary republican citizens and the new society they were creating.

Yet, unlike their revolutionary counterparts in France and Russia, Americans did not try to reset the historical clock or erase their pre-revolutionary past.[5] Rather, the American Revolution actually made the past matter more than ever before. How colonists and, later, Americans understood the past is crucial to understanding how they understood the Revolution. Changes in Americans' historical understandings of a variety of shared pasts both shaped and were shaped by the political and cultural developments of the Revolution. Therefore, understanding the interrelationship between history, culture, and politics in this period is crucial to understanding why the Revolution came about and why it played out as it did.

Before 1760, most British American colonists thought of British history as their own. That is, they held a form of cultural ownership over the British past. By the 1780s and 1790s, however, that was no longer the case, as the British past came to be replaced by a newly shared American past. This transformation played a critical role in shaping both the political dynamics of the coming of the Revolution and the political and cultural origins of early American national identity.

In the eighteenth century, history mattered. If you were to walk into a Boston courtroom in the 1760s, the first thing you would probably notice would be the enormous gold-framed portraits of Charles II and James II—Stuart monarchs of seventeenth-century England—hanging on the walls. If you were to walk into a Philadelphia coffeehouse in 1775 and express support for the local Committee of Safety, potential loyalists might call you a "Leveller" or a "Whig" and you would likely refer to them as "Tories," all terms dating back to and drawing on connotations from the British past of the previous century. If you were to walk into a bookshop or printer's office in the 1790s, you would see a significant number of publications in all genres drawing on the new nation's historical past, from general and state histories to popular poems, drama, and fiction. Indeed, the historical past pervaded revolutionary politics and culture in the eighteenth century in a way that historians are yet to fully recognize or reckon with.

"Nations," the historian Ronald Grigor Suny wrote, "are congealed histories."[6] Similarly, Anthony Kemp argued, "The idea of history is one of the most fundamental determinants of social imagination."[7] As the tangible political and cultural expression of a collective identity forged in a society's social imagination, a nation cannot long exist as such without a shared past. That being the case, to understand the creation of the United States as a nation it is necessary to understand the ways in which colonists shed their previously shared British past and created a newly shared American past. But how are such shared pasts created?

Memory lives in the shadow cast by history. Rather than trying to arrive at an accurate rendering of the past—which is a relatively contemporary academic development—the cultural and political use of history is primarily about providing the "shared sentiments, symbols, and social explanations necessary for an integrative national identity."[8] Indeed, "the stories people tell about their pasts have more to do with the continuing shoring up of self-understanding than with historical 'truths.'"[9] This often requires "using the present as evidence for its own past" as part of a "search for a past which is palpably and visibly present."[10] Shared pasts are, by nature, fundamentally constructed and present-minded. Therefore, uncovering how shared pasts were constructed by revolutionary Americans will tell us much about how they understood the revolutionary moment in which they were living and why they navigated as they did the twists and turns along the way.

Benedict Anderson, one of the foremost historians of nationalism over the last two decades, has argued, "If nation-states are widely conceded to be 'new' and 'historical,' the nations to which they give political expression always loom out of an immemorial past."[11] However, the postcolonial nations of the Western Hemisphere, with their origins in the more recent recorded past, have never fit easily within the mold created by scholars of European nationalism. Because of that, historians of New World nationalism have defined it primarily by its differences from European nationalism. They have argued that the diversity of the new nations of the Western Hemisphere, particularly the United States, "undermined any attempt to envision the nation along the lines of the European paradigm as a people bound and distinguished by common descent, a deep collective past, or homogenous cultural traditions." As a result, historians have argued, these new nations were forced to rely on "grievances and interests rather than on ethno-nationalist ideas of primordial differences with their mother country or myths of some previous common history as a nation."[12] Historians of early national America have largely concurred, with one concluding that "[early American] nationalism rejected the past."[13]

This book challenges this exceptionalist understanding of the nature and development of early American nationalism. Rather, it argues that Americans of the revolutionary era did indeed begin creating for themselves a sense of a "collective past" and "previous common history as a nation," which were crucial to the origins and development of early American nationalism. The role of history in that development manifested itself throughout the revolutionary era in three ways. Before independence, in response to the unprecedented political events of the imperial crisis, American patriots in the 1760s and 1770s began deconstructing their relationship to the British past and, hence, to Britain itself. Concurrently, they also began constructing a newly shared colonial past for the first time. After the war, they reimagined that shared colonial past in light of what was most important in the political and cultural circumstances of the early republic. Also after the war, they began the cultural construction of a "deep national past," built on mythical symbolism, epic renderings of the American past, and the nationalization of the natural history of the continent by appropriating the past of its Indigenous Peoples. All the while, these processes were informed by distinct cultural understandings of the relationship between the past and present and the period's shifting political and cultural circumstances. Taken together, they formed a core part of the civic identity transformation from British subject to American citizen that lies at the cultural heart of the Revolution.

To uncover and trace these processes, I employ the analytical concept of "history culture," which encompasses all references to and uses of the past in a given society.[14] History culture goes beyond just traditional historical works by considering articulations of the past throughout a society's culture. Like the concept of "print culture," it also includes the relationships, networks, and institutions that fostered "historical cultural production"—cultural works that drew on historical content or themes—and created and perpetuated historical memories. The scope of history culture includes "all the layers and processes of social historical consciousness, paying attention to the agents who create it, the media by means of which it is disseminated, the representations that it popularizes and the creative reception on the part of citizens."[15] Through the lens of history culture, we can begin to develop a much fuller understanding of a society's relationship to the past and the various roles played by the past in its culture and politics.

By allowing us to see connections otherwise obscured, history culture provides us with useful means for investigating "historical memory."[16] Historians and social scientists have used a variety of terms to describe similar phenomena, including cultural memory, collective memory, and social memory. I have chosen to use "historical memory" and my own euphemism, "shared past" interchangeably. Historical memories are built on specific interpretations of the past—either created or adopted—primarily for the purposes of forging group identity. A shared past, embedded with their ideals, principles, and sense of unity, allows a group to reproduce its identity.[17] The potential purposes behind the need for a coherent and reproducible group identity in the eighteenth century were many. They could be used to define a religious group, to create and manage political alliances, factions, or even individual conflicts, and to foster social and political unity in the face of a common enemy.

The primary challenge in analyzing historical memories is the lack of an accepted methodology.[18] Because of that, each historian must determine the criteria necessary to identify and define a "historical memory" specific to the place and time they are studying. As eighteenth-century America lacked many of the social and institutional structures that define a significant portion of modern memory studies, it requires its own distinct set of criteria. Herein, a historical memory can be identified when a specific interpretation or understanding of a historical event or series of events is employed by a variety of individuals for the same rhetorical purpose and widely circulated throughout the society's cultural production. One argument regarding the historical past in a single book or a pamphlet or newspaper does not constitute a historical memory. However, when a historical interpretation or understanding can be found in works from a variety of regions or backgrounds, when it can be found being employed for the same purposes, and when it can be found in a variety of the society's available media forms, then we can begin to think in terms of "historical memory."

As such, this book's source base focuses heavily on the rapidly growing print production of the revolutionary era. Research for this book involved systematic readings of colonial and British historical works produced before the Revolution and of American and British newspapers and pamphlets produced during the imperial crisis of the 1760s and 1770s. The latter has been well-trodden ground by intellectual and political historians of the Revolution, but in this book I seek to culturally contextualize that debate in a new way. For the postwar period, the source base expanded from largely political writings to include a broader array of cultural production. This included the wide variety of print forms, including books, pamphlets, broadsides, magazines, and almanacs, as well as newly emerging American literary genres such as poetry, historical fiction, drama, and art. It also required looking into educational texts, including textbooks in a variety of subjects and theoretical essays about education generally, as well as documents related the establishment of the nation's first historical institutions, including historical societies and museums. Finally, the manuscript source base drew on private correspondence, antiquarian collections, library and booksellers' records, and institutional records, as well as prepublication drafts of historical cultural productions. Because various chapters draw on different types of sources and methodologies, this book as a whole—rather than each discrete chapter—incorporates the broad perspective afforded by the concept of history culture.

One of the chief theorists of collective memory, Alon Confino, has described the "history of memory" as a "fragmented field" largely defined "in terms of topics of inquiry." Such a focus on static renderings of individual topics—such as the Holocaust, the French Revolution, or, in the American sphere, the Confederacy—"runs the danger of becoming an assemblage of distinct topics that describe in a predictable way how people construct the past." Instead, he called on historians of memory to focus on "articulating the connections between the cultural, the social, and the political, between representation and social experience." "Memory," Confino argued, "does not offer any true additional explanatory power. Only when linked to historical questions and problems . . . can memory be illuminating."[19] By linking memory to the history of mentalités, Confino argued that memory studies should not focus primarily on "how people remember the past after the fact, but how memory structures behavior and thoughts."[20] That is, instead of simply looking at how a specific event was remembered through static explications, historians need to look at how those memories changed over time and how they interacted with other political and cultural forms and events and use those investigations to answer "historical questions and problems."

This book does explicitly that. By focusing on how historical memories of the British and colonial pasts changed over time and their interrelationship with the political and cultural developments of the American Revolution and the origins of early American national identity, it seeks to shed new light on the historical question at the center of the origins of American nationalism: How did colonists go from thinking of themselves as British subjects to American citizens? In the process, I show the cultural malleability and political utility of the historical past in the American revolutionary era.

The first chapter, "History Culture in Eighteenth-Century British America," gives an overview of the role of the past in British North America during the pre-revolutionary decades. It begins by offering a survey of historical thinking and access to historical knowledge in British America in the middle of the eighteenth century. Next, it examines the structural role played by the past in colonial culture and political, religious, and legal thought, showing the cultural and political importance of ideas such as "first principles," custom, and precedent. It also explores the degree to which colonists relied on the British past for their imperial identities and on historical works and interpretations imported from Britain to shape those identities.

Building off the cultural context established in the first chapter, the second chapter, "The Colonial Past in the Imperial Crisis," begins to examine the explosion of historical writing that took place in the political literature of the imperial crisis. In their political rhetoric, patriots began creating a newly shared colonial past, particularly by forging a new historical memory of their colonial origins. This newly shared past contributed to both colonists' sense of themselves as part of a community with their fellow colonies and their sense of cultural difference with Britain. It then shows how colonists' cultural reverence for the authority of the past shaped the ways in which they understood the actions of Parliament and the rhetoric of its supporters, whereas British actions and rhetoric were based largely on the exigencies of the present. These different conceptions of the relationship between the past and present, I argue, contributed greatly to the intractability of the debate and colonists' emerging sense of cultural difference with Britain.

The third chapter, "The British Past in the Imperial Crisis," follows on from the previous chapter by examining the use of the British past in the political writings of the imperial crisis. Primarily, it explores how colonists' interpretations of the Glorious Revolution changed during the crisis and how their new understanding of that event helped shape patriot rhetoric after 1767. Having previously served as the foundation of their identities as British subjects, patriots came to understand the Glorious Revolution not as having restored the balance of the "ancient constitution" but as having given rise to the doctrine of "parliamentary supremacy," which allowed Parliament, in colonists' minds, to exert absolute authority over the colonies and act as arbitrarily as any seventeenth-century Stuart monarch. This fundamental shift in their historical understanding brought colonists' cultural relationship to the Glorious Revolution, and hence the British past, into question and resulted in the turn toward more universal arguments based on natural law after 1773.

The interlude, "Natural Law, Independence, and Revolutionary History Culture, 1772–1776," explores the emergence of natural law as a primary feature of patriot rhetoric in the early 1770s. Once colonists had begun questioning the British past and its relationship to their current circumstances, adopting natural law arguments more widely allowed them to continue to argue the same principles they had previously based on the British past by universalizing them under the rhetoric of "natural law" and "natural rights." In the years just prior to independence, arguments based on the authority of the past began to diminish in favor of natural law arguments. This shift is evident in the most important revolutionary texts from this period: Thomas Jefferson's *A Summary View of the Rights of British America,* Thomas Paine's *Common Sense,* and the Declaration of Independence.

Part II begins with the fourth chapter, "The Expansion of History Culture in the Early Republic," which examines the rapid growth in the presence and role of the past in the cultural production of the early republic. The first half of the chapter charts the vast increase in historical cultural production in a variety of print forms and literary genres. The second half of the chapter explores one of the processes behind this increase in production by uncovering an informal network—including historians, antiquarians, poets, essayists, painters, publishers, politicians, and others—that provided supportive relationships for those engaged in historical cultural production. Ultimately, that network, and the support it offered, provided the impetus and model for the institutionalization of history culture in this period through the establishment of the nation's first historical societies and museums.

The fifth chapter, "The Colonial Past in the Early Republic," examines representations of the colonial past in the two decades following the end of the war. It explores how postwar Americans reimagined their shared colonial past in light of the present by stressing the colonies' practical independence from Britain and internal unity from the earliest days of settlement. In doing so, this new shared colonial past contributed to both a sense of historical and cultural independence from the former mother country and a historical narrative that de-radicalized the Revolution by stressing continuity between the colonial past and present. I argue that reimagining the colonial past was a critical part of the efforts to create a shared national history that would foster national identity in the new republic.

The sixth and final chapter, "Creating a Deep Past for a New Nation," examines the ways in which Americans sought, created, and promoted a "deep national past," or American antiquity, for the new republic. The first half of the chapter explores how the use of Columbian, biblical, and epic symbolism all contributed to Americans' sense of a past deeper even than that of the colonial period. The second half of the chapter explores the nationalization of both natural history and the indigenous pasts of Native Americans and their expression in the nation's first natural history museums. The creation of a deep past grounded both in myth and the land was—like the simultaneously reimagined colonial past—part of a broader attempt to establish cultural independence from Britain, in this case by fostering a sense of national origins that transcended British imperialism and the British past altogether. The nature and purpose of the creation of this deep national past reveal two conflicting tendencies at the core of American history: the anti-colonial impulse to create national origins that transcend the former imperial ruler and the cultural settler colonialism of appropriating the history of Native peoples to foster the kind of national sentiment that would ultimately help justify the appropriation of Native land through the policies of removal.

When, in the 1830s, Alexis de Tocqueville sought out the "principal circumstances" that favored the establishment and maintenance of the United States as a democratic republic, he concluded the first to be the nature of "the origin of the American settlements." The second circumstance was the "nature of the territory" or the "boundless continent" the Americans inhabited which "God himself gave them."[21] In examining the historical causes of the young nation he was seeing on his travels in the summer of 1831, Tocqueville understandably drew upon the narrative and interpretations that were established by the first generation of cultural nationalists and revolutionary historians decades before. As for the revolutionary generation of nationalists and then for the Americans of the early nineteenth century, the historical memories of the colonial past and of the deep national past had come to define the first national historical narrative, much of which still retains significant purchase in the minds of many contemporary Americans.

This book makes contributions to and interventions into a number of historiographies, including memory and history in early America, the coming of the American Revolution, the origins of American national identity, and the early United States as a postcolonial society. Though early America, as a field, largely missed out on the "memory boom" of the 1980s and 1990s, there have been a fair number of studies of memory and history in early America over the last two decades, exploring regional memory, memory of specific events, the memorialization of individuals, and the legacy of classical Rome and Greece. Many of these studies, however, have focused on the collective memory of the Revolution in the early national period and beyond. Likewise, studies of historical writing in the eighteenth century—most of which came out forty years ago in a brief spurt around the Bicentennial—also focused on the Revolution from the perspective of the early republic, thereby missing the broader changes in historical understanding occurring over the course of the entire revolutionary era and their longer-term context and significance to the Revolution itself.[22] Moreover, as products of their time, they largely focused on the role of republican ideology in a few of the period's most popular historical works. While many works have looked at the role of the classical past in the Revolution, surprisingly few works have explored the meaning of the British past in the revolutionary era.[23] None have tried to understand the broader cultural importance of that past and its interrelationship with the politics of the Revolution. In spanning the long revolutionary era, exploring the role of the colonial and British pasts in both American culture and politics, and going beyond traditional historical works, this work contributes to our understanding of both memory and history in this period.

This book also makes a number of contributions to the historiography of the coming of the American Revolution. In the late 1960s and 1970s, historians, such as Bernard Bailyn, Gordon S. Wood, and J. G. A. Pocock, offered a very influential interpretation of the coming of the Revolution based on the ideology of classical republicanism.[24] Through the writings of seventeenth-century "commonwealthmen" and early eighteenth-century polemicists in England, they argued, colonists supposedly learned to be ever mindful of the conspiratorial designs of those in power who sought to seize the liberties of virtuous, public-minded citizens for their own political and material gain.[25] In the 1980s and 1990s, historians, such as Jack P. Greene and John Phillip Reid, offered constitutional and legal interpretations of the coming of the Revolution.[26] In multiple works, Greene argued that the Revolution arose out of "a disagreement over the nature of the constitution of the British Empire" between those on the peripheries, who over the previous century and a half had developed their own colonial constitutions, and those at the metropolitan center still trying to define the "imperial constitution."[27] Reid, in his four-volume *Constitutional History of the American Revolution,* took a decidedly legal approach, arguing that the conflict was the result of "competing constitutional doctrines," with colonists subscribing to the seventeenth-century "constitution of prescriptive, customary rights" and the British subscribing to the newer "constitution of parliamentary command."[28] Despite both of these interpretations incorporating connections with the past, popular understandings of the historical past have never been foregrounded in the scholarship of the period. In addition, both interpretations have offered largely static renderings of colonial thought and rhetoric throughout the imperial crisis. That is, colonists appear to have come into the imperial crisis with certain ideas, and they seem to have changed little, if at all, throughout the crisis.

Progressive historians in the early twentieth century argued that the fact that patriot arguments changed showed they were merely opportunistic rhetoric and, therefore, not worthy of serious consideration. In the 1940s and 1950s, Edmund Morgan argued that patriot arguments did *not* fundamentally change and, therefore, *should* be taken seriously. Morgan's work in this period marked the beginning of a return to an intellectual approach to understanding the coming of the Revolution that culminated in the 1960s and 1970s with the focus on classical republican ideology. The problem, however, was that Morgan defined the value of his argument (and, thereby, of patriot ideas) on the terms set by Progressive historians, with consistency as the primary criteria of both sincerity and significance. That fundamental understanding led to a lot of intellectual history that acknowledged long-term changes between the pre- and post-revolutionary eras but left us with a rendering of patriot thought as largely static during the imperial crisis, a period of unprecedented political and cultural upheaval. Yet, it seems unlikely that patriots went through the many and varied upheavals, confrontations, and debates of the decade-long imperial crisis without any significant modification or change in the ideas that informed their response to imperial reform, the arguments that supported it, and the actions that sought to achieve it. For colonists to go from resistance to revolution required changes in thinking on a number of levels, without which the Revolution appears to be inevitable from the start. It is the great irony of the 1960s revival of the intellectual approach to the coming of the Revolution that in trying to offer a more complex alternative to the Progressives' economic determinism, its proponents ended up coming up with an interpretation that one might describe as intellectual determinism. I contend that patriot arguments and ideas are that much more interesting, significant, and worthy of serious consideration precisely *because* they changed. Those changes were not predetermined by history culture but were interrelated with it.

This book seeks to understand the reasons behind those rhetorical changes by tracing how historical understandings framed and supported various patriot arguments throughout the crisis and how the political events of the crisis in turn shaped those historical interpretations. More broadly, it seeks to place patriot rhetoric within the context of colonial history culture and its interrelationship with the dynamic politics of the imperial crisis. After all, the most elemental question faced by historians of the coming of the Revolution is: How did colonists get from 1763 to 1776 in only thirteen years? That is, how did they go from being proud British subjects in the wake of the Seven Years' War to declaring independence less than a decade and a half later? This book does not pretend to disprove or replace the long-standing constitutional, ideological, and economic interpretations of the Revolution. Rather, it provides an additional avenue of understanding by offering one example of how historians might approach thinking about and uncovering the *cultural* origins and causes of the Revolution. It suggests that cultural breaks wrought by the imperial crisis were important precursors to the political break of independence and help explain how that political break came about so quickly.

In doing so, it also offers a number of readings of the imperial debate that differ from recent scholarship. For example, Progressive historians of the early twentieth century understood the seemingly overblown patriot rhetoric about British tyranny as mere cover for elites' own personal economic interests. Their successors, proponents of the "republican synthesis," understood that same rhetoric as the product of a near-paranoid worldview in which power was always encroaching on liberty aided by the corruptibility of human nature. That is, for much of the twentieth century, scholars of the intellectual history of the Revolution have started from a need to explain the exaggerated nature of patriot rhetoric. However, recent scholarship on eighteenth-century politics in Britain (as well as France and Spain) argues that there was indeed a distinct political and economic turn in imperial administration in the wake of the Seven Years' War.[29] The war and the accession of George III brought to power a group of politicians, including George Grenville and Lord North, with a decidedly more authoritarian ideology of empire and, most importantly, the will and means to implement it. Taking work by contemporary historians of Britain into account—as Edmund S. Morgan and T. H. Breen famously implored early Americanists to do—it would appear that patriot rhetoric about the increasing exercise of absolute power by Parliament and the Ministry over the colonies was not primarily paranoid alarmism so much as it was grounded in a vague but not mistaken understanding of contemporary political developments in Britain and Europe, much of which filled colonial newspapers.[30]

In part thanks to this recent scholarship on Britain and European politics, this book takes patriot rhetoric seriously in a way that has not often been the case in recent scholarship. I argue that the imperial debate was fought primarily over two succeeding issues. First, from the Sugar Act of 1764 to the Townshend Acts of 1767, the debate was fundamentally about civic equality. Were colonists equal to native-born Britons or were they second-class citizens within the empire? The legal and constitutional issues of representation and taxation were part of this broader political and cultural question of imperial identity and civic status. After the Townshend Acts of 1767, the debate shifted to focus more on parliamentary supremacy and the legitimacy of Parliament's arbitrary authority over the colonies.

This book suggests that rhetoric about British tyranny was not necessarily as hyperbolic or paranoid as historians have long contended. Rather, it represented, to a significant extent, a genuine understanding by colonists of their own circumstances in the 1760s and 1770s being subject to a Parliament and Ministry attempting to create a more authoritarian and centralized British Empire. Hence, the Revolution was not a revolution against the king or Parliament, let alone government per se. Instead, it represented a rejection of the exercise of arbitrary power over the colonies without recourse or redress. Just as their British ancestors had resisted the arbitrary rule of Charles I and James II in the seventeenth century, so did the colonists in the eighteenth century, with the seriously complicating twist that they were resisting an arbitrary Parliament—which had long been understood as the guardian of the peoples' rights—rather than an arbitrary monarch.

Moreover, the republican and constitutional historians have tended to focus on the minutiae of strands of the imperial debate that were often cited by obscure European thinkers, British legal cases, and constitutional theory. But the full power of those debates was limited in its reach, largely to elites with significant education. For common colonists without much education and legal training, these debates were refracted, in part, through their history culture and their cultural understanding of the relationship between the past and present. As such, colonial history culture helped translate the broader issues behind those more technical legal and constitutional debates into a colonial vernacular, giving them a much broader reach and, I argue, a greater cultural immediacy.

This book also makes a contribution to recent scholarship on nationalism in the early republic. In the last few decades, the field of early American history has shifted considerably toward the early national period. In the process, American nationalism has come to be seen as indigenous to the early republic, a product of the unique political circumstances of the post-revolutionary period.[31] Indeed, in a recent edited volume on the American Revolution, Michael Zuckerman praised the contributors (and, by proxy, the field as a whole) by saying, "They have no trouble with the notion of a nation not yet born on the Fourth of July."[32] In addition to offering the alternative perspective on New World nationalism previously mentioned, this book complicates that notion by arguing that origins of early American national identity can be found prior to independence and that they played an important role in bringing the Revolution about, not just defining it afterward.[33] Also, by focusing on cultural nationalism—that is, attempts to use cultural productions to create, define, and foster a shared national identity—in the early republic, this work seeks to contribute to scholarship that has tended to focus more on political nationalism, namely the processes through which the new national polity was defined, initially by focusing on who was included and, more recently, on the roles of race and gender in who was excluded.[34] The creation of a national history both reflected and reinforced those processes of definition, inclusion, and exclusion.

Furthermore, accounting for the early national reckoning with the colonial past extends recent work on the post-revolutionary relationship between the United States and Britain, particularly the recent scholarly development of treating the early national United States as a "postcolonial" society.[35] Sam W. Haynes has argued, "The young republic exhibited a set of anxieties not uncommon among nation-states that have emerged from long periods of colonial rule."[36] Similarly, Kariann Yokota recently argued, "The project of nation building and developing national identity in the young United States was as much about its people's struggles in 'unbecoming' what had made them British subjects before independence as it was about 'becoming' citizens of a new country." She has also argued, "The revolutionary victory was the first, rather than the last step in gaining freedom from the mother country." For the citizens of a new republic, "lingering colonial dependence—and a corresponding sense of inferiority—shaped the budding nation." Ultimately, these "colonials-turned-citizens had to create an interstitial space between their former identity as British subjects and the new political and cultural context in which they now found themselves."[37] One of those created spaces was the past. By looking at how the colonial past was represented in a variety of historical cultural productions in the early national period, we can begin to develop a more complex picture of Americans' cultural attempts to reconcile their dependent, colonial past with their independent, republican present. We can also identify the seemingly paradoxical ways in which Americans rejected their European imperial heritage, in part, by embracing their colonial past.

Finally, this book adds a historical component to the increasing scholarship on settler colonialism in the early national period. The creation of a deep national past highlights the fundamental contradiction in the postcolonial culture of the early republic between the lingering anti-colonial rhetoric of the Revolution and the settler colonial approach of American governments (both federal and state) to dealing with the non-whites among them. During the pre-revolutionary period, Indigenous Peoples appeared in histories of individual colonies primarily as antagonists, as the uncivilized Others against whom successful and honorable wars were waged. Such a characterization helped reinforce colonists' own sense of their retained British-ness and European-ness. During the 1760s and 1770s, however, as the historical stakes of the colonial period complicated those identities, Native Americans largely disappeared from the historical memory being created about a shared colonial past, their bodies effectively erased by a narrative that reduced them to merely part of the landscape of the "wilderness" of the "new world." In the early national period, Indigenous Peoples suddenly became quite visible in the revised postwar historical memory of the colonial past at the very same time that the federal government was systematically seeking to displace them from their ancestral homes in the borderlands of the Southeast and Northwest. Whether Native Americans' bodies or their histories were being erased, the historical memories of the revolutionary era could not help but be shaped by the settler colonial ideology that had defined both the colonial history and the present. As a result, the process of creating a deep national past for the new national history relied on an applied cultural form of settler colonialism.

Ultimately, this is a book about the creation of the very idea of "American history," which, as a concept, did not exist in any recognizable or substantive way before the conflict with Britain that led to independence. Moreover, it is a book about how the idea (and initial practice) of American history was not so much a product of the Revolution, as many historians have long assumed, but rather was actually a driving force behind it. It is also a story about how the rhetoric of the Revolution and the reality of the early national period embedded from the start the tension between anti-colonialism and colonialism and between anti-imperialism and imperialism into our national historical memories. How Americans thought about their colonial and revolutionary pasts were critical in shaping how the Revolution played out and how Americans sought to make their republican experiment stick in the early national period. And those ideas became the basis for a national origins myth that, for better or worse, still lives today in the minds of many Americans.

Studies produced each year by various civic organizations reveal that Americans think their history is important. Yet, those same studies simultaneously reveal that Americans generally know very little about that history. In our current political moment, public debates about the relationship between the past and present seemingly rage anew, centered around issues of memorializing slavery, the Confederacy, Christopher Columbus, and other parts of our past. But as contemporary Americans increasingly debate the meanings and legacies of American history and their implications for our current political and cultural lives, it is important to understand that such debates are not new. They have been a fundamental part of each generation's fashioning of their own national identities, from the revolutionary generation itself right down to our own. Indeed, these tensions between conflicting historical memories and different perceptions of the relationship between the past and present have been with us from the very beginning, having been embedded in American culture and politics through the roles they played in the American Revolution and the construction of our national origins myth. As partisan political pundits mourn for a mythical time when Americans were not engaged in historical "revisionism," I hope this book will make clear that reimagining the past is a tradition as old as the republic itself, one which played an important role in its birth.

PART I

Colonial History Culture in British America, 1730–1776

CHAPTER ONE

HISTORY CULTURE IN PRE-REVOLUTIONARY BRITISH AMERICA

For a long time, the paucity of historical works written by colonists and published in the colonies during the first half of the eighteenth century allowed historians to overlook the importance of history and the past generally in colonial culture and politics. When one looks beyond the narrow category of published historical works, however, we find a society in which the past mattered greatly. We can begin to develop a sense of colonial society's relationship with the past by looking at historical thinking and writing in the colonies in the middle of the eighteenth century, colonists' access to historical knowledge, and the structural importance of the past in colonial politics, religion, and law. Some of these aspects of British American history culture mirrored that of Britain, while others diverged. Nevertheless, the most defining features make clear that the colonies did have a significant history culture and it was a decidedly *colonial* history culture, in many ways derivative of and dependent on that of the metropole.

This chapter offers a synthetic overview of how colonial Americans in the middle of the eighteenth century engaged with and related to the past, both historical and otherwise. How did colonists think about history? How did they understand the relationship between the past and present? Why was the past so important in colonial culture? What kind of history did colonists write? Who had access to historical knowledge and in what ways and forms did they access it? What was the role of history in shaping how colonists thought about and engaged in government, politics, law, religion, and family? How did their understandings of the past manifest in colonial political and religious culture? And what role did history play in providing colonists a cultural lifeline to a mother country three thousand miles and an ocean away? While each could form the basis of individual studies, a broad inquiry into all of these questions is crucial to understanding the relationship between the past and present in colonial culture and society on the eve of the imperial crisis and, subsequently, how it changed during the Revolution.

To begin our examination of colonial history culture in eighteenth-century British America, we must first develop a sense of how colonists thought about the past and its relationship to the present. To do that, we must look at the most common prevailing perceptions of history in the middle of the eighteenth century. From there, we will look at how colonists understood the pragmatic utility of history as a form of learning by example and the methods they used to study it. Finally, we will examine the state of colonial and British historical writing on the eve of the Revolution.

In the British North American colonies, as in the broader Anglophone world, there existed three seemingly distinct understandings of history and the relationship between the past and present. First, there was the millennialist understanding that underpinned much of the evangelical revivals of the 1740s and 1750s. Second, there was a cyclical understanding of history, often expressed in the rise and fall of empires and civilizations. And, finally, there was the emerging sense of history as a linear story of progress. There is a significant amount of literature on each of these understandings of the relationship between the past and present, so we will explore each only briefly. Instead, I want to focus on just how indiscrete each of these understandings actually were and suggest some of the ways in which ideas and aspects of each were actually shared among all of them.

Millennialism—an eschatological Christian belief derived from the book of Revelations that Jesus Christ would establish a one-thousand-year reign of the saints on earth prior to the Last Judgment—came to America with the Puritans. New England Puritans, like their English counterparts, debated the theology of various millennial theories throughout the seventeenth century. Contrary to popular myth, however, most seventeenth-century Puritans, including the first settlers, did not think of their settling the New World as a sign of the coming of the millennium. Those ideas developed over the course of the seventeenth century. By the turn of the eighteenth century, the popularity of millennialism had declined in New England, where it enjoyed the most prominence. With its popularity waxing and waning, millennialism took on renewed prominence during the religious revivals of the 1740s known as the Great Awakening, with some religious leaders claiming the revivals themselves marked the onset of the millennium.

Central to the millennial view of history was the idea that God governed the world according to his own divine plan and actively intervened in human affairs. This idea defined much historical writing prior to the eighteenth century throughout Europe, including the sparse historical writing in late seventeenth-century and early eighteenth-century British North America. The idea of history as primarily the story of divine providence was shared, whether wholeheartedly or by default, well beyond fundamentalist Protestants. In such a context, it is hard to lend too much weight to history. Revivalists looked to history as a supplement to Scripture in trying to discern God's divine plan. Yet, the core of the fundamentalist interpretation of history was its representation of not just the manifestation of providence but also divine judgment. According to this perspective, when humans, societies, and civilizations acted in ways contrary to God's plan, they were punished for their immorality. Just as God had passed judgment on Sodom and Gomorrah, the reasoning went, so had he must have done on the Roman Empire and countless other societies since.

The second and likely most common understanding of history in the eighteenth century was the cyclical theory of history.[1] The classical origins of such a perspective can be found in the writings of Plato and Aristotle, but they were most fully formed by the ancient Roman historian Polybius. His theory, known as "anacyclosis," posited three simple, benign forms of government: monarchy, aristocracy, and democracy. Each of these, he claimed, would inevitably devolve into their malignant counterpart: tyranny, oligarchy, and anarchy.[2] In 1763, John Adams concluded an essay with a paragraph in which he reiterated Polybius's cycle, writing, "Simple Monarchy will soon mould itself into Despotism, Aristocracy will soon commence an Oligarchy, and Democracy, will soon degenerate into an Anarchy."[3] Upon coming across his draft of the essay over four decades later, he added a notation at the bottom of the page in which he called the cyclical theory of history the "Creed of my whole Life." To avoid these fates required a mixed government that incorporated monarchy, aristocracy, and democracy in such a way as each provided a check on the others. Throughout the first half of the eighteenth century, colonists, native Britons, and many enlightened thinkers throughout Europe believed the British constitution did just that.

In the cyclical theory, it was understood that empires and civilizations naturally rose and fell, though for different reasons. Colonists most commonly understood this process as morally driven. As Scottish historian and philosopher David Hume related, writing history was to "remark the Rise, Progress, Declension, and final Extinction of the most flourishing Empires; the Virtues, which contributed to the Greatness; and the Vices, which drew on their Ruin."[4] In addition to the moral interpretation of the cyclical nature of history, societies were also commonly understood in a manner analogous to the natural life cycle. They are born, rise from their infancy to their peak and, as with humans, decline and die away. This analogy gave rise to the double meaning of the term "constitution." For example, someone in the eighteenth century with a strong physical build was understood as having a strong *physical* constitution. As with human lives, the rate at which societies would inevitably decay was determined by the strength of their *political* constitutions. As Lord Bolingbroke wrote in *The Patriot King* (1738): "The best instituted governments, like the best constituted animal bodies, carry in them the seeds of their destruction, and though they grow and improve for a time, they will soon tend visibly to their dissolution. Every hour they live is an hour the less that they have to live."[5]

The idea behind this cycle was that the people in an up-and-coming society desired above all to improve their lives and acquire wealth, status, and power. These desires coupled with their lack of economic prosperity and cultural development led to frugality and a masculine, Spartan-like virtue, defined in classical terms as the individual putting the public good ahead of their own self-interest, all qualities that contributed to a society's rise.

Once they achieved the luxury that came with economic prosperity, cultural development, and political power, however, individuals inevitably became more concerned with their own self-interest and their manners became more effeminate and profligate, ultimately leading to the loss of virtue, the growth of corruption, and the beginning of their decline.[6] Bolingbroke explicated this common understanding of history and the relationship between the past and present when he claimed that "physical and moral systems are carried around in one perpetual revolution, from generation to corruption, and from corruption to generation; from ignorance to knowledge, and from knowledge to ignorance; from barbarity to civility, and from civility to barbarity."

In the middle of the eighteenth century, the cyclical theory manifested itself not only in historical texts but also mechanically and visually. For example, in 1753, the Frenchman Jacques Barbeu-Dubourg, a friend of Benjamin Franklin, created a mechanical historical timeline. Lodged in a wooden box with a roller on each side, his timeline was written on a fifty-four-foot scroll, allowing the reader (or operator) of his *Chronographie Universelle* to move backward and forward in historical time.[7] Such an invention received significant notoriety, including its own entry in the *Encylcopédie.* Around the same time, in England, another friend of Franklin, Joseph Priestley, set out to create a more useful and intuitive historical timeline, according to "the principles of Sir Isaac Newton." His chart organized history scientifically, at a uniform scale, and presented that information graphically. Through visual representation, Priestley's charts "impressed [information] upon the mind more forcibly by means of sensible images excited in the brain." "The capital use," he wrote, "of any chart of this kind is, that it is a most excellent mechanical help to the knowledge of history, impressing the imagination indelibly with a just image of the rise, progress, extent, duration and contemporary state of all the considerable empires that have ever existed in the world."[8] In 1765, Priestley published *A Chart of Biography* and followed that up in 1769 with *A New Chart of History,* which he dedicated to Franklin. The charts measured three feet in width and two feet in height and came with accompanying pamphlets that described the persons and empires depicted (as well as the methodology behind the charts).[9] Both Barbeu-Dubourg and Priestley tried to accurately represent the temporal relationship between the rise and inevitable fall of civilizations and empires throughout human history by creating visual and mechanical manifestations of the cyclical theory.

But if a society's declension was inevitable, how could it be delayed? "All that can be done to prolong the duration of a good government," Bolingbroke wrote, "is to draw it back, on every favorable occasion, to the *first good principles* on which it was founded."[10] Here he echoed, among others, the seventeenth-century radical Whig Algernon Sidney, who similarly wrote in his *Discourses Concerning Government:* "All human constitutions are subject to corruption and must perish unless they are timely renewed and reduced to their first principles."[11] The value of promoting "first principles" was a widely accepted notion in the Anglo-American world that contributed to the cultural reverence for and weight given to the ancient constitution in the eighteenth century by subjects on both sides of the Atlantic.[12] Moreover, this inherently conservative idea retains significant power in contemporary American political culture, informing ideas like originalism and movements like the Tea Party.

The idea of the ancient constitution, which preceded the Norman Conquest of 1066, was rooted in the balance between authority and liberty, between the three estates of the Crown, the nobility, and the common people, and, especially after the seventeenth-century Civil Wars and Glorious Revolution, the balance between king and Parliament. While the mythic idea that the British constitution and Parliament derived their authority from their ancient origins declined among many Whig elites in Britain during the eighteenth century, it continued to hold broad purchase throughout the colonies.[13] Therefore, for many colonists, their "first principles" were embodied in the idea of the ancient constitution.

By returning to its first principles, a nation could forestall the inevitable decline. The manifestation of the British past—in the form of the ancient constitution—was seen as one of the primary bulwarks against the inevitable erosion of the nation and its society. Many colonists and Britons believed that learning about and heeding the lessons of the British past could, in a sense, delay the future. This perspective attributed tremendous cultural and political weight to the past and its force in shaping the present and future. It also provided a crucial historical and temporal connection for a people separated by three thousand miles of ocean from their mother country, because colonists believed they too were the inheritors of Britain's ancient constitution, or "our ancient constitution," as it was commonly called in colonial newspapers and pamphlets.

The cyclical theory—and the notion of first principles—is also evident in the eighteenth-century meaning of the term "revolution."[14] Today, we generally understand a revolution as a violent uprising that produces a change in a society's ruling class, such as the French and Russian Revolutions. In other words, revolutions are now seen as an almost total disruption between the present and the past. In the seventeenth and eighteenth centuries, however, a revolution described the "course of any thing which returns to the point at which it began."[15] As the cycles of societies and governments were likened to the natural world, so was the civil definition tied to the natural "*Revolution of the Heavens.*"[16] That is, a "revolution"—natural, political, or otherwise—described a cyclical process of rotation rather than the onset of something new. In his *Dictionary of the English Language,* Samuel Johnson also defined a revolution as a "change in the state of a government or country" but also noted it was "used among us [most commonly], for the change produced by the admission of king William and queen Mary." A political revolution, therefore, was defined as a return to first principles, by force if necessary, often due to unusual or unprecedented circumstances.

Johnson's definition speaks to something very fundamental about how some Britons and many colonists viewed the Glorious Revolution of 1688. That is, many understood the events of 1688–89 as a "revolution" in the sense that it had restored the balance, or first principles, of the English constitution after being corrupted by the Stuart monarchs, who had tried to enlarge the authority of the king at the expense of Parliament.[17] Like many fellow Britons, colonists in the eighteenth century gloried in their Britishness and the history that defined it. To many, the ancient constitution had been saved in 1688 by a Parliament that represented the people. Parliament had also preserved the Protestant succession, by removing James II and his Catholic heir. In the minds of many colonists, Britain—despite multiple instances of its rulers seeking to expand their prerogative and exercise arbitrary power—had emerged from the turbulent seventeenth century the freest nation in the world. And it had done so because Britons had retained their faith in the ancient constitution and its first principle of "mixed government," which held the balance between king, Lords, and Commons.

By mid-century in Britain, however, many establishment Whigs had moved away from this cyclical idea of the Glorious Revolution. Rather, they came to see the Glorious Revolution as a pivotal turning point—or "Year Zero," as one historian has described it—that set the foundation for the development of most of the aspects that they believed had come to define Britain. In their view, the ability to secure subjects' liberty and promote commerce was a product not of the ancient constitution but of the post-1688 limited constitutional monarchy and the subsequent emergence of the fiscal-military state. This mainstream Whig interpretation in Britain reflected a very different perspective on history than that of many colonists, who continued to subscribe to the cyclical interpretations being made by the establishment Whigs' political opponents, like Lord Bolingbroke, about the Glorious Revolution's restoration of the ancient constitution. To these "country Whigs," the Glorious Revolution had restored the ancient constitution but it was then subsequently corrupted by the revolutionary settlement, which included such innovations as the establishment of the national debt, the Bank of England, the stock market, and a standing army. Ironically, Whigs had proffered the cyclical interpretation during the Glorious Revolution. For political purposes, by mid-century many establishment Whigs had adopted the interpretation of the 1680s and 1690s held by the Glorious Revolution's Tory opponents, who saw 1688 was a decisive break with the past.[18] But, for both establishment and country Whigs, the Glorious Revolution was the seminal moment in the historical memory of Britain with great political stakes in how it was understood both in England and its North American colonies.

Throughout the first half of the eighteenth century, many colonists agreed that the Glorious Revolution had restored the balance of the ancient constitution by checking the royal privilege in favor of the authority of Parliament, while also acknowledging that its restoration had helped set the stage for the eighteenth-century rise of the British Empire. They were not inclined to criticize the revolutionary settlement because, to that point, it seemed to be working for them.[19] As historian Jack P. Greene pointed out, not only the event itself but this interpretation of it was at the core of

British North American colonists' "intense British patriotism." In other words, this interpretation of the Glorious Revolution served as the foundation of their imperial identity as subjects of Britain, a nation defined in opposition to the rest of Europe (especially absolutist France) by its liberty, constitutional monarchy, Protestantism, and commerce, all of which had been created, reaffirmed, or restored by the Glorious Revolution.[20] As their fellow subjects in Britain came to understand 1688 and the history of Britain quite differently, this historical disconnect would result in significant consequences when those competing historical memories clashed during the imperial crisis.

The third and final understanding of history in the mid to late eighteenth century was based on the idea of progress.[21] Derived from the Enlightenment, the idea of progress posited that history and time were not circular but linear. Its proponents understood the process through which Europe had emerged from the darkness of the Middle Ages into the scientific, rational, and literate age begun in the sixteenth century and reaching its fruition in the eighteenth century as one of progress. Later in the eighteenth century, French *philosophes* such as Condorcet would argue that history was inevitably leading to the perfectibility of humankind. As he wrote, "No bounds have been fixed to the improvement of the human faculties." The "perfectibility of man is absolutely indefinite," he argued, and the "course of this progress may doubtless be more or less rapid, but it can never be retrograde."[22] This radical French Enlightenment idea, however, was not yet circulated widely in either Britain or its colonies in the middle of the eighteenth century.[23]

Instead, the primary development of the idea of history as defined by progress in the middle of the eighteenth century came from a number of Scottish Enlightenment thinkers, including Adam Smith, Adam Ferguson, John Millar, David Hume, Lord Kames, and William Robertson. Sometimes referred to as "the four stages theory," Scottish *philosophes* looked back at the past writ large in an attempt to describe the development of civilization. Later in the century, another fellow Scot, Dugald Stewart, would refer to their work as "theoretical or conjectural history." "There is in human society," wrote John Millar, "a natural progress from ignorance to knowledge, and from rude to civilized manners, the several stages of which are usually accompanied with peculiar laws and customs."[24] They were also marked by differing modes of economic subsistence as noted by Adam Smith, the famous Scottish economist, who described the "four distinct states" through which "mankind pass": "1st, the Age of Hunters; 2dly, the Age of Shepherds; 3dly, the Age of Agriculture; and 4thly, the Age of Commerce."[25] This theory marked one of the Scottish Enlightenment's primary contributions to historical thought and had a much more significant impact in colonial and revolutionary America than its radical French counterpart.[26]

Of these three understandings of history—millennial, cyclical, and progressive—the cyclical theory appears to have been the most generally accepted in the British North American colonies at the middle of eighteenth century. Nevertheless, it is important to recognize that, beyond the written page, these understandings seemed to mesh together and did not appear as distinct as they might seem. We might be inclined to see millennialism as a religious theory, progress as a secular theory, and the cyclical theory as perhaps a combination of both, but we should resist such characterizations. For example, all three of these understandings were decidedly moralistic. In societies that had declined, millennialists saw God's judgment for their lack of morality, while many proponents of the cyclical theory believed that moral decay brought about declension. Meanwhile, the progressive theory saw morality (or "manners") as something that could (and would) be perfected. Similarly, the movement toward both the millennium and human perfectibility were fundamentally linear and progressive. Moreover, many millennialists believed that the millennium itself, once begun, would undergo a cycle that would include both judgment and war against the forces of evil. Particularly by incorporating morality in these ways, each of these understandings recognized a significant sense of human agency that, in relative terms, was quite new to Western historical thinking, which had for centuries before understood historical causation in terms of divine providence.

Many historians have characterized historical thinking and practice in the eighteenth century as newly progressive and secular. But while these ideas were developed in this period, they were hardly triumphant in eighteenth-century British North America. What emerges is a much more complex picture that combined these perspectives in varying measures. That singularly indefinite combination of varying and, from our modern perspective, opposing conceptions of the nature of history gave historical thinking and writing in this period the complexity that defines its character. We can see ways in which these understandings overlapped with one another. Because of that, aspects of each helped form the matrix of historical thinking that, in part, shaped colonial history culture, particularly at a time when Britons were shifting away from the cyclical understanding toward the progressive conception of history. The progressive conception was much more comforting to people living at the height of the first British Empire than the cyclical theory, which effectively promised their demise.

While preserving first principles was a critical function of history and historical writing for society as a whole, colonists also inherited other ideas from Britain about the utility of history for individuals. As an anonymous writer noted in a front-page essay on the value of history in the *Maryland Gazette* in 1745, history served the "two Purposes of Instruction and Amusement."[27] For the children of elites and the upwardly mobile portion of the middling class, history served primarily as a form of moral education. Its tendency was "to inspire us with a noble Esteem of Virtue, and a just Contempt of Vice; hence naturally will arise an Ambition to imitate the first, and shun the latter." History was seen as a tool for teaching elites morality and political virtue; for everyone else, it was supposed to be a form of entertainment.

In 1732, when twenty-two-year-old Harvard graduate Jonathan Belcher was in England studying law at the Middle Temple, his father—then royal governor of Massachusetts and New Hampshire—offered suggestions on preparing for his anticipated career as a member of Parliament. It would be "a duty to yourself, as well as to the borough you may represent, and I shou'd say above all, to God & your country, to get yourself well grounded in the Roman history, as well as that of Europe, and of Gt Britain in particular, that your part of all debates may be wisely conducted, & issue in the good of mankind & more especially in that of your country."[28] For many young elite males, acquiring a knowledge of the past, particularly of their own country's history, was a significant part of laying the foundation for their political careers and their ability to discern and serve the public good.

History's dual purposes were starkly delineated by class. "Civil History," as opposed to ecclesiastical and natural history, was "the most agreable Amusement to an idle Man, and the most instructive Entertainment to a

Man of Business."[29] One of the most popular guides to studying history in the early eighteenth century noted, "Every one knowing the state of life he is placed in, ought to regulate himself in the study of History accordingly." It elaborated this point further: "We know for certain, that it would be very dangerous for a private person in applying himself to the reading of Historians, to turn his head to political reflexions, and those means made use of to make an appearance, and advance himself in the courts of great men."[30] Such a statement shows the perceived cultural status accorded historical knowledge, particularly regarding politics. That is, knowledge of history was so powerful that it could allow a commoner to pass for a "great man."

It was fine for non-elites to read history of the kind that focused on customs and manners, but it was "very dangerous" for them to read political history because it would likely spark their ambition to reach beyond their social status and even help give them the means of passing themselves off as gentlemen. Indeed, there had been a distinct difference between studying history for instruction and studying it for amusement. Especially in these study guides written by elites in the late seventeenth and early eighteenth centuries, an individual's relationship to the past was defined, in part, by their social status. By the middle of the eighteenth century, however, historical works were being read in Britain and the colonies for self-education and self-improvement well beyond just elites. Its broadening popularity was noted by Gilbert Stuart who claimed it was "certainly a compliment to the taste and wisdom of the present age, that history is the prevailing and most fashionable reading."[31]

Increasing access to historical literature and knowledge reinforced the degree to which the past shaped how colonists understood the present and how they perceived the relationship between the past and present. In the eighteenth century, historical distance—or how far removed from the present a given point in the past seems—was truncated to a degree that even the distant past retained an immediacy and practical resonance hard to understand from our own contemporary perspective. Although the colonies underwent rapid changes in terms of economic and social development, for the vast majority of colonists engaged in rural agriculture, the basic rhythms of their daily lives were not all that different from those of their ancestors of hundreds of years past. To them, the past did not seem as far away as we might assume. After all, we live in a contemporary society in which technological and other developments have inflated our sense of historical distance, where photographs from a few decades ago seem to be from another world. This shortened sense of historical distance contributed to a more intimate and intertwined relationship between the past and present than is typical in postindustrial, technological societies like our own or even that of the industrialized nineteenth century.

We can begin to get a sense of the intimacy of the relationship between the past and present in the way colonists used the term "history." In his *Dictionary of the English Language* (1755), Samuel Johnson defined it as "1. A narration of events and facts delivered with dignity; 2. Narration; relation; 3. The knowledge of facts and events." While the first relates most obviously to the work of historians and the third relates to history as a specific field of study, the second definition is much broader and more colloquial. Unlike in our contemporary culture, where we debate whether we are too close in time to an event to produce a history of it, the truncation of historical distance meant that last week was, in some sense, just as "historical" as the previous century. People in the eighteenth century did not just read histories; they lived them. In accordance with Johnson's second definition, they also told their own "histories" in conversation. As John Adams recalled upon visiting Mrs. Palmers, a very talkative neighbor, who "gave us history's of her Journeys with her Brother, to Connecticutt, to Barnstable, Plymouth, Middleborough, Norton, &c." She also recounted the "History of her Loves" which was "curious, but not uncommon."[32] People also spoke of "the History of [their] illness," and to gossip about someone was to "whisper the[ir] Secret History."[33]

This rhetorical mixture of the quotidian events of one's daily life with the grand political and religious events of the past is evident in the uses of the term throughout the pre-revolutionary period. For example, on a broader scale, the *Annual Register,* published yearly in London as a compilation of the notable events of the previous year, was subtitled, "Or a complete View of History, Politics and Literature" for the given year. Similarly, one of the first colonial periodicals was entitled the *American Magazine and Historical Chronicle* (1743–46). The section entitled the "Historical Chronicle," like the *Annual Register,* predictably aggregated a list of the most recent political and military events in Europe. Whether it was speaking or writing about a battle between national armies or the vagaries of an individual's love life, the term "history" was used widely and included both the distant and most recent past, the civic and the personal. Such usage speaks to both the truncation of historical distance and the intimate sense of the relationship between the past and present in eighteenth-century British America.

The historical works that circulated in the eighteenth-century British North American colonies focused on a variety of pasts, including the British, European, classical, and biblical pasts. Relatively speaking, historical works regarding the colonial past, however, were few and far between. In the first half of the eighteenth century, only a small number of works dealing with the histories of individual colonies had been published and most appear to have had very small circulation, both in terms of overall numbers and geographic reach. In 1702, Cotton Mather published his *Magnalia Christi Americana,* an ecclesiastical history of New England written in the seventeenth-century providential style of historical writing. In 1705, Robert Beverley, a member of the Virginia gentry, published *The History and Present State of Virginia.* These works were followed through mid-century by Daniel Neal's *History of New England* (1720), Cadwallader Colden's *History of the Five Nations* (1727), Thomas Prince's *Chronological History of New England* (1736), and William Stith's *History of the First Discovery and Settlement of Virginia* (1747). In the period between 1700 and 1750, only two works were published, both in London, that attempted to tell a history of all British American colonies. *The British Empire in America* (1708), written by John Oldmixon, a partisan Grub Street hack who had never visited the colonies, was primarily a compilation of previously published histories of individual colonies. *A Summary, Historical and Political, of the First Planting, Progressive Improvements, and Present State of the British Settlements in North-America* (1747–52) was written by William Douglass, a physician who had emigrated from Scotland to Boston, where he became involved in colonial politics, particularly regarding economic policy.[34] These latter two volumes turn up in a number of private libraries, though that seems more a result of their being the only compendious histories of the British American colonies than because of their quality. Either way, they were not widely known beyond a fraction of the small book-buying public of colonial elites.

Most of the relatively few historical works published on the colonial past in this period focused on the history of an individual colony. Many of these early works of colonial history were published in London for a primarily British audience. These colonial historians intended to show native Britons how economically important the colonies were and how culturally British the elite colonists were. They often included much information about the natural history, or "present state," of the colony, in part to show the credentials of the author (and his fellow elite colonists) as gentlemen interested in natural philosophy. More importantly, natural history was incorporated into these individual colonial histories as a way of arguing for the value of the colony's natural resources to the empire. Indeed, just as the British American colonies were, in some ways, culturally distinct from one another, so too were they historically distinct. And just as they felt a deeper cultural connection to Britain than to other colonies, they also had a deeper cultural connection to the British past than those of their fellow colonies. By the eve of the imperial crisis of the 1760s, there was as yet no sense of a shared colonial past, or "American history."

Instead, colonists read much more of and were more often exposed to the history of the Britain—through works written and published in Britain—than they were to the history of their own colonies, let alone that of other colonies. British historical writing underwent tremendous changes in the first half of the eighteenth century.[35] Before 1700, the primary form of historical works was the annal. These works—including Camden's *Britannia* (1586) and John Rushworth's popular *Historical Collections* (1659–1701)—were effectively glorified timelines and collections of historical documents that focused on political and military events. The turn of the eighteenth century, however, witnessed the publication of a number of important histories of England that would shape how colonists understood the British past. Among these were Clarendon's *History of the Rebellion and Civil Wars in England* (1702–4) and Bishop Burnet's *History of His Own Time* (1724–34). These works signaled a shift from the older form of historical writing toward narrative history, which, in turn, led to a more interpretative history. Yet, they were not complete histories of England, and many Britons bemoaned the absence of such. Literate and increasingly national-minded Britons desired a complete or general history that met the classical standards and style of Herodotus, Thucydides, and Livy, which was mimicked by the most popular recent continental historians.[36] The early eighteenth century had seen an explosion of highly partisan historical writing in Britain. Grub Street hacks, such as Oldmixon, with the support of the patronage of Whigs and Tories quickly produced ephemeral partial histories of England that supported their parties' interpretations of the English past. Two very different histories published before the Revolution came closest to meeting those standards of completeness and style and their popularity and interpretations require reckoning.[37]

The first truly popular general history of England was written by a French Huguenot, Paul de Rapin de Thoyras. Rapin had accompanied William III to England in 1688 and fought with him in Ireland before returning to Holland to settle down. Upon doing so, he began researching and writing his ten-volume *Histoire d'Angleterre.* It took seventeen years to complete. Quickly translated by Nicholas Tindal into a fourteen-volume English edition, it was published between 1726 and 1731 to great interest and acclaim.[38] Rapin's work was reprinted countless times in large, expensive folio volumes; smaller, cheaper duodecimo volumes; and every size in between. Both the volumes and the reputation of the author and his interpretation quickly made their way to the colonies. Unabashedly secular, Rapin notably projected a veneer of impartiality. As Voltaire wrote of his fellow countryman, "England is indebted to him for the best history of that Kingdom that has yet appeared, and the only one that is impartial, of a nation wherein few write without being actuated by the spirit of party."[39] Nevertheless, due to its forthright Whiggish interpretation and pretensions to objectivity, it found greater public favor than the more baldly partisan histories written by English writers during the Whig ascendancy that followed Queen Anne's reign and the Jacobite uprising of 1715.

Rapin's *History of England* was innovative in a number of ways. First, he took a critical and analytical approach to his primary sources, unlike most English historians. Second, he wrote in a direct narrative style, eschewing the common practice of fabricating speeches for his subjects, which European historians had adopted to mimic the classical histories of ancient Greece and Rome. One of the key aspects of Rapin's interpretation was his acknowledgment of and praise for the ancient constitution and its balance between king and Parliament. He argued Parliament had existed among the Anglo-Saxons before the Norman Invasion in 1066.[40] He also detailed the ancient constitution's usurpation by the Stuart monarchs throughout the seventeenth century, which took up a significantly large proportion of the work as a whole. Rapin blamed the Stuarts not only for the Civil Wars of the 1640s but also for the subsequent rise of political parties, then seen by many as a highly negative development in British politics.

Most of all, he trumpeted the Glorious Revolution, arguing that it had restored the ancient constitution. As a writer in one of the colonies' first magazines, the *American Magazine & Historical Chronicle*, wrote in 1746, "Rapin excels all our other Historians in [his] just Representation of the *English* Constitution." Speaking of the Glorious Revolution and its settlement, the writer noted, "He hath shewn that the People had their *Rights,* as well as the Kings their *Prerogatives;* that our Monarchy was not *absolutely hereditary* . . . and how dreadful were the Effects of our Kings struggling with the People for *absolute Power.*" For that reason, the writer concluded, "*This Book* should be in every *Englishman*'s Hand" and, like the Glorious Revolution itself, "engraven upon his Heart."[41] Rapin's interpretation lost favor with mainstream Whigs in Britain, who by mid-century saw 1688 as having marked the beginning of something new: the British Empire.

A look at the available library catalogs and bookseller lists from the middle of the eighteenth century, however, shows the great popularity of Rapin's work in the colonies.[42] As the *New-York Gazette* noted, "Perhaps no Book published of late Years has done more Service to General Liberty, than Rapin's History of England" thanks to its "right Understanding of our History."[43] Its popularity was due both to its style and its interpretation of the ancient constitution and the seventeenth-century British past, particularly the Glorious Revolution. Favor for subsequent works of similar interpretation reinforce this fact, including Lord Kames's *British Antiquities* (1745) and eighteenth-century updates of Henry Care's *English Liberties, or the Free-Born Subject's Inheritance* (1682), which was basically a guide to being English that sold freely and was included in many libraries throughout the first half of the eighteenth century.

Rapin's popularity can also be seen in the unusual availability of his *History.* Cheap editions were sold not just by booksellers but even by dry goods merchants. One 1737 advertisement in the *South-Carolina Gazette* listed newly imported items for sale, including "men, women, & childrens shoes, mens and boys hatts, cordage, *Rapin*'s History of England, wine glasses & decanters, [and] sewing silk."[44] Similarly, an advertisement in Boston in 1744 declared, "To be sold, a good Milch Cow, that will Calve next Month, a parcel of choice Allewives, repack'd, also Rapin's *History of England*."[45] The historian Richard Beale Davis found a case in which, "In Maryland in 1770, one poor man's three books included Rapin's *History of England* (volume 1)."[46] In the 1750s, individual volumes of Rapin's *History* could be had for around six shillings per volume. That is approximately 1.2 percent of the average annual income of the period, or the relative cost of an iPhone to someone earning the median annual income today.[47] In addition, it was held by most of the colonies' first social libraries and excerpted and cited by political polemicists in newspapers, pamphlets, and magazines, giving Rapin's reputation and general interpretation a public reach far beyond those who could afford to purchase his books.[48]

The second most important general history read in the colonies before the Revolution was David Hume's *History of England*.[49] Published in six volumes between 1754 and 1761 in England, it too quickly made its way to the colonies. Hume's *History* purported to take an even more objective approach than Rapin, whom he considered little better in terms of impartiality than the Grub Street hacks who had been producing quickly written partisan histories of England through the patronage of Whig and Tory leaders for decades.

Hume distinguished his work from both Rapin and the partisan Whig historians in a number of ways. First, he claimed that the modern Parliament only truly came into being during the reign of James I, thereby countering the myth that the Parliament dated back to England's Anglo-Saxon ancestors. This argument was significant because many attributed Parliament's authority to its ancient origins. He also argued that, due to its "encroachments" on the royal "prerogative," Parliament shared a significant portion of the blame for the Civil Wars. Second, Hume argued that the Glorious Revolution had produced a new, improved constitution rather than it having restored the ancient constitution. Third, he offered a relatively sympathetic portrayal of the Stuart monarchs, particularly James I and Charles I.

Taken together, it should not be surprising that some of his contemporaries, both in Britain and the colonies, characterized it as a "Tory" history. Indeed, its interpretations were attacked by a number of soon-to-be prominent revolutionaries both publicly and in their private correspondence, including Daniel Dulany ("a studied apology for the Stuarts"), John

Adams ("elegant lies" that "had nearly laughed into contempt Rapin"), and Thomas Jefferson ("made Tories of all England").[50] Jefferson went so far as to argue that Hume's *History* "seems intended to disguise & discredit the good principles of the government" by being "so plausible & pleasing in it's [*sic*] style & manner, as to instil it's errors & heresies insensibly into the minds of unwary readers."[51]

Historians have long assumed that, beyond the contempt in which he was held by lawyers like Adams and Jefferson, colonists generally ignored Hume and his *History of England*. The argument that Hume was unpopular is often based on the failed attempt by Philadelphia bookseller Robert Bell to procure subscriptions for an American edition of the *History* in 1771.[52] As historian Mark Spencer recently pointed out, however, there were also failed subscription attempts to produce editions of genuinely popular works like John Dickinson's *Letters from a Pennsylvania Farmer* in the same period. Indeed, Spencer argues that the failure of the subscription for an American edition was because the market was already flooded with British editions of Hume's *History*.[53] The response of the lawyers above did not represent the broader colonial response as the book appears in most library catalogues published shortly after the work began appearing. Both Jefferson and Adams, who despised Hume and his interpretation, nevertheless included it in a number of reading lists they drew up for friends and family over the course of their lives. By 1775, after the imperial crisis had forced colonists to reconsider their understanding of the Glorious Revolution, "Hume's History, despite its alleged Tory tendencies, [was] far more popular than the radically Whig histories by Rapin and Macaulay."[54]

The popularity of Hume's *History of England* has been hard for historians who have understood the coming of the Revolution in terms of radical Whig ideology to reckon with. Were not colonists supposed to be ever suspicious of power? If so, why would they so widely read Hume's apparent apologia to the absolutist Stuart monarchs? As we will see in chapter 3, the imperial crisis caused colonists to begin rethinking their own interpretations of the British past and their relationship to it. Over the course of the crisis, colonists came to see the Glorious Revolution's legacy primarily in terms of parliamentary supremacy—the doctrine at the heart of the imperial reforms of the 1760s and 1770s—not the reestablishment of the ancient constitution. As such, by the eve of independence, their ideas about the

British past actually came to rest much closer to Hume than Rapin. Hume had argued that Charles I did not deserve to be executed because it was Parliament that first overstepped the traditional bounds of its authority. Similarly, he saw Parliament's actions in 1688–89 as a necessary response to James II overstepping the bounds of royal authority.

What mattered to Hume in assessing historical blame was the action of a king or a Parliament taking it upon themselves to arbitrarily expand their authority. For Hume, such an act—so contrary to the balance of the British constitution—justified resistance and, in the case of 1688, revolution. Despite their mistrust of Hume, colonial patriots would apply a similar perspective to the contemporary politics of the imperial crisis. One cannot possibly argue a direct causal link between the reading of Hume or any single history and support for resistance to and independence from Britain. Yet, his seemingly inexplicable popularity is indicative of how previous understandings of the British past were coming into question throughout the Anglo-American world and the influence of those changing understandings on how both sides perceived the crisis.

In addition to works on British history, colonial elites also read a good number of works of European and, of course, classical history. Much work has been done on the reading of classics in the colonies, so it needs no retreading here, but it is worth noting that familiarity with the classical past was the type of history most limited to a small number of elites. Colonial elites also read widely in the history of Europe. Works such as Puffendorf's *History of Europe,* Davila's *History of the Civil Wars of France,* Voltaire's *History of Charles XII* and *History of Lewis XIV,* Buchanan's *History of Scotland,* Robertson's *History of Scotland* and *History of Charles V,* and Ricaut's *History of the Turks* were especially popular, as were histories of Geneva, France, Germany, the Italian and Dutch republics, Poland, Portugal, and Ireland, among others.

No small number of these popular European histories focused on revolutions, civil wars, and tyrannical monarchs. Beyond culturally insecure colonial gentry reaching for a cosmopolitanism they believed represented British high culture, the reading of European histories provided a broader context within which colonial elites could feel they were developing a deeper understanding of Britain's world-historical role as the Protestant empire of liberty and commerce. To their minds, the seventeenth century had put the ancient constitution's principles to the test, and it had passed by quickly reversing in England the wave of tyranny that had overswept and overpowered many of its continental neighbors.

Now that we have a sense of historical writing in eighteenth-century British America, we can ask: How did colonists—elite and non-elite—access these historical works and, more importantly, the information and interpretations they contained? Colonial elites, of course, had direct access. Imports from Britain dominated the book trade in the colonies at mid-century.[55] Because of their high cost, imported books were a visible status marker, with large, expensively bound libraries conspicuously displayed as appointments in the finely upholstered parlors of wealthy merchants and planters.[56] Books also represented their owner's enlightened participation in metropolitan and European literary cultures, or the so-called Republic of Letters. By buying books imported from London, the capital of the empire, colonial elites strengthened their cultural connection to the metropole. Many booksellers' printed catalogues and newspaper advertisements regularly touted their lists as "just imported from London." In the 1760s, there were three shops in Boston alone named "the London Book-store," one of which offered the very imperial description of its location: "The London Book-store, Second Door above the British Coffee-House, North-Side of King Street."[57]

With each passing decade, colonial elites' libraries swelled with more and more imported books, and history was an important part of their libraries. Historical works comprised about one-third of typical private libraries in the Middle Colonies. In New England, theology predictably dominated all other topics, but history was the second most popular subject and twice as prevalent as the next.[58] In the South, religious titles were also the most popular in number, but, again, historical titles took a "strong second."[59] Those proportions are especially significant when considering the range of other genres available and often present in such libraries, including natural philosophy, law, classics, applied science, novels, poetry, philosophy, and reference works.

Young elites (and some aspiring middling youth) had access to large collections of books through their college libraries. By 1770, the British American colonies had eight colleges thanks to a feverish two-decade period of college building spurred on by the Great Awakening.[60] The official curriculum at colonial colleges consisted of the three key liberal arts: grammar, rhetoric, and logic.[61] Since the colonial colleges were still largely seminaries, the curriculum also included theology and moral philosophy. Admission required a firm grasp on Latin and ancient Greek. Those admitted likely had also studied classical history. While history was not yet a discrete subject of study in college curricula, it was expected that students would do the necessary reading in history on their own time.

A look at published college library catalogues, therefore, is instructive regarding the role of history in colonial higher education beyond the classical curriculum. Yale College published its first library catalogue in 1741 as part of new Rector Thomas Clap's efforts to boost the ill-managed institution's reputation. Much of the collection consisted of old, seventeenth-century theological works, which had formed a major part of the library's initial foundation from donors. As in private New England libraries, however, by the 1740s history was the second largest subject of the college's collection. Divinity titles took up nearly half of the forty-four-page catalogue. History—including its correlative subjects of "antiquities," "lives of famous men," and "chronology"—accounted for almost seven pages in the catalog. No other subject required more than a single page. The library held approximately 2,600 volumes, of which about 233 were historical. That ratio would grow steadily as the century went on. Out of those 233 volumes, British and ecclesiastical history were the most predominant topics. Only 2 works related directly to the history of the colonies were held.

Meanwhile, the library at Harvard College by the early 1760s contained more than a half dozen multivolume general histories of England alone, a number in the most expensive folio editions. On a snowy, "tempestuous night" in January 1764, errant sparks from a fireplace in the "ancient" Harvard Hall set the library ablaze with a fire that consumed 90 percent of its books. In the years just before the fire, students borrowed Rapin's *History of England* more than twice as much as any other title.[62] History accounted for more than one-third of the individual volumes loaned in that period, topping even theology. The percentage of works of "general history" borrowed more than doubled from 19 percent to 40 percent between 1763 and 1776—the years of the imperial crisis—while "divinity" volumes declined from 34 percent to less than 10 percent.[63] By 1773, even with the vast increase of historical works in its collection thanks to post-fire donations, the Harvard College library still only held fewer than a dozen titles dealing specifically with the history of any of the British American colonies and none of them the works by Douglass and Oldmixon that sought to tell the history of the British American colonies in a single title.[64] More colleges meant more young men were attending college, all of whom were reading more British history than their counterparts of the previous generation. Moreover, more attendees meant more aspiring young men of lesser means attending college than ever before. Beyond these fortunate few, however, non-elites also had a relatively surprising degree of access to historical knowledge.

In addition to the small but growing number of rising middling-class youth attending college, non-elites also accessed imported books through social and circulating libraries, the forerunners to the modern public library. Social libraries were a way for individuals to pool together their money and buy far more books than they could on their own. Members purchased shares that went toward setting up the library and then yearly dues for its maintenance. Since these libraries were spending their members' own money and those funds were limited, their choice of books is a good representation of what the members wanted to read most and what offerings they thought would attract new members. While the Library Company of Philadelphia, established in 1731, was the first and perhaps most famous example, by mid-century a number of social and circulating libraries had sprung up in the colonies. That growth quickened between 1763 and 1776. By the time of independence, such libraries could be found in Philadelphia, New York, Boston, Charleston, and Providence, as well as in less urban areas, such as Burlington and Bridgetown, New Jersey, and Lancaster, Pennsylvania. There were over fifty social libraries established in New England alone between 1733 and 1780.[65] In Pennsylvania, a 1766 catalogue for the Juliana Library in Lancaster noted there were "not less than four in the Metropolis, and in almost every Town of Note, one."[66] Urban booksellers like Henry Knox in Boston offered discounts to "those Gentlemen in the Country who are actuated with the most genuine Principles of Benevolence in their Exertions to Exterminate Ignorance and Darkness, by the noble medium of social libraries."[67] These libraries, depending on the size of the membership or community, might hold anywhere from a few hundred volumes to a few thousand.

Unlike social libraries, which were community-driven efforts, circulating libraries were set up by individuals, usually booksellers. They, in turn, charged annual, half-year, or quarterly membership fees, no upfront share purchase required. For example, the New-York Society Library, established in 1754, charged five pounds for a share and annual dues of ten shillings. Meanwhile, Mein's Circulating Library in Boston, whose proportion of historical titles and volumes was even higher than most social libraries, required no share purchase. Borrowers paid twenty-eight shillings for a year, eighteen for a half year, or "Ten and Eight Pence per Quarter." Some libraries, like the still-extant Redwood Library Company established in Newport, Rhode Island, in 1747, also charged a "security" fee with prices set by the size of the book. The deposit fee was returned when the book was returned unharmed. Fees of a few shillings per month were certainly not out of reach for middling-class individuals intent on self-cultivation and self-improvement through reading.

An examination of the holdings of social and circulating libraries between 1741 and 1770 show that historical works formed an even bigger proportion of their collections than the college libraries.[68] For example, the Library Company of Philadelphia (one of four in the city by 1766) listed 375 titles in its 1741 catalogue, of which approximately one-third were historical works.[69] The 1765 catalogue cover for John Mein's Circulating Library listed the subjects in which he, as a bookseller, expected his potential clients would be most interested. "History" stood at the head of the list, accounting for near half of the library's more than 1,200 volumes.[70] Anywhere from one-third to one-half of all folio volumes (that is, the most expensive) in many of these libraries were historical titles. That means an even greater proportion of these libraries' limited purchasing funds was spent on procuring historical works than even the percentage of historical works among all titles (many of which were in smaller, cheaper quarto, octavo, and duodecimo sizes).

In a number of libraries, historical works accounted for approximately one-third of all titles. And, since many historical titles were multivolume sets, they took up a far greater percentage of a library's total number of volumes. Because many of these libraries often gave their purchasing agents in England lists of the titles their members wanted most, we can assume that the membership of these many libraries had a strong desire for access to a substantial number of historical works, particularly those regarding English history. Indeed, English history formed a larger percentage of the historical titles in total than in the college libraries where ecclesiastical and classical histories were more predominant (though many of those works were older and often acquired through donations). The collections of social libraries, bought with their members' own money, were based on the reading tastes and priorities of their members, and those of circulating libraries were based on the proprietors' often well-informed understanding of their potential readers' tastes. Taken together, the prominence of historical works in these collections serves as a fair representation of the place and priority of history in eighteenth-century colonial reading habits.

Non-elites also had access to historical information, particularly regarding the British past, in printed forms beyond books. Colonial newspapers often published essays that made references to historical events, particularly from the British past. On occasion they also published excerpts from well-known historical works, when deemed relevant to current affairs. One reader of John Peter Zenger's *New-York Weekly Journal* in 1733—in the midst of great political upheaval in the colony—took the liberty of suggesting to the printer that "some pieces of History would be full as Entertaining to your Readers, as your political Pieces."[71] In 1745, an anonymous writer contributed a full front-page essay to the *Maryland Gazette* extolling the virtues and value of history: "It is, in short, a great Step, by which we may attain to a competent Knowledge of Mankind; a Knowledge so necessary and useful in Life, that all Science and Learning without it, appears pedantic, insignificant, and vain." Historical works regarding England were most important because they "tend to inspire us with generous Sentiments, worthy of our happy Constitution, and instill into us [its] Principles . . . and enable us to secure our valuable Liberties and Privileges."[72] Historical references to the British past were also common in the regular reprinting of pieces from the British press as well as the partisan domestic political and religious debates that increasingly filled the columns and pages of colonial newspapers and pamphlets, many of which assumed a very basic general knowledge of the outline of the seventeenth-century British past on the part of their audience.

Almanacs too played a role in spreading such basic general historical knowledge. After the Bible, almanacs were the most widely owned form of print throughout the colonies. Many almanacs printed throughout the colonies in the 1740s and 1750s noted historical events by date in their calendar. The most common events were the regicide of King Charles I on January 30 and the Gunpowder Plot on November 5, which commemorated the uncovering of a Catholic conspiracy against Parliament, as well as the birthday and coronation of the current monarch. In some cases, the restoration of King Charles II was included. Many almanacs also included brief timelines denoting "things Remarkable" from both the British and colonial pasts. During the imperial crisis, a number of almanacs became increasingly politicized to the point that, in 1774, Nathanael Low included a woodcut of Oliver Cromwell on the front page of his *An Astronomical Diary; Or, Almanack.* On the first page, Low included a famous excerpt from Cromwell's speech in which "he put an end to the 'Long Parliament.'" The corollary between the past and present—a corrupt Parliament—would have been obvious to many of Low's readers: "It is high time for me to put an end to your sitting in this Place, which you have dishonored by your contempt of all Virtue, and defiled by your Practice of every Vice. Ye are a factious Crew, and Enemies to all good Government."[73]

Sermons, too, exposed colonists to historical information. They were a prominent and regular feature of colonial life. Clergy often delivered political sermons on election days as well as on the annual anniversaries of the regicide and the Gunpowder Plot. Many popular sermons were subsequently printed, but sermons were heard weekly throughout the colonies. Perhaps the most famous of the printed sermons was *A Discourse concerning Unlimited Submission and Nonresistance to the Higher Powers* (1750) by Jonathan Mayhew, a very liberal Congregationalist minister in Boston.[74] Following the Restoration of Charles II in 1660, the anniversary of the regicide of Charles I was declared a religious holiday, though it had never been celebrated by non-Anglicans in the colonies. Preaching on the centennial of the regicide, his sermon was inspired by recent attempts by Anglicans in

New England to publicly rehabilitate the image of Charles I from tyrant to martyr.

Mayhew began by laying out a Scripture-based version of John Locke's famous argument regarding the people's right to resist "when the Legislative, or the Prince . . . act contrary to their Trust."[75] Then he moved on to the historical question at hand: "For what reason the resistance to King *Charles* the *First* was made?" Charles I, he argued, had governed "in a perfectly wild and arbitrary manner, paying no regard to the constitution."[76] By "assuming a power above the laws," he had effectively "*unkinged* himself."[77] That is, when either the legislature or the king acts arbitrarily, they are breaking their contract (or "trust") with the people and the latter have the right to rebel and replace them. Both the social contract between ruler and ruled and an understanding of the dangers of unrestrained arbitrary rule were common throughout colonial political culture, and their foundations were to be found in contemporary understandings of the seventeenth-century British past. Within two decades, colonists would come to see attempts to reorganize the empire as evidence of the "wild and arbitrary manner" of Parliament. Because Parliament had historically served as the people's bulwark against absolute or arbitrary monarchs, such a notion flipped the British past on its head, both to colonists, who subsequently reconsidered their understandings of the British past, and to Britons, to whom the idea that Parliament could act arbitrarily or against the will of the people was effectively unintelligible.

Colonists of all ranks had a significant degree of access to historical information through a variety of modes. Based on the most common historical references in the forms discussed, particularly those that assume prior knowledge, we can surmise the degree of historical information generally possessed by the average colonist, though this would differ to some extent depending on region. Nevertheless, it seems likely that the average colonist would have had enough exposure to historical information to understand a basic outline of the major events of the seventeenth-century British past: the Civil Wars, Restoration, and Glorious Revolution. They would also likely have understood a very basic outline of the major events of their own colony, perhaps a rough idea of when, why, and by whom it was settled. Colonists in New England were likely to have more knowledge of their colony's past than non-elite colonists in the Chesapeake and Deep South. Just as colonists were more likely to know about current events in Britain than in other colonies, they were also likely to know more about the British past than the histories of their fellow colonies. Elites in the Middle Colonies and Chesapeake, however, appear to have been relatively aware of the history of New England's settlement, at least enough to offer a general critique of that history and its current inhabitants. Yet, what matters is that colonists had understandings of historical events, regardless of their thoroughness or accuracy. In fact, the relatively modest depth of historical information of such events held by many colonists made those interpretations more malleable than they might otherwise have been, thereby leaving them open to both question and change in the kind of moments of instability and uncertainty brought about by the imperial crisis of the 1760s and 1770s.

History culture manifested itself in mid-eighteenth-century colonial culture in other fundamental ways as well. Most notably, it played a key structural role in how colonists thought about, understood, and practiced government, politics, law, religion, and the family, all of which contributed to colonists' imperial identities as British subjects. A number of key ideas and events from the seventeenth-century British past helped shape how colonists understood government and politics, including the ancient constitution and the Glorious Revolution. The "ancient constitution" was an idea that emerged from late sixteenth- and early seventeenth-century English domestic politics. Sir Edward Coke, a prominent jurist, developed the mythology of the "ancient constitution," and it gained prominence during the seventeenth-century conflicts between the early Stuart monarchs and their Parliaments. The former sought to expand the royal prerogative and the latter sought to limit it. Royal proponents argued that the monarch's right to rule was divinely ordained. This meant the royal prerogative was unlimited and unchallengeable, because only God could render judgment on a monarch. The subject's primary civic and religious responsibility was to obey the monarch.

To counter the divine right theory, Parliament and its supporters argued that the ancient constitution, which though itself was unwritten, consisted of the common law and other precedents that defined the relationship between the Crown and its people and between the Crown and Parliament, including Magna Carta. To bolster the authority of their claims, they argued that Parliament itself predated the English monarchy. Despite a lack of evidence, the ideas of the "ancient constitution" and "precedent, common law, and ancient custom" were fundamentally historical. However, they also spoke to the perceived relationship between the past and present, as they encompassed "significant information . . . regarding the supposed mode and manner of [British] society's existence in time and history."[78] In a culture that invested great authority in the past, the origins of institutions and ideas was a fiercely contested topic laden with significant political and cultural implications.

In the early seventeenth century and before, Parliament was a very different institution than it would become by the eve of the American Revolution. It met infrequently, being called and dissolved at the monarch's whim. As a matter of custom, the House of Commons was the only body that could originate bills related to raising and granting revenue. When the monarch did call a Parliament, it was usually for the purpose of getting it to grant revenue to the king, either for his own personal expenses or for war. As members of Parliament in the early seventeenth century sought a larger role in governing the kingdom, they began arguing that Parliament was older than the monarchy itself, tracing its origins all the way back to a governing council, called the Witagemot, that existed before the Norman Invasion. Though there were some parallels between the Anglo-Saxon Witagemot and Parliament, it was a very specious argument in strictly historical terms. Yet, by arguing that the Parliament had ancient origins that predated the monarchy and was therefore a part of the ancient constitution, Parliament's supporters were increasing its claim to legitimacy by imparting to it an even greater sense of the authority of the past than it already had. The authority of the past in seventeenth-century English culture meant that the older something was—whether a law, institution, or religious practice—the more authority it had, because it had stood the test of time. Most importantly, seventeenth-century colonists had brought this reverence for the authority of the past across the ocean as part of their cultural inheritance from the mother country.

By the eighteenth century, however, educated Britons largely understood the lack of an actual historical basis for arguments regarding the ancient constitution and Parliament's antiquity. And its use, even by many Whigs, fell out of favor relative to the previous century. But such had not been the case in the colonies, which had been established during the period in which these arguments had defined the anti-royalist position in England. Colonists continued to refer to the "ancient constitution" as the source of their shared first principles with the Britain. Indeed, the hold of the ancient constitution remained so strong in the colonies that in the middle of the eighteenth century, colonial lawyers and law students were still engaging among themselves in the historical debate regarding the origins of the common law and the ancient constitution that had taken place in England in the seventeenth century.[79]

The Glorious Revolution of 1688 played a key role in colonists' identity as British subjects, just as it did for native Britons. Throughout the period between 1730 and 1760, colonial writers referred often in print to their "firm Attachment to the glorious Revolution, and the happy Establishment founded thereon."[80] These types of devotional statements became even more common during political crises, including the wars with Spain and the Jacobite Rebellion of 1745. In the wake of the latter, newspapers throughout the colonies reprinted Parliament's address to the king, which praised the "happy Revolution wrought by our great Deliverer King William the Third" and saw the rejection of Jacobitism as "clear Demonstrations that this Nation is determined to preserve the Structure built upon that glorious Foundation."[81]

In print, 1688 was just as often referred to as "our happy Revolution" as it was called the "glorious revolution."[82] Such a formulation gave priority not to the individual facts that the revolution of 1688 had been (relatively) bloodless or even had restored the Protestant monarchy so much as to colonists' understanding that it "laid the foundation of our present government" and for subjects' present "happiness." Happiness in the eighteenth-century sense meant the enjoyment of civic equality by white males, which provided the basis and opportunity for those individuals to pursue their own interests and pleasure in a manner congruent with the public good. For many Britons and colonists, the Glorious Revolution had done just that by giving British subjects "the peculiar Happiness to be born under a Constitution, the best calculated in the World for the Dignity and Welfare of Mankind."[83]

The Glorious Revolution also played a fundamental role in both colonists' and Britons' identities as British subjects. Throughout the eighteenth century, colonists' understanding of the legacy of 1688 and revolutionary settlement mirrored the "intensely nationalistic" role of that legacy in Britain.[84] As the historian Jack P. Greene noted, "The intense British patriotism of the colonists . . . depended upon the continuing credibility of the colonists' belief that they shared in the legacy of the Glorious Revolution."[85] James Otis echoed the belief of most colonists when he wrote that "no country has been more distinguished" for the "principles of equity, moderation and justice" than "Great-Britain, since the Revolution." And that Revolution had been "as joyful an event to the colonies as to Great-Britain." Colonists' ideas about the historical past and their ideas about government were interrelated and intersected with their own imperial identities as eighteenth-century British subjects.

The past also fundamentally shaped how colonists (and Britons, for that matter) understood the law. Unlike statutory law, the English common law was built on precedent and custom. Precedents set over time became customary. John Adams, writing in the *Boston Gazette* in 1773, described the common law as being "of higher antiquity than memory or history can reach" and used from "time out of mind, or for a time whereof the memory of man runneth not to the contrary."[86] Colonists had largely adopted the English common law from the start of settlement (if more in theory than in practice). Many colonists, particularly lawyers, understood that adoption as a crucial cultural connection between the colonies and the mother country. As Jack Greene has argued, "In their efforts to imprint Europeanness upon colonial landscapes, the legal systems by which they defined the new social spaces they were creating were critical."[87] The common law, like the British constitution, was the product of history itself. It was "a form of history . . . [that] helped explain the movement of events and the meaning of the present."[88] As a cumulative collection of precedents, it represented the sum wisdom of the past and a foundation for expectations about the future.

The broader interrelationship between history and law was understood at the time. Writing from London where he was studying law to his father in Maryland, Charles Carroll wrote, "Without a perfect knowledge of history and mankind, which latter is acquired from the study of History and personal experience, there is no possibility of excelling in the law."[89] Those laws, statutes, and decisions that remained in force had done so because they had stood the test of time. The passage of time conferred authority on them. This idea forms the very foundation of the cultural reverence in the colonies for the "authority of the past." This concept will be developed more fully in the next chapter, particularly its implications for the imperial crisis, but it is important to understand that the reach of this concept went well beyond the law. As historian John Demos has noted, the "common-law tradition was so deeply threaded into the cultural experience of early America" that these notions of custom, precedent, and tradition helped shape and define colonial society and thought well beyond the law.[90]

In addition to government and the law, the past also shaped how colonists thought about and understood religion. Religion in the eighteenth century was fundamentally historicized. The understandings of Protestantism that shaped colonial religion were inescapably rooted in the historical past, namely in a good-versus-evil interpretation of the Reformation and the Catholic Church. Moreover, individual denominational identities within the colonies—such as Congregationalist, Presbyterian, Anglican, Quaker, and Baptist—were simultaneously rooted in colonists' understandings of the origins of their denominations and their historical relationship, both in England and in the colonies, with their counterparts, particularly their suffering at the hands of the Church of England in the seventeenth century. Those historical understandings shaped colonial religious identities and, thereby, shaped the many religious conflicts in the colonies during the eighteenth century, including the Great Awakening.

Beyond denominational identities and conflicts, the past fundamentally informed religious understandings in other ways. First, and most obviously, many colonists read the Bible as history. To them, it told a tale of the historical past (or what we today would call a fundamentalist interpretation of the Bible). Not only did they read the Bible as history, they read "ecclesiastical histories," or historical works that offered a more traditional and complete historical narrative of the history of the Bible and of the church. Second, individual doctrines that helped define the denominations were also rooted in historical interpretations. For example, Anglicans understood their bishops as part of a lineal episcopacy that could be traced directly back to the apostles. It was, in part, for that reason that they rejected the validity of the ordination of ministers in the dissenting denominations that had been created by breaking away from the Church of England, such as the Puritans, Congregationalists, Quakers, and others. Meanwhile, Presbyterians believed their system of ecclesiastical rule by a council of elders was derived from the early Christian church. Similarly, Congregationalists' system of local governance by individual congregations was rooted in the historical experience of their Puritan ancestors who had been persecuted by the centralized, state-sponsored Church of England. In these ways and others, the historical past shaped how colonists in the eighteenth century understood their religious identities and the relationship between their religious and imperial identities.

Finally, the past also shaped colonial understandings of the family.[91] The dynastic sense of living under a monarchy translated in a cultural sense to the colonies.[92] Family histories, including births, deaths, and marriages, were kept in the family Bible as a record of the family's history. But a family's historical genealogy also took on social significance. Common colonists, in New England for example, took added pride in their family name if they were descended from early settlers of the colonies. As the eighteenth century wore on, Karin Wulf has argued, issues regarding family lineage would become an "object of state utility" as they increasingly factored into colonists' interactions with both developing legal and religious institutions. For colonial elites, though, their family's lineage had additional significance.[93]

Tracing family connections back to British nobility (or even gentry) allowed one to claim gentility through birth. The colonial gentry was looked down upon by their British counterparts, who they could neither match in status nor wealth. To assuage the social inferiority they felt in comparison, many elites sought to establish the gentility of their lineage, including subsequent revolutionaries such as Benjamin Franklin and Thomas Jefferson.[94] To do so, they corresponded with potential distant family members or "pedigree experts" back in Britain looking for historical information about relations and family crests. Some of those who could not trace their lineage back to more genteel British origins simply created their own. In seventeenth-century Virginia and New England, rising gentry without elite lineage had coats of arms created for their families, justified by their newfound wealth and status. The practice became so widespread in the eighteenth century that "heraldic painters" advertised their services regularly in colonial newspapers. These coats of arms would be included in portraits, engraved into silverware, and carved into tombstones. Unlike in England, where heraldry was highly regulated by the Crown, colonists were free to craft their own pedigrees, sometimes out of thin air, if necessary. Non-elite colonists also sought to trace their family histories back to Britain.[95] As in England, both the recent and distant pasts served as a common topic of conversation at family gatherings of colonists of all social ranks. Such occasions, famously parodied by Laurence Sterne in *Tristram Shandy*, provided opportunities for the sharing and perpetuation of oral family histories. As François Weil has argued, "Genealogy suggested a psychological, intellectual, and affective relation to time, ancestors, and family."[96] Indeed, "widespread kin-related genealogical practices developed during the eighteenth century in the British Atlantic world," and this "genealogical consciousness" formed "a bedrock of British American culture" in the eighteenth century.[97] As such, it reflected colonial society's relationship to the past and the role of the broader colonial history culture at the most immediate and intimate local and familial levels.

In this chapter, I have offered a broad overview of British America's history culture in the middle of the eighteenth century. In many ways, this history culture was decidedly colonial. It relied on Britain both materially and intellectually. Regional history cultures existed to varying degrees, with New England's being perhaps the most developed. Nevertheless, for our purposes going forward, it is important to understand a few key aspects of colonial history culture in the pre-revolutionary era. First, the perceived past—historical and otherwise—played an important role in colonial culture generally, especially because historical distance was truncated to such a degree that it fostered a very intimate sense of the relationship between the past and present. Second, colonial history culture was defined in no small measure by its relationship to that of Britain, especially colonists' understanding of their own shared past as British subjects. Colonists held that shared British past in common, and even though they defined it differently than many of their fellow subjects in Britain, it provided an important cultural lifeline for them as subjects living on the peripheries of a rapidly expanding global empire and separated from the metropole by three thousand miles of ocean. The divergence of colonial historical understanding, especially regarding 1688, from Britain that developed in the first half of the century went largely unnoticed, only to be starkly revealed in the 1760s and 1770s. Confronting this important cultural difference was all the more shocking to colonists who had developed a strong sense of confidence in their shared culture with Britain through the process of Anglicization and the consumer revolution. Finally, that shared British past was the only past colonists from different colonies held in common. Before the Revolution, there was as of yet no sense of a shared colonial past and no coherent sense of an "American history." All of these key factors would begin to change during the imperial crisis of the 1760s and 1770s.

CHAPTER TWO

THE COLONIAL PAST IN THE IMPERIAL CRISIS

On January 13, 1769, seven young men from the town of Plymouth came together to form the "Old Colony Club," to commemorate the colony's origins and avoid the "inconveniencies that arise from intermixing with the company at the taverns." After meeting throughout the year, they voted that December 2 would be "kept by this club in commemoration of the first landing of our worthy ancestors in this place." These festivities to celebrate the arrival of the Pilgrims drew out the entire town. The day started with the discharging of a cannon and the "hoist[ing] upon the Hall an elegant silk flag with the following inscription, 'Old Colony 1620.'" In the afternoon, they invited the town elders to a dinner at which the attendees and the food were "dressed in the plainest manner (all appearances of luxury and extravagance being avoided, in imitation of our worthy ancestors whose memory we shall ever respect)." After dinner, the members led a procession through the town to their Old Colony Hall led by the club steward, who carried "a folio volume of the laws of the Old Colony." There, "a number of descendants from the first settlers in the Old Colony drew up in a regular file and discharged a volley of small arms, succeeded by three cheers." Out of "respect for the memory of their ancestors," students of the local grammar school joined the crowd and sang "a song very applicable to the day."

In the evening, the members and invitees gathered in the club's Hall to deliver twelve toasts. Sitting in a chair previously owned by William Bradford, the club president Isaac Lothrop offered the first toast: "To the memory of our brave and pious ancestors the first settlers of the Old Colony." They spent the rest of the evening "recapitulating and conversing upon the many and various adventures of our forefathers in the first settlement of this country."[1] The club continued to celebrate this new holiday—known as both "Old Colony Day" and, later, "Forefathers' Day"—until 1773, when its twelve members split between loyalists and patriots. Residents of Plymouth resurrected both the club and the holiday in 1820. Forefathers' Day, through its commemoration of the Pilgrims, its use of symbolic dress and food, and its commemoration of Native American assistance to the settlers, served as a template for Thanksgiving, which became a federal holiday during the Civil War. The establishment of both the club and the holiday in 1769 speaks to the growing sense of connection both felt and sought by colonists during the imperial crisis with the original settlers, the act of settlement, and the colonial past more generally. Indeed, how colonists—both patriots and loyalists—thought about and used the colonial past in the political rhetoric of the imperial crisis helped shape the dynamics of the imperial debate and, thereby, of the coming of the American Revolution.

In engaging with the most crucial questions of the imperial debate, colonists repeatedly based their arguments on the past in a variety of ways. They created and employed historical memories of both the British and colonial pasts designed to reconcile the present with the past and begin fostering a collective sense among the inhabitants of Britain's North American varied colonies. Colonists also appealed constantly to the historical past itself as a source of authority. They used it in every type and form of resistance rhetoric throughout the entire imperial crisis, from newspaper essays and pamphlets to sermons, orations, and songs, from the resolves of farmers and artisans in town meetings to the official resolutions of lawyers in congress, from New England to Georgia, from 1764 to 1776.

Colonists' use of the past was just as prevalent, direct, and fundamental in the patriot rhetoric of resistance during the imperial crisis as constitutional theory or the influence of radical Whig writers and, arguably, was more visceral to a broader portion of colonial society. Since only a small portion of colonists truly understood the subtleties of the legal and constitutional arguments made and debated by lawyers, history culture served as one of the modes through which those subtleties were translated into the colonial vernacular. That is, history culture did not trump or diminish the importance of the legal and constitutional issues at stake in the crisis but rather served as one important additional lens through which those issues, and the crisis itself, were understood.

In light of a colonial history culture in which the cyclical perspective on history was predominant, the conflict with Britain caused colonists to look to the past in search of the first principles that could help forestay the inevitable decline of the British Empire, the beginning of which, patriots believed, was represented by the imperial reforms of the 1760s and 1770s. Before the crisis, their searches for such first principles reflexively turned primarily to the ancient or British constitution. Almost immediately, the imperial crisis began changing the dynamic of the relationship between the colonies and Britain. Colonists began crafting a sense of a new, shared colonial past from which they could derive new first principles and employ them in their responses to Parliament's actions and to the pro-reform British rhetoric that made its way into the colonies' prints.

Colonial history culture—particularly through historical memories and colonists' cultural reverence for the authority of the past—played an important role in shaping debate during the imperial crisis. Recognizing that role helps us better understand both colonists' arguments against imperial reform and how those arguments evolved. Most notably, colonists made arguments that drew on their changing historical memories of both their colonial and British pasts. Through these arguments, they employed a shared historical grammar that took for granted the authority of the past, itself a cultural inheritance from the mother country. The authority of the past was an important part of colonial history culture and shaped colonists' cultural understanding of the intimate relationship between the past and present. The intimate nature of this relationship produced expectations that the past would explain and make sense of the present. That is, the past allowed colonists to understand the present and develop reasonable expectations about what they could expect in the future, especially in terms of their relationship with the empire. Confidence in those expectations offered a sense of security and stability to colonists living on the peripheries of an otherwise rapidly changing Atlantic world.

The weight afforded to the past as a source of authority in colonial culture weighed that much heavier during the imperial crisis as Britain instituted a program of imperial reforms to address its new geopolitical and economic circumstances following its victory in the Seven Years' War. In a colonial culture in which custom and precedent defined the force of law and in which the past itself justified the legitimacy of the present, the unprecedented imperial reforms of the 1760s seemed inexplicable to many colonists not just legally, constitutionally, or politically but also culturally. Indeed, imperial reforms set colonists' reverence for the authority of the past on a collision course with Britain's determination to deal with the immediate exigencies of empire through unprecedented means, if necessary.

That Parliament and the Ministry appeared to be no longer bound by the authority of the past caused political *and* cultural anxiety on the part of colonists during the crisis. It also made increasingly obvious a new and significant cultural difference between them and their counterparts in Britain, who had developed very different ideas about the relationship between the past and present over the previous half century.[2] The changes in patriot rhetoric throughout the imperial crisis were produced by a combination of shifting political circumstances, colonists' continuing appeals to the authority of the past, and their attempts to reconcile the past and the present in a way that made cultural as well as political sense. Therefore, the reciprocal interrelationship between colonial history culture and imperial politics is important for understanding the dynamics of the imperial crisis.

Broadly speaking, the imperial crisis was brought on by shifting ideas of authority in the mid-eighteenth-century Anglo-American and Atlantic world. Yet, it was not only a difference of opinion over where political authority within the empire should lie. It was also brought about by changing and conflicting notions of cultural authority on a number of levels, including the authority of the past. Throughout the imperial crisis the two sides seemed to be talking past each other, each seemingly unable to understand the other. This ultimately fatal disconnect, however, was not just the result of fundamentally different conceptions of the imperial constitution or mutual conspiratorial suspicions of one another, as historians have argued. Colonists and their contemporaries in Britain also held different cultural conceptions about the relationship between the past and present that, in many cases, informed their core positions and arguments as much as constitutional theory or radical Whig ideology and contributed greatly toward their mutual unintelligibility. Therefore, the role of colonial history culture in the imperial crisis—through the construction and use of historical memories and the authority of the past—helps uncover a part of these cultural origins of the American Revolution and contributes to our current constitutional, ideological, and economic understandings.

In the wake of the coronation of George III and the end of the Seven Years' War, British imperial policy took a concerted turn away from the previous approach to governing the empire. George III distrusted the Whig politicians who had dominated the levers of domestic and imperial policy for decades since the end of the reign of Queen Anne. Upon assuming the throne, he put in place a new Ministry in the early 1760s. Excepting the very brief terms of Rockingham and Pitt in the wake of the Stamp Act, the ministers of the 1760s and 1770s—the Earl of Bute, George Grenville, and Lord North—subscribed to a very different view of the British Empire than their predecessors. Rather than continuing policies to grow trade, domestic manufacturing, and colonial markets for those manufactures, men like Grenville and North believed Britain should emulate the Spanish model of empire by prioritizing extraction of natural resources from their colonies rather than promoting trade and adopting a more authoritarian and centralized approach to imperial administration. They could then use the revenue from taxes and duties on their colonies to pay down the large national debt incurred during the Seven Years' War and relieve the tax burdens of their primary constituency at home, the landholding gentry, at the expense of merchants and the colonies with which they traded.

As a result, decades of policies began to come to a seemingly abrupt end in the mid-1760s. In 1764, Parliament passed the Sugar Act, which sought to tighten collection of trade duties. The next year Parliament passed the Stamp Act, which required a wide variety of items be printed on taxed paper, from newspapers and legal documents to marriage licenses and playing cards. It was repealed in 1766 after boycotts by colonists and protests by London merchants. In 1767, it was followed by the Townshend Acts, which placed duties on imported lead, glass, and other items. Again, after further colonial protests and boycotts, most of the Townshend duties were ultimately repealed by Parliament in 1770. In 1773, colonists responded to passage of the Tea Act, which tried to establish a monopoly in the colonies for the East India Company, by confiscating or destroying the tea. Parliament subsequently passed a set of bills known collectively as the Coercive Acts, with the purpose of punishing Massachusetts for the Boston Tea Party and setting an example to the other colonies of their renewed zero-tolerance policy regarding colonial dissent.

Yet, the British North American colonies had really come of age—both economically and politically—in the first half of the eighteenth century when British authority was exercised primarily in regulating trade. Most colonists viewed them not as merely temporary policies that could be changed depending on the whim of the Ministry or Parliament at any given moment. Rather, they believed those policies defined the customary (and, hence, legal) relationship between Britain and its colonies. As such, their economic and political stability was based on the expectation that those policies would remain the same in the present and into the future. So, when the Ministry began to fundamentally reshape the nature of the British Empire, colonists tried to make sense of these developments, in part, through the lens of their colonial past. Their expectation that the past would make sense of the present was tested to its limits as Parliament took unprecedented actions in the 1760s and 1770s to reorganize the empire and redefine the colonies' (and, by extension, colonists') relationship to Britain.[3]

In the first half of the eighteenth century, the North American colonies underwent a process the historian John Murrin famously referred to as "Anglicization."[4] The colonies had been founded by groups of people escaping the vicissitudes of seventeenth-century England. At first, they created societies that, in many ways, looked very little like the one they had left behind. By the close of the seventeenth century, however, the colonies had been racked by a series of tumultuous events, such as King Philip's War, Bacon's Rebellion, the Dominion of New England, Leisler's Rebellion, and the Salem witch hunts. Clamoring for a sense of stability, colonists increasingly fashioned their political institutions, social hierarchy, economy, and culture after the successful and stable model of post-1688 Britain. From the patronage of royal governors to the creation of an elite American ruling class, from the increasing importance of the colonies in the imperial economy to the consumer revolution that brought British goods to an ever-growing number of colonists with the disposable income to buy them, by mid-century colonists had never been more culturally British. Therefore, when Parliament usurped the authority of the past with unprecedented legislation in the 1760s and 1770s, it created a cultural as well as political crisis as colonists repeatedly sought to reconcile their understandings of the past with their new unprecedented present and unpredictable future.

The creation of a new historical memory of the colonial past served two primary functions during the imperial crisis. First, it fostered a sense of a shared past among many colonists throughout British America where they had only heretofore shared the British past in common. In so doing, it contributed to the development of colonial unity and a burgeoning sense of being part of a shared community, which was crucial to the success of resistance and, ultimately, the move toward independence. Second, it provided an effective origins myth for this emerging community of a people who were not yet a nation. This new historical memory of a shared colonial past reflected the interrelationship between history culture and the politics of the period. The colonies had developed to a place of stature within the economy of the British Empire. Yet, to preserve that place, especially in the face of such unprecedented actions by Parliament, would require a return to first principles. Those first principles, for many British American colonists, were increasingly found not just in the British constitution but in the origins of the colonies themselves.

From the very earliest protests against the Sugar Act in 1764, colonists' efforts to foster united resistance to imperial reforms began producing a historical memory of a shared colonial past, particularly by focusing on the colonies' settlement. The discussion about the colonial past is one of the most prominent and recurring features of patriot rhetoric throughout the imperial crisis. Accounts and interpretations of the colonies' settlement, development, and charters appear in countless pamphlets, newspaper essays, letters to officials, sermons, almanacs, songs, and official resolutions. One patriot writer in 1769 made clear the necessity of understanding the colonial past in adjudicating the current crisis: "The present dispute therefore can only be determined, by considering what were generally understood to be the rights and privileges of the colonies at, and soon after, their settlement, as they appear from their most ancient charters."[5] The past was central to how colonists understood the imperial crisis and their burgeoning historical memory of the colonial past served as a foundation on which they built most of their arguments.

Because the colonies had very different origins and histories, patriot rhetoric about their pasts employed generality as a way of incorporating all of the colonies. Since only New England had anything resembling a developed regional history culture, this generality allowed those in other colonies and regions of mainland British America to adopt this historical memory without the potential contradiction of their own less predominant regional memories. Indeed, the rhetoric around settlement became remarkably similar, in both meaning and phraseology, whether written in Massachusetts or Virginia, by elite lawyers or local farmers gathered at a town or country meeting. Certain aspects of the interpretation expressed by the rhetoric had been developing in often isolated debates over constitutional issues in various colonies over the previous decades.[6] The rhetorical and political demands produced by the imperial crisis, however, led to the coalescence of these ideas into the beginnings of a historical memory created, shared, and echoed by a variety of individuals in a variety of media throughout the colonies. This historical memory came to form an important part of the foundation for colonists' interpretations of the actions of Parliament and the rhetoric of pro-ministerial British writers. Its simple, visceral, and narrative terms contributed to the nascent sense of the colonies as comprising, in some respects, a single polity with not only shared interests but a shared identity that went beyond their all being British subjects.

Forged in the crucible of resistance, the historical memory of the colonial past, particularly regarding settlement, addressed one of the most fundamental questions—from colonists' perspective—raised at the start of Britain's program of imperial reforms in 1764: Were the British American colonists equal to native-born subjects of Britain? To answer that question required first answering a number of historical questions. For example, why were the colonies settled? What were the original motivations of both settlers and the English government? Under what authority and at whose expense were they settled? And, finally, what were the terms of the agreement between settlers and the English government? In addition to the specifics of the debate between 1764 and 1766 over taxation and representation, the broader question of colonists' civic equality within the empire was at stake. That subjects could not be taxed without representation was a widely accepted constitutional—and, hence, historical—proposition in the Anglo-American world. Colonists also believed that the previous fifty years of precedent meant that their status within the empire was also an accepted historical and, hence, legal fact. The new reforms, however, suggested that was not the case for George III and his new Ministry. Therefore, such historical questions were understood by colonists as crucial to a proper understanding of the relationship between the colonies and the mother country.

Petitions and remonstrances against the Sugar and Currency Acts in 1764 from New York and Virginia made reference to the settlement of the colonies when arguing that colonists were entitled to the same rights as Britons. Virginia's House of Burgesses claimed that the privilege of not being taxed without being represented was "inherent in the persons who discovered and settled these regions, [and] could not be renounced or forfeited by their removal hither, not as vagabonds or fugitives, but licensed and encouraged by their prince and animated with a laudable desire of enlarging the British dominion, and extending its commerce." This continued with resolves against the Stamp Act the following year. The House of Burgesses' Stamp Act resolutions began: "*Resolved,* That the first Adventurers and Settlers of this his Majesty's Colony and Dominion of *Virginia* brought with them, and transmitted to their Posterity, and all other his Majesty's Subjects inhabiting in this his Majesty's said Colony, all the Liberties, Privileges, Franchises, and Immunities, that have at any Time been held, enjoyed, and possessed, by the people of *Great Britain.*" Indeed, the Virginia Resolves catalyzed colonial resistance to the Stamp Act, in part due to the inclusion in multiple reprints throughout the colonies of two additional radical resolutions that were never actually passed.[7]

As one of the most widely circulated documents of early colonial resistance to parliamentary legislation, their language played a key role in shaping the rhetoric of patriot resistance. A number of colonies' subsequent resolutions against the Stamp Act copied both their form and content, including Rhode Island, Maryland, and South Carolina.[8] The form of the Virginia Resolves—starting with a resolution that referred back to settlement as the means of framing an argument for equality with Britons—is also evident in numerous resolves passed by towns and counties against the

Stamp Act and, later, the Townshend Acts.[9] Even those colonies that did not copy Virginia in the form of their official resolutions against the Stamp Act—such as Massachusetts, Connecticut, Pennsylvania, and New York—still referred back to their own settlements in making their arguments for colonists' equality with Britons.[10] Having set a rhetorical foundation, references to settlement moved increasingly away from the particulars of individual colonies toward a more general rendering that could encompass the seventeenth-century settlement of most colonies and helped create the foundation of a shared characterization and narrative of the origins of the British North American colonies.

Commemoration of settlement played an important role in this new general rendering of the colonial past. For example, colonists commonly referred to the first generation of settlers as "adventurers." Since the seventeenth century, this terminology was most commonly employed in a mercantile context. During the imperial crisis, however, the mercantile connotation of the adventurer as a risk-taker and one setting out for a distant journey was increasingly colloquialized and historicized to refer to the first settlers. In a piece first printed in New York and reprinted throughout the colonies in 1764, a "proprietor" from the "West India islands" argued that the Sugar Act (and proposed Stamp Act) violated "the faith whereof the adventurers embarked their lives and fortunes."[11] The same year in Massachusetts, James Otis described the settlers as "*the noble discoverers and settlers of a new world.*"[12] Near a decade later in Virginia, Thomas Jefferson wrote in his *Summary View of the Rights of British America* (1774) that the colonies "had been acquired by the lives, labours, and the fortunes of individual adventurers."[13] These types of phrases were common in patriot writings from all regions throughout the imperial crisis.

Through this kind of shared commemorative language, colonists expressed a sense of reverence for the first settlers and sought to strengthen their connection with them, much like the young men who formed the Old Colony Club in 1769. Most importantly, these common references—like many of the shared historical references throughout the crisis—reflected the importance of the past not just in patriots' attempts at political persuasion but also in their understanding of the present. After all, patriot writers and orators, whose primary goal was to persuade their fellow colonists, would not have bothered to use such references so prominently and so often if they did not believe they carried significant weight among those they were hoping to persuade. Their increasingly widespread use reflected both the development of a shared historical grammar that would form the foundation of a newly shared colonial past and the rhetorical and cultural power of the past in colonial society generally.

Colonists commemorated their forbearers during the crisis in a variety of forms. In the summer of 1768, a number of newspapers in Philadelphia and New England printed a song set to the melody of the popular tune "Heart of Oak" that offered a lyrical tribute to the settlement generation:

> Our worthy Forefathers—let's give them a Cheer—
> To Climates unknown did couragiously steer;
> Thro' Oceans to Desarts for Freedom they came,
> And dying bequeath'd us their Freedom and Fame—
> Their generous Bosoms all Dangers despis'd.
> So highly, so wisely, their Birthrights they priz'd;
> We'll keep what they gave,—we will piously keep,
> Nor Frustrate their Toils on the Land or the Deep.[14]

In delivering an oration commemorating the Boston Massacre in 1771, James Lovell began by noting, "Our fathers left their native land, risqued all the dangers of the sea, and came to this then-savage desart, with that true undaunted courage which is excited by a confidence in God."[15] Similarly, when the township of Gloucester passed resolves regarding boycotts in the wake of the Townshend Acts, their first resolution began, "Voted unanimously, That the first settlers of this country left their native land and . . . risqued their lives and spent their fortunes" in settling the colonies.[16]

In this narrative, not only had the first settlers taken such risks, they had succeeded to the benefit of the mother country, as the Stamp Act Congress had pointed out multiple times in their "Petition to the King." Held at New York in October 1765 and composed of delegates from nine colonies, the Stamp Act Congress was the first organized body of intercolonial resistance to imperial reform. Despite the historical diversity of their colonies, they framed their petition with a shared narrative of settlement and the colonial past. Through "their successful perseverance in the midst of innumerable Dangers and Difficulties," they argued, the settlers had "happily added these vast and valuable Dominions to the Empire of *Great-Britain.*" In the following paragraph, the Congress noted that through their ancestors' efforts, "the inhospitable Desarts of *America* have been converted into Flourishing Countries . . . and the Wealth and Power of *Great-Britain* proportionably Augmented." In case the king had not yet grasped the point, the Congress stated clearly, "That by Means of these Settlements . . . a Foundation is now laid for rendering the *British* Empire the most Extensive and Powerful of any Recorded in History."[17] The use of the plural—"settlements"—by the Stamp Act Congress in 1765 was an early example of how the historical rhetoric around the colonial past began to be generalized to create a narrative that encompassed the origins of all the colonies.

This "wilderness" narrative implicitly dehumanized the indigenous inhabitants, who were often referred to as "savages" or "savage men." This long-standing trope in colonial and European writing about Native Americans denied any notion that might include or define Indigenous Peoples as participants in civilization, as defined in eighteenth-century European terms. In turn, colonial writers expected that highlighting Native Americans in their wilderness narrative as "savage men" needing to be conquered would render their ancestors' commitment and achievement that much more impressive. They likely also hoped that referencing the indigenous Other would inspire a sense of solidarity in native Britons with the colonists that would prove beneficial to the latter's cause.

Such rhetoric stripped all Indigenous Peoples of not just claims to civilization but to humanity itself, reducing them to the same status as the continent's animal inhabitants. In doing so, colonists sought to render their ancestors' deeds more admirable while also rhetorically justifying the intentions and results of the settler colonial project of continental confiscation. The settlement narrative generally and these characterizations held Native Americans up as a negative standard by which the settlers and their colonial descendants could define their increasingly tenuous cultural connection to Britain. By the time of the Boston Tea Party in 1773, colonists would begin appropriating Native American identity, revealing the increasing tenuousness of that cultural connection.

For colonists, this shared colonial past came with a shared responsibility to live up to the legacy of "the first Settlers of this Wilderness," by "maintain[ing] the liberty which we have derived from our Ancestors," as one Pennsylvania writer noted.[18] In the song above, the first settlers had "bequeath'd" their "Freedom and Fame" to the colonists of the 1760s. This rhetoric defined colonists as the direct beneficiaries of the settlers' actions (that is, their "Freedom"), but it also bequeathed the responsibility of perpetuating and honoring their achievements (or "Fame"). They were exhorted to "piously keep" their legacy and not "Frustrate their Toils." The historian Catherine Albanese has argued that such rhetoric was also prominent in religious contexts during the crisis, especially sermons, forming part of the basis for what she called "the civil religion of the American Revolution."

Colonial resisters typically made two arguments regarding the original intent or motivation behind earliest settlements. In the earliest writings against the Sugar Act during 1764, patriots from New England to Virginia argued that the settlers, "with the Approbation of their Sovereign" and "under national Encouragements," had "left the Mother Kingdom to extend its Commerce and Dominion."[19] Indeed, Virginia's House of Burgesses, in petitioning the House of Commons in 1764, claimed the first settlers were "animated with a laudable Desire of enlarging the British Dominion, and extending its Commerce."[20] And they reminded Britons that had their ancestors not undertaken those endeavors, North America would likely have become "an appendage of France or the Netherlands, or perhaps divided between both; in either of which cases, Britain would have made a quite different figure from what she does at present."[21] The intimate interrelationship between the past and present was central to colonists' arguments affirming the value of the colonies to the empire.

As the crisis developed and their sense of alienation from Britain grew, patriot writers' historical arguments increasingly reflected that alienation. The first settlers, they began to claim, had fled England not to extend her dominions and commerce but to escape persecution. Such an argument had very different implications.[22] In 1765, under the historical pseudonym "Hampden," James Otis wrote, "The origin of the British colonies was in the cruel persecutions set on foot in church and state under the family of *Stuart*."[23] Decades after the Revolution, John Adams recalled, "The Reigns of the Stewarts, the Two Jameses, and the two Charleses were in general disgrace in England. In America they had always been held in Abhorrence. The Persecutions and Cruelties Suffered by their Ancestors under those Reigns, had been transmitted by History and Tradition."[24] Both historical traditions—settlement driven by the desire to extend the dominions of England and by the persecution of the Stuarts—lived side-by-side in New England's colonial history culture (and, to a lesser extent, in the Middle Colonies), but the nature and political circumstances of the imperial crisis caused the latter to begin taking precedence in New England and beyond.

"Drove from their native country, in those reigns which by oppression stain'd the glory of Britain," their "forefathers fled into the wilderness to avoid the intolerable oppression and arbitrary power of the faithless Stuarts," one writer claimed in the *Boston Evening-Post.*[25] This narrative spread beyond New England as an anonymous pamphleteer in the Middle Colonies in 1768 wrote, "The impolitic imprudent reign of the Stuart race, raised such disturbances in Britain, as obliged numbers to seek abroad that civil and religious liberty which they could not enjoy at home."[26] By generalizing the blame upon the Stuarts as a dynasty that spanned almost the entire seventeenth century, the rhetoric incorporated chronologically the settlement of almost all of the North American colonies. Such an interpretation was not new to the 1760s, though among the mainland colonies it had previously been most common in New England. Yet, through its repeated use in widely circulated resistance literature, its reach was new.

By 1774, however, this interpretation had changed again. In the late 1760s and early 1770s, patriots began denying any jurisdiction for Parliament over the colonies and sought the king to intervene on their behalf. In accordance with the new political circumstances, some patriot writers reinterpreted the causes behind settlement in a way that would reconcile the past with their increasingly unprecedented present. To do that, they stopped arguing that the first settlers had left England because of the tyranny of the Stuarts. As a young Alexander Hamilton claimed in 1775, "The principal design of the enterprize was to be emancipated from their sufferings, under the authority of parliament."[27]

Such an argument was not based on historical facts, but historical memories do not require historical accuracy and the power of the past does not rely on it. By making such arguments patriots imparted the weight and authority of the past to patriot rhetoric against Parliament. Most importantly, such an argument reconciled the present with the past, which colonists both expected and took for granted, at a time when Parliament's actions were making the past and present irreconcilable in unprecedented ways. This specific argument put the historical onus for settlement on the overreaching authority of Parliament, drawing a direct analogy between settlement and colonists' experiences during the imperial crisis. In addition, by removing blame from the Stuart monarchs, the argument tried to assuage King George III, whose family were dynastically linked to the Stuarts and whom, as of 1774, patriots still hoped would personally redress their grievances against Parliament. This argument also offered crucial historical context for patriots seeking to drum up support, particularly as the crisis reached its final stage following the Coercive Acts and the establishment of the Continental Congress in 1774. These changing arguments about the motivations behind settlement show the interrelationship between patriot interpretations of the past and the shifting political circumstances and rhetorical needs of the crisis with Britain. As the custom and precedent of the colonies' relationship with Britain became increasingly malleable in the hands of Parliament and the Ministry so too did colonists' understandings and use of their own past.

Both of these specific arguments about the origins of the colonies—that settlers were motivated by either a desire to expand the British Empire or to escape persecution in Britain—were made primarily to assert colonists' equality with Britons. Though they are seemingly incompatible, both arguments were built on a narrative in which the first settlers left England voluntarily and settled a new world at their own expense. To stress this, the Stamp Act Congress in New York described them as "*private* adventurers" who had settled the colonies through the "Profusion of their Blood and Treasure."[28] Indeed, the British settlements had been "firmly established, at the expence of individuals, and not of the British public." "Not a shilling," Thomas Jefferson wrote in Virginia in 1774, "was ever issued from the public treasures of his Majesty, or his ancestors, for their assistance, till of very late times, after the colonies had become established on a firm and permanent footing."[29] This argument became increasingly common as the crisis went on and served the dual purpose of stressing the cost in "Blood and Treasure" expended by the settlers, thereby having earned the right to retain their English liberty and minimizing the contribution of England to the settlement of the colonies.

Unsurprisingly, many British writers largely ignored the persecution arguments and attributed the act and expense of settlement to England. "The great end of colonization every body will acknowledge," a British polemicist wrote, "is to provide a residence for any exuberance of people, which may be found amongst us, and to supply those with an opportunity of subsisting in another part of the world, who found that opportunity difficult to be obtained at home."[30] A writer in the *London Chronicle* asserted, "The colonies were acquired with no other view than to be a convenience to us."[31] Colonizing was "the act of a powerful and parental people."[32] From this perspective, the colonists were "Children of one common Mother" who had "one common Cause, *the Welfare of their Parent.*"[33] By reducing the settlers to the infantile refuse of British society and settlement to a mere transaction undertaken by England solely for its own benefit, these writers appeared to be minimizing the settlers' expense of blood, treasure, and toil in the eyes of the colonists and challenged an important historical foundation of patriot arguments.

These competing historical memories of colonial settlement came head-to-head in Parliament early in the conflict in 1765. As the Commons debated the well-supported Stamp Act, Colonel Isaac Barré, an Irishman who had spent time in the colonies during the Seven Years' War, challenged the bill. In reply to Barré, Charles Townshend said, "And now will these Americans, children planted by our care, nourished up by our indulgence until they are grown to a degree of strength & opulence, and protected by our arms, will they grudge to contribute their mite to relieve us from the heavy weight of that burden which we lie under?" Townshend offered what was a common historical interpretation in Britain of the origins and development of the colonies.[34] When he finished, Barré stood up and replied in a "most spirited and . . . almost inimitable manner." "They planted by your care?" he bellowed, "No! your oppressions planted them in America. They fled from your tyranny to a then uncultivated and unhospitable country—where they exposed themselves to almost all the hardships to which human nature is liable. . . . And yet, actuated by principles of true English liberty, they met all these hardships with pleasure, compared with those they suffered in their own country, from the hands of those who should have been their friends."[35]

Having refuted Townshend's interpretation of settlement, Barré went on to refute his narrative of the development of the colonies. "They nourished up by *your* indulgence?" he boomed. "They grew up by your neglect of them: as soon as you began to care about them, that care was exercised in sending persons to rule over them, in one department and another, who were perhaps the deputies of deputies to some member of this House—sent to spy out their liberty, to misrepresent their actions and to prey upon them." Jared Ingersoll, a colonist observing this scene in Parliament, later wrote, "I own I felt emotions that I never felt before and went the next morning and thanked Colonel Barré in behalf of my country for his noble and spirited speech."[36]

When news of Barré's speech reached the colonies in the spring of 1765, newspapers throughout the colonies reprinted it. Some argued that "a Column ought to be erected to him in *America,* as a lasting Monument of the Gratitude of the People." Barré's historical defense of the colonies had such an impact in further rousing opposition that those hoping to defuse the increasingly volatile situation in the colonies planted stories in the newspapers about another letter from London that claimed "Col. Barré, a Member of the House of Commons, did not say one Word in Opposition to the laying a *Stamp-Duty* on the Colonies." "If this is true," another paper wrote, "there cannot be a Word of Truth in that *Pompous* Account which we Published in our last."[37] These attempts to discredit or downplay Barre's speech were largely unsuccessful, and in 1769, a new town in Pennsylvania was named Wilkes-Barre, in honor of him and John Wilkes for being supporters of the colonies in England.

This famous exchange shows the importance of competing interpretations of the colonies' settlement and development to the political arguments being made by both sides from the very start. It also shows their importance in both sides' perceptions of each other, which grew as the crisis developed. Over the next few years, patriot writers employed an increasingly shared historical grammar, based in part on these characterizations of settlement, which helped create a historical memory of the colonial past that would serve as part of the foundation of their rhetoric and political arguments for the rest of the crisis.

That foundation was critical for colonists, who argued that the act of settlement entailed a compact between the settlers and the Crown.[38] As Stephen Hopkins, the patriot governor of Rhode Island, noted at the start of the imperial crisis, the settlers had "left the delights of their native country, parted from their homes, and all their conveniencies, searched out and subdued a foreign country with the most amazing travail and fortitude, to the infinite advantage and emolument of the mother state." They did all of this on "a firm reliance of a solemn compact" that they would be "partakers and sharers in all the privileges and advantages of the then English, now British constitution."[39] Of the Stamp Act, one writer asked, "Would it not be a direct breach of that compact and those conditions, on the faith whereof the adventurers embarked their lives and fortunes?"[40]

While some writers argued the legal particularities over whether the settlers had brought their rights with them or forfeited them by the act of migration, patriots in 1765 Boston reprinted a thirty-year-old pamphlet by Jeremiah Dummer. The reprint value of *A Defence of the New-England Charters* lay, in part, in the fact that Dummer had put the question in commonsense, rather than legal, terms, which echoed patriots' settlement rhetoric during the crisis. "Must the brave adventurer," Dummer asked, "who with hazard of his life and fortune seeks out new climates to enrich his mother country, be denied these common rights, which his countrymen enjoy at home in ease and indolence?" The supposition led Dummer to exclaim with a decidedly eighteenth-century sense of drama, "Monstrous absurdity! Horrid inverted order!"[41] Colonists assumed that their ancestors' "native Privileges" as Englishmen "could not be forfeited by their Migration to America" and "must be derived to us from them."[42] Andrew Eliot clearly stated this idea in a sermon in 1765: "Our fathers dearly bought the privileges we enjoy."[43] Similarly, when the town of Pomfret issued its own resolves against the Stamp Act, they succinctly summed up both the connection and responsibility colonists in the 1760s felt for the first settlers noting, "We are as natural Heirs, as to our Fathers Inheritance."[44] For many patriots, the risk, hardships, and success of the settlers had earned the protection and inheritance of those rights for their posterity.

This popular connection with the act of settlement and with the sense of inheritance that infused its meaning stretched all the way to the frontier. In 1775, the freeholders of Botetourt County, almost two hundred miles west of Williamsburg, wrote to inform the House of Burgesses of their take on the conflict with Britain, "My liberty to range these woods on the same terms my father has done is not mine to give up; It was not purchased by me, and purchased it was; it is entailed on my Son and the tenure is sacred Watch over it, Gentlemen, for to him it must descent inviolated if my arm can defend it."[45] Indeed, as the crisis wore on, patriots throughout the colonies increasingly voiced their displeasure with the actions of Parliament and the Ministry in terms that made clear that they felt their historical inheritance was fundamentally at stake, ultimately framing the first resolves passed and published by the First Continental Congress.[46] No legal training or constitutional understanding was necessary to comprehend this argument's emotional power because its power came from the context of colonial history culture.

While historians have noted the importance of the familial metaphor used by both sides during the crisis, they have largely focused on Britain as "the mother country" and on personifications of the colonies as its children. British writers depicted the colonies and colonists as the insolent young children of the mother country. Meanwhile, American colonists saw the colonies as children who had grown to a degree of maturity. Nevertheless, a look at the historical aspects of the rhetoric used during the crisis shows the "father" in this metaphor was not absent. Rather, colonists employed the familial language when referring specifically to their direct ancestors who settled the colonies as their metaphorical "fathers." Seen through the lens of eighteenth-century gender roles, in which the father held the decisive role in familial matters, such language implied not just the predominance of the experiences of their ancestors in settling the issues at stake in the crisis but also the growing, relevant importance of the colonial past in patriots' civic identities.

While the New England colonies were predominant in shaping that generalized colonial past, they were not alone in drawing directly on their own regional history cultures to try and make sense of their contemporary political situation. Elizabeth Graeme Fergusson, an elite woman from Pennsylvania who was actually engaged for a time to Benjamin Franklin's son, hosted regular literary gatherings at her family home, Graeme Park. These salon-type events drew Philadelphia's elite, including John Dickinson, who often attended during the time he was writing his famous patriot essays, "Letters from a Pennsylvania Farmer." Though not published until after the war when she had lost everything along with her loyalist husband, in 1768, Fergusson wrote and shared a long poem entitled "The Dream." In it, she responded directly to Dickinson's popular essays and to the imperial crisis enveloping the colonies.[47]

In the poem, the narrator, along with the colony of Pennsylvania, are reprimanded "with haughty warmth" by Albion, a mythical female personification of Britain. "Dare they reject my Commerce and my Power," she asked, "And spurn my Influence in a fatal Hour?" In response, William Penn, the colony's "pious Founder" and the most prominent figure in Pennsylvanian history culture, descends from the sky on a cloud. Drawing on the settlement memory that increasingly pervaded the news and political polemics Fergusson was surely reading, Penn exclaims:

> I once claimd Britain, for my Natal Soil;
> And thence I led a hardy Race for Toil,
> These Western Woods from Savage Steps we cleared
> And just Industry her rich ensigns reard.

Penn gives the narrator "a fair long written scroll" and commands her to "go show my Children what is written here / May Pennsylvania hold my precepts dear" before vanishing. In the poem, she gives the scroll to a character representing Dickinson who proceeds to deliver the founder's reassuring message to his troubled posterity stressing the importance of continuing the colony's history of self-sufficiency from Britain established since its settlement. The poem provides a striking example of female participation in and perspective on both politics and history culture. It also shows how local or regional history cultures converged with the politics of the period and with the developing historical memory of a shared colonial past.

Ultimately, colonists argued that their ancestors had been assured that they would retain all the rights and privileges they had held in England and that they and their posterity were not to be treated differently than native-born subjects. When they felt those rights were being challenged by imperial reforms in the 1760s and 1770s, colonists turned to the idea of settlement-as-a-compact to lay the basis for their arguments that they were entitled to the same rights and privileges as Britons. While elite lawyers argued over legal minutiae through arcane references to obscure cases, patriots from cities to small towns drew on and contributed to the historical dimension of colonial identity through their use of this historical memory of the colonial past, based on a conflation of their emotional connection with the first settlers and the easily understood notions of compact and equality with Britons.[48]

This historical memory of the colonial past served as an important part of the foundation of the fundamental claim in resolutions passed by various bodies, large and small, from the beginning of the crisis to the end that colonists were "entitled to all the inherent rights and privileges of [the king's] natural born subjects within the kingdom of Great Britain."[49] Like many newspaper essays and many of the pamphlets usually deemed the most important and most influential, official colonial resolves often began by establishing the historical premise of their argument. As one "plain yeoman" correctly observed in 1765, "All the colonies on the continent, in their several petitions and remonstrances, dutifully, though firmly, assert their right of exclusion from parliamentary taxation, founded upon the principles of the *British* government, and the terms of their colonization."[50]

Though the specifics of patriot arguments changed over the course of the crisis, the same language used above can be found consistently, from the colonial assemblies' various resolves against the Sugar Act and Stamp Act in 1764 and 1765 to the resolves of the First Continental Congress in 1774.[51] Colonists often referred to the British past in these resolves—particularly referencing Magna Carta, the Petition of Right, and the Bill of Rights—when arguing against a specific action by Parliament. Yet, in making the broader case for their equal status with native Britons, they ironically drew just as heavily, and in many cases more so, on their own colonial past to lay the foundation for that claim. In the process, they were helping create a shared past for themselves that went beyond their long-shared British past.

For colonists, their colonial charters were the primary evidence that settlement had been a contractual arrangement between the settlers and the Crown. The compact rhetoric around the charters was decidedly vague because often the charters themselves were vague. The legal historian John Phillip Reid, who has written most about the charters in the imperial crisis, concluded it was "the weakest of the constitutional arguments."[52] Reid based his judgment of the charter argument strictly on its legal merits. But, in the popular cultural context of resistance, what was actually in the charters mattered less than what they meant and signified to patriot writers and their audiences. After all, Reid admitted that they were "so frequently cited and so effectively argued." Though the vagueness of the charter rhetoric may be problematic for legal historians on an analytical level, it was a rhetorical advantage for patriot writers. That ambiguity made the charters rhetorically malleable, which is partly why colonists referred to them so frequently and effectively.

Even those colonies without charters understood themselves as having earned the equivalent of a de facto charter in the form of "a civil Constitution, which, so far at least as the Rights and Privileges of the People were concerned, would remain permanent, and be transmitted to their latest Posterity."[53] One patriot in the *Boston Evening-Post* in 1765 expressed this idea succinctly when he asked, "Are not our charters,—and also—all the rights of the other governments in America, fully confirmed to us by the usage and law of parliament, for a century past, and ever since their first institution?" In New York a decade later Alexander Hamilton argued that even though "it is true, that New-York has no Charter," it could support its "claim to liberty" by referring to "the common principles of colonization."[54] That is, actual charters were only a written expression of the implied compact that colonists believed existed between all of the original settlers and England, charter or no charter. In Virginia, the compact was expressed clearly: the colonists had "generously offered to let England partake of the advantages of their conquests, in consideration of securing to themselves the rights of Englishmen in their new settlements."[55] Moreover, the subsequent past from settlement to the start of the crisis in 1764 could only be understood as having affirmed the original compact. Like the rhetoric surrounding settlement, generality allowed the compact rhetoric (even when using the specific term of "charter") to be utilized by and have meaning for colonists from different types of colonies with different charters or frames of government in New England, the Middle Colonies, and the South.

Despite the generality, colonists imparted great significance to their charters and the historical compact they represented. They were, James Otis argued in 1764, "given to their ancestors, in consideration of their sufferings and merit, in discovering and settling America."[56] According to a writer in the *Massachusetts Gazette,* the "solemn Charter Compact and Agreement" granted to the settlers "and their posterity, all the rights, liberties, privileges and immunities of natural subjects, born within the realm."[57] The people of the town of Weymouth declared, "We have ever supposed our Charter, the greatest security that could be had in human affairs.—This was the sentiment of our forefathers."[58] Yet, charters had come under attack a number of times since the Restoration, whether through the Dominion of New

England under James II in 1686, calls to revoke all the colonial charters in the 1720s, or in attempts to gain an administrative handle on the empire in the 1740s.[59] In the context of the imperial crisis, however, the threat to charters and the settlement compact seemed much greater because of the bold assertiveness and unprecedented actions of Parliament, which had previously protected their charters from revocation by the Board of Trade.

In such a situation, colonists gave that much greater significance to their charters and the implied compact, in part by analogizing them to British history. As Richard Bland wrote in Virginia in 1766, "The terms of the Compact must be obligatory and binding upon the Parties; they must be the Magna Charta, the fundamental Principles of Government."[60] Very similarly, a decade later in Connecticut, Moses Mather argued, "[The colonies'] constitutions are the original compacts, containing the first great principles, or stamina of their governments . . . those compacts are permanent and perpetual, as unalterable as Magna Charta, or the primary principles of the English constitution."[61] In some sense, as above, we can see in these analogies a manifestation of the growing priority of the colonial over the British past that will be the focus of the following chapter.

Unsurprisingly, supporters of the Grenville ministry and Parliament disagreed with these analogies. A pro–Stamp Act British writer in 1765 remarked, "The people in our American Colonies lay a very great stress upon the importance of their Charters, and imagine that the privileges granted to their Ancestors, at the time of their original establishment, must infallibly exempt them from participating in the least inconvenience of the Mother-country, though the Mother-country must share in every inconvenience of theirs." While granting "these Charters should be as inviolably adhered to as the nature of contingencies will admit," he nevertheless felt the need to "inform my fellow-subjects of America, that a resolution of the British Parliament can at any time set aside all the charters." Therefore, "nothing can be more idle than this pompous exclamation about their Charter exemptions. "[62] As the imperial crisis neared an end, Britons and loyalists had grown quite tired of colonists who "arrogantly" and "with very Ill Grace . . . upbraid us with their original Terms of Colonization."[63] They rejected the notion that colonists could claim any privileges not enjoyed by native Britons, particularly exemption from parliamentary legislation, due to their "original Charter Rights, or Motives of their first Settlement, or Covenants of Colonization, as they now call them."[64] For many, however, the charters and the "terms of colonization" they represented served as a new set of first principles to guard themselves against or perhaps even forestall the decline of the British Empire into an oligarchy led by the king's ministers and Parliament.

In the face of these counterarguments, many colonists continued to believe and argue that their charters and compacts were permanent, perpetual, and unalterable, becoming the American equivalents of Magna Carta.[65] Similarly, they continued to argue that, as the posterity of the original settlers, they were party to a compact with the British Crown. Both arguments employed a generality in their rhetoric that allowed them to be adopted, or at the very least identified with, by the inhabitants of the colonies. Along with the political use of prints and other forms of intercolonial cooperation, like the Stamp Act Congress and boycotts of British goods, the settlement and compact rhetoric contributed to the creation of a shared historical memory of the colonial past that fostered the early development of the colonies as an "imagined community" and the burgeoning sense of intercolonial unity.

The importance of the colonial past in this debate, particularly from its outset, is significant. As we have seen in the previous chapter, the British past had provided colonists with their most useful and meaningful historical frame of reference in the decades before the imperial crisis (particularly beyond New England). The imperial crisis and the creation of this shared historical memory of their colonial origins—defined by the similarities of interpretation and language and their repetition in a variety of writings from different regions by persons from various stations throughout the imperial crisis—started a shift in which the colonial past began taking on increasing importance. Before the imperial crisis, colonists primarily thought of themselves as British subjects. Their sense of ownership of the British past offered them a cultural lifeline to the mother country and played an important part in shaping their imperial identities in the eighteenth century. As the imperial crisis made the colonial past more important, however, it brought into question some of the connections on which those identities were based. Colonists' reconception of their colonial past began the process of shifting their imperial identity as proud subjects within an empire into a decidedly colonial identity that set them within but also somehow apart from that empire.

The primary question of the first stage of the imperial debate had to do with whether colonists were equal to native-born subjects (and, therefore, should not be taxed without representation). The settlement argument both framed and complicated their answer, as colonists sought to define their current standing within the empire based on the first principles of the relationship between the colonists and England at the beginning of settlement. On the one hand, colonists protested that even though their forefathers had left England, they and their posterity were still "Englishmen" and, therefore, entitled to the same rights and privileges guaranteed by their shared British past. Yet, at the same time, the settlement argument—through its adoption and repeated use throughout the colonies—began to create a shared colonial past, one that allowed colonists to begin seeing themselves as different and, to some extent, apart from their fellow British subjects.

These debates over charters and over the terms of settlement were also carried on by both sides in many pamphlets by lawyers who cited obscure European thinkers and British legal cases and constitutional theory. And most historians have tended to focus on the minutiae of those debates. But for common colonists without the extensive education and legal training of most elites, these debates were refracted through their history culture and their cultural understanding of the relationship between the past and present. Indeed, history culture translated the broad ideas behind those more technical legal and constitutional debates into a colonial vernacular.

British commentators, unaware of the developing sense of a shared colonial past, thought that colonists' ownership of the British past would eventually bring them around. In 1765, one British writer argued, "One would scarcely imagine, if [the colonists] forgot us, that they would entirely lose all remembrance of themselves."[66] But, as the crisis went on, the settlement argument provided the foundation for a historical memory of a shared colonial past that would become increasingly important to both their identities and the rhetoric throughout the crisis. Coming on the heels of the rise of patriotic sentiment in Britain and Europe in the decades before the crisis, the historical memory of settlement created during the crisis stands as an early attempt by colonists to think of themselves as sharing a history other than the British past. Indeed, it served the purposes of an origins myth for disparate colonists beginning to think of themselves as "a people" who were not yet a nation but were nevertheless being forced by political circumstances into a process of reconsidering their own identities and, ultimately, redefining themselves.

If, as one historian has argued, "Nations are congealed histories," then the imperial crisis and this historical memory in particular marks the beginning of that process for Americans, a process that would accelerate after independence had been secured.[67] Yet, to fully understand why colonists framed the debate with their colonial origins and the explanatory power it held for them, we must also explore the role of the cultural authority of the past in the patriot rhetoric of the imperial crisis.

As we have seen, the past played an important structural role in colonial society and culture. Yet, the impact of the past on colonial culture in British North America—and, therefore, on the imperial debate—has generally been obscured by historians who have often sought out what was new, or proto-American, about the colonies.[68] In addition, those who have focused on the role of the Enlightenment in the Revolution have also obscured it. Colonists, like their European counterparts, were supposedly committed to using reason as a means of not only questioning but of escaping tradition and the "heavy crust of custom."[69] Colonial societies, however, were still very much steeped in customs and traditions they had inherited from the Old World, and the past continued to play an important role in colonial culture through the imperial crisis.[70] Daniel R. Woolf, the leading scholar of British historical culture, has noted how "the appeal to the past saturates early modern discourse."[71] The same was true in the colonies.

This cultural power—which I refer to as the "authority of the past"—was embodied by (though certainly not limited to) the concepts of custom, precedent, and tradition. Admittedly, these terms are typically understood as legal expressions, but they had a cultural power beyond the law. The broad concept of custom contributed to the authority of the past the tendency in colonial culture to bestow legitimacy on something because it had existed for a significant period of time. The fact that a law, institution, social arrangement, or religious or governance practice had stood the test of time invested it with authority.[72]

The authority of the past, however, was not absolute. Therefore, we should not understand it as suggesting that colonial culture was either reactionary or regressive. After all, in the first half of the eighteenth century, the colonies experienced changes to long-standing institutional and religious arrangements, as well as significant and rapid economic, political, and demographic changes. Bernard Bailyn, echoing Frederick Jackson Turner of a hundred years earlier, has argued that colonists' "provincialism"—due to being located not only outside the metropolitan center but on the perceived fringes of "civilization"—played a crucial role in the development of colonial political creativity.[73] At the same time, in the face of such flux, many colonists clung to the authority of the past, particularly regarding their political and cultural relationship with Britain.

Indeed, neither the connection to the past nor the willingness to innovate when necessary precluded the other. Rather, they coexisted in colonial culture, politics, society, religion, and economy. Michael Zuckerman has noted this "dialectic" between colonists' reverence for tradition and their dislocation from the source of those traditions. "Reaction entailed innovation," he wrote. "Conservation of tradition compelled cultural creativity."[74] Michael Kammen has similarly argued that "in seeking to preserve the past under difficult circumstances, the colonists would move, crablike, sideways into the future."[75] The existence of the authority of the past did not make innovation impossible. Rather, one could argue colonists' expectations regarding stability and the continuance of their customary relationship with Britain provided the space in which they could comfortably deal with change. This intersection between the cultural authority of the past and the political, economic, and demographic exigencies of the present can actually help account for the dynamics of the imperial crisis. For, while authority of all kinds—royal, imperial, political, social, legal, and cultural—could often be tenuous, the authority of the past retained its salience in the colonies in the middle of the eighteenth century.[76]

The authority of the past helped define colonists' perceptions of the relationship between the past and the present. Historical distance in the eighteenth century was truncated to a degree that even the distant past retained an immediate, contemporary resonance, which itself resulted in a more intimate and intertwined relationship between the past and present than is common in later periods. This intimate relationship with the past made for an intensely historicized present. Colonists expected and, in a cultural sense, needed the past to explain the present. Their present was contextualized and understood through a number of shared pasts, including those of Britain, their individual colonies, and their communities, denominations, and families. The authority of the past and the intimate relationship between the past and present gave to the settlement and compact rhetoric both its explanatory and persuasive power.

Simply put, colonists viewed the present through the lens of the past. The past allowed colonists to make sense of the present. Indeed, they relied on it to do so. The authority of the past offered colonists a sense of security and stability in a dynamic early modern Atlantic world because it allowed them to have certain expectations about the present and the near future. The custom and precedent of the colonies' relationship with Britain allowed them to feel secure in their expectations that that relationship would not suddenly change. In fact, the authority of the past mattered even more because that relationship had been so ill defined for so long. Colonists' expectations and understandings of their relationship with Britain were reinforced by their sense of the authority of the past and the intimate relationship between the past and present inherited from—and ostensibly shared with—the mother country.

Yet, the onset of the imperial crisis warned that perhaps this was no longer so. The unprecedented nature of the steps taken by Parliament in the 1760s to redefine Britain's relationship with the colonies caused such alarm because it undermined these senses of security and stability and the expectations regarding their relationship with Britain. In implementing such unprecedented imperial reforms, Parliament could not "justify the proceedings of the present age by those of the past," which, as John Oldmixon noted in his history of England, was one of the primary purposes of history.[77] Britain's seemingly utter disregard for the authority of the past created anxiety for both elites and white non-elites. New Englander John Adams expressed this anxiety in addressing a British commentator in 1765 when he asked, "Are we not to prophecy the future by the experience of the past?"[78] His Virginia counterpart Patrick Henry, in his famous "Speech to the Virginia Convention" in 1775 framed his remarks by saying, "I know of no way of judging of the future but by the past." Offering a middling-class perspective, a patriot pamphleteer asked pointedly, "For what Encouragment hath the Merchant to expose his Interest to Chances and Dangers, the Farmer, the Mechanic and the common Labourer to weary themselves" if their situation was no longer "as they have heretofore been led to think?"[79]

After all, in their eyes, what sense of stability could be had if colonists had no way of expecting what Parliament would do next? What sense of security—in property and otherwise—could be had if Parliament could willfully ignore a century of custom regarding its relationship with the colonies and centuries of English custom and precedent regarding taxation? Echoing John Adams above, one colonist asked simply, "Is not the mind of parliament known by their usages?"[80] The incredulity behind these rhetorical questions reflects just how fundamental such assumptions about the authority of the past were to colonists. As Brendan McConville has noted, the sense of "a rupture with the past . . . troubled many," forcing them to "[look] backward as much if not more than forward" in trying to "resolve these tensions."[81] With the onset of Britain's program of imperial reform, however, the past could no longer explain the present and colonists were in danger of losing their political and cultural mooring and being set adrift on a sea of uncertainty.

To many colonists, reading Britons defending Parliament seemed to reveal a significant cultural disconnect between the colonies and the mother country. By the 1760s, it made no sense to Britons to rely so rigidly on the past. Already by the end of the seventeenth century in England, according to Daniel Woolf, "the past had lost some of its power to authorize individual behaviour and validate social practices in a world that increasingly planned for present needs and future contingencies."[82] Also, in a little over the previous half century, the nation had been transformed. A revolution had radically altered the nature of its monarchy, legislature, and economy followed by rapid commercial and military expansion and, after the Seven Years' War, sudden geographic expansion and the debt that had achieved it. The British, and Parliament in particular, now faced unprecedented problems and issues, particularly regarding imperial administration. To their minds, it was logical that these unprecedented problems would perhaps require unprecedented solutions.

This perspective was utterly alien and just as highly troubling to many colonists as the actual unprecedented solution of centralizing and tightening imperial administration. The authority of the past colonists had inherited from the mother country seemed to now be shunted aside by their fellow subjects in Britain. Even worse, it was being disregarded for the exigencies of the present and the immediate short term, which was exactly the type of perspective and actions against which the authority of the past was supposed to preclude. This proved disconcerting for two reasons. First, it usurped the authority of the past and colonists' ability to have expectations regarding the future, thereby promoting an anxious sense of instability and insecurity. Second, the British past specifically had long given colonists on the peripheries a meaningful sense of cultural connection to the mother country and their fellow subjects. The rejection of the authority of the past by Parliament made many colonists feel insecure and uncertain and created an opening for them to question their cultural relationship with the British past and with Britain itself.

The seeming rejection of the authority of the past by Britons during the 1760s and 1770s began revealing a cultural distinction between how the colonies and Britain understood the relationship between the past and present. Because the colonies had been becoming increasingly British in their institutions, society, and politics, one might expect that upon recognizing this cultural difference they would have sought to imitate the new ways in which Britons were relating to the past. But instead colonists clung to the authority of the past, which, for much of the early years of the crisis, seemed to them to be more British in behavior than that of Britons themselves. As a result, colonial history culture contributed a cultural difference with Britain that would help define the rest of the debate during the imperial crisis and, ultimately, help make the political break possible.

The authority of the past manifested itself in patriot rhetoric during the imperial crisis in a number of ways, particularly through the concepts of custom and precedent. In making their arguments against Parliament's imperial reforms, colonists repeatedly pointed out their contradiction of longstanding arrangements and assumptions about the colonies' relationship to

Parliament and the metropole. Colonists' rights to self-legislation were supposedly confirmed not only by their charters but also, as Connecticut Governor Thomas Fitch argued in a 1765 pamphlet, by "having been in the Possession, Enjoyment and Exercise of them for so long a Time." Fitch concluded, "And what better Foundation for, or greater Evidence of such Rights can be demanded or produced, is certainly difficult to be imagined."[83] The town of Providence instructed their delegates to the assembly the same year that their rights as colonists had been "long since precisely known and ascertained, by uninterrupted Practice and Usage from the first Settlement of this Country, down to this term."[84] Similarly, when New York petitioned the House of Commons in 1764 against the Sugar Act and proposed Stamp Act, it "appeal[ed] to all the Records of their past Transactions" as the logical basis of its expectations regarding Parliament's relationship to the colony.[85]

Lack of precedent itself was also deemed customary. For example, in 1769, the Pennsylvania House of Representatives petitioned George III for redress from the Townshend duties. In doing so, it argued that exemption from parliamentary taxation "has been recognized by long established usage and custom, ever since the settlement thereof, without one precedent to the contrary, until the passing of the late Stamp-Act."[86] Similarly, Richard Henry Lee noted that colonial rights with regard to Parliament had been "rendered sacred by a possession of near two hundred years, that is . . . from the first settlements of North America, until a late period."[87] This logic led colonists to conclude that "they cannot now be deprived of a right they have so long enjoyed."[88] These appeals to precedent and the authority of the past were a common feature in patriot rhetoric of all forms throughout the crisis.

In addition to these simplified vernacular references to customary practice, the cultural power of custom and the authority of the past are found often in the phraseology of patriot rhetoric. Colonists used a number of keywords as shorthand for the authority of the past, including the adjective "ancient" to impart a sense of authority. In petitioning the king, the Virginia House of Burgesses, representing the "most ancient and loyal colony," sought to protect "their ancient and inestimable Right of being governed . . . from their own Consent."[89] They believed implicitly that Virginia's status among Britain's North American colonies was due not solely to the relative import of its economic contribution to the empire or its accumulated wealth but also to the fact that it was the first (and, therefore, oldest) of the mainland colonies. The juxtaposition of "ancient" and "loyal" reflects a perception of the inherent relationship between the unmatched depth of Virginia's historical relationship with England and its loyalty to the empire. Such a statement implied the colony's history of having supported the Crown against Parliament and Cromwell during the English Civil Wars in the 1640s. Similarly, the repeal of the Stamp Act, Jonathan Mayhew noted, meant that colonists had been "reinstated in the enjoyment of their ancient rights and privileges."[90] Colonists often referred to their "ancient colony," "ancient charters," "ancient principles" established by "the glorious revolution," and, even, the "ancient established method of calling on their assemblies by requisitory letters from the crown" in lieu of being directly taxed by Parliament, even though none of these principles or methods were much more than a hundred years old.[91] That is because, unlike our contemporary usage, the appellation of "ancient" did not relate merely to age but to the meaningful passage of time, which resulted in the establishment of custom and, its colloquial cultural equivalent, expectation.

Colonists also repeatedly used the term "innovation," but not, as we do today, as a positive descriptor carrying constructive or beneficial connotations. In eighteenth-century colonial culture it carried entirely opposite connotations. An "innovation" was something not rooted in the authority of the past. That meant it warranted caution and, even, suspicion. In this sense, colonists' use of "innovation" reflected the uncertainty and anxiety caused by Parliament's actions. "Innovation" could also carry the connotation of an attack or unprovoked aggression. For example, in 1764, a news item addressing French and Spanish complaints about British naval preparations noted, "To which reply has been made, That the men of war fitting out are intended only for the protection of our possessions, and not to make the least innovation on the rights and properties of any nation whatsoever."[92] The aggressiveness and suspicion of the potential danger perceived in innovation (and its subversion of the authority of the past) were expressed at the outset of the crisis in 1765: "It is well observ'd by an ingenious political writer, 'That the first article of safety, in Princes and States, lies in avoiding all councils, *or designs of innovation, in ancient and established forms and laws*, especially those concerning *liberty, property* and *religion*, which are the possessions men *will ever have most at heart,* and be most tenacious of retaining. By avoiding which *designs of innovation,* they will leave the channel of *known and common Justice* clear and undisturbed.'"[93] In other words, subverting the authority of the past through a legislative or political innovation necessarily created the potential for injustices against the people's "liberty, property, and religion" and, therefore, rebellion.

Unsurprisingly then, "innovation" was a common descriptor for unprecedented parliamentary legislation in local instructions and resolves from New England to Pennsylvania to Virginia, from 1765 to 1775.[94] In pamphlets and essays as well, colonists referred to the concept throughout the imperial crisis. For example, in 1768, after conceding Parliament's authority to regulate trade during the Stamp Act debate, many patriots rejected the new duties imposed by the new Townshend Acts on the grounds that they were created "for the purpose of raising a revenue," which itself was an "innovation."[95] By referring to Parliament's various reforms as "innovations," colonists were saying much more than that they were new. They implied both the subversion of the authority of the past and aggression on the part of Parliament.

British reaction to colonists' appeals to the authority of the past generally ranged from bemusement to incredulity. One British writer in 1765, dismissed patriot rhetoric when he wrote, "The Americans pretend to be aggrieved by the late Stamp-Act, under pretence that it is *contrary to their charters,* and an *infringement of the rights and privileges of British subjects.*"[96] Inherent in this passage is an incredulity at the colonists' appeals to such an irrelevant, distant past. From the pro-Parliament and present-minded British perspective, it could only be a pretense. Surely colonial protests were driven by their desire to avoid bearing the immediate financial cost of the duties, many Britons assumed.

Both bemusement and incredulity are found in a pamphlet by William Knox, an undersecretary of state under Dartmouth and a Grenville acolyte, entitled *The Claim of the Colonies to an Exemption from Internal Taxes imposed by Authority of Parliament* (1765). Knox wrote, "If the novelty of a tax was to be admitted as an argument to prove a defect of jurisdiction in those who were about to impose it, we should probably have never seen either an excise or a land-tax in England; for there certainly was a time when neither of those modes of taxation were used." Knox's argument reflected both the pragmatism required by Ministry officials reorganizing a new and greatly expanded empire and the gulf between how the two sides understood the relationship between the past and present and its role in structuring colonial and imperial politics.

For many Britons, such an unprecedented situation required sufficient flexibility, even to the point of novelty or innovation. After all, with nothing in the "records of history to serve as a precedent, or clew, to direct their steps," all members of Parliament could do was "grope their way by their own industry, and to employ their reason, as the only compass which can steer their course aright."[97] No one and nothing, including colonists and the past, could bind Parliament to such limitations, Knox argued, particularly at a moment when it found itself in such new circumstances dealing with such new problems. To even suggest so seemed naïve, unreasonable, and even illogical to many British writers.

However, to those Britons who lived or had lived in the colonies, such as Colonel Barré, the colonial reaction was not altogether surprising. In the fall of 1765, following the Stamp Act riots in Boston, Massachusetts's royal governor Francis Bernard reflected on Parliament's naïveté of colonial culture and politics in passing the bill: "It must have been supposed that such an Innovation as a Parliamentary Taxation would cause a great Alarm & meet with much Opposition in most parts of America; It was quite new to the People, & had no visible Bounds set to it."[98] Bernard understood that such a significant innovation was never going to be received kindly by the colonists, in part because not having "visible Bounds set" by custom and precedent was the very definition of subverting the authority of the past. The interplay and relationship between patriot writers and British pamphleteers like Knox is emblematic of the debate as a whole. Both sides brought to the debate fundamental, underlying assumptions—in this case, regarding the relationship between the past and present—that shaped their perceptions of the other side and influenced their reactions to them. Ultimately, this cultural difference often helped render the other side either unpersuasive or, in some sense, even unintelligible.

In addition to subverting the authority of the past, another problem related to colonial history culture with an "innovation" was that, if it stood, it would become a "precedent."[99] This was feared just as much, if not more, for its practical political meaning than its strictly legal meaning. While some pamphleteers on both sides argued legal points over whether Parliament had taxed the colonies in the past, specific arguments about obscure pieces of legislation dating back over one hundred years mattered less to a broader audience than the commonsense premise inherent in the practical understanding and application of precedent within colonial history culture. The town of Rowley, in the fall of 1765, expressed this anxiety when it instructed its representatives to oppose the Stamp Act because it was likely to be "an introduction to a train of other acts of a similar oppressive nature."[100]

Failure to take "suitable Notice" and protest parliamentary reforms like the Stamp Act would be akin to approving of it, thereby setting a precedent on which the British could draw legally and, perhaps more importantly, politically.[101] That is, colonists knew that if they failed to resist, Parliament and British writers would later use that to argue they had already implicitly assented to such legislation. A writer from London stated the obvious when he wrote worried that colonists "will prevent a precedent . . . if they withhold their Assent to the Stamp Act."[102] Resistance was not only aimed at getting specific legislation repealed, but its mere existence was meant to be an obstruction to future reforms by the colonists having "borne our testimony against it."[103] After all, as one colonist supposed, "Has not the incomprehensible Policy of the present Ministry given Us Reason to suppose that future Ministers may be guilty of still greater Absurdities?"[104]

The suspicion and caution inherent in such logic derived from colonists' perceptions of Parliament's actions as doing violence to the authority of the past. To use an analogy, for colonists it seemed not so much that the rules were being changed in the middle of the game as that they were being thrown out completely. Moreover, the rules for the rest of the game would now be determined by their opponent at each turn. Historians have understood patriots' reactions as rooted in the colonists' propensity toward conspiracy, supposedly fostered by reading the radical Whig writers of Britain.[105] Without rejecting that interpretation outright, we can also see how Parliament's actions sparked such reactions even among those patriots who had not been devoted readers of those somewhat obscure writers like many of the elite lawyers we often refer to as "founders." Parliament's actions in subverting the authority of the past warranted suspicion and caution and increased colonists' sense of the instability and uncertainty of the moment, which exacerbated the political and cultural anxiety of the crisis.

When added alongside the previous ideological and constitutional interpretations, this increased sense of social instability and economic uncertainty combined with the implication of parliamentary legislation and British rhetoric that colonists were second-class citizens within the empire seems to make the visceral (and, at times, violent) response by non-elite colonists much more understandable.

Patriots used this fear of a precedent being set to foster unity among the colonies. For example, in the summer of 1767, Parliament suspended the New York assembly for failing to comply with the Quartering Act, which required the assembly to pay to support British soldiers garrisoned in the city. John Dickinson, in his immensely popular series of essays, "Letters from a Farmer in Pennsylvania," asked his fellow colonists, "Why may not every colony be treated in the same manner?" After all, "if the parliament may lawfully deprive New York of any of her rights, it may deprive any, or all the other colonies of their rights, and nothing can possibly so much encourage such attempts, as a mutual inattention to the interests of each other."[106] Similarly, when Parliament passed the Coercive Acts in 1774 in the wake of the Boston Tea Party, shutting down port of Boston and taking away the Massachusetts charter, colonists again understood these actions as attempting to set a precedent for its authority over all the colonies. Rather than distancing themselves from Massachusetts, as Parliament and the Ministry expected, colonists throughout North America sent aid and comfort to their sister colony in part to register the dissent necessary to preclude the setting of a precedent.

The present would soon be the past, and the two would remain intimately connected. What Parliament could do and what colonists could expect was continuously being redefined throughout the imperial crisis with each action by Parliament and each reaction by the colonists. Ultimately, the authority of the past did not impact the imperial crisis only through colonists' looking backward but forward as well, thereby revealing the intimacy of the relationship between the past and present that helped define both colonial history culture and the colonial response to imperial reform.

Colonists' sense of the authority of the past was intertwined with their newly shared colonial past. While that sense of the authority of the past led them to have certain assumptions and expectations regarding their relationship with Britain (and Parliament), equality with native-born Britons was perhaps the most elemental assumption (and expectation) that colonists had. That is why their arguments for that equality were fundamentally historical and based on a historical memory of a newly shared colonial past. Colonists had built up expectations about their relationship with Britain based on the customary development of that relationship and on their understandings of the meanings and motivations behind settlement. Parliament's attempts at imperial reform in the 1760s and 1770s were fundamentally at odds with both of those historical perspectives, and they would only become even more conflicting as the crisis continued, ultimately resulting in colonists beginning to question their understandings not only of the colonial past but of the British past and their relationship to it.

By looking through the lens of history culture, we can begin to see how references to settlement and arguments about charters, custom, precedent, and time derived from a coherent shared colonial perspective on the relationship between the past and present. We can also see how the cultural understanding of that relationship in the colonies differed from that of Britain. Additionally, the historical context of the imperial debate offers us a window into culturally derived popular attitudes that did not rely on familiarity with British writers from the early eighteenth century or legal and constitutional theorists from the seventeenth century. In this new context, we can understand the imperial crisis and debate as having also been about defining the meaning of the past just as much as defining the immediate grievances of the present or the direction of the future. Moreover, we can see an interrelationship between them. In this process of defining the meaning of the past and its relationship to the present in ways that differed from Britons, we can begin to uncover part of the cultural origins of the American Revolution.

Both sides came into the imperial crisis with very different understandings of the relationship between the past and present. In 1775, Josiah Tucker, a British political and economic writer, summed up how this fundamental disconnect between the two sides had affected the debate when he wrote: "The first thing observable in this controversy is, that there is no common principle to rest upon, no common medium to appeal to. The Colonists reason principally from what they apprehend ought originally to be the case,—to what in the future shall or must be:—And the Mother Country from what actually was,—to what still ought to be."[107]

That is, Tucker recognized the degree to which the colonists' started their position from the past and expected that the present and immediate future would reflect the past, largely because of the authority they invested in it. They expected the present and immediate future (what "shall or must be") would be an extension of the past (that which "ought originally to be the case"). Meanwhile, the British had determined to judge their courses of action throughout the previous ten years of the crisis based on the various situations-at-hand, or "what actually was," at any given moment in pursuit of the ultimate goal of imperial reform, or what "ought to be." The colonists' perspective on the relationship between the past and present—itself a cultural inheritance from England in the previous century—had shifted in Britain considerably over the course of the eighteenth century.

For many Britons, particularly those engaged in responding to colonial resistance arguments, the present offered unprecedented challenges and, logically, called for unprecedented solutions. If the best way to manage unprecedented debt and an enlarged empire was to impose a stamp tax on the colonists, so be it. That it had never been done before was not a consideration most MPs appeared to have had during its debate and passage or most Britons had afterward. By the 1760s, the colonists' perspective seemed to Britons to be antiquated and naïve, with many convinced it was merely an insincere rhetorical tactic. In Britain, the "antiquarian"—someone who loved the past for its own sake and often collected historical relics such as coins and inscriptions—was a common target of ridicule and satire.[108] Satirists often portrayed them as isolated, pedantic, and local-minded individuals with no interest in or knowledge of the broader world in which they lived. By repeatedly invoking the authority of the past over present exigency, colonists seemed to many Britons be just as deserving of ridicule, which was indeed how pro-reform British writers treated their arguments from the authority of the past. In Britain, this ridicule reinforced popular perceptions of colonists' provincialism and cultural inferiority, while in the colonies, the abandonment of the authority of the past reinforced perceptions of both political corruption and cultural declension in Britain. The disconnect between the two sides, which became apparent as early as the

Stamp Act crisis of 1765, continued throughout the imperial crisis and, as Tucker realized toward the end of it, offered an explanation for the inability of each side to take the other side's arguments seriously and engage in a meaningful dialogue aimed at reconciliation and compromise.

Finally, the settlement and compact rhetoric, which represented colonists' search for their own first principles, and the appeals to the authority of the past combined to form the basis of a historical memory of a newly shared colonial past. That these ideas about the colonial past were shared and replicated throughout the colonies using similar language for similar purposes shows its reach. Moreover, its ubiquity and conspicuousness in patriot arguments show how important this past was to the arguments colonists made throughout the crisis. The new shared colonial past served as one of the new ties that bound disparate colonists together in their resistance to imperial reform and contributing to colonists' growing sense of being part of a collective public that encompassed all of the British mainland colonies as a polity apart from Britain itself. By the time independence was declared, Americans had already created the beginnings of a shared history. As we will see in the following chapter, the imperial crisis also forced colonists to begin reconsidering the British past and their relationship to it in new ways that also had a profound effect on how they perceived their relationship with Britain, how they navigated the politics of the crisis, and, ultimately, how they came to declare independence.

CHAPTER THREE

THE BRITISH PAST IN THE IMPERIAL CRISIS

On a cold winter's day in February 1761, people ambled down King Street in Boston past the Old State House. There, in the Royal Council Chamber on the east side of the second floor, the General Court heard arguments in the infamous Writs of Assistance case. As James Otis, Jr., a lawyer for the defense, began his four-hour speech that day, he did so in front of "Two Portraits at more than full length of King Charles the second, and King James the second, in splendid golden frames" hung on the chamber wall. John Adams called them "the finest Pictures I have seen." Under these imposing portraits, Otis argued against the legality of the writs, which were effectively broad search warrants, by going "back to the old Saxon Laws and to Magna Charta and the fifty Confirmations of it in Parliament and the Execrations ordained against the Violators of it, and the National Vengeance which had been taken on them from time to time down to the James's & Charles's, and to the Petition of Rights and the Bill of Rights, and the Revolution."[1] As with Otis in the courtroom on that day in 1761, the British past hung over the impending imperial crisis, casting a long shadow indeed that helped shape the perceptions and arguments of both sides and, thereby, the coming of the American Revolution.

Having looked at the role of the colonial past and the authority of the past generally in patriot rhetoric, particularly in the early years of the imperial crisis, let us now turn our attention to the role of the British past in shaping the imperial debate, particularly between 1768 and 1776. During the imperial crisis, many patriots began to reconsider the British past and their relationship to it. The broadest question at stake in the Stamp Act debate was whether colonists were considered equal with native-born British subjects and therefore entitled to the same rights and liberties. One of the primary ways colonists asserted their civic status was by denying the right of Parliament to tax them without being represented in that body. Many colonists viewed their arguments over the issues of taxation and representation through the lens of the British past, while simultaneously drawing on their colonial past to frame the broader question of their equality with native Britons. With the passage of the Townshend Acts in 1767, however, the primary question of the imperial debate changed.

In the late 1760s, the major issue of the imperial debate began shifting to parliamentary supremacy, which was the idea that sovereignty was lodged solely in the "king-in-Parliament," and its implications for the colonies. In other words, sovereignty was understood as being held by the combination of Crown, Lords, and Commons, rather than the Crown alone. The English Civil Wars of the 1640s had been brought about by a decades-long struggle between Parliament and Charles I, as the former sought to expand its own prerogative and limit that of the king. This conflict continued throughout the seventeenth century through the Protectorate of Oliver Cromwell and the restoration of the Stuart monarchy in 1660 following his death. With the accession of James II in the 1680s, the struggle took on new meaning due to the new king's Catholicism and the birth of his son, a Catholic heir to the throne of Protestant England. When Prince William of Orange, a Dutchman and son-in-law of James II, invaded England at the behest of prominent Whigs seeking to secure the Protestant succession, the king abdicated his throne by fleeing to France. Parliament then bestowed the crown on William with the condition that he agree to restrictions on the royal prerogative and to the enlarged prerogative of Parliament.

In the early decades of the eighteenth century, Britain was too occupied with wars with France and Spain for Parliament to use its newfound supremacy to attempt broad imperial reform in the colonies. Imperial policy in this period was largely determined by a Whig ideology of imperial political economy that enforced the Navigation Acts but prioritized fostering trade with the colonies, thereby generating revenue through customs and duties rather than taxing them directly. In the wake of the Seven Years' War, however, George III brought new men to power who shared a very different idea of empire. Men like George Grenville and Lord North sought to fashion Britain's new, enlarged empire according to the Spanish model by focusing on centralizing and tightening oversight, extracting natural resources, and directly taxing colonies to pay for the empire's domestic national debt. Parliamentary supremacy would be one of their primary tools. This reform program would define the ministries of the years between 1763 and 1776, only temporarily stalled by the brief tenures of the Marquis of Rockingham, who helped secure repeal of the Stamp Act, and William Pitt between 1765 and 1768.

In the Declaratory Act that accompanied the repeal of the Stamp Act in 1766, Parliament declared its supremacy over the colonies "in all cases whatsoever." For many colonists, the passage of the Townshend Acts in 1767 seemed to signal that Parliament had begun reasserting that supremacy. Patriots understood the Townshend Acts' duties on glass, lead, paper, and tea as a way to get colonists to assent to paying taxes in the form of import duties. Looking back on it in 1773, the New York Sons of Liberty described the acts and their intent as a "necessary badge of Parliamentary supremacy."[2] The application of the doctrine of parliamentary supremacy to the colonies for the first time in the late 1760s caused colonists to begin reconsidering the British past, particularly the Glorious Revolution, which gave birth to the doctrine. They also began questioning their relationship to the Glorious Revolution and the British past generally, which fundamentally changed patriots' understanding of the crisis and, as a result, their rhetoric of resistance, which helped clear the way for independence less than a decade later.

Before the Revolution, colonists held the British past in common, but by the 1780s and 1790s Americans no longer thought of the British past as their own. This change, however, did not occur overnight when the colonists declared independence in 1776. Rather, it was a process begun during the imperial crisis and continued into the first decades of the early republic. It consisted, in part, of the construction of a newly shared colonial past and the deconstruction of colonists' British historical memory. The latter was no small task considering just how fundamental the British past had been in shaping colonists' imperial identities. Such identities were defined by colonists' understanding of what the empire represented, their role within it, and their sense of belonging to not just the empire but to Britain itself. Their knowledge and celebration of the British past had provided a critical cultural lifeline between the provinces and the mother country. That lifeline allowed colonists—many removed from Britain by generations and all by three thousand miles of ocean—to believe they were just as British as native-born subjects. Colonists believed they were British not only by virtue of their political ties to the empire but also by their cultural ties to Britain. Indeed, as the colonies became more important to the imperial economy through the first half of the eighteenth century, the cultural ties came to matter even more. Yet, as Parliament's actions and the rhetoric of its defenders brought the British past into question, it, in turn, brought colonists' imperial identities into question. That process contributed to a cultural break with Britain that was a necessary prerequisite for declaring political independence.

While patriots were beginning to create a shared historical memory of their colonial past during the imperial crisis, the British past was equally important in shaping the dynamic of the imperial debate. In resisting the Stamp Act, colonists repeatedly referenced the history of the English Civil Wars to bolster their arguments regarding taxation and representation. All spending bills, including those granting revenues to the Crown for its maintenance as well as for wars, could originate only in the House of Commons in Parliament. Beginning in the late 1620s, however, Charles I sought revenue without calling a Parliament by taking advantage of a medieval tax, known as "ship money," that did not require Parliament's approval. Until then, the tax had been assessed only in wartime and only on communities near the coasts to help pay for the Royal Navy. In the 1630s, Charles I levied the tax during peacetime and on communities far afield from the coasts, thereby sidestepping the long-standing prerogative of the House of Commons. Colonists seized on this famous historical example of the government skirting representation in search of revenue. They, unsurprisingly, referenced ship money early and often in the imperial debate as analogous to the

Stamp Act and Townshend duties, that is, an example of the people being taxed without consent of their representatives. In his 1764 pamphlet, *Rights of the British Colonies,* James Otis drew the analogy simply by saying, "King Charles I his ship money everyone has heard of."[3] The incident was so well known and the reference was so ubiquitous, both in print and generally, that the analogy needed no further explanation.

Colonists saw distinct parallels between the years leading up to the Civil Wars and their circumstances early in the imperial crisis. "As the King," one patriot noted, "cannot by his sole authority lay a tax on the people of Britain without their consent, as in the famous case of ship money . . . so the King and Parliament cannot, *for the same reason,* lay a tax on America without their consent."[4] Another asked rhetorically, "Was not the raising taxes by ship money, &c. Without the consent of the good people of England who were to pay them, and arbitrary courts of trial, contrary to the rights of Englishmen and the . . . principal grievances and causes of civil war in the reign of Charles I?"[5] The issue of taxation at the start of the imperial crisis—and, more broadly, the issue of the relationship between the authority of the state and the liberty of the subject—brought colonists' historical memories of Charles I and the Civil Wars to the fore.

After not calling a Parliament for eleven years, Charles had no choice but to do so in 1640 because he needed funds to pay for an army to turn back a Scottish invasion of the northern border. After a contentious year, in December of 1641 Parliament passed the "Grand Remonstrance." In it, Parliament detailed its long-standing grievances against the king, including the ship money taxes, and called for weakening the royal prerogative. Charles rejected the proposed changes and unsuccessfully tried to arrest five parliamentary leaders in the House of Commons. These tensions between the royal prerogative and that of Parliament ultimately led to the start of the Civil Wars the following year. Describing the situation in 1768, the Reverend Andrew Eliot wrote to a friend, "I am sure this will put you in mind of 1641."[6] Besides the sure assumption, Eliot's analogy referred to the use of arbitrary power by Charles I, who believed he ruled by divine right and was therefore above being questioned by anyone, including Parliament. Moreover, the analogy betrayed Eliot's sense that the current crisis had the potential to become a military conflict as he was writing just days before British troops arrived in Boston to restore order following protests against the Townshend Acts. Eliot's fears came to fruition on the cold, snowy evening of March 5, 1770, when five colonists were killed by British troops in the so-called Boston Massacre.

One example of how much the English Civil Wars were on patriot minds right from the start of the imperial crisis can be found in an exchange between a British polemicist named "Wm. Pym" and James Otis and John Adams.[7] Pym published a series of letters in the *Public Ledger* in the fall of 1765 denouncing colonial resistance. British leniency, Pym argued, had "filled their little assemblies with a notion, that they were every whit as important as a British Parliament." "This behaviour has absolutely intoxicated them," he continued, "and they now talk of their privileges with as great an air, as if they were the actual representatives of the Mother Country."[8] Soon after these letters were reprinted in the colonies, James Otis and, later, John Adams responded in a series of letters written under the historical pseudonyms of Hampden and Clarendon. Both of these men had been leading figures in Parliament against the Crown, but as the conflict wore on, Clarendon became disenchanted with the increasingly popular nature of parliamentary resistance. When war broke out, he sided with the king. Years later, he wrote the most widely read history of the Civil Wars, which was well respected by colonial elites for its moderate and even-handed treatment of the events. While Adams never commented on the reasons for his adoption of the pseudonym, he was an admirer of Clarendon, whom he called "one of the greatest English ministers." He also greatly admired Clarendon's *History of the Rebellion and Civil Wars Begun in England in the Year 1641*, which he recommended to his son Charles as a work of admirable objectivity.[9] The moderate, anti-popular nature of Clarendon's history and political career would have resonated deeply with Adams, who in the 1760s was a strong critic of Parliament but also deeply uncomfortable with the popular mobs and destruction of property that marked the early resistance in Boston.

Historians have long believed that Pym's moniker was a "strange mistake," claiming "the author had intended to refer to John Pym, the opposition leader in the Long Parliament, but had mistakenly rendered it as William Pym."[10] Yet, there is no textual or contextual reason to support this assumption, and those historians' analysis seems to have been influenced more by Otis's and Adams's subsequent adoption of pseudonyms related to the Civil Wars. Nothing in any of the letters suggests that Pym was adopting a historical pseudonym (let alone a historical persona, as Adams did), and there are no significant references to the Civil Wars in his pieces. Indeed, one recent historian has found evidence that suggests "Wm. Pym" was actually the author's real name and not a pseudonym at all.[11] In this case, we can see the degree to which the Civil Wars were on these patriots' minds early in the crisis by the fact that their adoptions of Civil Wars–related pseudonyms and personas were triggered by the mere similarity of the author's last name to the historical parliamentary leader. Adams adopted only one other historical persona in his many writings during the crisis, that of John Winthrop, showing both the dichotomous presence of the colonial and British pasts in Adams's thinking and his assumptions about the rhetorical and persuasive power of both pasts on his audience.[12] While much has been made of patriot writers' adoption of classical pseudonyms, they also used pseudonyms drawn from England's seventeenth-century past, the meaning of which would have been familiar to a far broader audience than the meaning behind most classical pseudonyms. Ultimately, the Civil Wars provided many similarities and allegories on which patriot rhetoric could draw and retained a varying degree of cultural salience in colonial politics.[13]

The Civil Wars had produced conflicted historical memories in the colonies.[14] New Englanders generally saw the actions of Parliament in waging war against and ultimately killing the king as justified. But while there was a general consensus on the causes of the Civil Wars, the consequences were a more complicated issue. New Englanders had an on-again-off-again relationship with Oliver Cromwell. The pious Puritan leader of the Parliamentarian forces played a major role in the military defeat of Charles I and his subsequent execution in January 1649 before declaring England a commonwealth and himself its Lord Protector. Though he enjoyed a degree of popularity as a folk hero to the laboring classes, in times of relative peace, many New Englanders saw Cromwell as a tyrant.[15] Anglicans and Puritan elites with the most to lose especially despised the middling-class celebration of a man they saw as an enthusiastic demagogue promoting anarchy. In times of war, however, particularly against the Spanish, his image was often very quickly rehabilitated. His imperial legacy of seizing Jamaica from the Spanish in 1655 was useful to those seeking to bolster their arguments for dealing more aggressively with Spain, especially during the War of Jenkins' Ear (1739–48).

During the imperial crisis, Cromwell appeared in New England literature as a popular patriotic counterpoint to Anglicans' commemoration of the Stuarts and to the moderate approach of most colonial elites, particularly at the start of the crisis.[16] In 1765, an altered Anglican litany circulated in Connecticut that exclaimed, "O, Cromwell, deliver us!"[17] In 1771, a patriot writer adopted Cromwell's persona to decry the "tyrannical ministers and their infamous tools (the genuine offspring of my ancient enemies and the Popish Stuarts)."[18] In 1774, Nathanael Low included a woodcut of Oliver Cromwell on the front page of his almanac published in Boston, and two years later the first privateer sanctioned by the new Commonwealth of Massachusetts in 1776 was named the *Oliver Cromwell.* Because so many supporters of Charles I had settled in the Chesapeake, however, Cromwell's legacy in Virginia remained primarily that of traitor and tyrant.[19]

The use of Civil War terminology to denigrate one's political or religious opponents was a common rhetorical device in eighteenth-century colonial political and religious culture. Loyalists continued to draw on that tradition. They referred to patriots as "republicans" and "levellers" and dubbed their leaders "Cromwells." A Boston innkeeper and British informant, Richard Sylvester, reported to army officers in 1769 that the Sons of Liberty believed "that Oliver Cromwell was a glorious fellow, and what a pitty it was that they had not such another to espouse their cause at present."[20] In New England, particularly among Anglicans, these references continued to carry heavy rhetorical weight because of the historical understanding that the region was settled by anti-monarchical, radical Puritan republicans. Peter Oliver, a prominent loyalist historian whose family's history went back to the earliest years of the Massachusetts Bay Colony, understood the "Sympathy of Soul" between the New Englanders of the 1760s and the first settlers, who were ardent supporters of the Commonwealth. Even Britons who supported the Americans' grievances understood this. One anonymous pamphleteer pondering the possibility of Britain needing to send troops to enforce the Stamp Act predicted, "It is not to be expected that the spawn of the old Cromwelians [*sic*] will submit without a blow."[21] As a contemporary British historian noted after the war, "The source of the Rebellion [was] founded in the principles and dispositions of the first settlers of New England."[22] It was a common rhetorical move by Britons and some loyalists to argue that due to their Puritan origins in the period of the Civil Wars, New Englanders were by their very nature anti-monarchical, rebellious, and even seditious. As the crisis wore on, it became more common to extrapolate those characterizations to describe the American colonists as a whole.

British and loyalist writers took great exception to patriots' analogies of the current situation with that of the Civil Wars, particularly in the earliest years of the crisis. Faction, disorder, violence, and radicalism defined Britain's popular memory of the Civil Wars. Eighteenth-century Britain prided itself on being nothing like that dark time in the nation's past. The "Whig supremacy" in English politics had largely neutralized political factionalism and popular politics and maintained relatively peaceful order domestically over the previous three decades. So when Stephen Hopkins, the elected governor of Rhode Island, included an epigram in his pamphlet *The Rights of the Colonies Examined* (1764) that quoted a line from the poem "Liberty" by James Thomson referencing "Hambden," it provoked a swift and virulent reaction: "I might challenge all sons of discontent and faction, in the British dominions, to shew the least similitude between the years one thousand six hundred and forty-one, and one thousand seven hundred and sixty-four. How cruel and invidious is it to insinuate the most distant likeness between the two periods? How much like sedition does it seem, to associate the present transactions of the nation with those of one thousand six hundred and forty-one, which soon after kindled into a civil war, and in the end overturned the English constitution?"[23] For this writer, even "insinuating" any similarity between 1641 and the present times—let alone making a direct analogy—was a "cruel and invidious" act akin to "sedition." He was not alone, and colonial references to the Civil Wars fostered the sense among some Britons that the colonists' ultimate aim was independence.

By the 1770s, however, Britons and loyalists were beginning to see their own analogies. Thomas Bradbury Chandler, an Anglican clergyman and loyalist from New Jersey, analogized the Continental Congress delegates with the Parliamentarians: "You may still profess yourselves to be *his Majesty's most dutiful and loyal subjects,* as you did in your late RESOLVES, and as the leaders in the grand rebellion of 1641 did, in their messages to the King immediately after the battle of *Edge-Hill,* where they had fought against him in person."[24] Furthermore, he charged his fellow colonists with aiming "to plunge [their sword] into the bowels of our ancient and venerable Constitution," just as he believed Cromwell had done. Similarly, in 1772, a writer in London's *Gazetteer and New Daily Advertiser* related, "The Proceedings of Fanaticks and Republicans, under the Conduct of Cromwell, is so fresh in our Minds, that there is not one honest and sober thinking monarchical Englishman, but thinks the Bostonians have been governed rather by too slack than too tight a rein; and that the Administration cannot keep too vigilant an Eye over them."[25] At the start of the crisis, Britons and loyalists were offended at analogies with the Civil Wars, but as the crisis wore on they began to see and make their own analogies based on their characterization of the Civil Wars that stressed colonial dissemblance and disloyalty.

Colonists saw these similarities between the 1760s and the English Civil Wars that much more vividly because of their more intimate cultural relationship between the past and present and the truncated historical distance between them. For Britons, however, the tumults of the 1640s and 1650s were a stain on the nation's history, something that deeply offended the order and moderation-based sensibilities of Augustan England. As a result, Britons in the mid-eighteenth century were largely intent on extending the historical distance between themselves and the Civil Wars. In the late nineteenth century, it was reported that when British troops arrived in Boston in 1768, they forced Joshua Brackett, the patriot owner of a tavern on School Street called "Cromwell's Head," to take down its sign because it included a large portrait of the Lord Protector himself, rendered by Paul Revere. Brackett's sign was said to have "hung so low that all who passed were compelled to make an involuntary reverence."[26] There are no contemporaneous sources for this story, but whether this tale was apocryphal or not, the existence of Brackett's inn was not. The sign allegedly remained down until the British evacuated the city in spring 1775, at which time it was restored. In the early years of the imperial crisis, patriots made common use of the English Civil Wars as reference points in their arguments. But, of course, taxation was only one issue that contributed to the English Civil Wars. For many colonists the most common interpretation of the Civil Wars had been that the upheavals of the mid-seventeenth century were, broadly speaking, the product of the arbitrary rule of Charles I. That basic understanding would continue to inform patriot rhetoric, and after 1768 the theme of arbitrary power would be central to colonists' shifting perceptions of the Glorious Revolution, Parliament, and the crisis itself.

Patriot arguments changed a number of times following the passage of the Townshend Acts, which imposed duties on certain goods imported from Britain and set up a new customs bureaucracy of commissioners and vice-admiralty courts to enforce the new duties. In the winter of 1767–68, John Dickinson, a lawyer from Delaware, responded to the new acts with a series of newspaper essays entitled "Letters from a Pennsylvania Farmer." Perhaps the most widely read and discussed piece of patriot rhetoric until *Common Sense* almost a decade later, Dickinson's essays drew heavily on both the authority of the past and the British past specifically.[27] At the start of the first letter, Dickinson assumed the appealing persona of an independent, learned farmer, establishing his credentials by claiming, "Being generally master of my time, I spend a good deal of it in a library." His particular qualification followed: "I believe I have acquired a greater knowledge in history, and the laws and constitution of my country, than is generally attained by men of my class."[28] In his role as "Farmer-scholar," Dickinson was "praised for his 'painful study' and 'deep Researches.'" To the actions of Parliament, he "annex[ed] that meaning which the constitution and history of England require to be annexed to it."[29] Dickinson understood and harnessed the persuasive and rhetorical power of the authority of the past and the cultural meaning of the British past in the colonies, which contributed significantly to the attraction, appeal, and persuasiveness of the "Letters."

In attacking the Townshend Acts, Dickinson argued that though colonists continued to acknowledge the sovereignty of Parliament, its legislative authority in the colonies was limited by the custom and precedent of the past. "Never did the British Parliament, till the period above mentioned, think of imposing duties in America for the purpose of raising a revenue," he pointed out.[30] To use those regulations, as the Townshend Acts did, for the "sole purpose of levying money" was an "innovation," which, as we saw in the previous chapter, was a highly negative descriptor to colonists living in a history culture defined by custom, precedent, and tradition, or, in other words, the authority of the past.[31] The Townshend Acts made it plain to many that the Sugar and Stamp Acts were not isolated incidents but instead were part of a plan of imperial reform by Britain. Dickinson, one of the patriots' most renowned moderates, had not yet come to that conclusion but declared: "If at length it becomes undoubted that an inveterate resolution is formed to annihilate the liberties of the governed, the *English* history affords frequent examples of resistance by force."[32] Throughout the letters he displayed his deep familiarity with British history, adding even greater weight to his otherwise direct and easily understood arguments. As historian Pauline Maier has noted, "The colonists viewed their opposition as more justified by English tradition than were Parliament's innovations."[33] Dickinson's "Letters," which were reprinted, read, and discussed widely throughout the colonies, did not single-handedly spur colonial resistance to the Townshend Acts, but they did inform that resistance as it developed over the course of 1769, helping set the stage for an important turn in patriot rhetoric.

From the wake of the Townshend Acts through the end of the crisis, the debate came to center on the issue of parliamentary supremacy. The legacy of the Glorious Revolution had been a cornerstone of national identity in the Anglophone world, both in Britain and the colonies. "The revolution," as colonists referred to 1688, had secured the Protestant succession by inviting William of Orange to invade England and force James II, a devout Catholic, off the throne. But, most importantly, the Glorious Revolution had limited the royal prerogative and increased the authority of Parliament by investing it with an unprecedented degree of sovereignty.

In doing so, the Glorious Revolution fundamentally changed the relationship between Parliament and the Crown, giving all power to initiate legislation to Parliament but requiring the king's assent to all acts passed. In the years that followed the Glorious Revolution, however, William was more concerned with using his new position as king of England to aid his long-standing fight against France than he was with domestic politics. The result was the weakening of the monarch's role in legislative matters, which meant that, in reality, sovereignty had come to rest solely in Parliament by the middle of the eighteenth century. Technically the king retained the prerogative to veto bills passed by Parliament, but no Hanoverian monarch dared exercise it. Therefore, the royal veto was, for all intents and purposes, effectively defunct.

As a result, during the course of the eighteenth century, the doctrine of parliamentary sovereignty transformed into "parliamentary supremacy." By mid-century, Britons increasingly understood that whatever Parliament did was, by definition, constitutional. Therefore, Parliament could not act unconstitutionally, even if it tried, and its actions were beyond the authority of all but a subsequent Parliament. Based on the widely accepted notion that sovereignty within a state must be indivisible, this understanding of parliamentary supremacy was "hardening into an orthodoxy" by the end of the Seven Years' War.[34] The imperial crisis was, at its heart, the extension of this doctrine to the empire, as a means of asserting greater centralized control than had been achieved previously by the Ministry and Board of Trade. Over the course of the crisis, however, colonists developed a critique of parliamentary supremacy that forced them to reconsider the meaning of the Glorious Revolution's legacy, and that reconsideration profoundly affected the imperial crisis and, ultimately, their path to independence.

Early in the imperial crisis, following the Stamp Act, patriot rhetoric regarding the Glorious Revolution remained much the same as it had been in the decades before. In 1764, Stephen Hopkins praised "the *British* constitution, as it at present stands, on revolution principles."[35] Likewise, James Otis believed that the "great doctrines of British liberty taught in 1640" had been "tempered and refined by the revolution."[36] "The British constitution," he argued, had been "re-established at the revolution."[37] Many patriots had long believed that the Glorious Revolution—"that grand æra of British liberty"—had restored the constitution "on its free and ancient principles."[38] Establishment Whigs in Britain, however, came to understand 1688 as a radically transformative event, that is, "Year One" of a new type of limited monarchy and a new and improved constitution.[39] As Lord Hervey claimed in 1734, "From King James the Second's Banishment, Abdication, Deposition, or whatever People please to call it, I date the Birth of real liberty in this kingdom."[40] In Britain, he was not alone. By the late 1760s, however, colonists too began to recognize that the Glorious Revolution had been a fundamental break with the past, one which, for them, became increasingly problematic.

The most pressing change was the development of parliamentary supremacy, an important part of the Whig legacy of the Glorious Revolution that effectively put Parliament beyond the authority of any other individual or body within the realm.[41] In 1764, Otis, like most colonists, acknowledged parliamentary supremacy, "The power of parliament is uncontroulable, but by themselves, and we must obey." He continued, "They only can repeal their own acts. There would be an end of all government, if one or a number of subjects or subordinate provinces should take upon them so far to judge of the justice of an act of parliament, as to refuse obedience to it."[42] In another pamphlet, Otis wrote of colonists' understanding of parliamentary authority prior to the crisis and before the shift in colonial rhetoric later in the decade, saying, "I never heard one man of sense and knowledge, in the laws and British constitution, call the parliamentary authority arbitrary."[43] Early in the crisis, patriot writers repeatedly professed their loyalty and subjection to both king and Parliament, but in the years to come they increasingly came to see Parliament's authority as arbitrary and the nature of their subjection to Parliament as problematic, both ultimately resulting from the Revolution Settlement.[44]

Parliament had passed the Stamp Act in 1765 but it also had been responsive to colonial remonstrances and repealed it the following year. In the years that followed, however, as Parliament began making good on the promise of the subsequent Declaratory Act, its response to colonial petitions and protests became equally problematic. In 1768, at Providence, a patriot orator declared, "Upon the whole, the conduct of Great-Britain shews that they have formed a plan to subject us so effectually to their absolute commands. . . . We are insulted and menaced only for petitioning. Our prayers are prevented from reaching the royal ear, and our humble supplications to the throne are wickedly and maliciously represented as so many marks of faction and disloyalty."[45] Similarly, George Washington wrote to George Mason in Virginia in 1769, "Addresses to the Throne, and remonstrances to parliament, we have already, it is said, proved the inefficacy of."[46] A few years later, in 1772, the Boston Committee of Correspondence noted, "The Colonists have been branded with the odious Names of Traitors and Rebels, only for complaining of their Grievances."[47]

Following the Declaratory Act, Parliament made clear that subsequent legislation was not to be questioned. When the New York assembly sent a petition to Parliament in the wake of the Coercive Acts in 1774, Lord North responded, "The honour of Parliament required, that no paper should be presented to that House, which tended to call in question the unlimited rights of Parliament."[48] From the patriot perspective, if Parliament had "unlimited rights," or absolute power, to which there was no direct recourse, then Parliament was free to act as arbitrarily as any seventeenth-century monarch. For colonists, acting arbitrarily meant effectively to act ahistorically, or in a way that was unrestrained and not bound in any way by the authority of the past.

From the late 1760s onward, patriots were compelled to try to come to terms with what they perceived as the increasing ahistoricity of Britain's commitment to the notion of parliamentary supremacy and its legislative results. For colonists who had long developed expectations about the present based on the past, this caused no small sense of anxiety. That anxiety was reflected in the degree and nature of the subsequent shifts in their rhetoric. The first significant shift came in the late 1760s as some patriot writers began to make a historical argument that Parliament actually had no authority over the colonies at all. Instead, they used the settlement and charter rhetoric as a foundation for arguing that the colonies had never been annexed to the Realm of England and, therefore, had always been under the authority of the Crown alone. The degree of the shift from just a few years earlier can be seen in the way James Otis addressed the "error" of such thinking in 1765: "This is a hard doctrine for a Colonist to believe, harder still to swallow, and the man lives not who can cram it down the throat of a Hampden.—How abhorrent such a position is to all the colony charters."[49] By the early 1770s, however, many patriots had indeed come to understand their charters as "the ligaments and bonds that connect the colonies with the king of Great-Britain, and the king with them," a relationship that patriots increasingly argued was beyond the jurisdiction of Parliament entirely.[50]

This argument—referred to by historians as the "dominion" or "commonwealth" theory—is, perhaps, first addressed so directly and in such detail in a pamphlet by Edward Bancroft published in London in 1769, and in the colonies in 1771, entitled, *Remarks on the Review of the Controversy between Great Britain and her Colonies.*[51] Bancroft's pamphlet is, at its core, a historical work recounting the history of the colonies' settlement. He began by noting that to "expose the Fallacy of this ministerial Position, so injurious to the Colonies" he must go back to "the Terms, Principles, and Designs of their Settlement; and the Degree and Mode of Connection." "To effect this," he continued, "it will be necessary to review their Political History, the Charters on which they were settled, the Circumstances attending their Settlement, and the Conduct of the King and Parliament towards them since that Æra."[52] For Bancroft, the history of settlement made clear that the colonies "belonged to the Crown alone."[53] The implication was that the history of the colonies showed that they were beyond the jurisdiction of Parliament. Though the pamphlet was not widely circulated at the time, it drew on and reflected patriot rhetoric generally. Like many other patriot writers in this period, Bancroft incorporated the historical memory of the colonial past discussed in the previous chapter into his critique of interpretations of the British past.

Traces of this argument among patriots had existed before 1769. One writer in New York in 1766 dramatically expressed the sentiment behind the argument, declaring: "I am very far from being an Enemy to Parliamentary Power. I revere the House of Commons as the Watchful Guardians presiding over the Liberty of their Constituents; but when I see Them grasping at a Power altogether foreign, and inconsistent with the Principles of their own Constitution; I could wish to see Them reduc'd within their natural Bounds, and would even shelter myself under the Wings of the Royal Prerogative."[54] That same year, Benjamin Franklin noted in his marginalia on a pamphlet containing the protests of the House of Lords against the repeal of the Stamp Act, "The Sovereignty of the Crown I understand. The sovereignty of the British legislature outside of Britain I do not understand. . . . America not in the Realm of England or G.B. . . . Parliament has the power only within the realm."[55] These new arguments were a tentative response to these imperial reforms, which, as a usurpation of the authority of the past, colonists referred to as a "new system of politics." Wrought initially by the Glorious Revolution, this "new system of politics"—based on parliamentary supremacy—manifested itself in Parliament's unprecedented attempts to declare and exercise its legislative supremacy over the colonies.

In the years after 1768, the argument that the colonies were solely under the authority of the Crown and not Parliament could be found increasingly in pamphlets and newspaper essays throughout the colonies. It was also found in patriot oratory. Patriots used the settlement and charter rhetoric that contributed to the historical memory of the colonial past created in the early years of the crisis as a foundation for their reconsideration of the British past. After 1767, Parliament was increasingly and conspicuously missing from the opening platitudes so common in many resistance writings during the Stamp Act crisis. Others were more direct. On July 25, 1768, Silas Downer gave a rousing public sermon in Providence, Rhode Island, to dedicate the town's liberty tree. He began: "On this occasion we chearfully recognize our allegiance to our sovereign Lord, George the third, King of Great-Britain, and supreme Lord of these dominions, but utterly deny any other dependence on the inhabitants of that island, than what is mutual and reciprocal between all mankind."[56] Unsurprisingly, Downer then moved into a long historical disquisition on both settlement and the British past that stressed the endeavors of the settlers in escaping tyranny in England and the subsequent hands-off approach of British governance toward the colonies for the rest of the seventeenth century. Two years later, a letter to the Earl of Hillsborough published in both pamphlet form and excerpted in newspapers also began with a lengthy disquisition on the history of the colonies' settlement that provided "so many accumulated proofs, that the colonies, before the act of navigation, not only considered themselves, but were considered by the King, Parliament, and people of England, as free distinct states, not depending on the Parliament of this kingdom, though owing allegiance to its sovereign."[57]

In his 1771 oration to commemorate the first anniversary of the Boston Massacre, James Lovell, shortly to become a Massachusetts delegate to the Continental Congress, necessarily began his speech by "once more look[ing] into the early history of this province." There, he found "that our English ancestors, disgusted in their native country at a legislation, which they saw was sacrificing all their rights, left its jurisdiction, and sought, like wandering birds of passage, some happier climate. Here at length they settled down." "The king of England," he continued, "was said to be the royal landlord of this territory; with HIM they entered into mutual, sacred compact. . . . It is in this compact that we find OUR ONLY TRUE LEGISLATIVE AUTHORITY."[58] Lovell then clarified directly, "We are rebels against parliament;—we adore the King."[59] And, in case his audience had any doubt left as to the target of his ire, he professed, "I had an eye *solely* to parliamentary supremacy."[60]

Just as during the Stamp Act crisis when colonists argued for their equality with native Britons, they founded their arguments against parliamentary supremacy upon their historical memory of their colonial origins, modifying when and where necessary to account for their new political circumstances and historical perspective. In these writings and published speeches, colonists' construction of their own colonial past in the early years of the crisis necessarily shaped the dismantling of their relationship to the British past as the crisis wore on.

In one of many newspaper essays written by "The British American" in 1774 and 1775, the author stated what had become increasingly accepted over the previous five years or more when he wrote, "The first stab given to the constitution was the crown's losing its independence on the other two branches of the legislature."[61] Refuting the "general opinion" among Britons and loyalists, the writer argued that the Glorious Revolution and its settlement had not restored the Parliament of the ancient constitution. Instead, it had produced "this self-created aristocracy, though assuming the specious name of a British Parliament."[62] By, and in the wake of, the Glorious Revolution, the "Constitution hath been altered" and its "excellence almost annihilated" by the rise of Parliament at the expense of the Crown.[63] In 1767, one reader of the *Pennsylvania Chronicle* wrote a letter imploring the printer to reprint the English Bill of Rights in his paper as it would "please many of your readers" and "give them the Pleasure of examining a beautiful and strong Pillar of the English Constitution."[64] The reader's goal was to remind fellow colonists of what had been the original intentions (or first principles) behind the Glorious Revolution before its corruption by parliamentary supremacy. The printer included both the letter and the Bill of Rights together on the front page of the next issue of the newspaper.

The degree to which the debate had come to focus on parliamentary supremacy by the 1770s is further indicated in *The Address of the People of Great Britain to the Inhabitants of America* (1775). The pamphlet's author noted that "there was a time when our ancestors seemed to differ as much about the terms resistance and non-resistance" in relation to the monarchy "as their posterity do now upon the terms supremacy and independence" in relation to Parliament.[65] The most direct expression of parliamentary supremacy before the Coercive Acts had been the Declaratory Act passed in 1766, in which Parliament declared the right to "bind the colonies . . . in all cases whatsoever." That phrase encapsulated both the position and threat of parliamentary supremacy applied to the colonies. As a result, it was one of the most repeated in patriot rhetoric between 1767 and 1776, from pamphlets and newspapers to myriad resolutions and instructions from towns and counties from New England to South Carolina.

Some patriot writers refashioned the historical memory of the colonial past in an attempt to better make sense of the present and incorporate this emerging narrative of the British past in which the Glorious Revolution no longer seemed so glorious. For some, the motive behind settlement changed from Stuart oppression to parliamentary oppression. As Edward Bancroft wrote, "The Settlement of New England followed that of Virginia, and was occasioned by a noble Disdain of civil and religious Tyranny, the very object for which it was solely undertaken being an Emancipation from the Authority of Parliament." Another patriot writer in 1769 argued that the original settlers "conveyed themselves to the wilds of America, in quell of that freedom which they were denied within the jurisdiction of parliament."[66] In 1775, a young Alexander Hamilton characterized settlement thusly, "The principal design of the enterprize was to be emancipated from their sufferings, under the authority of parliament and the laws of England."[67] These arguments represented colonial attempts to reconcile the present with the past in a way that had often not been possible since the start of the imperial crisis. But such changes in argument were not necessary for most patriots. Many continued to cyclically argue that just as the revolution against the absolutism of Charles I had produced an absolute and tyrannical Parliament, so had the revolution against the absolutism of James II. Such a realization planted the seeds for the notion that independence via revolution might be the only recourse.

Supporters of Parliament and the Ministry reacted incredulously to patriot arguments that they were under the sole jurisdiction of the Crown. In response, they took the patriot argument to its logical conclusion. The colonists, William Knox wrote, "have been deluded into the absurd and vain attempt of exchanging the mild and equal government of the laws of England, for prerogative mandates." It made no sense to British writers that colonists were "seeking to inlarge [their] liberties, by disenfranchising [themselves] of the rights of British subjects."[68] "They must see," Knox argued, "that if they reject parliamentary authority, they make themselves to be still the subjects of the abjured Stuart race."[69] Lord North was not alone in perceiving colonists as speaking the "language . . . of Toryism" or, worse, Jacobitism, the eighteenth-century movement to restore the Stuart dynasty to its rightful throne.[70] As the historian P. D. G. Thomas has written, "Men like George Grenville and Lord North saw themselves as defending what they believed to be the great victory won at the Glorious Revolution of 1688–9, the supremacy of Parliament in the state."[71] Lord Hillsborough, addressing the colonists, wrote, "It is essential to the constitution to preserve the supremacy of Parliament inviolate."[72] In British eyes, as in those of the colonists, to deny parliamentary supremacy was to deny the legacy of the Glorious Revolution itself. And to deny the legacy of the Glorious Revolution was to deny not only the meaning but the very heart of their Britishness.

The period between the repeal of the Townshend Acts in 1770 and the Tea Act of 1773 is often seen as a time of restored, though temporary, calm in the colonies. Yet, public debate continued throughout British America as colonists tried to reconcile "the odious and arbitrary powers" of Parliament with their understanding of the British past.[73] As one writer in the *New-Hampshire Gazette* asked, "Why was the British Constitution framed as it is, and secured with so much zeal and caution by *Magna Charta* and the *Bill of Rights!* Undoubtedly because the Nation was determined not to be subject to arbitrary power."[74] In New York, an anonymous patriot wrote of Parliament's "alarming Encroachments . . . by arbitrary power."[75] The idea that the Glorious Revolution had fundamentally upset the balance of the English constitution was echoed by the same writer who lamented Parliament as "the Aristocracy introduced at the Revolution." The *Virginia Gazette* reprinted a piece from the *Public Advertiser,* a London newspaper, in which the writer echoed patriot sentiments succinctly saying, "It is indifferent to me, whether the Crown, by its own immediate act, imposes new, and dispenses with old laws, or whether the same arbitrary power produces the same effects through the medium of the House of Commons."[76] The British past served as the lens through which Parliament's exercise of arbitrary power was understood. As "A Citizen" explained in the *New-York Gazette:* "Thus will the History of our mother Country, and Examination of its happy Constitution, sufficiently explain to us the dangerous Nature of our present Situation."[77]

At the same time, events in Britain and throughout Europe seemed to suggest that absolutism and arbitrary rule were on the march in Europe.[78] Colonial newspapers often printed news regarding European conflicts in this period, including the rise of an absolute monarchy in Sweden under King Gustav III, the Russian and Ottoman Empires' war over Eastern Europe, and the fall of the Polish-Lithuanian Commonwealth. In the winter of 1773 and 1774, a number of colonial newspapers printed a news item about the continuing suffering in Poland that proclaimed, "The age of liberty has passed away, and that of the most violent arbitrary power has succeeded."[79] In May 1774, the *Pennsylvania Journal* offered more news from Poland before concluding with this ominous warning: "*View this O Americans and tremble, for the arm of power is stretched over you! . . . No one knows where arbitrary power will stop!*"[80] Later in 1774, the connection was made even more explicit, as one writer pointed out, "The Situations of the Citizens of Dantzick, and that of the People of Boston, is in many Instances, says a Correspondent nearly similar; both plead for their ancient Rights, Customs, and Privileges; both unheard, both distressed by the rapacious Paw of that Monster, Arbitrary Power."[81] Rather than being a period of restored calm and amity due to a lack of new reform legislation, the years between 1770 and 1773 allowed colonists time to think through the historical implications of the last half decade or more of parliamentary attempts at imperial reform and their relation to geopolitical developments in the present.

The public debate over parliamentary supremacy in the colonies culminated in some sense in early 1773 in a public conflict between the arch-loyalist governor Thomas Hutchinson and the Massachusetts House of Representatives. Hutchinson was a scion of one of the oldest families in Massachusetts, a direct descendant of Anne Hutchinson who did not inherit her disdain for colonial authority. In the previous two decades, he had held many offices, often simultaneously, which made him a lightning rod for patriot discontent in Boston. In the fall of 1765, Stamp Act protesters destroyed his house along with that of his brother-in-law, Andrew Oliver. In addition to being a colonial bureaucrat, Hutchinson was also the foremost historian of Massachusetts, publishing the first two volumes of his *History of the Province of Massachusetts Bay* in 1764 and 1767. During the attack on his home, his unrivaled collection of historical documents—the product of his research and elite family status—was largely destroyed by protesters, a grievous loss for all subsequent generations of historians of Massachusetts and New England.

As a civil servant of the colony's royal government and a subject of the British Empire, Hutchinson sought to quell the discontent in his colony. He attacked it at the root by publicly dispelling patriot arguments about Parliament's lack of jurisdiction over the colonies. Prior to the legislative session, Committees of Correspondence had been established in towns throughout Massachusetts. In town meetings, they published resolves "denying in the most express Terms the Supremacy of Parliament, and inviting every other Town and District in the Province to adopt the same Principle." Hutchinson was so alarmed by these developments that he asked to address the opening session of the assembly.

As a product of colonial history culture, Hutchinson's original impulse in making the case against resistance was the same as many patriots in making the case for resistance. That is, he would draw on both the memory of settlement and the authority of the past in laying the foundation for his argument. In beginning his speech, Hutchinson said, "When our Predecessors first took Possession of this Plantation or Colony, under a Grant and Charter from the Crown of England, it was their Sense, and it was the Sense of the Kingdom, that they were to remain subject to the supreme Authority of Parliament. This appears from the Charter itself and from other irresistable Evidence."[82] Yet, as a historian of the Massachusetts Bay Colony, Hutchinson knew full well that Parliament did not yet enjoy "supreme Authority" in the 1630s when Massachusetts was first settled. He was attempting to use the authority of the past to bolster the legitimacy of parliamentary supremacy by stretching its existence farther back in time. But he was also laying the basis for another turn in his argument that tried to flip resistance arguments from the authority of the past on their head.

If Parliament's jurisdiction over the colonies did indeed date back to settlement, he argued, then the denial of parliamentary supremacy was itself an "innovation."[83] "I think I may very safely say," Hutchinson claimed, "that the oldest Person in the Province has never heard the Supremacy called in Question until within a few Years past." Hutchinson, ever the historian, then offered examples meant to show that Parliament had exercised its supremacy over the colonies numerous times in the past and that the colonies had assented, thereby trying establish precedents (another constituent form of the authority of the past). His speech is an excellent example of the cultural relevance of both the authority of the past on all colonists as both patriots and eventual loyalists developed new ways of thinking and talking about the colonial past.

He also took aim at the patriots' historical memory of settlement, which stressed the compact inherent in the colonial charters. Hutchinson argued that Parliament's jurisdiction over the colony was enshrined in the common charter provision prohibiting them (and other colonies) from "mak[ing] Laws *repugnant to the Laws of England*." For Hutchinson, as for many in Britain, to deny parliamentary supremacy was to question not only the British constitution but the entire foundation of the British Empire. "I know of no Line," he declared, "that can be drawn between the supreme Authority of Parliament and the total Independence of the Colonies." From these two implications, Hutchinson argued that denying parliamentary supremacy was to effectively invite the "Misery of Independence."[84] Indeed, Hutchinson saw more clearly even than many patriots in early 1773 that the development of a consensus for denying parliamentary supremacy (and thereby the Glorious Revolution) would ultimately make conceiving and declaring independence possible.

Three weeks later, the House responded. Unsurprisingly, its members found his arguments less than persuasive. In their replies, they too referred back to the memory of settlement, referencing Hutchinson's own *History of the Province of Massachusetts Bay* as well as other historical works and documents. Settlement, they argued, was fundamentally "an Acquisition of Foreign Territory, not annexed to the Realm of England, and therefore at the absolute Disposal of the Crown." This meant "the Colonies were not intended or considered to be within the Realm of England, though within the Allegiance of the English Crown." The House then turned the common British argument that there could be only one supreme legislative authority on its head by arguing that "to suppose a Parliamentary Authority over the Colonies under such Charters, would necessarily induce that Solecism in Politics *Imperium in Imperio*," which British writers had decried during the Stamp Act debates.

The representatives argued the original settlers and subsequent generations of colonists did not believe themselves to be under the "Supreme Authority of Parliament." Therefore, the supremacy of Parliament itself was an innovation, or a "new and unprecedented Measure." Ultimately, they, like Hutchinson, concluded that it could only be the case "either that the Colonies are the Vassals of the Parliament, or, that they are totally Independent." And "as it cannot be supposed to have been the Intention of the Parties in the Compact, that we should be reduced to a State of Vassallage." "It was [the settlers'] Sense," they argued, "that we were thus Independent." And to be clear about their understanding of parliamentary supremacy, they concluded, "There is more Reason to dread the Consequences of absolute uncontrouled Supreme Power, whether of a Nation or a Monarch, than those of a total Independence."[85] Over the course of the next year, the proceedings of the House and Hutchinson's speeches were published in pamphlet form and excerpted in various newspapers throughout the colonies.

Near the end of 1773, a group of patriots, some thinly disguised as Native Americans, dumped 342 chests of the East India Company's tea into Boston Harbor. In retaliation for their disobedience, Parliament passed a series of laws in the spring of 1774 known as the Coercive Acts (or, in patriot parlance, the "Intolerable Acts"). By establishing a military occupation of Boston and royal control over Massachusetts, British officials hoped that these measures would force the city and colony to turn on the radical patriots and send a clear warning to patriots in other colonies of the consequences of destroying the property of the empire and defying the will of Parliament.

In the wake of the Coercive Acts, colonists appealed directly to the king for his protection from what they deemed to be the arbitrary authority of Parliament. They hoped to persuade him to convince Parliament to rescind the acts. Should it be necessary, they hoped he would exercise the royal veto that had fallen into disuse after the Glorious Revolution. Their appeals were earnest but not driven, as one political scientist has recently argued, by an ideology of royalism or a desire to return to monarchical absolutism. Rather, they made such appeals because, practically speaking, they saw the king as their last hope for stemming the arbitrary authority of Parliament over the colonies. In May of 1775, Lieutenant John Barker, stationed with the British army in Boston during the aftermath of Lexington and Concord, recorded, "The Rebels have erected the Standard at Cambridge; they call themselves the King's Troops and us the Parliaments. Pretty Burlesque!"

Another British soldier writing from "the Camp at Cambridge" referred to pro-British arguments as being of "the parliamentary strain." Patriots marching in New York City carried a flag that read: "*George* III. *Rex, and the Liberties of America; No Popery.*"[86]

"No Popery" referred to the Quebec Act of 1774, which Parliament passed just a few months after the Coercive Acts. It sought to establish a new government and boundaries for the Canadian province, the latter of which included large portions of the Northwest frontier and even part of the Ohio Valley. Lands coveted by British colonial settlers since the end of the Seven Years' War but denied them by the Proclamation Line of 1763 were now handed over to French Catholics. Most distressing to the Protestant British colonists was the act's provision guaranteeing freedom to practice Catholicism. From the patriots' perspective, at least in New England, the British government seemed to be methodically hemming them in, on the coast by the British army in Boston and on the frontier by French Catholics and their indigenous allies.

The cries of "No Popery" reflected colonists' primary association of Catholicism with arbitrary rule. In addition, its place on the sign above with the king's name expressed both their desire for the king to save them from the arbitrary rule of Parliament and their equating of the current Parliament with the deeply despised Vatican. Responding to the Quebec Act, one writer scolded Parliament, "You have *not been ashamed* to vote for the ESTABLISHMENT OF POPERY AND ARBITRARY POWER!—Is there *no* enormity too gross for your digestion?"[87] This sense, however, was not limited to New Englanders. In a pamphlet published in New York in December 1774, Alexander Hamilton rhetorically asked, "Does not your blood run cold, to think an English parliament should pass an act for the establishment of arbitrary power and popery in such an extensive country?"[88] With the combination of the Quebec Act and the king's "Proclamation for Suppressing Rebellion and Sedition" of August 1775, in which he forthrightly refused to assert his historical prerogative over the colonies, patriots began to consider the king—their last hope for redress—as actively complicit in Parliament's actions.

On April 23, 1776, Chief Justice William Henry Drayton addressed a grand jury in Charlestown, South Carolina. His lengthy charge drew on both the colonial and British pasts to make the argument that by declaring the colonies to be in open rebellion, the actions of Parliament and the king were just as bad if not worse than those of James II, who had been guilty of "two points of criminality—breach of the original contract, and violation of fundamental laws." If the king refused the colonies his protection, what loyalty did they owe to him and his empire? He went on to compare the actions of the two kings: "Wherefore, if James the Second broke the original contract, it is undeniable that George the Third has also broken the original contract between King and People." The colonists' subjection to the king of Great Britain, he argued, was "due only as a return for protection."

The implication was clear. The Glorious Revolution had not restored the ancient constitution. Rather, it had merely created different conditions for producing similarly "evil machinations tending to nothing less than absolute tyranny." Drayton even went so far as to argue that the arbitrary rule of the king that had stoked "the famous Revolution in England, in the year 1688, [was] much inferior" to that of the King and Parliament over the colonies in the 1760s and 1770s.[89]

The context of colonists' reckoning with their British past is crucial to understanding the patriots' rhetorical turn toward the king in the late 1760s and early 1770s.[90] This turn was the result of colonists struggling to come to terms with their relationship to Britain and to the British past itself, which had been a crucial part of their identity as British subjects before being usurped by Parliament's program of imperial reform.[91] Without that context, historians have seen these appeals to the Crown much as Lord North did when he described colonists as espousing a form of absolutist Toryism. Their appeals to the king to rein in Parliament, however, were actually a rejection of the absolutism practiced by the Stuarts and now manifested in the power and actions of Parliament. Yet, this realization of the arbitrariness of Parliament was not consistent with their earlier interpretation of the Glorious Revolution, on which so much of their British patriotism rested. As Ezra Stiles noted in a letter to the famed British historian Catherine Macaulay in 1773, "My Ideas of the English Constitution have much diminished. It seems to have become or arisen into a kind of fortuitous Consolidation of Powers now in opposition to the true Interest of the people."[92] Similarly, in his 1776 valedictory address to the students of Yale College, Timothy Dwight claimed that "the boasted *British-constitution* is but an uncouth *Gothic* pile, covered and adorned by the elegance of modern architecture."[93] The Glorious Revolution had produced a new kind of limited monarchy, for sure, but many patriots came to understand that it had, in fact, also produced a new kind of unlimited Parliament, one so beyond reproach and unbounded by the authority of the past that it could act as arbitrarily as Charles I and James II ever had.

Patriots' rhetorical turn to the Crown in the late 1760s and 1770s did not reflect their seeking "absolutist" or "royalist" rule. Rather, it represented their resistance to absolutism and arbitrary authority in the form of parliamentary supremacy.[94] Most patriots did not want or expect their arguments to result in ambitious Crown rule over the colonies or England. They were not seeking to merely substitute the arbitrary rule of Parliament for that of the Crown. As Judge William Henry Drayton noted in 1775, colonists hoped to "vest the King of *Great Britain* with such a limited dominion over us as may tend, *bona fide,* to promote our true commercial interests, and to secure our freedom and safety—the only just ends of any dominion." They wanted the jurisdiction over the colonies returned to the Crown, after which many expected the king to restore the colonies' customary autonomy within the empire as enjoyed prior to 1764.

Over the course of the crisis, patriots started trying to reconcile the past with the present rather than vice versa. In their British past, when one branch of the government began acting in an absolutist manner, another branch of government had to step in. This had happened with Charles I and Parliament in the 1640s and with James II and Parliament in the 1680s. But in both of those cases, patriots understood that the Parliament that emerged itself became absolutist, first the Rump Parliament, which eventually required the restoration of the monarchy, and now the post-1688 Parliament, which, to patriot minds, appeared to also require the intercession of the Crown. In the 1650s, the English had turned to Charles II to restore balance to an English constitution disrupted by the Rump Parliament and the Protectorate. In the 1760s, colonists turned to George III to do the same. This is why the First Continental Congress's *Declaration and Resolves* of 1774 describe themselves as acting "as Englishmen, [and as] their ancestors in like cases have usually done."[95]

The strategy, therefore, of appealing to the king after 1768 was not drawn from their adoption of a royalist or pro-Stuart ideology but from the fact that, in light of Parliament's supremacy, the Crown was the only possible source of redress left to them. The imperial crisis had created a disconnect between the past and the present that colonists tried to reconcile in a number of ways, including their creation of a shared colonial past and the questioning of their previous understandings of the British past and their relationship to it, as reflected by their reconsideration of the legacy of the Glorious Revolution and their rhetorical turn toward the Crown to restrain Parliament's arbitrary rule at the end of the 1760s.

When Captain Levi Preston, a teenage minuteman in Massachusetts in 1775, was interviewed at the age of ninety-one years old, his interlocutor, seeking insight into why common colonists had revolted, asked Preston why he had participated in the Revolution. Was he oppressed by the Stamp Act? By the Tea Act? "Oppressions," Preston replied, "I didn't feel them." Was it from reading "Harrington or Sidney or Locke about the eternal principles of liberty?" "Never heard of 'em," he said. Exasperated, the interviewer asked, "Well, then, what was the matter? And what did you mean in going to the fight?" "Young man," Preston said, "what we meant in going for those red-coats was this: we always had governed ourselves, and we always meant to. They didn't mean we should." Another man interviewed at the same time whose father had participated in the Revolution said that the colonists had "fought seven years against a declaration." He was referring to the Declaratory Act, Parliament's most succinct statement of its supremacy and arbitrary authority over the colonies.[96] Ultimately, the American Revolution was not fundamentally a war against Parliament or against the monarchy per se as institutions. It was also not primarily a revolt against unrepresentative or centralized government. Rather, it should be understood, at least in part, as it was by colonists, as a revolt against arbitrary rule and against a single power beyond redress or reproach.[97]

According to the shared colonial past being created during the imperial crisis, the colonies had been settled, in part, by Englishmen fleeing the arbitrary rule of the Stuarts. By the 1760s, arbitrary rule—this time by Parliament—had seemingly made its way across the ocean and had to be resisted. As the "Old Colony Club" of Plymouth toasted its members in 1769, "May every person be possessed of the same noble sentiments against arbitrary power that our worthy ancestors were endowed with."[98] Colonists turned to the Crown and the royal prerogative because they believed it was the only possible counter left to parliamentary supremacy, their last hope to stem Parliament's arbitrary rule. Having begun over the question of colonists' equality with native Britons, by 1768, the crisis that led to independence and revolution was, for colonists, about arbitrary power, which they were determined to resist just as they believed their ancestors and fellow countrymen had, whether exercised by a king or Parliament or king-in-Parliament.

Broadly speaking, patriots repeatedly drew on the seventeenth-century past in these debates, while Britons and loyalists generally drew on the more recent past. The former drew predominantly on long-standing customs in making their arguments, while the latter tried to counter by drawing on contemporary circumstances and, when resorting to supporting their arguments historically, individual precedents. These modes of argument were shaped by each sides' different perceptions of the relationship between the past and present. For many Britons, particularly those in power in the 1760s and 1770s, the Glorious Revolution had produced a new beginning, and therefore more recent examples of the colonies submitting to Parliament's authority held more weight for them. Patriots, however, continued to draw on the seventeenth-century past, but, after 1768, it was to argue that the Glorious Revolution had indeed brought about a fundamental change in both the English constitution and the relationship between the colonies and Britain, the full implications of which were not fully revealed to them until the 1760s and 1770s. Over the course of the imperial crisis, they came to see the Glorious Revolution as the beginning of the end of their loyal autonomy. This perspective lived on in the early republic, as evidenced by David Ramsay's *A Map, Historical and Biographical Chart of the United States* (1810). The chart's color-coded historical timeline dates the start of "free government" in many colonies with settlement and the end of it at the Glorious Revolution, only to be restored following independence (figure 1). Indeed, Ramsay's chart provides a visual rendering of how the Glorious Revolution came to be perceived by Americans, beginning during the imperial crisis.

Colonists had struggled throughout the crisis to keep trying to make sense of the present through the past, but Parliament's repeated subversion of the authority of the past made it increasingly difficult. Their ideas about the

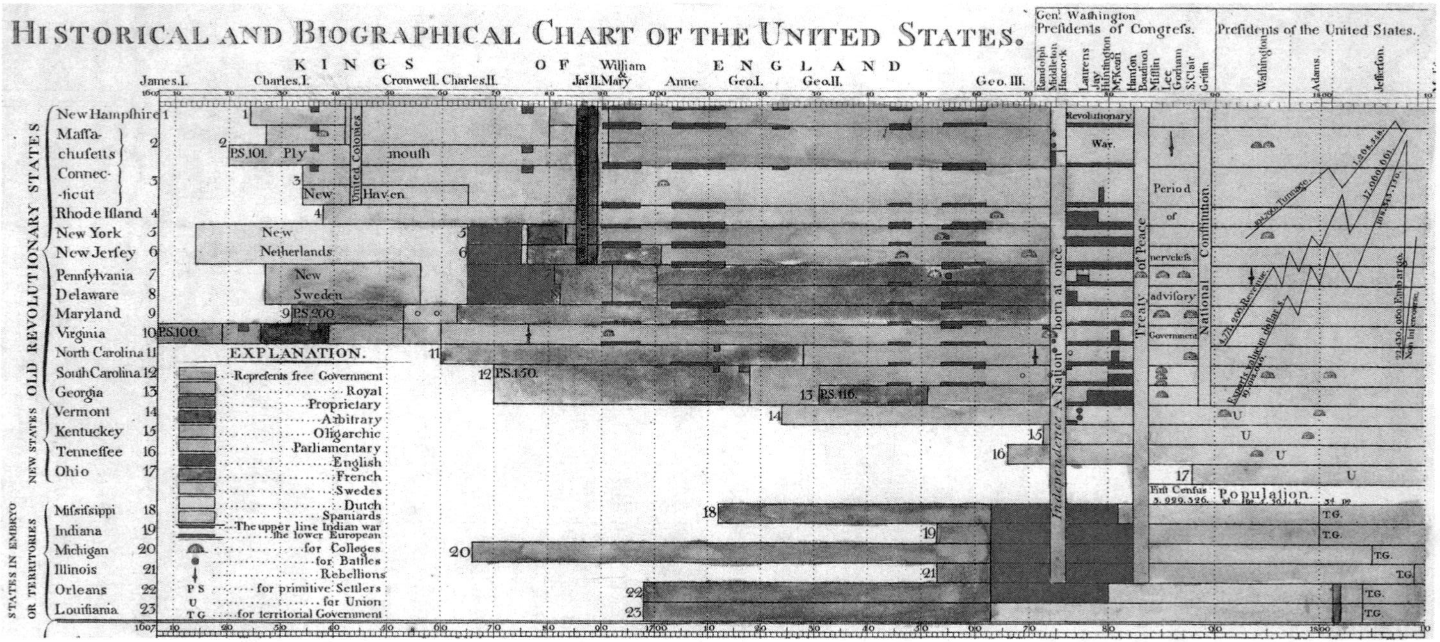

FIG. 1. David Ramsay, *A Map, Historical and Biographical Chart of the United States* (Charleston, 1810). Courtesy of the American Philosophical Society, Philadelphia.

British past and their relationship to it were changing in fundamental ways that were direct responses to the events and rhetoric of the imperial crisis and their political, cultural, and historical implications. After the Coercive Acts, however, attempts at reconciliation decreased rapidly as many patriots came to realize the impossibility of reconciling the present with the past in their current situation. The turn to the Crown ended in late 1775 when George III issued a proclamation that declared the patriots to be in "open Arms and Rebellion against our Government" after their protests against the Coercive Acts.[99] By 1776, many colonists had become convinced that Parliament was irredeemable and that the king had been misguided by his corrupted ministers, thereby dispelling their last hopes for a bulwark against Parliament's arbitrary rule. This left them in circumstances without historical precedent because in the 1640s and 1680s the arbitrary rule of either the king or Parliament had been willingly challenged and checked by the other. By 1776, many patriots came to the stark realization that this repeated historical precedent was no longer a possibility. With all historical avenues exhausted for making sense of the present, they were forced to abandon the British past, both rhetorically and culturally, and adopt an ostensibly ahistorical argument that could justify their resistance and, ultimately, the "innovation" of independence.

Interlude

Natural Law, Independence, and Revolutionary History Culture, 1772–1776

The immediate impact of colonists' reconsideration of the British past is most clearly evident in their adoption of natural law and natural rights as the foundation of their arguments after 1772, which served as a necessary cultural bridge from resistance to independence. Britons' repeated rejection of arguments made from the authority of the past had both pointed out a significant cultural difference between the two sides and frustrated patriots rhetorically. They came to understand that if Parliament was no longer bound by the authority of the past, they would need a counterargument that was similarly unbound from the memorial past. Hence, their language over the last few years of the imperial crisis increasingly appealed to natural law and natural rights, rather than the common law or the rights of the British constitution specifically.[1]

Noting the shift by 1775, Josiah Tucker pointed out that the patriots now primarily had "recourse to what they call immutable truths,—the abstract reasonings, and eternal fitnesses of things,—and, in short, to such rights of human nature, which they suppose to be unalienable and indefeasible. Former laws and precedents carry little or no conviction to people who argue after this manner."[2] That is, the importance of the British past in resistance rhetoric had been minimized by the eve of independence. Patriots understood natural law as encompassing all the rights and privileges guaranteed by the historically constructed British constitution *and more.* Most importantly, the natural law arguments relieved the rhetorical and cultural burden the crisis had placed on colonists' memories of the British past throughout the conflict. These arguments still relied on the authority of the past, but they could now bypass the British past completely, drawing instead on the much more nebulous but deeper past of "time immemorial."

"Natural rights" and "natural law" were by no means absent in patriot rhetoric prior to the 1770s, but their place and emphasis in that rhetoric was minor relative to the last few years of the crisis.[3] They simply were not a predominant part of patriot arguments against the Stamp Act and Townshend Acts. This began to change in the early 1770s, as colonists' relationship to the British past became increasingly complicated. In November 1772, the Boston Committee of Correspondence issued a report that in some ways represents the patriots' pivot toward prioritizing natural law in their arguments. Also known as "The Rights of the Colonists," the pamphlet begins not with a disquisition on the settlement of the colonies as had been so common throughout the crisis to this point but with a section entitled "Natural Rights of the Colonists as Men." The pamphlet enumerated those rights: "First, a Right to Life; secondly, to Liberty; thirdly, to Property." It goes on to assert, "All positive and civil Laws should conform, as far as possible, to the Law of natural Reason and equity." It concludes the section by arguing, "In short, it is the greatest Absurdity to suppose it in the Power of one or any Number of Men, at the entering into Society, to renounce their essential natural Rights or the Means of preserving those Rights, when the grand End of civil Government, from the very Nature of its Institution, is for the Support, Protection and Defense of those very Rights."[4]

In the report's final section, entitled "The Rights of the Colonists as Subjects [of England]," it argued, "All Persons born in the British American Colonies are, by the Laws of GOD and Nature and by the common Law of England, *exclusive of all Charters* from *the Crown,* well entitled, and by Acts of the British Parliament are declared to be entitled to all the natural, essential, inherent and inseparable Rights, Liberties and Privileges of Subjects born in Great Britain or within the Realm."[5] This quote is especially interesting and emblematic for a number of reasons. First, in the order ascribed to the sources of colonists' rights, "the Laws of GOD and Nature" are given precedence over "the common Law of England," thereby reflecting the order of the chapters and reflecting the diminishing importance of the British past. In the eighteenth century, the order of items in lists such as these were rarely incidental, especially when included in texts produced by debate and approved by groups such as town or county meetings. Like many others, Alexander Hamilton used this new ordering regularly. For example, in a pamphlet from 1774, he argued that "the voice of nature, the *spirit* of the British constitution, and the charters of the colonies in general [show] the absolute non-existence of that parliamentary supremacy."[6] This wording directly reversed the order used more commonly early in the crisis. The ordering was neither incidental nor unique to the report. It could be found repeatedly in pamphlet essays as well as local resolves after 1772. Indeed, the commonality of this reordering of the foundation of their resistance arguments in patriot writings from 1773 to 1776 reveals the shifting priorities of patriot arguments, particularly that given to natural law over common law (which represented the British past) and the charters (which represented the colonial past).

Second, the report argued that the colonists' "inherent and inseparable Rights" were "*exclusive of all Charters*" (italicized by the original writers for emphasis) thereby minimizing the political and rhetorical need even for the settlement and charter arguments that, at this point, comprised a good part of the newly shared colonial past.[7] This report is one of the most coherent and plainly written expositions of natural law in all of the patriots' writings throughout the crisis, and it is one of the first to rely almost entirely on natural law in resisting imperial reform. Furthermore, it represents the beginnings of the broader rhetorical shift toward natural law and away from arguments built on historical memories, which had defined patriot rhetoric up to this point, while retaining their critical sense of the authority of the past.

This rhetorical shift is even more apparent in the local town and county resolves passed in Massachusetts in 1773 and those published throughout the colonies in the summer and fall of 1774 to protest the Coercive Acts and British treatment of Boston.[8] Whereas local resolves against the Stamp Act and Townshend Acts in the 1760s and early 1770s were often framed by the historical memory of settlement and rooted in the authority of the past, those passed and published in 1774 against the Coercive Acts read very differently. Many often make no mention of the past whatsoever. For example, the town of Providence's first resolve contained a promise to stand with Massachusetts and the rest of the colonies, not for protecting their rights as British subjects derived from their colonial and British pasts, as they had argued for much of the previous decade, but "for the protecting and securing their invaluable natural rights and privileges."[9] Farther south, the inhabitants of the county of Salem, New Jersey, called the Coercive Acts "a most arbitrary exertion of Tyranny over a free and loyal people." They continued, "That this meeting think it their duty to declare, that they consider the acts of the British Parliament . . . an absolute infringement of the natural Rights of the subject."[10] In Goshen, Connecticut, the inhabitants resolved "that the act for shutting up the port of Boston, is contrary to the natural rights of mankind, and threatens the liberties of the colonies in general."[11] These constructions run similarly throughout the resolves, from New England towns to southern counties.

For much of the imperial crisis, natural law and the British constitution were often spoken of as if they were one and the same. Yet, in the years just before independence, this conflation was no longer intended to augment the authority (or validity) of the British constitution. Rather, it was intended to deny the British constitution (and the British past from which it was constructed) its singular importance, effectively stripping it of its Britishness. This point was not lost on some of the British writers who dismissed patriots' natural law arguments. Patriots' natural law arguments avoided relying on the British constitution for their justification by retroactively suggesting that its principles, which they had held so dear for so long, were not, in fact, the product of the British past. Once this understanding became widely circulated and accepted among patriots, they increasingly dropped their specific references to the British constitution and relied on "natural law" as the foundation for their arguments. Ultimately, natural law arguments allowed colonists to retain the principles on which their previous arguments had been based because the rhetoric of natural law universalized those principles and disassociated them from the British constitution and, hence, the British past.

Even when some colonists did still declare for specific British rights in addition to their "natural rights," the latter often took precedence. In Hartford, the Coercive Acts were declared "an Innovation of their natural Rights as Men, and constitutional Rights as English Subjects." The residents of Dumfries, Virginia, resolved that Parliament's actions were "subversive of our natural rights, and contrary to the first principles of the constitution." The inhabitants of Queen Anne's County also noted that the Coercive Acts were "a cruel and oppressive invasion of their natural rights as men, and constitutional rights as English subjects."[12] Colonists had made reference to natural law and natural rights earlier in the crisis, but they had done so far less and with less prominence and emphasis. For example, see this common 1765 construction referring to the Stamp Act as "a violation of their charter, of their constitutional rights as Englishmen, and their natural rights as men."[13] The order of construction in patriot writing was rarely incidental, here prioritizing the colonial past over the British past and both over "natural rights." By 1774, however, patriots were arguing that "he must be blind indeed who does not see" that "our natural rights, which we value as our lives" were being "threatned to be vacated, or quite taken away."[14] All throughout the colonies in the spring and summer of 1774, colonists gathered at their town greens and county courthouses and, in some cases, taverns to argue against Parliament's actions in new ways that minimized the need for historical framing by prioritizing their "natural rights" over their "British" rights.

Interestingly, though Thomas Jefferson would ground the Declaration of Independence in ideas of natural law just two years later, his *Summary View of the Rights of British America* from 1774 was very much rooted in both the British and colonial pasts. Indeed, *Summary View* encapsulates nearly all the historical aspects of patriot rhetoric that we have discussed in this and the previous chapter. First, Jefferson began his pamphlet by drawing on the historical memory of settlement noting that understanding colonists' rights required "a view of them from the origin and first settlement of these countries." Jefferson went even further saying their "Saxon ancestors" had "in like manner left their native wilds and woods in the North of Europe."

According to Jefferson, they, like the first English settlers, had carried their rights with them. He then characterized the past decade of the imperial crisis from the colonial perspective: "Scarcely have our minds been able to emerge from the astonishment into which one stroke of parliamentary thunder has involved us, before another more heavy, and more alarming, is fallen on us." As a result, he concluded that Parliament was "a body of men, foreign to our constitutions." For the remainder of the pamphlet, he "earnestly entreat[ed] his majesty," who was "the central link connecting the several parts of the empire" to "recommend to his parliament of Great Britain the total revocation" of the Coercive Acts.[15] Jefferson's *Summary View* was the product of the previous ten years of patriot rhetoric as shaped by the historical grammar of resistance, incorporating the historical memory of settlement, the authority of the past, and appeals to the king as a rejection of parliamentary supremacy.

All of these developments between 1773 and 1776 regarding natural law and the minimizing of the importance of the distant past helped give rhetorical power to Thomas Paine's arguments in *Common Sense* (1776) that effectively denied the cultural authority of the past. He exhorted colonists to drop their "ancient prejudices" and declared, "We have it in our power to begin the world over again."[16] Later, in his *Rights of Man,* Paine expanded on this idea: "The case and circumstances of America present themselves as in the beginning of the world." "We are brought at once," he wrote, "to the point of seeing government begin, as if we had lived in the beginning of time. The real volume, not of history, but of facts, is directly before us, unmutilated by contrivance, or the errors of tradition."[17]

Common Sense used the historical past to frame a resistance argument but with a different intent. Rather than trying to reconcile the past with the present, Paine used the historical past to make a case for the irreconcilability of the past and the present. He was effectively telling colonists that they could end the uncertainty and instability of being unable to reconcile the present with the past by embarking on the innovation of independence. Stop trying to reconcile the present with history, Paine was saying; the present moment *is* history. Part of Paine's unprecedented reception was because his arguments—including his historical critique of monarchy and an "old world" that was "overrun with oppression"—offered colonists a way out of the cultural disconnect with the past brought about by the imperial crisis.[18]

The past, for Paine, was inherently corrupt and the colonists' destiny was to effectively put an end to the history of the Old World by truly beginning the history of the New World with American independence. Let go of the authority of the past and begin a new history, he said, a "new epoch," where authority would come from living citizens themselves, not from long-dead monarchs and their hereditary successors or failed traditions. While he persuaded his American readers that, through independence, they could redefine themselves and their governments, they were never willing, as we will see, to make as radical a break with the past as Paine envisioned. History culture in the colonies ran too deep.

If the arbitrariness of Parliament and ideas of natural law had helped loosen colonists' connection to the British past, Paine's *Common Sense* sought to put the final nail in the coffin of that connection. The "so much boasted constitution of England," he declared, had been "noble for the dark and slavish times in which it was erected." But by the 1770s, it had become "imperfect, subject to convulsion, and incapable of producing what it seems to promise." The constitution was "so exceedingly complex, that the nation may suffer for years together without being able to discover in which part the fault lies." He summarized the British constitution as the product of the "base remains of two ancient tyrannies, compounded with some new Republican materials." The king and Lords represented the two ancient tyrannies and the Commons represented Paine's republican materials. Yet, it was clear that the colonists had lost faith in the Commons and in the balance between them. Paine reinforced that loss of faith when he argued, "To say that the constitution of England is an UNION of three powers, reciprocally CHECKING each other, is farcical." In the wake of the king's forthright siding with Parliament against the colonists at the end of 1775, Paine played to colonists' disappointment with George III claiming that "the will of the king is as much the law of the land in Britain as in France, with this difference, that instead of proceeding directly from his mouth, it is handed to the people under the formidable shape of an act of parliament."

These statements, had they been written even a decade earlier, would have been viewed by many colonists as near heretical. Yet, their perspective on the historical development of the British constitution in the wake of the Glorious Revolution had changed rapidly since 1765, dramatically changing how they understood what it meant to British. As Paine wrote, "The prejudice of Englishmen, in favour of their own government, by King, Lords and Commons, arises as much or more from national pride than reason." Because the Glorious Revolution had been such a critical part of colonists' perception of Britishness and patriotism, a shift in their understanding of its legacy also meant a shift in their understanding of their relationship to Britain itself and in their civic identity, as they increasingly came to see themselves primarily as part of a continental rather than imperial polity.

For much of the spring of 1776, the Continental Congress dragged its feet toward independence, being otherwise occupied by trying to supply and maintain an army in Massachusetts. Popular will, however, pushed it forward. Through a series of resolutions beginning in May 1776, the Congress called first for colonies to begin establishing their own state governments, followed a month later by Richard Henry Lee's resolution for independence. On July 2, the Congress passed the resolution and two days later approved their final draft of the Declaration of Independence. The historian Benedict Anderson noted the document's lack of historical references, writing, "The Declaration of Independence of 1776 makes absolutely no reference to Christopher Columbus, Roanoke, or the Pilgrim Fathers, nor are the grounds put forward to justify independence in any way 'historical,' in the sense of highlighting the antiquity of the American people." As we will see in the chapter 5, the specific narrative of the colonial past that Anderson implies would be created shortly after the war ended. But, in the specific moment of July 1776, the universalism of the preamble reflected the turn toward natural law in the years prior to independence. Unlike when writing *Summary View* two years earlier, in drafting the Declaration Jefferson no longer felt the same rhetorical need to draw on the distant historical past. Instead he, and the Continental Congress, produced a document framed by "the Laws of Nature" and colonists' "unalienable Rights."

The Declaration, however, did have a clear historical dimension. Its focus was on the more recent revolutionary past found in the long list of grievances against the Crown and Parliament. As discussed in chapter 1, the important events mentioned in that portion of the Declaration were no less understood as "historical" just because they were recent. Just as *Summary View* reflected history culture's influence on patriot rhetoric during the first decade of the crisis, the Declaration of Independence, too, reflected the changes in patriot rhetoric that had occurred since *Summary View* had been published in 1774, namely the turn toward natural law, the minimizing of the distant past in favor of the more recent revolutionary past, and, ultimately, the diminishing of the authority of the past.

While these rhetorical changes between 1773 and 1776 that the Declaration reflected had become predominant in the years leading to independence, after the war there would be much less rhetorical and ideological consensus around the place of the past in both politics and the nation. The authority of the past, as such, would be transformed in the postwar era into what we might call the "usability of the past." That is, the value of the past came to be found in how well it could be made to justify the present rather than an inherent authority embedded in the past that necessarily had to explain to the present. After the war, many supporters of a strong federal government in the 1780s and then the Constitution in the 1790s went back to the longer historical perspective developed throughout the crisis because they saw it as an important tool for developing a shared national sentiment among its new citizens. Anti-federalists in the 1780s, and later, for a time, Jeffersonian Republicans, were uninterested in combining the distant colonial pasts into a new national narrative, focusing instead, in a national context, on the more recent revolutionary past covered in the Declaration's grievances and the pasts of individual states. They also used the distant classical past to argue against the likely success of a large republic and the British past to historicize their experiences of the imperial crisis. Their influence during the ratification process of the Constitution brought about the Bill of Rights and their frame of historical reference was most immediately drawn from their experiences in the more recent past of the imperial crisis: when the royal governments made attempts to squash patriot resistance with restrictions on protest and print; when local militias had had their ammunition confiscated; when the Royal Army quartered soldiers in homes; and when unlawful searches were used to catch smugglers who were then sent to trial decided in non-local arbitrary courts. The new historical perspective that defined patriot rhetoric between 1773 and 1776 most memorably in the Declaration of Independence retained salience into the postwar era—primarily for anti-federalists—though its time of predominant consensus was short-lived.

In addition to their severance from the British past, colonists' emotional and cultural ties of all kinds were being torn asunder after 1773, including their emotional ties with the Crown, economic and cultural ties with Britain, and, in many cases, their social ties with neighbors.[19] At the same time, political and social structures and authority began to break down.[20] A weighty haze of instability and uncertainty hung over the colonies in the two years before independence. Within this context, patriots wrestled with the growing realization that the British past they had held so firmly and so dearly had been nothing more than a chimera. This can be easy to downplay or even overlook until one stops to consider what that experience might have felt like. What might it feel like to realize that the past that had played such a crucial role in defining your civic and self-identity was not what you thought it was? One can imagine such a sense of disconnection, disillusionment, and discontinuity as a deeply discomfiting psychological event, particularly at a time of broader uncertainty and instability and all the more so in a society that had invested significant cultural authority in the past. Colonists, however, were not completely unmoored. At the same time as the wall of their British past was being torn down, they were beginning to construct a shared colonial past, which somewhat helped redirect their sense of civic connection and purpose.

Patriots lost a good deal of their imperial identity as Britons and began creating their own collective identity during the imperial crisis. Historians often implicitly conflate the two, failing to recognize that these were two different processes, complementary to be sure but unique nonetheless. Looking at how colonists came to create, transmit, and adopt their new shared colonial past, as we did in chapter 2, allows us to glimpse a more complex understanding of the role of identity in the imperial crisis. During the Stamp Act resistance, colonists used a historical memory of the colonial past to stress their equality with native Britons, while simultaneously fostering unity between the inhabitants of the various colonies through the creation of a shared past. After 1768, colonists' continued use of that historical memory increasingly served to foster a sense of difference between them and native Britons, compounded by Parliament's unprecedented actions and their own reconsideration of their relationship to the British past.

This burgeoning sense of difference between colonists and native Britons was deepened by the opinions of a number of pro-ministerial British writers. In the 1770s, they increasingly referred to American colonists as "our subjects" and the colonies as "our possessions."[21] One writer in the *Public Advertiser* named "Brittanicus" argued that the American colonists were "not their fellow-citizens, but their subjects." In another piece, the same writer described colonists as "our tenants."[22] This rhetoric sought to define American colonists as second-class citizens within the empire, which was exactly the notion that colonists refuted in their resistance of the Stamp Act. In addition, the pointed and repeated use of the possessive in this rhetoric sought successfully to give some native British commoners a false sense of authority and ownership over the colonies and its inhabitants. Such rhetoric sought to turn public opinion against the colonists by getting common Britons to see colonial resistance as a personal affront to their own identity as the real Britons standing at the head of a diverse empire. As a result, by spring 1776 the prospect of colonial independence was an insult to the British nation felt by many on a personal level.

The desire for independence may seem sudden in retrospect, but it was the result of a combination of long-term processes and short-term events. The political fights that drove colonists' developing sense of difference from native Britons over the previous decade led communities throughout the colonies to begin calling for independence from Britain as early as 1775.[23] The king's proclamation, arriving eight months after the first shots fired at Lexington and Concord, declared patriots outside of the king's protection, after a previous decade that had brought their sense of Britishness and their relationship to Britain into question. Having argued that their primary connection to the empire was defined by colonists' shared subjecthood of the king, the proclamation tore that connection asunder in the eyes of patriots. *Common Sense* put a particular voice to this multivalent alienation, but even before its wide circulation, the proclamation had made clear that their last hope for redress by the king was gone and with it the last hopes for reconciliation.

Ultimately, declaring independence was an unprecedented action, an "innovation" that, like parliamentary legislation of the previous decade, would disconnect colonists from the past. Ironically, Americans had been forced into embarking on such an innovation precisely because of their long-standing commitment to the authority of the past throughout a decade of unprecedented parliamentary actions. In 1778, a Briton, William

Meredith, expressed a retrospective realization of the degree to which Parliament's actions had alienated colonists from the mother country writing, "For, if the constitution is once changed upon the colonist, the country is no longer his country; he becomes an alien."[24] Both Parliament's actions and colonists' questioning of the British past contributed to that alienation and the sense of cultural distinction that preceded the political break. In 1765, the British polemicist, "William Pym," said of the colonists, "One would scarcely imagine, if they forgot us, that they would entirely lose all remembrance of themselves."[25] While that may have been the case in 1765, by the end of the crisis, questioning the meaning of the British past and their relationship to it—alongside creating a shared colonial history—helped colonists begin the process of effectively abandoning the British past as their own. In doing so, they severed one of their most important cultural connections to the mother country and thereby helped make it possible to conceive of severing their political connection. The role of the past in the imperial crisis—defined by the importance of different perceptions of the relationship between the past and present, the construction of a shared colonial past, and the discarding of a formerly shared British past—helped shape the rhetoric and dynamics of the resistance that led to the ultimate "innovation" of declaring independence, partly because these factors all contributed to a sense on the part of colonists that perhaps they were not as "British" as they had once believed. Ultimately, in creating these historical memories, colonists began developing a far more instrumental relationship with the past, beginning to look at the past through the lens of the present instead of the other way around. This new relationship with the past would play a crucial part in the efforts of cultural nationalists after the war to begin developing a shared identity for the new nation.

PART II

National History Culture in the Early Republic, 1776–1812

CHAPTER FOUR

THE EXPANSION OF EARLY NATIONAL HISTORY CULTURE

In February 1787, the *New-Haven Gazette* published "An Essay on American Genius" by Timothy Dwight, the soon-to-be president of Yale College and a respected clergyman and poet.[1] Dwight's essay took up the issue's entire front page and half of its second page. He began by ruing the low opinion in which the new United States was held both culturally and scientifically by the learned class of Europe. As Dwight explained, "The idea had become prevalent among the naturalists and literati in Europe who have written on American subjects, that almost every species of animal and vegetable-life, has degenerated by being transported across the Atlantic to this country." For decades, a number of prominent European natural philosophers had extrapolated that argument to apply to Americans themselves, who they claimed were both physically and culturally degenerated compared to Europeans. In the wake of the Revolution, Dwight declared, "The time is come to explode this European creed."

To do so, he recounted the most impressive American cultural achievements in its first decade of independence, much of it spent in the midst of war. First, he mentioned David Ramsay's *History of the Revolution of South-Carolina* (1785), the first American historical work on the Revolution. He then remarked, "A history of the war in the Eastern and Middle States, is a *desideratum* earnestly longed for, by every genuine patriot." From there, Dwight moved on to praise Americans' "peculiarly strong talents for painting," mentioning Benjamin West and John Singleton Copley as being among "the first historical painters of the age" and John Trumbull's recent "series of historical designs," including "the *battle of Bunker-Hill* and the *death of Montgomery*." Dwight then turned his attention toward poetry. Despite a number of previously published poems from which to choose, he singled out Joel Barlow's epic historical poem about the history of the New World from settlement to revolution, *The Vision of Columbus,* which was still in press and not yet published. Dwight acknowledged, "The age of ultimate refinement in America is yet to arrive," but, to his mind, a good start had been made toward that goal. Similarly, in his *Defence of the Constitutions of the United States* (1787), John Adams listed American cultural achievements, "As Copley painted Chatham; West, Wolf; and Trumbull, Warren and Montgomery; as Dwight, Barlow, Trumbull and Humphries composed their verse, and Belknap and Ramsay history."[2] All of Dwight's and Adams's examples of "American genius" in the 1780s—from writing to poetry to painting—were works that drew on historical content or themes and served as the vanguard of an explosion of historical cultural production in the new nation.

At the same time that Americans were creating new state and federal governments and institutions, they were also engaged in creating new American cultural forms. Indeed, the revolutionary era begat a long-anticipated cultural explosion. Just a few years after the war's end, a writer in the *Massachusetts Centinel* noted, "At no time did Literature make so rapid a progress in America, as since the peace."[3] As the historian Kenneth Silverman has summarized, "In a quarter-century of startling innovation, the country had produced its first novel, first epic poem, first composer, first professionally acted play, first actor and dancer, first museum, its first important painters, musical-instrument makers, magazines, engravers—indeed most of the defining features of traditional high culture."[4] Yet, as Richard Bushman has shown, forms that were considered "high culture" when produced by Europeans assumed a more "vernacular gentility" in the United States and were beginning to be consumed by a more middle-class audience in this period. American commentators dating back to the 1750s had believed such cultural development was only a matter of time. Yet, it was the Revolution that ultimately brought it about, not least by providing compelling subject matter derived from Americans' individual and collective memories for a variety of literary and artistic historical cultural productions.

History culture expanded both quantitatively and qualitatively in the early republic, becoming an increasingly important part of the cultural world of the new nation. This expansion of history culture relative to that of the pre-revolutionary period is most evident through the growth of historical cultural production and the new prominence of historical content and themes in a variety of print forms, literary and artistic genres, and educational texts, particularly regarding the American past. Quantitatively, more works of history were written and published. Historical content and themes were found more regularly in far more newspapers, magazines, and almanacs than ever before. Qualitatively, historical themes informed many of the most prominent works of American literature and art. Historical content also served as the glue that bound together various subjects in their educational texts, providing a foundation for an idealized national form of education. Accounting for the quantitative growth of historical cultural production in the first half of this chapter reveals the qualitative expansion of history culture as the American past became a far more important form of cultural currency than it had been before the Revolution, building on the development begun during the imperial crisis.

The second half of this chapter examines some of the underlying processes that fostered the expansion of historical cultural production. It uncovers an informal historical network consisting of historians, antiquarians, essayists, poets, painters, politicians, publishers, and booksellers. In a time when there was no institutional support, the mutual relationships cultivated by participants in the network served a number of key functions related to historical cultural production in this period, particularly aiding collection, preservation, and sharing of broadly scattered primary sources; providing feedback on each other's written work in manuscript; and creating relationships between authors and publishers. Ultimately, a number of participants in this informal network went on to help establish the nation's first historical societies and museums, thereby fostering the institutionalization of history culture in the early republic.

During the war, the significant growth of print experienced during the imperial crisis stagnated as the availability of supplies diminished. Many cities and towns ended the war with the same or fewer printers than when it had begun, and the number of newspapers being published at the start of the war in 1775 was cut nearly in half by its conclusion in 1783. In turn, historical cultural production diminished significantly once the war began in earnest. Indeed, no significant historical works were published during the years of the Revolutionary War. Once the war was over and Americans found themselves in a new and unfamiliar place, historical cultural production resumed with an unprecedented earnestness.

Both older and recent scholarship has explored the important role of the military, of mobilization, and of wartime experiences in shaping the origins of American national identity. For example, Charles Royster has explored the importance of the military in this period, including the contentious relationship between the Continental Army and the American people and its role in the developing sense of "American character." Edwin G. Burrows and T. Cole Jones have examined the treatment of prisoners of war on both sides and its broader implications for how the war was perceived, and Robert Parkinson has shown the importance of race in patriot rhetoric aimed at mobilization. Recent scholarship on loyalists and patriots has also highlighted the role of the war in creating, maintaining, and shaping senses of allegiance. If the imperial crisis and independence had not forced all to choose a side, the war would. Allegiances declared and confirmed in the heat and fog of war had to be maintained and strengthened in the peacetime context of the new republic. In this way, the war and the dynamics of allegiance it created helped set the stage on which early national history culture would play out.

The expansion of history culture in the decades after the Revolution happened alongside the expansion of both print and the cultural marketplace of the early republic. History culture relied on cultural productions, many of which were print-based. But it was not a one-way relationship. The expansion of history culture, in part, also helped fuel the rapid growth of print in this period. It was a symbiotic relationship that went beyond just an increase in the number of historical works being written, published, and read. In these unprecedented times, the past enjoyed increasing cultural importance after the Revolution. During the colonial period, historical cultural production (and cultural production generally) had been limited. A few colonial elites wrote historical works about their own individual colonies, but the vast majority of the most popular historical works of the period focused on British history, written by British historians and imported from British booksellers. Indeed, colonial history culture was defined largely by both material and intellectual dependence on the mother country. After the war, however, the burgeoning print culture, the rise of literary and artistic production, the growing importance of education, and the establishment of historical institutions all contributed to the growth of historical cultural production and the origins of a national history culture.

Imports from Britain had long dominated the colonial book trade. But in the decades after the Revolution a domestic book trade began to take shape thanks to growing literacy and an increase in the number of printers.[5] In addition to the growth in demand and production, there was also a growth in supply in the work of American authors, who, like domestically published books, were relatively scarce before the Revolution. Writing and printing books remained a significant financial risk for all parties, but the passage of the first state copyright laws in 1783 and the first federal copyright law in 1790 began to offer American authors and publishers limited, but previously unenjoyed, protections in a trade that had long been dominated by "unauthorized" reprint editions.[6] These protections provided added impetus for authors, many of whom, unlike their colonial forbearers, were not men of leisure but working professionals, and for printers, who were beginning the transition into the more entrepreneurial role of "publisher." As such, the number of historical works on American history being published grew rapidly.

In the three decades after the end of the war, significant and often multivolume works of American history by native authors were being published in the United States in far greater numbers and more regularly than during the colonial period. These included a number of histories of the recent revolution.[7] In 1785, David Ramsay published the first—*History of the Revolution of South-Carolina*—less than two years after the war had ended. He was followed by William Gordon, who wrote the first general history of the Revolution in his four-volume *History of the Rise, Progress, and Establishment of the Independence of the United States,* published in London in 1788. The following year, Ramsay published his own general history, the two-volume *History of the American Revolution*. And, in 1805, Mercy Otis Warren published her three-volume *History of the Rise, Progress, and Termination of the American Revolution*. Other accounts of the war published in both the United States and England circulated in the United States as well.[8] A number of these works went through multiple editions between their publication and 1815.

The majority of scholarship on early republic historiography has focused on those three major histories of the Revolution, but many state histories were published between 1783 and 1812. These included histories of New Hampshire, Maine, Pennsylvania, Connecticut, South Carolina, and Georgia, and two each on Massachusetts, Virginia, and Vermont.[9] Historians, including Hannah Adams, Isaac Backus, and Jedidiah Morse, also wrote a number of histories of New England.[10] Pedagogical works such as Jedidiah Morse's *American Geography* and Noah Webster's readers likewise incorporated historical accounts and themes related to individual states' revolutionary and colonial pasts.

While some historians have argued that these histories represent a continuation of the colonial period's localist tradition of historical writing, they actually formed an important part of postwar nationalist literary production.[11] As one newspaper piece reprinted multiple times in 1795 argued, "A separate history of each State in the union has for some time been a desideratum with every man of letters in America."[12] Similarly, a few years earlier, David Ramsay had clearly stated the necessity and nationalist utility of these state histories, arguing that they helped Americans "become acquainted with each other in that intimate familiar manner which would wear away prejudices—rub off asperities & mould us into an homogeneous people loving esteeming & rightly appreciating each other."[13] After all, Ramsay argued, "We are one people in name but do not know half enough of each other to make our commerce reciprocally serviceable & to cement our friendship & intercourse."[14] Ramsay, like many other like-minded cultural nationalists in the postwar era, understood the work of writing and reading state histories as a crucial part of fostering a sense of familiarity among Americans that could in turn foster a sense of being part of a shared community, or "one people."

The availability of these many state histories contributed to the appearance of the first general histories of the United States beginning in the mid to late 1790s.[15] Compilers of general histories often drew heavily on the published state histories. After all, it took Jeremy Belknap nearly ten years to research and write the first volume of his three-volume *History of New-Hampshire.* One of the first to do this was John Lendrum's two-volume *A Concise and Impartial History of the American Revolution,* the first volume of which consisted of "A General History of America" from settlement to the 1760s. In his preface Lendrum noted, "The writings of Dr. Belknap, Dr. Ramsay, Dr. Gordon, and Dr. Morse, have been freely made use of in what regarded American Affairs."[16] The practice of copying passages (or, in some cases, entire chapters) was widely accepted and practiced. The availability of information about individual states provided by the publication of so many state histories made the appearance of general histories of the United States possible.

Of course, the general histories were intended to do the same nationalist work as the state histories. Benjamin Trumbull, in the "Preface" to his *General History of the United States* (1810), evinced a similar sentiment to Ramsay, arguing that general histories would "bring the inhabitants of our country into a more general acquaintance with each other, awaken their mutual sympathies, promote their union and general welfare."[17] In that regard, one general history could do the work of many state histories. Accordingly, three major multivolume general histories were published between 1805 and 1810, which were followed by David Ramsay's highly anticipated *History of the United States,* published posthumously in 1816 following his assassination by a deranged former patient on the streets of Charleston. General histories synthesized the many already published state histories into a form "within the reach of every purse [and] the leisure of every reader."[18]

This period also saw the publication of the first anthologized collections of primary source documents from the colonial past in book form, including two volumes of Ebenezer Hazard's *Historical Collections, State Papers, and Other Authentic Documents* (1792–94) and Morgan Edwards's *Materials Toward a History of the Baptists* (1792).[19] A number of important colonial documents were also published for the first time in the 1790s, including the first two volumes of John Winthrop's journal covering 1630 to 1644. Beginning in 1792, the newly established Massachusetts Historical Society began publishing annual *Collections* volumes consisting largely of colonial era documents, including the "Historical Collections of the Indians in New-England," written by Daniel Gookin in the mid-seventeenth century.[20] Another major reference project in this decade, Jeremy Belknap's two-volume *American Biography* (1794–98) compiled biographical narratives of sixteenth-century explorers and important figures in the settlement of New England and the Chesapeake. Widely excerpted in newspapers and magazines, it earned Belknap the title of "the American Plutarch," though his was just the most prominent of a number of biographical dictionaries published in this period, including John Eliot's *A Biographical Dictionary* (1809).

Those dictionaries heralded the emergence of biography as another important book-based form of historical cultural production in the early nineteenth century. As before the Revolution, biographies of classical figures—namely in the form of Plutarch's *Lives*—and European rulers remained available and popular with readers. But after the Revolution, the first full-length biographies of American political figures were published. Unsurprisingly, George Washington was the first great American biographical subject. In 1800, Mason Weems published *The Life and Memorable Actions of George Washington* as a tribute to the recently deceased former president. He revised and expanded this work in 1806. Though the revision was aimed at a younger audience—introducing into American culture the infamous cherry tree story—it became an early American bestseller, going through twenty-eight editions in two decades. Weems was an itinerant bookseller and, in addition to its strikingly moralistic and nationalistic tone that especially appealed to revivalists, the success of his book was also due partly to his constant promotion of it on his travels throughout the country.

At the same time, Chief Justice John Marshall published his multivolume *The Life of George Washington* (1804–7) and David Ramsay published the single volume *Life of George Washington* (1807). Marshall's work was aimed at a more sophisticated audience and used Washington's life as a means to tell the history of the Revolution. It was very popular, particularly in the South and with northern Federalists, while Ramsay's work appears to have been more popular with Republicans in northern cities.[21] Weems subsequently published numerous other biographies of revolutionary figures, including Benjamin Franklin, Marquis de Lafayette, and General Francis Marion. The Revolution provided the first American national heroes suitable for such biographical treatment. Moreover, their biographies provided a model for republican citizens to emulate, in a form and style that proved highly popular and effective in bringing the American past to an even broader reading public than traditional historical works.[22]

Though limited largely to elites before the Revolution, books became increasingly affordable and accessible to a broader range of citizens after the war.[23] Relatively speaking, Americans were, generally, "highly literate and schooled."[24] To serve this ever-growing reading public, printers and booksellers multiplied throughout the country, including in the territories. The growth of domestic production made books much more affordable. Yet, Americans did not only have access to books that they owned personally. In the 1790s alone, communities, large and small, throughout the United States, established over 250 social and circulating libraries.[25] And, like before the Revolution, historical works of all kinds, including biographies, formed the "substantial backbone" of these libraries' catalogs.[26] Ultimately, these postwar developments meant far more historical works written by Americans were being published and were achieving a significantly greater reach among the American reading public than before the Revolution.

Even more so than books, Americans learned about their past from newspapers and magazines. The publication of newspapers grew rapidly in this period. In 1776, there were only 37 weekly newspapers in the new United States, but by 1810 there were 365, many of which were daily newspapers.[27] This rapid proliferation of newspapers throughout the country greatly expanded their reach compared to the decades before the Revolution. More newspapers being published more regularly required more content. Unsurprisingly, newspapers began featuring historical content and themes to a greater degree than before the war. Indeed, many newspapers began giving significant amounts of column inches to serialized and excerpted historical narratives of the American past immediately upon the war's conclusion.

However, since there was as yet no history of the Revolution or the United States as a whole written by an American in the years immediately after the war, newspaper publishers were initially forced to excerpt from British works to satiate readers' desire for historical content. In 1784, Isaiah Thomas used his *Massachusetts Spy* to reprint almost the entirety of the first three volumes of *The History of America* (1777) by acclaimed Scottish historian William Robertson, which covered the history of Spain's New

World colonies. Thomas did this by serializing the work over an almost unbroken run of seventeen months.[28] The publishers of the *Continental Journal* in Boston picked up the idea and began serializing it as well in eighty-two consecutive installments.[29] Also in 1784, shortly after taking over the *Vermont Gazette,* printer Anthony Haswell chose to serialize *An Impartial History of the War in America* (1780), which had been written by the Reverend James Murray of England before the war had even ended. Haswell gave over the entirety of pages 2 and 3 to the first installment with a header for the title on page 2 larger than the paper's own front-page masthead.[30] That is, he considered its inclusion such a huge selling point that he subverted the traditional design of a newspaper to accommodate and promote it.

When the first general history of the Revolution—William Gordon's *History of the Rise, Progress, and Establishment of the Independence of the United States*—was published in 1788, at least eighteen newspapers began serializing it almost immediately, including *The Massachusetts Spy.* Parts of Ramsay's *History of the American Revolution* appear to have been serialized prior to publication under the heading "Sketches of American History" in the *City Gazette and Daily Advertiser* in Charleston, South Carolina, through most of 1788.[31] Magazines and newspapers throughout the country also excerpted Ramsay's two histories of the Revolution. Numerous other historical works, including a number of state histories, were excerpted regularly, and newspapers often included original and reprinted historical essays, including biographical essays.[32]

Newspapers brought historical works to a larger audience beyond those who could afford to buy many books. In March 1789, William Morton, the printer of the *Morning Post* in New York City, announced his intention to serialize all four volumes of Gordon's *History* in their entirety and thereby furnish the public "with a valuable historical Treasure at a very inconsiderable price." He did this by giving it one and a half to two columns on page 2, six days per week for eighty-five weeks, or 507 issues.[33] Following the final installment of Robertson's *History of America* in the *Massachusetts Spy,* Isaiah Thomas reminded his readers, "We have now gone through the three first volumes, which would have cost the reader *six dollars,* had he purchased the books."[34] These kinds of serializations were profitable for printers because they turned newspapers from an ephemeron to a collectible item, increasing the demand for the newspaper.

In the 1780s, histories of the Revolution were so highly anticipated that newspapers reported on the progress of William Gordon, who was widely known to be writing the first general history of the Revolution by someone living in America. In the summer and fall of 1784, newspapers in New England and Charleston, South Carolina, reported that Gordon had petitioned Congress for access to its papers as part of his research for the history.[35] Gordon was a pastor at Roxbury, Massachusetts, who had emigrated to the colonies from England in 1770 and had been a vocal supporter of the patriot cause. Nevertheless, his *History*—and his suitability for the job of being the first historian of the Revolution—was a topic of acrimonious prepublication debate in public prints from Massachusetts to South Carolina over a period of two years.[36] Some expressed concern upon hearing of Gordon's plan to sail to his native England to have his manuscript published in London, a development also reported in newspapers throughout the country. In reality, Gordon decided to publish in London because he thought it would help minimize the appearance unauthorized editions.

That the first history of the Revolution would be written by an Englishman and published in London clearly aroused anger and suspicion. One writer, who signed his name, "An American of Republican Principles," referred to Gordon as "the Divine Beggar of Roxbury" for having asked advance subscribers to his book to pay a down payment of half. Others feared that he was publishing in London because his *History* was unfavorable to Americans.[37] He was referred to, snidely, as "the British Historian of our Revolution."[38] A piece on Gordon's as-yet-unpublished history in the *Massachusetts Centinel* carried the dramatic headline: "Anti-American HISTORY!!"[39] After all, from the Americans' perspective, why would a London printer publish a work that was sufficiently critical of Britain (as, in their minds, any accurate American history of the Revolution must be)?[40]

Their fears, however, were not wholly irrational. By the time Gordon's work was published in London, it had changed significantly, in both form and content, from the original manuscript with which he had left America. Aside from being changed from narrative to epistolary form, later rumors suggested that the original manuscript was deemed unsaleable by British publishers. They also suggest that Gordon conceded to allow a "professional gentleman" to make it "agreeable to English readers." Indeed, the marginalia in the preface of John Adams's copy of the first volume claims (with names) that publishers refused to take it if "the sincerity of reflexion on the English were not softened, and if the Praises of the Americans were not moderated." Adams's marginalia continued, "All this was done. And if Gordon's original manuscript should be preserved, all this in substance will appear."[41] These claims have never been substantiated because the original manuscript has never been located. Nevertheless, the suspicion, anxiety, and angst that surrounded its publication was very real. In late 1786, a New England newspaper gleefully reported that Gordon's *History* had either not yet been published or, even better, had but had gone unnoticed. The piece read: "We have search'd . . . the London news-papers, for intelligence respecting Dr. Gordon, and his History—but none can we find—both the History and the Historian appear there to be wholly 'unnoticed or unknown.' "[42]

Newspapers did not only excerpt, serialize, and review historical works, publish historical essays, and circulate subscription proposals. They also served as a forum in which the progress and direction of the production of the nation's history was debated, at times quite vehemently and with high stakes. As a result, newspapers had an intimate relationship with historical cultural production in the early republic, helping circulate far more historical content than they ever had during the colonial period.

Magazines, too, were an important print vehicle for historical content and themes in the decades after the war. Only a small handful of short-lived magazines were published before the Revolution. Between 1783 and 1800, however, at least eighty new titles were published, of which a significant number were national magazines that circulated directly to subscribers and readers beyond the region in which they were published.[43] Like newspapers, magazines serialized excerpts of historical works with the intention of bringing them to a broader audience and with the understanding that they served as an additional selling point for their publications.

In an editorial statement in the first issue of the *American Monitor and Republican Magazine* (1785), publisher Ezekiel Russell noted, "To convince [his readers] that he intends to serve the Publick in general, but the less affluent part of them in particular, he shall insert in this work (if proper support is offered) the interesting, useful and entertaining History of the State of *New-Hampshire,* wrote by that eminent Historian, the ingenious and learned Mr. Jeremy Belknap."[44] The *Columbian Magazine,* the most successful of the period's periodicals, serialized Ramsay's *History of the American Revolution* as soon as it was published. The serialization stretched continuously for three and a half years, from March 1789 to November 1792. More commonly, though, magazines excerpted historical works into self-contained essays.

Magazine editors, who in most cases were also the printer and publisher, regularly commissioned original essays and brief historical and biographical sketches by historians, who were highly sought out and valued as contributors. Magazines were also a common venue for poetry, particularly poems dealing with national historical themes.[45] In addition, the nationalist-minded magazine editors published reviews of most new works of American history by American authors. Like newspapers, they provided a venue for discussing the value of history itself, as well as education more generally. Taken together, magazines circulated a broader array of historical cultural production than any other print form in the early republic.[46]

Almanacs, too, continued to serve as an important venue for history and contributed to the increased availability of historical knowledge after the Revolution. Colonial almanacs had included some historical information, primarily the most important dates in British monarchical history incorporated into their calendars. Some almanacs also included brief imperial chronologies (or timelines). The most prominent inclusions in the almanac calendar during the colonial period had been the regicide of Charles I, the Restoration, and the Gunpowder Plot. After independence (and, for some almanacs, even before), compilers began dropping these events from the calendar and replacing them with events from the imperial crisis and the war. Almanacs, therefore, served as a manifestation of how the American past had come to replace the British past. In doing so, they helped make more historical knowledge of the past more accessible than during the colonial period.[47]

Beyond specific forms of print, American history and historical themes also played an important role in the emergence of American literature and art. The poetry of the revolutionary generation after the war was decidedly nationalistic and showed a propensity toward using historical themes, particularly the work of the most prominent writers. Indeed, as with the period's historians, many of the most important poets were cultural nationalists dedicated to fostering nationalist sentiment through the creation of a national culture. Poetry of this sort was published often in both magazines and newspapers, which provided writers with the "advantage . . . of having them known to every body."[48] They wrote poems about the Revolution itself, but they also played a significant role in creating a new shared national past.[49]

Building on the "Rising Glory poets" of the 1770s, the poets of the 1780s and 1790s wrote a large number of "prospect poems." Prospect poems were a popular form, particularly among cultural nationalists, that were essentially paeans to the inevitable future glory of the nation. These poems circulated widely in pamphlet form, as well as in magazines, newspapers, and anthologies.[50] One of the earliest anthologies of American poetry, *American Poems, Selected and Original* (1793), declared in its preface that the volume was intended to provide "a more thorough acquaintance . . . of the state of the belles-lettres in the individual parts of the Union; and hereby will be promoted a more intimate combination of literary interests."[51] Though most of the volume consisted of the works of the Connecticut poets, including Trumbull, Dwight, Barlow, Humphreys, and Hopkins, the themes of their poems were largely national, intending, like the general and state histories, to create "a more intimate combination" of the states.

Historical scenes and subjects played an important part in the development of American art.[52] In April 1790, John Trumbull circulated a subscription proposal in New York for prints drawn from two paintings depicting the deaths of Generals Warren and Montgomery.[53] In his subscription proposal, he was explicit about the historical and nationalist value of his work, explaining that his paintings and prints would "assist in preserving the Memory of the illustrious Events which have marked this Period of our Country's Glory." Abigail Adams agreed, writing that the paintings would "transmit to Posterity Characters and actions which will command the admiration of future ages and prevent the period which gave birth to them from ever passing away into the dark abiss of time whilst he teaches, mankind, that it is not rank, or titles, but character alone which interest Posterity." Painting, for Trumbull, was an ideal form of historical cultural production. "Historians will do Justice to an Æra so important," he admitted, "but to be read, the Language in which they write, must be understood;—the Language of Painting is universal."[54]

Among the most popular historical scenes of the period was Trumbull's *The Death of General Warren at Bunker Hill,* which was available commercially

FIG. 2. John Norman, after John Trumbull, *The Battle at Bunker's Hill, or The Death of General Warren.* Engraved prints were made from Trumbull's historical paintings for sale to the public, such as this early nineteenth-century example. Yale University Art Gallery, New Haven, Connecticut.

as engraved prints (figure 2).[55] Abigail Adams saw the painting itself in London in 1786, and she was immediately struck by its inherent nationalist and historical power and the potent relationship between them. She wrote of her reaction to her sister, "To speak of its merit, I can only say; that in looking at it, my whole frame contracted, my Blood Shiverd and I felt a faintness at my Heart. He is the first painter who has undertaking to immortalize by his Pencil those great actions; that gave Birth to our Nation."[56] Adams's reaction likely was not unusual. It can be hard for us, who live in a highly visual culture, to comprehend the visceral and emotional reaction that could be wrought by such a visual representation in the eighteenth century. That was likely even more the case for Americans seeing for the first time visual renderings of their revolution. Trumbull concluded his proposal with a list of the scenes that would make up the rest of the series, many of which remain important to our historical memories of the American Revolution. His nationalist efforts came full circle in 1817 when he was commissioned by Congress to paint four life-sized versions of his previous revolutionary paintings to be placed in the Capitol Rotunda for the princely sum of $32,000.[57]

Most American painters, however, primarily produced portraits. Yet, contemporary portraits of revolutionary leaders, including Gilbert Stuart's hugely popular 1797 portrait of George Washington, were also historical in intention. Done during and following a successful revolution, those portraits were commissioned, produced, and preserved with posterity in mind. Trumbull believed the artist's true purpose was not just "to diffuse the knowledge and preserve the memory of the noblest series of Actions which have ever dignified the History of Man" but also "to transmit to their descendants the personal resemblance of those who have been the great actors in these illustrious scenes."[58] The display of portraits of revolutionary leaders, as in Charles Willson Peale's museum in Philadelphia, could be employed to significant historical and nationalist effect. They also contributed toward the initial mythologizing of the Revolution and, especially, to the iconography of the cult of the individual that began in this period and continues to retain a strong hold on American popular memory.[59] In addition to the Revolution, scenes from the colonial past also became important subjects in art, a favorite being William Penn's signing of a "treaty with the Indians."[60] As such, the birth of American art in this period, in the form of paintings and innumerable locally produced woodcuts and engravings, contributed to the broader growth of historical cultural production.

Historical themes, particularly of the recent revolution, were also prevalent in some of the most popular dramatic works of the period.[61] Two of the most popular plays were William Dunlap's still-appreciated *André* and John Daly Burk's less timeless *Bunker-Hill, or The Death of General Warren,* named loosely after Trumbull's popular painting. Burk was a highly political Irish immigrant who fled his homeland after a failed attempt to rescue a fellow anti-British rebel from the gallows. His play, like Trumbull's painting, was built on a popular fascination with Warren that lasted well into the nineteenth century. It premiered at the Hay-Market Theatre in Boston on February 17, 1797, to "a larger and more respectable auditory than perhaps was ever contained in any other theatre on the continent."[62] As one reviewer noted in the *Columbian Centinel,* "The very name of this piece, without any knowledge of its real merits, was enough to excite the curiosity and attention of the public."[63] This was not just a theatrical premiere but also a public event that concluded with a parade, including "Young Women dressed in White, holding Flowers in their hands." The notice also assured the presumed nationalist audience that "American Music only, will be play'd between the Acts."[64]

Though panned by critics, it was "received with the most lively and flattering approbation" and a "high degree of incitement" by the city's working-class population.[65] The play was staged nine times in Boston and multiple times in Philadelphia over the course of the next year.[66] It was also staged at least half a dozen times in New York City in the fall of 1797, where it was said to have been shown to "the largest and most respectable Assembly that ever graced a Theatre in America." Among the audience one evening was President John Adams, who left displeased with Burk's more working-class portrayal of his deceased friend as "a bully and a blackguard."[67] Within a year, Burk found himself imprisoned under the recently passed Sedition Act for libeling Adams's administration in his New York newspaper, the *Time-Piece.* Upon his release, he moved to Petersburg, Virginia, where he began writing a three-volume history of the state before being killed in a duel with a Frenchman on April 11, 1808.[68]

Revolutionary themes and events were popular in early American theater partly because they gave a working-class audience the chance to relive events in which many took part. Even more importantly, they enabled that audience to see themselves portrayed in a heroic light on the stage of history, thereby bolstering their sense of having played an important part in the national past. This interrelationship and affinity between history, theater, and the people were clear enough to be obvious to Burk, an immigrant from Ireland, who wrote the play just a few months after first arriving in the United States in 1796.[69]

Plays set in the colonial period were also popular around the turn of the nineteenth century. James Nelson Barker's *The Indian Princess; or, La Belle Sauvage,* a musical comedy that debuted at the Chestnut Street Theatre in Philadelphia on April 6, 1808, was one of the foundational pieces of American theater and one of the first to feature Native Americans as characters.

In telling the story of Pocahontas and the settlement of Virginia, the play referred to settlers as "Europeans" and to Native Americans as "Virginians," as Barker used Pocahontas and the Powhatans to represent the American continent in contrast to Europe. This interest in the colonial period and in the original settlers' relations with Native Americans became a powerful theme in the early national period, as we will see in chapter 5.

The late eighteenth and early nineteenth century also saw the beginnings of American fiction, including historical novels, which helped bring the national past to a growing audience.[70] Many of the most popular novels and short stories were set in the colonial period. Washington Irving, for example, wrote not only about colonial history but also about historians of that history. In his satirical *History of New-York from the Creation of the World to the End of the Dutch Dynasty,* Irving adopted the identity of a crusty, old historian of colonial New York named Diedrich Knickerbocker. Perhaps his most timeless work, "Rip Van Winkle," told the tale of a man who had fallen asleep during the colonial period and awakened in the early republic. From the South, the stories of John Smith, Pocahontas, and Bacon's Rebellion were increasingly treated in literature in the early decades of the nineteenth century, and even earlier in many northern histories and educational texts.[71] Ultimately, the popularity of historical themes in early national literary production shows the purchase the colonial past retained on the American popular imagination into the nineteenth century. Simply put, the American past, of both the recent revolution and the colonial period, formed an important part of the content and themes in all of the major forms and genres of American cultural production in the decades following the war.

The growing importance of and access to education in the new nation also contributed to the expansion of history culture.[72] David Ramsay noted in 1778, "A zeal for promoting learning, unknown in the days of our subjection, has already begun to overspread these United States."[73] In 1792, Noah Webster exhorted his fellow citizens, "Americans, unshackle your minds, and act like independent beings . . . you have an empire to raise . . . and a national character to establish. . . . To effect these great objects, it is necessary to frame a liberal plan of policy and build it on a broad system of education."[74] As suggested by Webster's statement, cultural nationalism suffused efforts in these decades to create an American form of pedagogy, one that would banish the vestiges of British influence and therefore be suitable to a "free, independent, and virtuous people."[75]

Education was crucial to the formation of virtuous republican citizens, particularly civic education, of which history was a fundamental part.[76] Therefore, cultural nationalist educators, like Noah Webster and Jedidiah Morse, created distinctly American textbooks for reading and geography. Webster eventually went a step further trying, unsuccessfully, to codify an American form of the English language. These efforts were part of a broader educational impulse in the early republic that included the establishment (and expansion) of colleges, academies for both young men and women, and numerous national and local learned societies and institutions, such as the American Academy of Arts and Sciences, the American Philosophical Society, and the nation's first museums.

The American past figured prominently in these efforts to nationalize pedagogy. As Noah Webster noted in the *American Magazine*, "Every child should be acquainted with his own country. . . . [A]s soon as he opens his lips, he should rehearse the history of his own country."[77] Indeed, in the early 1790s, Webster argued that none of the current readers available were "calculated particularly for American schools." Their readings "respect distant nations or ages," but "in America, it will be useful to furnish schools with additional essays, containing the history, geography, and transactions of the United States." Webster believed that including carefully chosen historical stories in his reader would "transfuse [liberty and patriotism] into the breasts of the rising generation." During the colonial period, history was primarily exemplary in that it was meant to provide examples of virtuous and unvirtuous behavior, particularly for elites. In the early republic, however, the teaching of history became more emotive as it was intended to foster national unity and pride among the vast majority of the population. Such educational texts brought the national past to a much broader (and more impressionable) audience.

A new nationalist idea in historical education in this period was to begin a student's course of reading with the recent past and move backward in time, rather than starting with ancient history. The impetus behind this idea was that it was more necessary for students to know the recent national past followed by the recent past of other countries than it was for them to know about ancient Greece and Rome. The idea being that if they ended schooling early, students would at least have read the history most important for them as citizens of a new republic.[78] Such reconsiderations show an assumption that the study of history needed to be revised to account for the new circumstances in which that study was taking place. Methods that had served the purpose of elite moral instruction during the colonial period were no longer broadly useful in an emerging democratic republic. New circumstances required new methods that could serve the new goals history would play in the formative education of new republican citizens.

To that end, the most popular readers for young people featured many national historical stories. For example, Webster's very popular *The Little Reader's Assistant* (1790) began with "a number of Stories, mostly taken from the history of America," including the "The Story of Columbus," "The Story of Capt. John Smith, who first settled Virginia," and "The Story of the First Settlers in New-England."[79] These stories were meant to instill the type of nationalist connection with the first generation of settlers that had begun to develop during the imperial crisis. Webster's 1787 edition of the final part of his three-volume *Grammatical Institute, An American Selection of Lessons in Reading and Speaking,* included much historical material related to the Revolution, including both a political and military history of its events and a number of documents published by the Continental Congress between 1774 and 1776. He also included a chapter titled "Discovery and Settlement of *North America.*" Historians have estimated that Webster's texts sold upward of ten million copies between 1783 and 1843.[80] Morse's *American Geography,* one of the most popular and reprinted works of the period in any genre, included brief histories of every state and region of the nation often drawn directly from the increasing number of published state histories.[81] Also adapted for younger readers were historical works, such as *The History of America, abridged for the use of children of all denominations* (1795) and Hannah Adams's *An Abridgement of the History of New-England, for the use of Young Readers* (1806).

The cultural importance of the national past can be seen in the degree to which it was incorporated into instructional texts for other subjects and literary genres. These texts drew on the historical content and themes that were being published in this period in a variety of print forms directly and indirectly, from historical works to magazines. The incorporation of the national past into such works helped turn spellers and geography textbooks into civic texts. By extension, they turned those subjects into important components of civic education in the early republic. These texts, through their astoundingly wide circulation, are an excellent example of both the expansion of history culture and its interrelationship with American culture more generally in these decades.

Education also provided the platform for the origins of history culture's modest expansion in terms of gender. Before the Revolution, there were no published female historians in the colonies and female education had been minimal. After the Revolution, however, the notion of "republican motherhood" temporarily expanded women's civic role. Female education took on a greater importance as women were expected to provide the foundation at home for the civic education required to raise virtuous republican citizens.[82] It was important that "ladies should be qualified to a certain degree, by a peculiar and suitable education, to concur in instructing their sons in the principles of liberty and government."[83] History was an important part of that civic education.

Unlike the generations before them, young women in the early republic were expected to read and learn history. In 1787, Benjamin Rush wrote, "The attention of our young ladies should be directed, as soon as they are prepared for it, to the reading of history."[84] That reading of history was not intended to be passive. It was not enough for the female student "to store her memory with facts and anecdotes, and to ascertain dates and epochas." Rather, according to Hannah More, she must learn "to trace effects to their causes, to examine the secret springs of action, and accurately to observe the operation of the passions."[85] This degree of engagement by women with the study of history had been previously limited to elite males and thought too dangerous even for working-class males. In the early decades of the nineteenth century and beyond, however, there were an increasing number of female historians and female writers of all genres who incorporated historical themes and the national past into their work.[86] As another popular educational work aimed at young women (and excerpted in multiple magazines and newspapers in the 1790s) argued, "With the history of your own country, you cannot be decently unacquainted." For young women to be unlearned in history was to "betray an unpardonable ignorance."[87]

In the postwar decades, women slowly but increasingly incorporated themselves into the nation's history culture both as authors and readers. When Susannah Rowson, the most popular novelist in the United States in the 1790s and 1800s, spoke of her desire to use historical fiction to inspire an interest in history in her "young readers," she did so knowing that most of those readers were female. Also, a few of the most prominent historical works of the period were written by women, including Mercy Otis Warren, who produced what is perhaps the most original of the period's three major histories of the Revolution, and Hannah Adams, the prolific and well-respected author of *A Summary History of New-England* (1799).[88] In 1812, Timothy Alden, a Newark schoolmaster, held Adams's historical work up as an example to his female students saying, "In her researches after useful and important knowledge, she has long been a model of patience and perseverance worthy the imitation of the young ladies of America."[89] The profiles of Adams and Warren as historians set examples for younger women.

Noteworthy in the quote above is the implicit gendering of the practice of historical research as something suited to both men and women but to be learned through examples from one's own gender. Although it would be well into the nineteenth century before women were both producing and consuming history on a significant scale, the seeds for those developments were sown in the history culture of the early republic. Beyond their actual historical works, pioneers like Warren and Adams and female authors of historical fiction like Susannah Rowson contributed an important and authoritative female presence to an otherwise male-dominated national history culture.

Ultimately, it is impossible to quantify the exact number of historical cultural productions produced between 1783 and 1812, partly because historical content and themes suffused every form and genre of literary and print production in the period. The contrast in the visibility of the past between pre-revolutionary and postwar cultural production, however, is striking. Early national Americans sought to make sense of the present by constantly looking to the past in as wide a variety of contexts and forms as was available to them. The diffusion of historical content and themes throughout the cultural production of the period speaks broadly to the increased importance of the past in the culture of the early republic and represents the creation of a newly national history culture. Indeed, Americans in the early national period wrote, read, and thought about the past more than they ever had before.

To better understand the vast expansion of a national history culture in the early republic, it is necessary to go beyond the texts and circulation of historical cultural productions and look at how they were produced. In the 1780s, an informal network consisting of a web of personal and professional relationships began to emerge that significantly contributed to the growth in historical cultural production and, hence, the expansion of history culture in the early republic. It included historians, antiquarians, essayists, educators, poets, painters, printers/publishers, booksellers, and even a number of elite politicians, the vast majority of whom could be described as cultural nationalists (figure 3). Through their correspondence, travels, and publications, these men and women fed all forms of cultural production and spanned most regions of the new nation. These individuals produced a significant proportion of historical cultural production in the period, while a number of them went on to help establish the nation's first historical societies. Ultimately, the network played a critical role in the expansion and institutionalization of history culture after the Revolution.

The historians David Ramsay, Jeremy Belknap, William Gordon, Mercy Otis Warren, Ezra Stiles, and even the British historian Catherine Macaulay corresponded with one another and with antiquarians interested in collecting and preserving primary sources from the colonial past, such as Ebenezer Hazard, John Eliot, and John Pintard, among many others throughout the colonies. The network included poets and essayists, such as Benjamin Rush, Joel Barlow, and Timothy Dwight. It included men devoted to producing pedagogical works of nationalist value, for example, Noah Webster and Jedidiah Morse, as well as the painters John Trumbull and Charles Willson Peale. Also keyed into the network were a number of politicians—George Washington, John Adams, Thomas Jefferson, John Jay, and William Livingston, among many others—who corresponded with historians and antiquarians offering support and encouragement for their endeavors, as well as access to official and personal documents. Finally, the network included printers, publishers, and booksellers, who were integral to the process of disseminating the labors of the network's participants, such as Mathew Carey and Robert Aitken in Philadelphia, Isaiah Thomas

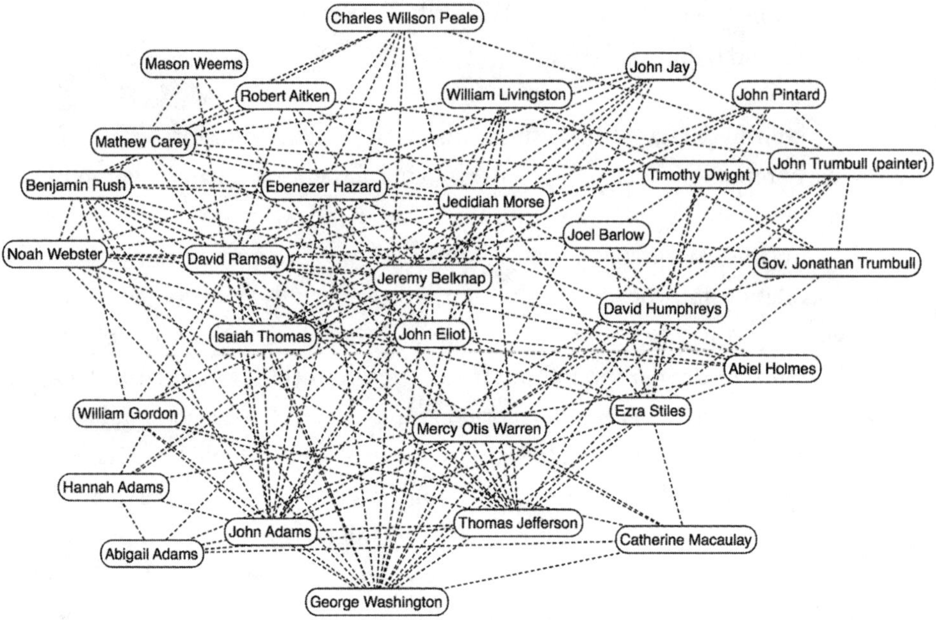

FIG. 3. This sociogram offers a visual representation of the core participants of the informal historical network that contributed to the growth in historical culture production. The lines represent the existence of correspondence between individuals related specifically to at least one of the four key functions described in this chapter: collecting, preserving, and sharing primary sources; offering and securing patronage; providing feedback on manuscripts; and fostering relationships between authors and publishers.

in Boston, Noah Webster in Connecticut (and New York), and Mason Weems, who traveled throughout the country selling books for Carey before becoming a popular biographer.

Participants used the relationships that made up the network for a number of functions related to supporting historical cultural production from its earliest research phases to writing through to publication and promotion. First, they created a supportive research community by sharing historical sources they had collected and transcribed, as well as news and leads on sources of interest to others. Second, some participants also used the network to request and receive patronage. They received crucial assistance in getting access to official sources from politicians who understood the political importance of creating a coherent national history after the Revolution. Third, participants shared drafts of their work and offered each other feedback and encouragement. Often isolated locally, they used their network relationships to effectively serve the functions of a modern-day writers' group. Finally, participants shared publishing information and advice with each other and created professional relationships with the printer/publishers connected to the network. Meanwhile, printers used their network relationships with writers to secure historical content, particularly for their magazines. Ultimately, a number of participants used their network experiences and relationships to begin establishing the nation's first historical societies and museums, thereby creating institutions that could provide the kind of support for historical endeavors for which they had previously relied on personal relationships.

The first function the network served was in aiding historical research as participants traded transcriptions and information about historical documents. Historical research in this period was not for the faint of heart; primary sources did not come cheap. Without any central repositories, private citizens held many important historical documents, often unknowingly. Historians in this period had no easy way of knowing whether a document they were looking for was even extant. Tracking down documents required both detective and social skills, as well as unrelenting commitment.

Jeremy Belknap, perhaps the period's most respected historian, recalled "search[ing] for his materials wheresoever they were likely or *not likely* to be found," including the "garrets and rat-holes of old houses." Historians, Belknap said, had to search as widely as possible knowing that "not one in a hundred that he was obliged to handle and decipher would repay him for the trouble."[90] As a new minister at Dover attempting to collect information for his *History of New-Hampshire,* he also used his professional travels around the state, particularly opportunities to give guest sermons at other churches, to do historical research. For example, in 1788, Belknap recalled that in between his morning and afternoon guest sermons at "Roxbury Old Church," he forewent socializing in favor of rummaging through the building's basement "looking over the ancient church records."[91] Indeed, Belknap spent over ten years collecting and transcribing documents for his three-volume *History of New-Hampshire.* The collections amassed by historians during their research were often among the largest collections of historical documents at the time, many of which would ultimately go on to form the foundation of the initial collections of the nation's first historical societies.

Yet, not all of those persons collecting sources were historians intending to write books. The latter decades of the eighteenth century saw a rise in antiquarianism in the new United States, as individuals throughout the country became obsessed with collecting and preserving documents from the past, with some of them amassing significant collections. Writing history in this period required not only searching for documents but also knowing who else was searching for them, in case they had already been collected or transcribed by someone else. With such effort and expense required, it made no sense to duplicate someone else's work if it could be avoided. It also required knowing who else was in the process of researching and writing histories. Therefore, relationships between historians and antiquarians were crucial to both historical research and the production of historical works in this period.

Those relationships and how they supported historical cultural production are best exemplified by the relationship between Jeremy Belknap and Ebenezer Hazard. Hazard, a former bookseller in New York City, served as postmaster general of the United States during the war and used his official travels throughout the country as a means to collect and transcribe a broad array of documents from the colonial past.[92] He embarked on a plan of collecting, editing, and publishing a collection of historical documents covering the entire national past beginning with the first settlements. He and Belknap struck up a friendship in the 1770s through their mutual interest in both national and natural history and corresponded regularly until Belknap's untimely death in 1798.[93]

Conversations about various primary sources are littered throughout their correspondence, ranging from seventeenth-century imperial and colonial documents to papers regarding the Siege of Louisbourg in 1745. For example, in early 1779, Belknap promised to send his transcriptions of a batch of documents he thought might be useful for Hazard's *Collections.* Because Hazard's positions as surveyor-general and postmaster general meant he was often traveling, he asked Belknap to send them to their mutual acquaintance and fellow historian, William Gordon, to forward. He then reminded Belknap, in the interests of historical accuracy, "to mention on each paper the *authority* or book from which it was taken, and please favour me with a line informing me whether they were transcribed *literatim*."[94] Belknap responded with a list of the "titles of sundry papers which are among those in my possession," which he offered to share with Hazard.[95]

Hazard was more often traveling than not, and he treated his work jaunts as research trips. During his frequent visits to New England, he became interested in collecting the records of the United Colonies of New England, a confederation of four colonies that began in 1643 and ended in the 1680s. The two corresponded about their efforts, potential leads, and successes in finding these records, with Hazard taking the lead. In a 1781 letter, Hazard detailed his progress (and dedication), writing, "My transcript is contained in two 4to volumes, the first of 242 pages, and the other of 399. The last is what I have lately transcribed."[96] Despite the immense amount of "labor and expence" involved in transcribing these hundreds of pages of documents, Hazard had "no objection" to sending them to Belknap, in case he might be able to make use of them.[97] By 1790, he strongly considered publishing the records from New England on their own by subscription.[98] Instead, he opted to include them in the second volume of his *Historical Collections* (1794).[99]

Without institutional repositories for historical documents, individual historians and antiquarians spread throughout the country had to collect, transcribe, and preserve them through their own efforts, at their own expense. Many, like Belknap and Hazard, also made those documents available to others engaged in these kinds of historical endeavors. This informal historical network allowed individual participants to find, learn about, and share historical documents to which they otherwise would not have had access, thereby supporting the research behind many published historical works.

The second function the network served was to provide historians with access to historical patronage from politicians and military officials. Historians used their relationships with these individuals to gain access to both official government documents and the private papers of those prominent figures. Politicians and military officials, such as George Washington, John Adams, Thomas Jefferson, Henry Knox, and others corresponded with many network participants about historical topics and their own historical endeavors. Jefferson and Washington actively encouraged the writing of histories of the Revolution. John Adams, however, wrote at length to numerous correspondents about his belief that a true and accurate history of the Revolution could not be written so soon after the event had ended because most of the necessary documents were "yet Secret."[100] Indeed, Adams at one point claimed that the amount of research necessary to write an accurate general history of the Revolution would "require the whole of the longest life."[101] Nevertheless, as early as 1786, Washington "regretted" that a "comprehensive view of the war" had not yet been published. All three of them willingly and repeatedly answered queries about the Revolution and requests from historians for relevant documents. They all understood the value and necessity of quickly establishing a national historical narrative for the young republic. As a result, they offered support, encouragement, and a bit of caution in the 1780s and 1790s to those seeking to craft the first histories of the Revolution and the new nation.[102]

As early as 1774, Hazard had already conceived of his project of collecting and publishing the most important documents of American history dating from settlement and secured a list of subscribers stretching from New Hampshire to South Carolina. At the start, he sent a draft of his "Proposals for Printing by Subscription a Collection of State Papers, intended as materials for an History of the United States of America" to potential subscribers, including Thomas Jefferson, whom he asked for assistance in collecting materials related to Virginia.[103] "It is an undertaking of great utility to the continent in general," Jefferson replied. He promised to send Hazard "copies of our charters, resolutions of assembly &c. and of our treaty with the commonwealth of England."[104] Hazard also sent his proposal to Benjamin Franklin and Washington, receiving favorable replies. In July of 1778, he petitioned the Continental Congress for "a certificate of their approbation" and "free access to the records of their respective states." Congress sent the request to a committee, which, after "having conversed with Mr. Hazard," was convinced enough of the project's value to give him access to its records and ordered the significant sum of "one thousand dollars be advanced to him."[105]

For his *History of the American Revolution,* David Ramsay sought out assistance and primary documents directly from the source. Beginning in 1782, and especially after the spring of 1785, he spent much of his time in Congress at New York "collecting facts & making extracts from official papers to enable me to write a general history of the American Revolution."[106] Ramsay also sent out a number of questionnaires to revolutionary political and military leaders in the spring of 1786. He was especially interested in "the general temper of the people in 1775" and the transition from royal governments to "the popular councils" in each state.[107] Upon his request, General Henry Knox sent Ramsay detailed military information about "the Campaign of 1777 & and the Affair of Trenton 1776."[108] By May 1786, his time in Congress—and, therefore, his ability to search and copy its papers—was nearing an end. To get as much copying done as possible, he had "for some months" spent "from five to 8 hours every day at this work."[109] Like fellow historians, Ramsay also corresponded regularly with political leaders, including John Adams, Thomas Jefferson, Benjamin Rush, and Charles Thomson about historical and research-related topics.

William Gordon began preparing to write the first general history of the Revolution not long after the Congress declared independence. He immediately started a correspondence with George Washington, whose acquaintance he made during the siege of Boston. As the Continental Army moved to New York and then New Jersey in the second half of 1776, Gordon took it upon himself to keep Washington updated on the minute affairs in Boston. He also offered him *a lot* of unsolicited (and unheeded) advice.[110] Toward the end of the year, he wrote to Washington about "preparing for that history in which you are so deeply concerned & make so eminent a figure" and thanked him for offering the assistance of "furnishing materials."[111] In October 1782, Washington suggested that it appeared to him "impracticable for the best Historiographer living, to write a full & correct history of the present Revolution who has not free access to the archives of Congress, those of Individual States—the Papers of the Commander in Chief, & Commanding Officers of separate departments."[112]

Accordingly, Gordon sought access to as many primary sources as he could, including the papers of Congress and a number of military figures, including Washington, Nathanael Greene, Henry Gates, and Henry Knox. In July 1783, Washington offered Gordon access to "all my Records & Papers . . . and I shall be happy in your Company at Mt Vernon while you are taking such Extracts from them, as you may find convenient."[113] The following spring Gordon applied for and received "access, under the necessary restraints, to the documents and records in the archives of Congress." Soon thereafter he began a southward trip during which he would also interview and inspect the papers of General Greene and visit Mount Vernon for two and a half weeks of intensive copying.[114]

Without any institutional repositories, historians looking for official documents and the papers of prominent figures had to turn directly to the governments and individuals who held them for patronage in the form of access. Their communications with political and military leaders proved invaluable, particularly to historians of the Revolution like Ramsay and Gordon, as a source of both information and credibility. Indeed, Ramsay noted in the brief preface to the first volume of his *History of the American Revolution* that "as a member of Congress, I had access to all the official papers of the United States . . . every letter written to Congress by General Washington . . . [and] the letters of other general officers, ministers of Congress, and others in public stations."[115] Similarly, Gordon traded often on his relationship with Washington as a means of bolstering the credibility and legitimacy of his history of the Revolution. As early as 1777, in a letter he wrote to the famed British historian Catherine Macaulay, he claimed that his upcoming history of "the American Revolution" was effectively authorized by "His Excellency Genl Washington," "Other Generals," and "many honourable members of the Congress."[116] In both the subscription notices and his preface, Gordon informed the reader that the work had been "known to the late commander in chief of the American army" and that he had received "the desired encouragement from him" as well as the "United States, in congress assembled."[117]

Men like Washington, Adams, and Jefferson, among many others, understood the importance and value of creating a national history, and particularly a history of the Revolution. They understood that Americans no longer had a shared past, having effectively disowned their previously shared British past, and that a new shared past in the form of a national historical narrative was needed to replace it. Jefferson supported, in some fashion or other, a number of historical projects, including Ebenezer Hazard's *Historical Collections*, John Trumbull's series of revolutionary paintings, David Ramsay's *History of the Revolution of South-Carolina*, John Daly Burk's *History of Virginia*, and an unfinished history of the Revolution undertaken by Joel Barlow at Jefferson's behest. Adams, too, corresponded with and assisted numerous individuals involved in historical cultural production, including Mercy Otis Warren, William Gordon, David Ramsay,

Benjamin Trumbull, Isaiah Thomas, Jeremy Belknap, and Catherine Macaulay, among others. Their correspondence with multiple participants drew them into the network where they played an important role in fostering historical cultural production and the expansion of history culture.

Beyond the collecting and sharing of historical sources and information, the network also provided authors with the means of sharing and receiving advice and feedback on their works prior to publication, providing an eighteenth-century version of a writers' support group. For example, after months of writing over the summer and fall of 1786, Ramsay offered a draft of six chapters to Charles Thomson, who had immigrated to the colonies from Ireland when he was ten years old and went on to serve as the secretary of the Continental Congress for its entire fifteen-year existence. Ramsay sent them to Thomson "in order that he may have it perused by the Eastern Gentlemen as it relates chiefly to their country."[118] Six weeks later, Thomson responded with a lengthy letter pointing out factual errors and offering suggestions on Ramsay's writing style. Thomson's critiques were sharp and blunt, but he also offered his own generous account of events in Pennsylvania leading to independence.[119] Thomson left it to the historian "to mould [the account] in any form you think proper," but Ramsay inserted a good deal of it into the fourth chapter of his manuscript verbatim, then a standard practice. Later, when preparing a revised edition of the *History* over two decades later in 1809, he had to write Thomson to ask him what he meant by specific phrases in his account. Ramsay also sought out feedback from Benjamin Rush, whom he hoped would submit the manuscript "to the perusal of well informed persons for their remarks before publication." While Thomson's is the only extant response, a comparison between one of the circulated drafts and the published volume reveals many significant changes, suggesting that the feedback Ramsay received very much shaped his revisions of the manuscript before publication.[120]

Similarly, Jedidiah Morse published his *American Geography* in 1789 with significant assistance from his fellow network participants. That is because Morse's geography textbook was not merely a collection of maps and descriptions of topography. His accounts of each state included brief histories, covering such topics as politics, government, religion, and educational and cultural institutions. To aid him in chronicling the histories of the new states, he enlisted the help of a number of historians, whom he referred to as "literary characters," including Jeremy Belknap and David Ramsay.[121] So desirous of Belknap's feedback was Morse that he sent his "first & only draught" of his historical "acct. of New Hampshire," which contained many excerpts from Belknap's own history of the state.[122] He also asked if he could send Belknap his account of Massachusetts's history when completed, which he did two months later, again sending his "first & only draught."[123] Ultimately, William Livingston, governor of New Jersey and network participant, contributed to the manuscript and helped with securing publication, as he did with Ramsay's *History of the American Revolution,* thereby earning Morse's dedication of the work.

Writers connected to the network were desperate to produce the best works possible. To do so, they were willing to draw on any and all potentially helpful relationships and resources. Or at least most writers were. While a few persons around Boston claimed to have seen the original manuscript of William Gordon's *History,* he did not circulate it for feedback among his colleagues. Knowing it would be the first history of the Revolution, he kept it close, especially as he came closer to finishing it. After its publication, Belknap, Hazard, Ramsay, and others judged the work harshly. Belknap called it "jejune, stiff, and unanimated," which Hazard concurred was "a just idea of the style."[124] Taking it a step further, Belknap remarked that it included much that was "below the dignity of history."[125] Hazard gave it a sly criticism wrapped in a compliment when he praised Gordon's "collection of facts."[126] Critiquing Gordon's practice of the discipline of history, Belknap replied, "I have heard it observed of him that the first report which he heard he would set down as true, and if anybody doubted his information . . . he would say, 'Sir, I have it from the best authority.'" Belknap attributed the book's issues to Gordon's failure to avail himself of the opportunities of getting feedback from his fellow historians. He wrote, "I only wish that Dr. Gordon had let his History be seen by some judicious friends. . . . I am persuaded he might have profited by their advice, but he had too much of the self-sufficient principle in him."[127] Unlike Gordon, however, many of those connected to the network sought to use their relationships not only at the beginning of a project to secure materials but also to improve the writing style and accuracy of their manuscripts.

Participants also turned to network relationships for help in navigating the nascent American publishing industry. Writers sought advice about publishing their work from other participants. In August 1784, as Ramsay completed the manuscript for his first work, *The History of the Revolution of South-Carolina* (1785), he wrote to Rush, "Where do you advise me to have it printed. In London or Philadelphia. I incline to the latter. The accuracy of a London printer would make me less concerned about my own inaccuracies & yet I hate to be beholden to our late enemies."[128] In 1787, as Ramsay was finishing work on his *History of the American Revolution,* he wrote to Morse, "You say printing is cheap in New Haven. Perhaps I may get my new work printed there. Will you favor me with estimates of your printer?"[129]

For his first volume, Belknap asked similar advice of Hazard, who had become well acquainted with many printers, including those in Philadelphia. Beyond accuracy, Belknap also weighed aesthetic concerns in his search for a printer, noting, "I like Bailey's *type* that Evans's sermon was printed with, but should choose better paper and a larger *page,* such as the Observations on the Revolution, printed by Styner and Cist in 1779."[130] Hazard replied, "Robert Aitken has the most taste of a printer of any man in this city; and, were I to have a book printed here, it should be done by him."[131] Accuracy, aesthetics, and, of course, costs were primary concerns of authors publishing in the immediate wake of the war, and they used their relationships within the network to seek out information about the best "terms" for the printing and binding of their works.[132]

This first generation of American historians differed significantly from their colonial predecessors, such as Robert Beverley, William Byrd II, Cadwallader Colden, and Thomas Hutchinson. Men like Ramsay, Belknap, Hazard, and Gordon (as well as many of participants in the network) may have fancied themselves gentlemen but they certainly were not men of leisure. They were working professionals, such as clergymen, doctors, or lawyers. During the war, Belknap was in frequent financial distress due to the Dover congregation's inability to pay his minister's salary. As a doctor, Ramsay's financial situation fluctuated, and it was not uncommon for him to find himself in significant debt periodically.[133] As postmaster general during the 1780s, Hazard was on the payroll of a Continental Congress that had a hard time raising money even to sustain the army that was fighting for its very existence.

These men understood what they were doing—preserving the past, educating the public, developing American letters, and promoting American culture—as being in service to the greater causes of fostering both a national culture and national identity. Nevertheless, they fully expected to be remunerated for the countless hours they had spent collecting and transcribing sources and writing and revising their manuscripts, essays, and magazine pieces. In doing so, they were engaged in a process of redefining and democratizing the idea of the historian and, along with numerous antiquarians of similar means and backgrounds, the practice of history itself.

Unfortunately, they suffered the bane of being pioneers and not only failed to profit greatly from their works in the 1780s and 1790s but often lost money. By 1787, Ramsay had complained to the poet Joel Barlow—who had written him seeking advice on publishing his epic historical poem, *The Vision of Columbus* (1787)—that publishing his *History of the Revolution of South-Carolina* (1785) had left him "in debt above fifteen hundred dollars."[134] Belknap, too, saw almost no profit from publishing the first volume of his *History of New Hampshire.* This was partly because, despite their best efforts to avoid it, London and Dublin publishers quickly produced pirated editions. Adding insult to injury, they soon made their way to American bookstores at cheaper prices than the authors' editions.[135] Gordon tried to avoid this fate for his work, which he expected to provide the funds for his retirement, by having his history of the Revolution published in London.[136] Unfortunately, his plan did not work. Just a few months after its publication, Hazard noted, "Dr. Gordon's History is reprinting here, in 3 vols., 8vo, at half the price of the London edition, and is daily retailed in two of our newspapers. It is not done in either case 'by the Doctor's desire,' or with his knowledge; though I am inclined to think he expected it would be done."[137]

The historians quickly learned their lesson. They had to be business-minded from the start. Noah Webster was perhaps the most acutely business-minded of the network's authors. In traveling throughout the country giving lectures, Webster made a point of visiting booksellers at each stop to assess the sales and availability of his books and report them back to his publishers in Hartford, Hudson and Goodwin, with whom he kept up a constant correspondence.[138] Yet, many of the other authors curbed their over-optimism and produced less costly volumes, often by eschewing the inclusion of costly plates, such as maps. Instead they increasingly relied on pre-publication subscriptions to print smaller but better selling editions.[139]

As Ramsay pointed out to Barlow, "It is too much to expend money in collecting materials and then again to lose money by printing. I am determined to adopt a cheaper plan."[140]

Publishing the books by subscription offered one such plan. William Gordon, like others after him, had subscription proposals for his work printed in newspapers throughout the country. Yet, doing so required having those subscriptions collected and managed by local contacts, which network relationships provided. For example, the proposal for Gordon's *History* that was printed in the *Pennsylvania Journal* noted, "Subscriptions are taken in by R. Aitkin, Printer, Market-street."[141] In the 1790s, many other writers, including Hazard and Belknap, also sought out subscribers prior to publication for their works.[142] As the federal Copyright Act of 1790 began to provide some protections, historians and publishers began figuring out how to produce and publish works that would, at the very least, not result in financial losses for both. Yet, it would be well into the nineteenth century before an American could even dream of being a "professional" writer or historian." Nevertheless, these works' less-than-anticipated profits for the author do not correspond with their reach, as many more unauthorized editions were sold, they were serialized and excerpted in newspapers and magazines, and single copies bought by a local social library would be read by many people.

Finally, participants in the network used their connections to support the production and publication of a number of important magazines. Publishers and editors of magazines, such as Mathew Carey, Robert Aitken, Noah Webster, and Isaiah Thomas, were in constant need of original material for their magazines and turned to their network relationships. Even before the war was officially over, Hazard wrote to Belknap to inform him that Aitken was looking for "half a dozen good stated writers, whom he might employ by the year . . . to furnish papers regularly."[143] Virtually all major magazine publishers were cultural nationalists. Indeed, Benjamin Rush, in a letter to Noah Webster, noted, "I wish always to see such publications wholly confined to the hands of men who possess *American hearts.*"[144] National historical content was especially desirable in the eyes of these publishers.

Being the nation's most prominent historian throughout the 1780s, Jeremy Belknap was in high demand. He received numerous proposals from magazine publishers to become a regular contributor. In early 1787, Belknap declined an offer to be the editor of the *Columbian Magazine,* though he did agree to provide content for the magazine—under the name "The American Plutarch"—for one year for the significant sum of fifty pounds.[145] Under this pseudonym, he published some of the entries from his work-in-progress, the two-volume *American Biography* (1794).[146]

A few months after starting the *American Museum,* Mathew Carey, an Irish immigrant and highly entrepreneurial publisher in Philadelphia, offered Belknap "20 guineas per annum for writing the historical part" of his magazine. When, as part of his pitch, he suggested that it would not take much effort, Belknap responded indignantly: "It might be an easy matter with writers of a certain sort to dish up a fricasee of newspaper intelligence & dignify it with the pompous title of The History of the United States. But a person who values his reputation as a writer would chuse to have the best materials, & even then would hesitate about many things an inconsiderate scribler would venture to throw out at random."[147] A few months later, Belknap received yet another offer from Noah Webster asking him to be part of a group of regular contributors to his new *American Magazine* made up of fellow network participants, including Barlow, Trumbull, Rush, and Ramsay.[148] Indeed, most of the writers in the network contributed to magazines, whether it was in the form of excerpts, poems, and essays, or even letters between participants and the editor/publishers.

The relationships formed between network participants helped make original historical content in a variety of forms an important part of early American magazines. More broadly, the network offered authors a means of navigating a new and, as yet, uncertain publishing industry, providing significant support not only in the production of historical-themed works but also in their publication and circulation. Until now, it may have been easy to have a mental picture of a late eighteenth-century American historian alone in his dark room sitting at a candlelit desk covered in ink marks and piles of manuscript pages. Yet, the uncovering of this network makes clear that historical cultural production in this period was a collaborative endeavor. Indeed, many of these historical cultural productions had many hands from all over the new nation involved in their creation and production.

Perhaps most significantly, the network helped provide the impetus and model behind the establishment of the nation's first historical institutions. During the colonial period, no institutional support existed, whether for the work of historians or for bringing the past to the public. The creation of such institutions, like the impulse behind it, is genuinely native to the early republic. The establishment by network participants of the Massachusetts Historical Society in 1791 (Jeremy Belknap and John Eliot), the New-York Historical Society in 1804 (John Pintard), and the American Antiquarian Society in 1812 (Isaiah Thomas), as well as the Peale museum in Philadelphia began the institutionalization of history culture in the early republic. The cultural nationalists who founded these institutions saw them as an important part of their broader efforts to lay the foundation for a national identity by creating and propagating a shared national past.

In many ways, the earliest historical societies were created to provide the supportive roles and functions previously served by the personal relationships that constituted the network. For much of the 1780s and 1790s, individuals produced historical works with little to no institutional support. In that absence, network relationships helped support that work, from research and writing to publication and promotion. Historians traveled many miles looking for historical documents and spent many hours transcribing them. They corresponded with antiquarians, who had taken it upon themselves to collect and preserve historical documents. They shared their collections and information with one another, and they used their network relationships to support the production and publication of historical works. In the decades following the war, however, new historical societies and museums began providing these types of support.

Even before the war, Jeremy Belknap and Ebenezer Hazard were conscious of the need to preserve the documents and printed ephemera produced by the resistance to British imperial reform. In 1774, Belknap wrote, "Political pamphlets, Newspapers, Letters, funeral and Election Sermons and many other papers which are now regarded only as beings of a day may if preserved give posterity a better idea of the Genius and Temper of the present age (and of our most material Transactions) than can be derived from any other source."[149] Hazard aided in securing "the records of the city of *New-York*" before and after the British invasion in 1776. In

December of that year, he recommended to the New-York Committee of Safety "that proper measures may be taken to secure those authentick documents, which may be of a great service in a future day."[150]

By the late 1780s, the need for "public repositories for historical materials" was becoming increasingly evident and urgent. "Many papers which are daily thrown away may in future be much wanted," Belknap noted.[151] John Pintard, an antiquarian and driving force behind the establishment of the New-York Historical Society in 1804, believed that establishing such repositories would "prove a public benefit by affording a safe deposit for many fugitive tracts which surviving the purpose of a day, are generally afterwards consigned to oblivion tho' ever so important in themselves, as useful to illustrate the manners of the times."[152] All the more maddening were the documents still held in private hands by people "who have suffered them to be wasted and destroyed as things of no value."[153] In a 1789 letter to John Adams, Belknap mourned, "There are in the Libraries and Custody of Gentlemen of the present age many materials which are now neglected and which may soon be scattered the loss of which posterity may regret as much as we do now the carelessness of former Times."[154] Adams replied with information about the state of various types of government documents and official correspondence.[155]

The establishment of institutional repositories would not only offer a safe home for the collections of antiquarians, but they would also spur individuals who perhaps held a few significant documents to entrust them to an institution committed to their preservation. Perhaps more importantly, the members of such societies would continue to seek out historical materials for their respective repositories. "There is nothing like having a *good repository*," Belknap wrote in 1795, four years after he helped establish the Massachusetts Historical Society, "and keeping a *good look-out,* not waiting at home for things to fall into the lap, but prowling about like a wolf for the prey."[156] Belknap worked indefatigably until his death in 1798 continually identifying and negotiating with potential donors for important documents.[157]

Just having a repository, however, did not guarantee the survival of historical documents, particularly in case of fire and war. When, on the brink of war in 1812, network participant Isaiah Thomas sought funds from the state legislature to help establish the American Antiquarian Society, he made the timely argument that the new society's non-urban location in

Worcester made it ideal "for the better preservation from the destruction so often experienced in large towns and cities by fire, as well as from the ravages of an enemy, to which seaports in particular are so much exposed in times of war."[158] Indeed, Thomas Jefferson had noted in 1791, "Time and accident are committing daily havoc on the originals deposited in our public offices; the late war has done the work of centuries in this business."[159] Truly ensuring the survival of precious historical documents required more than simply placing them in a repository.

The only guarantee that historical documents could survive such dire circumstances was through "the multiplication of Copies."[160] Historians and antiquarians all along had been transcribing and copying documents they had found in others' possession for their own collections. In his "Introductory Address from the Historical Society," Jeremy Belknap wrote, "There is no sure way of preserving historical records and materials, but by multiplying the copies."[161] He repeatedly echoed this sentiment in his own personal correspondence. And, of course, the easiest means of multiplying copies was "by printing them in some Voluminous work."[162] Accordingly, each of the first three historical societies made provisions for the publication of their collections immediately upon their establishment. The New-York Historical Society, in a letter "To the Public," justified the first volume of its *Collections* by arguing that it would "better secure our treasures by means of the press, from the corrosions of time and the power of accident." Publishing was an integral part of the process of preservation.

In addition to the function of collecting and preserving historical materials, historical societies would make those materials accessible to historians and the public. Preserving historical documents was necessary to "enable some future historian to delineate the present times in as full and perfect a manner as possible."[163] As John Pintard noted in a newspaper announcement of the establishment of the New-York Historical Society in 1805, "Without the aid of original records and authentic documents, history will be nothing more than a well-combined series of ingenious conjectures and amusing fables."[164] When Isaiah Thomas petitioned the Massachusetts General Court to incorporate the American Antiquarian Society in 1812, he defined the society's primary intention as to aid "in collecting, and preserving such materials" that would "assist the researches of future historians of our Country."[165]

In terms of access for the broader public, the published collections were crucial. As the New-York Historical Society pledged, "It will be our business to diffuse the information we may collect in such a manner as will best conduce to general instruction."[166] But public access did not end with the publications. In a letter to Hazard acknowledging the establishment of the Massachusetts Historical Society, Thomas Jefferson echoed the goal of preserving materials but "not by vaults and locks, which fence them from the public eye." Indeed, the Massachusetts Historical Society's first "Circular Letter" stated, "ANY PERSON desirous of making a search among the books or manuscripts, may have access to them."[167] Historians like Belknap, Hazard, Ramsay, Thomas, and Pintard were working professionals who did their research and writing on their own time, not elite men of leisure like their colonial predecessors. Therefore, the goal of making historical materials available beyond the immediate membership of the institutions and already recognized historians was a shared goal embedded in the societies they established.

Finally, these societies also shared the ideal of being *national* institutions. When founded in 1792, the original name of the Massachusetts Historical Society was, simply, "the Historical Society." "Massachusetts" was added when it was later incorporated by the state legislature in 1794. Upon its founding, Belknap sent a "Circular Letter" to be printed in newspapers and circulated among like-minded individuals throughout the country. It introduced the society and its purpose, which was "to collect, preserve and communicate, materials for a complete history of this country . . . from the beginning of its settlement." The society's focus was to be on "American Antiquities, natural, artificial and literary." Similarly, in Pintard's 1805 newspaper announcement of the establishment of the New-York Historical Society, he stated, "Our inquiries are not limited to a single State or district, but extend to the whole Continent."[168] And Isaiah Thomas described the scope of the American Antiquarian Society as "not confined to local purposes—not intended for the particular advantage of any one state or section of the union, or for the benefit of a few individuals."[169] Belknap, Pintard, and Thomas were cultural nationalists and their intent was to create national institutions that would preserve and propagate a national history.

Network participants played the lead role in establishing the nation's first historical societies. Their conversations and correspondence with one another spurred them on in those endeavors. Their shared experiences as practicing historians and antiquarians helped shape the nature and early development of those institutions. They designed their historical societies to meet many of the same needs previously met by their personal relationships with other network participants. They would institutionalize (and, thereby, centralize) the process of locating, collecting, and preserving historical documents in repositories and provide libraries where historians could perform their research. And as the network had provided them with a supportive, like-minded national community, the societies would replicate those same types of productive relationships by inviting individuals from other states to become "corresponding members," many of whom were initially fellow network participants. While these societies hoped to foster historical cultural production and the public's engagement with its national past, they also carved out a visible and tangible place for history culture within the cultural landscape of the early republic and promoted the historical memories detailed in the remaining chapters.

The transformation from a colonial history culture to a national history culture can be traced through four specific developments in this chapter. First, history culture underwent a significant expansion in the decades after the war. Far more historical cultural productions were produced. More historical works were written and published. Historical contents and themes could be found with much greater frequency in newspapers and magazines, which serialized and excerpted historical works and published other original historical material. Historical content and themes also became increasingly important in the literary and artistic production of this period compared to that of the colonial period. Just as historical content related to the American past was seeded throughout these various print forms and literary genres, it also formed an important part of the new, nationalist educational curriculum. This expansion was fostered, in no small part, by the informal network of historians, antiquarians, essayists, poets, painters, printers, and politicians, who supported each other's efforts.

Second, history culture became more democratized in this period. More people, including women, from more varied backgrounds engaged in and consumed historical cultural production than before the Revolution. The writing of historical works was no longer limited to a few elites. Indeed, the most popular historians of the 1780s and 1790s were working professionals, including doctors, lawyers, and clergymen, who came from a variety of socioeconomic backgrounds. Similarly, historical cultural productions of all forms and genres reached a much broader audience than they had during the colonial period. This larger audience was due to both the enormous growth of print after the war and the prevalence of historical content and themes in the most widely circulated forms of print.

Third, history culture in this period became nationalized in a way it had not been before the Revolution. During the colonial period, historical works often focused on individual colonies with an intended audience of that colony and the British public. During the imperial crisis, however, we began to see the creation of the idea of "American history" as a collective perspective on the colonial past that helped explain the Revolution. That perspective came to fruition in the 1780s and 1790s. General histories that included all the states and began with settlement were written for the first time. And many of the state histories written in this period were done with the intent of contributing to the larger national history and with a more national audience in mind.

Finally, history culture became institutionalized in the decades following the 1780s. Before the Revolution, there had been no dedicated historical societies or institutions in the colonies. In the 1780s, those engaged in historical cultural production sought each other out and supported one another's efforts through networking. With the establishment of the nation's first historical societies, those functions began to be provided on an institutional level, thereby offering more support and encouragement for historical endeavors. In addition, the establishment of other historical institutions, such as natural history museums, contributed to the increased cultural presence and importance of the past in this period. All four of these developments were either wholly or largely nonexistent in the colonial period, and the combination of them reveals the transition from a colonial history culture to a national history culture in the early republic. Ultimately, with American cultural production in these decades so saturated with history, the main challenge that stood before cultural nationalists was finding a way to reconcile the dependent colonial past with the independent present of the new republic.

CHAPTER FIVE

THE COLONIAL PAST IN THE EARLY REPUBLIC

In Washington Irving's tale "Rip Van Winkle," the protagonist fell asleep in the "Kaatskill Mountains" and awoke twenty years later, during which time the Revolution had come and gone. When Rip made it back to his village, things appeared quite different. The portrait of King George III that had hung above the local inn was replaced by someone named George Washington. The men gathered outside the inn were "haranguing vehemently about rights of citizens—elections—members of congress—liberty—Bunker's Hill—heroes of seventy-six." Are you "federal or democrat," he was asked, feeling very much like a stranger in a foreign land. Published in 1819, the story is often interpreted as an expression of Irving's "amazement at the transformation that had taken place in America" in just a few short decades following the Revolution.[1] But following his initial bewilderment, Rip found that—despite the appearance of great difference—much had not changed, and he settled back into the familiar rhythm of life in the village, "resum[ing] his old walks and habits." "Rip, in fact, was no politician," Irving wrote, "the changes of states and empires made but little impression on him." At the story's end, he "took his place once more on the bench at the inn door, and was reverenced as one of the patriarchs of the village." As "a chronicle of the old times 'before the war,'" Rip Van Winkle actually symbolized the continuing presence of the colonial past in the early republic and the inescapable necessity of reconciling it with the present.

Thirty years earlier, while preparing the manuscript of his *History of the American Revolution* in the summer of 1787, David Ramsay wrote regretfully to Benjamin Rush, "If I was sufficiently informed I would devote half or even whole of the first volume to a recapitulation of the history of the colonies from their settlement to the year 1761."[2] Instead, he ended up devoting his first chapter to the colonial past. In fact, Ramsay discarded much of a first draft of the chapter that had initially focused on the domestic history of seventeenth-century England and replaced it with histories of the settlement and development of the colonies.[3] The extant manuscript provides a tangible metaphor for how Americans as a society mirrored Ramsay's writing process by largely discarding the British past as their own after the Revolution and replacing it with a new, shared colonial past. At the same time, William Gordon devoted the first one hundred and fifty pages of *The History of the Rise, Progress, and Establishment, of the Independence of the United States of America* to the colonial era. These two most popular early national histories of the Revolution did not begin with the Stamp Act in 1765 or the Proclamation of 1763. Rather, they began with settlement because, as Ramsay noted, it was "at this last period the seeds of the revolution were sown." These early histories of the Revolution were actually the first attempts at producing national histories because the early historians believed that to understand both the Revolution and the present one had to understand the colonial past. These historical works—like historical cultural productions of all kinds in the decades following the war—exemplify the idea that the colonial past, rather than having become irrelevant, was actually an integral part of the new national history and the history culture of the new republic.

In the decades following the war, American writers, intellectuals, and artists reinterpreted the historical memory of a shared colonial past created during the imperial crisis—both its broad outlines and specific events—to reconcile it with the unprecedented circumstances of the postwar period. The cyclical perspective of history remained embedded in American history culture after the war, and the desire to reinterpret the colonial past came partly from the need to establish the basis for a new set of first principles for the new nation. Before the Revolution, individual colonial histories of the eighteenth century had stressed their value to the empire. They also stressed their similarities with and loyalty to the mother country. But with the war over, cultural nationalists began to reconstruct the historical memory of the colonial past, primarily by reframing the relationship between the colonies and the mother country. This new historical memory reinterpreted the colonial past through the lens of the republican present and, thereby, made the past look more like the present. It also fostered the political ends of cultural nationalists, most of whom were staunch supporters of the Constitution and the new federal government. The general outlines of this historical memory were codified in the most popular histories of the Revolution and further circulated and reinforced in other types of historical cultural productions, including general and state histories, edited collections published by historical institutions, poetry, drama, and other cultural forms.

Most fundamentally, historians and other writers in the decades following the Revolution recast the relationship between the colonies and Britain in a way that stressed their effective independence from the former mother country and their internal unity. These two ideas formed a core part of the grammar of American historical nationalism in the early republic precisely because independence and unity were core issues in the politics of the period. During the eighteenth century, colonists had treasured their independence from Britain without any desire to be independent. Indeed, during the imperial crisis they believed that their "independence *within* the empire" had been a key factor in the British North American colonies' rapid economic and political development.[4] Only when the Coercive Acts and their aftermath threatened the loss of that independence within the empire did declaring themselves independent from Britain become a real option. In the context of a recently established republic, however, the meaning and connotations of the term "independence" took on new political and cultural significance. Cultural nationalists seized the rhetorical opportunity by effectively conflating the distinction between practical independence and being independent and collapsing multiple meanings of unity. Their efforts were intended to suggest cultural independence from the former mother country and a shared sense of national identity and purpose.

Independence as a concept in the immediate postwar period was multivalent and ambiguous. The Americans had won their political independence from Great Britain, but cultural independence—or the sense of truly feeling independent from the former mother country, feeling not British anymore—was another matter entirely. Also, what was the practical meaning of such political independence? They had taken five years to reluctantly put the Articles of Confederation into effect, partly due to the war but also due to disagreements over the degree of independence the individual states would have from the Confederation government. Furthermore, how independent would citizens be from that Confederation government or from their own state governments for that matter? Cultural nationalists in this period sought to define independence in national terms through historical narratives in all the forms and genres available to them in an effort to subsume these other vexing political questions about the relationship between individuals and the state.

The idea of unity was equally ambiguous. The Congress had declared the former colonies independent with the plural denomination of "these United States." Yet conflicts, large and small, between states began almost immediately and intensified over time. In the wake of the war, it appeared to many cultural nationalists that too much independence might make unity impossible. Therefore, they sought to use all the tools at their disposal to define those ideas in historical terms in ways that would temper the political sense of independence unleashed by the Revolution and promote a sense of union between the states toward a common national good. They did so by recasting the fundamental historical relationship between both the colonies and Great Britain and between the colonies themselves.

These characterizations of independence and unity are especially significant in the first two histories of the Revolution by Ramsay and Gordon, both of which appeared at the end of the 1780s and enjoyed great popularity for decades afterward. Beginning their accounts of the Revolution with settlement, they set a foundation for the national historical narrative that developed over the following two decades. Gordon's *History* was one of the most widely serialized and excerpted historical works of the 1790s, while Ramsay's most recent biographer described his *History of the American Revolution* as "the major event in the development of a distinctly national historical consciousness."[5] An obituary following his assassination in 1815 called it "unquestionably the most popular history of that great and glorious event which has been published."[6] Yet, because they copied wholesale so much of their accounts of the war itself directly from the British *Annual Register,* their writings on the colonial past are among the most original writing in these works.

Much of that originality manifested itself in their characterization of the settlement of the colonies. Gordon described Puritan Massachusetts in the seventeenth century as "very near to an independent commonwealth."[7] Similarly, Ramsay wrote of the colonies, "They had in effect the sole direction of their internal government." He went even further, saying, "The inhabitants of the colonies from the beginning . . . enjoyed a government, which was but little short of being independent."[8] Ramsay went on to make arguments about the development and coexistence of independence and "liberty" among the earliest settlers in New England, made possible by "the distance of America from Great Britain," the lack of "an extensive trade with England," and colonial religion, which "also nurtured a love for liberty."[9] "Under these favorable circumstances," he argued, "colonies in the new world had advanced nearly to the magnitude of a nation."[10] The use of the singular "nation" was intended to suggest a sense of common identity between colonists from multiple colonies. Even though some of his readers were old enough to remember the sharp distinctions made by colonists between different colonies on the eve of the imperial crisis, Ramsay wrote, "A sameness of circumstances and occupations created a great sense of equality, and disposed [colonists] to union in any common cause." While these assertions had, at best, a tenuous connection to historical reality, looking at the colonies' early history through the lens of the present rendered independence from Britain and unity not only visible but fundamental in defining the colonial past.

The independence of early colonists, Ramsay repeatedly argued, came from the abandonment in early New England and Virginia of a "community of goods" in favor of the adoption of private property. "In imitation of the primitive Christians," he wrote, "they threw all their property into a common stock, and, like members of one family, carried on every work of industry, by their joint labour, for common benefit."[11] This "community of goods" encouraged "idleness," and in 1615, he argued, Virginia introduced "private property" as an "incentive to industry."[12] The same occurred, according to Ramsay, in Plymouth in 1627. Once private property was established, representative legislatures soon followed. In 1634, "Representatives [were] first chosen in Massachusetts. The government hitherto has been a pure democracy."[13] For Ramsay, the rise of this republican combination of property ownership and local representative government defined the development of the British colonies in the seventeenth century. "With this new tenure," he proclaimed, "liberty was rooted in the soil."[14]

Historians and other writers reconciled the colonial past with the republican present in a variety of ways beyond foregrounding the idea of effective independence from Britain. In addition, they cast the earliest decades of the colonial past and its inhabitants in terms with which the revolutionary generation could understand and identify. This helped create a historical memory in which the colonial past looked very much like the present of the 1780s and 1790s. Of the early settlers of New England Ramsay wrote: "[The colonies] were settled with the yeomanry. Their inhabitants, unaccustomed to that distinction of ranks, which the policy of Europe has established, were strongly impressed with an opinion, that all men are by nature equal. . . . The political creed of an American Colonist was short but substantial. He believed that God made all mankind originally equal: That he endowed them with the rights of life, property, and as much liberty as was consistent with the rights of others. That . . . impressed with sentiments of this kind, they grew up, from their earliest infancy, with that confidence which is well calculated to inspire a love for liberty, and a prepossession in favour of independence."[15]

Here, the first settlers had abandoned both the social and political hierarchies of Britain and Europe in favor of the belief that "all men are by nature equal." Furthermore, they believed God had "endowed them with the rights of life, property, and . . . liberty." Ramsay effectively transformed the Puritan settlers into proto-signers of the Declaration of Independence, meaning the eighteenth-century colonists who revolted were part of a people who had grown up "from their earliest infancy" with a "favour of independence." This passage reads the history of early Massachusetts through the lens of the 1780s post-revolutionary afterglow, attributing the specific language and ideas of the Revolution to Puritans in the 1630s. Similarly, James Sullivan in his *History of the District of Maine* (1795) wrote, "[The colonies] were settled originally on the idea, expressed at this day in all their forms of government, that 'all men are born free, equal, and independent.'"[16] The historical inaccuracy of such statements notwithstanding, many state and general histories drew highly specific analogies between the colonies' earliest settlers and the revolutionary generation, thereby rendering the colonial past more recognizable and more useful to citizens of a new republic.[17]

Ramsay and others also applied this perspective to early colonists' affection for and emotional attachment to the mother country. By the time "the American Revolution commenced," he wrote, "affection for the mother Country . . . scarcely had any existence." Indeed, "the bulk of the [colonists]," he continued, "knew but little of the Mother Country, having only heard of her as a distant kingdom."[18] Alexander Hewat, in his *Historical Account of the Rise and Progress of the Colonies of South Carolina and Georgia* (1779), noted, "We allow, that the first generation of emigrants retained some affection for Britain during their lives, and gloried in calling her their home and their mother country; but this natural impression wears away from the second, and is entirely obliterated in the third."[19] Ramsay took it further, arguing that the colonists' "attachment to their sovereign" was already "diminished in the first emigrants to America" and "still farther diminished, in their descendants." Colonists, he contended, thought of Britain on the eve of independence only as a nation that "had in the preceding century persecuted and banished their ancestors to the woods of America."[20]

It was not enough, however, for the colonial settlers to share contemporary Americans' sentiments regarding Britain and the decision to declare independence. They also had to agree with the resistance principles that led to the latter. After his one-hundred-page account of the early histories of each colony, Gordon summarized, "On the review of what you have read, you will note, that the colonists were very early in declaring, that they ought not to be taxed, but by their own general courts, and that they considered subjection to the acts of a parliament in which they had no representatives from themselves, as a hardship—that like true born Englishmen, when grievously oppressed by governors or others, they resisted, deposed, and banished; and would not be quieted till grievances complained of were redressed."[21] By reading the colonial past through the lens of the present of the 1780s and 1790s and thereby collapsing the historical distance between them, the earliest colonists became proper patriot forbearers of the revolutionary generation and the revolutionary generation became tied even more closely to their colonial ancestors.

Drawing on the historical rhetoric of the imperial crisis, the subsequent development of the colonies was to be understood primarily within a framework based on independence from the mother country. While loyalist historians contended that the colonies' rapid growth was due "almost solely to the protection and patronage of the Parent State," Ramsay pointed out, as Jefferson did in his *Summary View* in 1774, that, of all the colonies, only Georgia had been "settled at the expence of the government."[22] The colonies, Ramsay claimed, had been settled by "private adventurers, without any advances from the national treasury." Samuel Williams, in his *History of Vermont,* noted, "The first settlers in the British colonies were left in a great measure by their sovereigns, to take care of themselves."[23] These settlers had tamed "the wilds of America" by themselves, a process that, Williams noted, "operated to produce that natural, easy, independent situation, and spirit" that marked the colonies and its inhabitants.[24] *America Invincible* (1779), a poem widely reprinted in the 1780s, gave lyrical voice to this idea:

> Thrice fifty years the golden sun has roll'd
> Since fam'd Columbia's sons, e'er uncontrol'd
> First beat the thicket with unweari'd pain,
> Subdu'd the soil the earnest of their gain.[25]

Likewise, in *America: or, a Poem on the Settlement of the British Colonies* (1780), Timothy Dwight recalled that it was the colonists' "rough-brow'd Labour" alone that had "Made fruitful gardens round the forests rise." Most importantly, it was understood that the "acquiescence of the parent state . . . toward her colonies, during the first century and half after their settlement, had a considerable influence in exalting them to this pre-eminence."[26] This commonplace argument found expression in numerous subsequent general histories by Benjamin Trumbull, John Lendrum, William Winterbotham, and others, as well as most state histories. That is, the colonies had "achieved consequence . . . without any aid from the mother country," thanks to "a predilection for independence" that defined their origins and development.

Beyond these characterizations of the colonies' settlement, which were reprinted in newspapers and magazines throughout the new nation in the 1790s in the form of excerpts of histories, the themes of historical independence and unity also figured into how writers dealt with other events from the colonial past in other literary genres. Two events from that past—a century apart—were of particular interest to historians, antiquarians, poets, dramatists, and textbook writers for these reasons: the United Colonies of New England of the 1640s and the Siege of Louisbourg at Cape Breton in 1745. Both were prominently covered in most general histories and New England state histories, as well as in a variety of literary historical cultural productions.

The United Colonies of New England—or the "New England Confederation"—was an agreement made in 1643 between the colonies of Massachusetts Bay, Plymouth, New Haven, and Connecticut for the purpose of coordinating defense against both Native Americans and the Dutch settlers of New Netherland to the south. In addition to coordinating their interactions with the Mohegans and Narragansetts, its charter also provided a mechanism for resolving intercolonial disputes. Ebenezer Hazard was particularly keen to document the confederation, actively searching out related records and transcribing them. By 1779, he had already collected "upwards of five hundred pages in folio."[27] Hazard spent over a decade tracking down and transcribing these records anywhere he could find them, with the assistance of other historians and antiquarians.[28]

In addition to most New England state and regional histories published in the 1780s and 1790s, a variety of other historical cultural productions highlighted the New England Confederation, including general histories, state histories, satirical histories, edited collections of historical documents, and reference works, such as readers for children, history and geography textbooks for students, and atlases. In 1794, Hazard included the documents he had collected in his multivolume edited series of primary sources, *Historical Collections,* where they took up almost the entirety of the second volume. In his satirical allegory of the history of the United States, *The Foresters: An American Tale* (1792), printed first in the *Columbian Magazine* and later in book form, Jeremy Belknap spoke of how colonists had "formed an association for their mutual safety" from the "wild beasts" of the forest.[29] The highlighting of the confederation is also found in general histories by John Lendrum, William Winterbotham, John M'Culloch, and Benjamin

Trumbull; highly popular textbooks for reading, geography, and history by Noah Webster and Jedidiah Morse; and reference works such as *Carey's American Pocket Atlas* (1796), *Gaine's Universal Register, or, Columbian Kalendar* (1786), and *Fleets Pocket Almanack* (1788).[30] But why pay such special interest and attention to this 150-year-old agreement between four colonies?

Describing the arrangement between the colonies in a letter to Belknap, Hazard wrote, "They had the direction and management of all matters of general concernment,—in short, very much such powers as the present Congress."[31] Jedidiah Morse, in his *Geography Made Easy* (1790), described the confederation: "The powers delegated to [its] commissioners, were much the same as those vested in Congress by the articles of confederation, agreed upon by the United States in 1778."[32] In his histories of Connecticut and the United States, Benjamin Trumbull had also described the New England Confederation in a way that drew parallels with the current Constitution: "It was happily adapted to maintain a general harmony among themselves, and to secure the peace and rights of the country."[33]

The New England Confederation was highlighted in historical cultural productions of all kinds because it could be fit perfectly into the specific historical memory of the colonial past being created in the 1780s and 1790s. It showed the colonies and colonists acting independently of Britain while also displaying unity among themselves. Perhaps, most importantly, the confederation could be seen through the lens of the 1780s and 1790s as a forerunner of the Articles of Confederation and the Confederation Congress, and, later, the Constitution and Federal Congress. Such a perspective created a narrative that gave those new political institutions a historical basis in the early colonial past. This, like the stressing of the establishment of assemblies in state and general histories, placed the new federal government within a historical institutional tradition they hoped would contribute to its popular legitimacy. This narrative was important for cultural nationalists trying to buttress institutional authority and federalism itself with a historical foundation that would imbue it with the authority of the past. Just as importantly, it also helped cultural nationalists minimize the sense of the new republic being a radical departure from the past and to.[34]

The Siege of Louisbourg in 1745 was also celebrated in a variety of historical cultural productions beyond historical works as an instance in which the colonial militias had achieved relatively independent and unified military success.[35] Often referred to during the imperial crisis as evidence of colonists' commitment and contribution to the British Empire, in the early republic, the Siege of Louisbourg came instead to represent colonists' independence from the empire. In early 1792, the recently established Massachusetts Historical Society published the first volume of its *Collections of the Massachusetts Historical Society*. Of all the materials at its disposal, it chose to lead the first volume with documents relating to the expedition of colonial forces to Cape Breton to seize Louisbourg, a French fortress in Nova Scotia, during the War of the Austrian Succession in 1745.[36] Approved by the Massachusetts assembly and organized by Governor William Shirley, the expedition received contributions of men, materiel, or funds from Connecticut, Rhode Island, New York, Pennsylvania, and New Jersey, while the Royal Navy provided ultimately unneeded support from sea. The "Introductory Address" to the *Collections* volume justified its pride of place noting, "One of the most remarkable events in the history of this country is the expedition to Cape Breton in 1745. . . . It displayed the enterprising spirit of New-England; and though it enabled Britain to purchase a peace; yet it excited her envy and jealousy against the colonies, by whose exertions it was acquired."[37]

This colonial military success, along with other military exploits of the Seven Years' War, was commemorated often in other cultural productions.[38] The poem *America Invincible* (1779) remembered it as a day of glory for America:

> For *Louisbourgh* the great design was fram'd,
> For this their strength, for this their courage arm'd
> With fourteen thousand there our Leaders steer'd;
> And near the bason the vast fleet appear'd:
> For thee, fair *Louisbourg*, to yield a prey,
> Heav'n e'er decreed before the solar day,
> Thus fell the city by our bold alarms,
> A place of commerce and the pride of arms.[39]

Even before the Revolution, the American colonists had conquered a French stronghold thanks to the "great design" their "Leaders steer'd." In the end, their bravery made them victorious, giving them "the pride of arms." In Jabez Peck's drama *Columbia and Britannia* (1787) the character of

Britannia is forced to acknowledge the value of the colonial militia, very much drawing on the memory of Louisbourg specifically:

> Yes, my dear Columbia
> Most justly thou deserv'st Britannia's
> Warmest thanks, for thy sincere
> Attachment to the general good,
> Which even beyond thy share has prompted thee
> To undertake, and bravely persevere
> In carrying on a dangerous and expensive war;
> And for the happy event, Britannia
> Acknowledges herself to thee indebted.[40]

The "happy event" of the Siege of Louisbourg was an important choice of subject for historians, antiquarians, and writers of various literary forms because it provided an example of intra-colonial unity and an example of independent military glory for colonial militia, who organized the expedition and made up the landing force of the siege. As David Ramsay noted, "One of the first events, which as an evidence of their increasing importance, drew on the colonies a share of public attention, was the taking of Louisbourg from France."[41] Hannah Adams, in her *Summary History of New-England,* echoed similar sentiments, "The enterprizing spirit of New-England gave a serious alarm to those jealous fears, which had long predicted the independence of the colonies."[42] For historians of the Revolution, it served as a pre-revolutionary example of the on-the-ground independence and martial spirit they thought so crucial to victory in the war against Britain. Meanwhile, in general histories of the United States, it became a precursor of "the general union" of the states.[43] As with the New England Confederation, the siege became an important recurring event in historical cultural productions because it reinforced the themes of independence and unity that defined the cultural nationalists' political goals of the 1780s and 1790s and, hence, their historical memory of the colonial past.

Unsurprisingly, New England enjoyed pride of place in this historical memory of the colonial past, particularly Massachusetts. The vast majority of the historians and cultural nationalists, more generally, of the postwar period were from New England. Gordon was, for a time, a transplanted New Englander. Ramsay, though he was born and educated in the Middle

Colonies and lived most of his adult professional life in Charleston, appreciated New Englanders' unmatched zeal in preserving their regional past, which was now part of a national history. In a 1792 letter to Jeremy Belknap, praising his *History of New-Hampshire,* he wrote, "Posterity will know much more about the early settlement of New-England than they ever will of the more southern states."[44] Alexis de Tocqueville's perspective on the United States a few decades later, like so many then and since, was shaped by this defining feature when he saw "the destiny of America embodied in the first Puritan who landed on those shores, just as the human race was represented by the first man."[45] This aspect of the new colonial past, however, was not without its critics. As Samuel Peters, the loyalist historian of Connecticut, noted ruefully, "The historians of New England have constantly endeavored to aggrandize Massachusetts Bay as the parent of the other colonies, and as comprehending all that is worthy of attention, in that country."[46] Relative social and political stability and a decidedly historical worldview, however, meant that more history was preserved in New England than in the Carolinas or even Virginia. And more historians from the region meant more history written about New England. Indeed, the first post-independence state history of Virginia did not appear in print until 1804.

John Daly Burk, who moved to Virginia following his short stint as a playwright and newspaper publisher in the North, took it upon himself to insert Virginia more decidedly into this new historical memory of the colonial past. Despite its seventeenth-century royalist past, Burk's *History of Virginia* (1804–5) described the colony as "the elder branch of a confederacy, which threw down the gauntlet to kings." It was, he claimed, "the faithful guardian and depository of the public spirit."[47] The *History of the American Revolution* had established Ramsay as the nation's most prominent historian, and it quickly became "the most influential scholarly narrative of the early national period."[48] Thus Burk attempted to fit Virginia into the historical memory of the colonial past initially outlined in Ramsay's *History* and subsequently adopted in many historical works and cultural productions. To do so, he had to paint a picture of early Virginia as effectively independent of the mother country with a genuinely representative assembly. That meant dispelling the "universally received opinion arising from the want of an authentic history, that Virginia was distinguished for her invariable loyalty, and her submissive and tractable temper, during the greater part of her colonial existence." Burk understood that "it has been customary to contrast her yielding policy with the sturdy patriotism of New-England." But a coherent national historical memory required consistency not contrast. Therefore, he argued that seeing Virginia as having been less independent than New England was an "unjust" comparison. "Nothing," Burk retorted, "is more untrue."[49]

Challenging this perception, however, was no small task and often required some specious interpretations. For example, most previous colonial and imperial historians of Virginia attributed the colony's initial struggles to the ineffectual direction by the Virginia Company of ill-prepared settlers. They attributed its turn toward prosperity to the revocation of the Virginia Company's charter and its becoming a royal colony in 1624.[50] Such a narrative effectively declared early Virginians' efforts at self-government a failure that required instituting a strong royal government to restore order and prosperity. From the perspective of the early republic, this would not do. To downplay the significance of the mother country and the colony's new royal government, Burk argued that the colony's early problems were merely "the difficulties incidental to new establishments," which "would have fallen with equal weight on any other imaginable form." Therefore, he counterfactually supposed, "the colony in a given time, under the government of the company, would have made strides equally rapid towards power and consequence."[51]

To further incorporate Virginia into a national narrative dominated by the experience of New England, Burk also downplayed the degree of change in governance after the institution of royal government by stressing the continued and growing importance of Virginia's assembly, the House of Burgesses. As Ramsay, Gordon, and others had done with New England, Burk attributed great weight to the establishment of representative government and political participation, even though in reality there was much less political representation and participation in early Virginia. Nevertheless, the first volume of his *History of Virginia* culminates with the rise of the House of Burgesses, which represented the "unfolding, in the midst of the wilderness, [of] the true principles of the representative system; universal suffrage, and equality."[52]

Likewise, colonial historians of Virginia generally interpreted the end of

Virginia's resistance to Cromwell's Commonwealth in 1651 as an act of unwillful submission. Burk, however, saw the "Articles for the surrendering of Virginia to the subjection of the parliament" as "rather like a contract between two sovereign and independent states." That is quite an interpretative leap considering the act includes the words "surrendering" and "subjection" in its title. According to Burk, Virginia's agreement to "a nominal dependance on the parent state" was nothing but "empty professions, which cost them nothing." He even went so far as to argue that through the act Virginia had actually "acquired a real and substantial independence."[53] Reimagining the colonial past, therefore, occurred on both the macro level of Gordon's and Ramsay's general readings of early New England and the micro level of Burk's granular treatment of early Virginia. In the early republic, the colonial past at all levels was up for grabs. Reconciling the inconsistent development of seventeenth-century New England and Virginia proved one of the bigger historical challenges in creating a coherent, unified narrative of the colonial past.

That challenge—as well as a historical memory based on the idea of independence, more generally—was complicated by slavery. Unsurprisingly, nationalist historical works downplayed the role of slaves and slavery in the development of the colonies. Despite the fact that many cultural nationalists opposed the institution, slavery simply was not a significant part of their historical memory of the colonial past.[54] In Benjamin Trumbull's well-circulated *A General History of the United States of America* (1810), which covered settlement to the Seven Years' War, slavery goes unmentioned. On the few occasions where slavery was addressed directly in national histories, its tension with the broader narrative was quite visible.

For example, in his *History of the American Revolution,* Ramsay devoted two long paragraphs to slavery in his first chapter on the settlement and growth of the colonies before 1761. It is a surprisingly awkward apologia from a man who shared an "indignation at slavery" with many of his fellow cultural nationalists.[55] Ramsay noted that in the "Southern Provinces, domestic slavery was common." He argued the southern colonies "must have remained without cultivation, if it had not been cultivated by black men," since they were more biologically suited to the climate. "From imagined necessity," he wrote, "domestic slavery seemed to be forced on the Southern provinces." As for the enslaved themselves, Ramsay claimed, "Negroes who have been born and bred in habits of slavery, are so well satisfied with their condition, that several have been known to reject proffered freedom."[56]

Reconciling slavery with a historical memory of the colonial past that was defined by the idea of independence forced Ramsay to negate enslaved persons' lack of independence by suggesting that they had not wanted it and, therefore, had not had independence denied them. This allowed Ramsay to absolve the supposedly independence-loving slaveholders who needed to be incorporated into the national historical narrative. The issue was further complicated by the fact that challenging the dedication to independence of seventeenth-century Virginia slaveholders would necessarily do the same for their direct descendants, many of whom were prominent leaders of the Revolution and the new federal government. Twenty-five years later, in his *History of the United States,* Ramsay's account of early Virginia mentioned slavery only once.[57] While Ramsay appears to have been the most willing prominent writer to address slavery within the context of the national historical narrative, the intellectual awkwardness with which he did it—simultaneously defending and criticizing, justifying and abhorring—reflects the problem that slavery posed for many early national historians attempting to incorporate the colonial past into a national history, even for those who, in other arenas both private and literary, expressed more decidedly antislavery sentiments.

For historians writing state histories of southern colonies, it was often easiest to just ignore slavery altogether.[58] In Burk's *History of Virginia,* slavery plays no significant role. He remarks on it only briefly noting, "[1620] was remarkable for the introduction of negro slaves into the colony, an evil, than which none can be conceived more portentous and afflicting."[59] Yet, beyond that, slavery remains largely invisible, even during his discussions about the development of tobacco as the colony's cash crop. Instead, Burk focused on the colonies' political relationships with Britain and Native Americans. Historians of the South downplayed the role of slavery in the development of their states, thereby consciously excluding African Americans from the first national historical narrative. But the absence of slavery in Burk's work, like the awkwardness of Ramsay, was also a result of trying to incorporate the history of Virginia into the new historical memory of the colonial past, specifically, and the national historical narrative, in general. As an institution based on coercion that increasingly divided the nation, slavery, in any form, simply did not fit into a historical memory of the colonial past that stressed the ideas of independence and unity.

Like their English counterparts seeking to restore order after the Glorious Revolution, Americans of the early republic would have to find a way to define the American Revolution by principles other than the right of resistance. In his *History of the United States,* Ramsay noted, "The right of the people to resist their rulers, when invading their liberties, forms the corner stone of the American republic." Yet, he concluded, "This principle, though just in itself, is not favourable to the tranquility of present establishments."[60]

As during the imperial crisis, this new historical memory of the colonial past created in the 1780s and 1790s was a product of contemporary political circumstances. The political and social turbulence of the period fostered a need to justify and frame the origins and causes of the Revolution. In the mid-1780s, the participants in Shays's Rebellion—a revolt against the state government by rural farmers in western Massachusetts seeking relief from eastern, urban creditors—"appropriate[ed] the symbols of the Revolution" in their cause.[61] Although the rebellion was put down, it highlighted not only the weakness of the Articles of Confederation but also the ambiguous issue of ownership of the revolutionary legacy. Shays's Rebellion and subsequent popular rebellions in the 1790s made clear the need for cultural nationalists to make the past less co-optable by the discontented. As a result, they sought to achieve that goal primarily by stressing continuities between the colonial past and the present, thereby minimizing the sense of historical change wrought by the Revolution.

During the war, patriots had argued that Britain's treatment of the colonies, particularly between 1773 and 1776, gave colonists no choice but to declare independence. Throughout the eighteenth century, British writers often speculated that the colonies had designs on independence. During the imperial crisis, many suspected openly that the colonies' ultimate goal was independence. After 1776, those accusations appeared validated. Such an interpretation of the causes of the Revolution, however, effectively absolved the Ministry, Parliament, and king of contributing to the colonies declaring independence. Americans felt compelled throughout the war to counter this argument. As Ebenezer Hazard told Jeremy Belknap in 1782 before the war ended, "The British Emissaries, even from Queen Anne's time, have diligently propagated an idea that the Colonies were disaffected to the royal government, and thirsted after independence; and I think it a duty incumbent on every American historian to use his endeavours to wipe off so unjust an aspersion."[62] Their declaring of independence, they argued, had been brought about by necessity due to the actions of Britain rather than their own ambition.

They countered by asserting that the colonies had been unfailingly loyal "as long as was practicable considering the immense provocation which we received." In other words, independence came about quickly in direct response to the actions of the British Ministry and Parliament. Yet, by emphasizing loyalty, this understanding was still very much rooted in the colonial mindset. Indeed, as late as 1789, Belknap still felt compelled to point out that "our Opposition to Great Britain did not originate in a desire of Independence."[63] Combined with "the myth of the Revolution as a spontaneous rising of the people" as expressed by the rebellious farmers in Western Massachusetts, these early understandings of the causes of the Revolution stressed political, economic, and social rupture.[64] Most of all, they argued for very short-term causes making independence seem like a sudden decision forced on colonists by the British.

Ironically, this initial short-term reading of the causes of the Revolution shared significant similarities with loyalist histories.[65] Jonathan Boucher, a former Maryland clergyman and loyalist, argued that the Revolution was brought on by inept ministers who "were really unequal to the management of the arduous business which was then imposed on them."[66] Imperial mismanagement was a recurring theme in loyalist histories of the Revolution, as was the idea that a small number of demagogues—or "a Catilinarian Combination of individual Scoundrels"—caused the Revolution by promoting social disorder, licentiousness, and disobedience.[67] At the same time, though, for many loyalist historians these propensities were part of the colonial character dating back to settlement.[68] As Boucher argued, "I believe the people of the four New England governments may challenge the whole world to produce another people, who, without actually rebelling, have, throughout their whole history, been so disaffected to government."[69] Yet, despite this disaffection to government, loyalists argued that the colonies had always been under the immediate authority of the mother country. In his *Political Annals* (1780), George Chalmers meticulously catalogued English exertions of imperial authority over the colonies, both large and small, in the seventeenth century to demonstrate that dependence—not independence—had always defined the relationship between the colonies and Britain. Ultimately, he concluded, "The various plantations formed therefore no more than the dependencies of a great kingdom, which directed their affairs. And they enjoyed no portion of sovereignty."[70]

Although these early understandings of the causes of the Revolution were not yet codified into coherent historical memories, they became increasingly problematic for cultural nationalists seeking to construct a national historical narrative that stressed the colonies' long-standing independence. They countered these short-term understandings of the causes of the Revolution with a much more long-term interpretation. In their historical memory of the colonial past, as we have seen, Americans had been largely independent of Britain from the "first settlement in America" (figure 4).[71] The Revolution, they argued, sought to preserve that independence. They also argued that the colonists' relationship with Britain had never been one of genuine affection or kinship but rather one of antagonism begrudgingly abided. Furthermore, the historical memory claimed that Americans' earliest colonial forbearers had shared the principles that defined the resistance to imperial reform and, ultimately, the Revolution. If all these were indeed the case, the Revolution, then, would appear to have been the product of deep, systemic long-term issues that had been baked into the imperial cake rather than a radical spontaneous reaction.

The historical memory of the colonial past minimized the changes wrought by the Revolution and stressed continuity between the colonial past and the post-revolutionary present. Yet, it still allowed cultural nationalists to attribute causal significance to British actions during the imperial crisis by embedding the American reaction within a much longer historical context that could explain independence as the result of long-term factors. That is, they argued that separation only happened so quickly after the end of the Seven Years' War because of the inherent independence of the colonies, their lack of affective bonds with the mother country, and their long-standing intercolonial unity. By creating a narrative in which independence represented continuity rather than rupture, this historical memory of the colonial past effectively deradicalized the Revolution at a time

FIG. 4. Carl Gottlieb Guttenberg, *The Tea-Tax-Tempest, or the Anglo-American Revolution* (1778). This engraving, which circulated throughout the 1780s, shows Father Time projecting the past with his magic lantern while personifications of the world's continents look on. Images like this one supported the wartime narrative that the Revolution was brought about primarily by short-term causes, such as "the tea-tax" of 1773. Yale University Art Gallery, New Haven, Connecticut.

when cultural nationalists sought to help rein in the popular spirit unleashed by the Revolution and prevent it from sowing further discord, especially in the years just before and after ratification of the Constitution.

The political goals of supporting ratification of the Constitution and the new government shaped cultural nationalists' historical endeavors. Most recognized the flaws in the Articles of Confederation and, ultimately, supported ratification of the Constitution. David Ramsay staunchly favored ratification of the new federal Constitution that had emerged from Philadelphia in the fall of 1787. "My first wish," he told John Eliot in early 1788, "is union."[72] By the spring of that year, he was "pretty confident that [the Constitution] will be ratifyed."[73] At the same time, Ramsay was finishing the manuscript of his *History of the American Revolution* and desperately wanted to see it in print. But seeing the ratification of the Constitution as the culmination of the Revolution, Ramsay decided to hold off publication of a work in which he had invested a decade of his life. As he wrote to Benjamin Rush in February 1788, "I shall wait the event of the new constitution. The revolution cannot be said to be compleated till that or something equivalent is established." Accordingly, the second and final volume of Ramsay's *History of the American Revolution* (1790) ended with an exhortation to his readers: "Citizens of the United States! You have a well-balanced constitution established by general consent, which is an improvement on all republican forms of government heretofore established. . . . The end and object of it is public good. If you are not happy it will be your own fault."[74] For Ramsay and his fellow cultural nationalists, the Constitution represented the culmination not only of the Revolution but also of the national historical narrative, of which the historical memory of the colonial past was a part.

This historical memory of the colonial past was one of the ways in which cultural nationalists promoted a conservative revolutionary legacy, primarily by attributing it to long-standing origins and causes and bestowing upon it an air of inevitability.[75] Contrary to the Declaration of Independence, this reading implied that fundamental political problems work themselves out over the long term in a way preferable to spontaneous and popular mob violence. Cultural nationalists defined the Revolution by this dynamic and hoped to impart it to contemporary politics.

This conservative post-revolutionary ideology has generally been attributed to elites who retained cultural or political affection for Britain, most notably John Adams or Alexander Hamilton. Yet, we can see that it also manifested itself in the context of a historical memory that sought to create historical and cultural distance between the new republic and its former mother country. Though this historical memory stressed the colonies' long-standing independence from Britain, the ideology behind it can be traced back to imperial crisis arguments justifying resistance on the grounds of preserving British liberty. The main difference, however, was that in historical cultural productions of the 1780s and 1790s what had been preserved turned from British liberty to independence from Britain. This reckoning with the meaning and character of the Revolution through a historical memory of the colonial past was an attempt to negotiate the paradoxical sense that the Revolution had produced, in the words of Linda

Kerber, both "a radical break with the past and a conservative affirmation of it."[76]

Many of the most important cultural nationalists were supporters of the new government and therefore, by default, supported the Federalists in the early 1790s. Yet, a number of them—such as David Ramsay and Joel Barlow—became Republicans over the course of the decade, as the party system began to take shape, without fundamentally changing their nationalist historical perspective. Though anti-federalists in the late 1780s and early 1790s used historical references in their writings, they did not produce historical cultural productions on a scale comparable to cultural nationalists. Because they were primarily concerned with maintaining the sovereignty of the states and minimizing the importance of the federal government, they did not create a complete, coherent national historical narrative that could compete with that of the cultural nationalists.

Anti-federalists' historical concerns and rhetoric were focused either on the relatively recent revolutionary past, the British past, or the very distant ancient past. Classical history, they argued, showed the impracticability of running a successful republic over such a large geographic scale.[77] More recent examples from European history—such as the Swiss Cantons—were cited as evidence that a "confederacy of states" was preferable to "one great republic." The British past provided examples of the necessity of written bills of rights and the ease with which the individual's liberty could be trampled by an all-powerful state.[78] But the eighteenth century and the imperial crisis provided the most immediate historical examples of how easily a powerful, distant, centralized state could result in arbitrary power, partly because they remained in living memory for many Americans. As one anti-federalist wrote during the ratification debates: "We are not sure that men have more virtue at this time and place than they had in England in the time of George the Second."[79] Ultimately, the discussions of English history in the anti-federalist writings served to offer deeper context for the problems experienced during the imperial crisis, including the importance of representation, trial by jury, and the dangers of a standing army.[80] In this sense, their historical perspective remained similar to the Declaration of Independence, which, after a decade of sustained discussion about the history of the colonies to contextualize the political moment, sought instead to focus primarily on the most recent past.

Anti-federalists wrote little about the seventeenth-century colonial past, certainly relative to their opponents. They used history in their writings primarily to support their arguments about the potential dangers of the Constitution. Without thinking synthetically about the colonial past, the anti-federalists did not produce any competing national historical narrative that incorporated the colonial past. The vacuum they left increased the visibility and power of the historical cultural productions produced by cultural nationalists who effectively constructed the first national historical narrative largely unopposed. This dynamic began to change after the turn of the century as both parties increasingly adopted historical cultural production as a tool of party politics. In the 1780s and 1790s, however, cultural nationalists wrote histories for the nation, not for parties, though in doing so they inevitably conferred legitimacy on the party in power and buttressed its authority.

That, however, is not to suggest that the anti-federalist perspective did not affect, or at least reflect, a part of Americans' historical understanding. In the early republic, independence and union—as interrelated historical and contemporary political themes—served to counter the realization by Americans that, as anti-federalists had argued, they had effectively traded one distant, centralized government for another. Similarly, the conservative interpretation of the Revolution in which those themes played a major role also sought to justify the perception that, while the persons in power were different, much seemingly had not changed from before the Revolution. Americans in the 1780s and 1790s were being taxed more heavily by their state governments than they ever had been by Parliament, leading to a number of popular rebellions. Many also felt those state governments—and, later, the new federal government wrought by the Constitution—had a similar ability to act as arbitrarily and without potential redress as Parliament had before independence.

The leaders of the Revolution—now proper state and federal officeholders—sought to quell these notions. By the 1780s and 1790s, men who had been the most radical of patriots during the imperial crisis were making arguments to their fellow citizens about the need to acquiesce to the authority of the state and federal governments. These arguments were often remarkably similar to those made by loyalists in defense of Parliament in the 1760s and 1770s. Responding to such discontent, Samuel Adams, organizer of Boston's Sons of Liberty and perhaps the most radical member of the Continental Congress, wrote to fellow cultural nationalist Noah Webster: "It is prudent for the People to keep a watchful Eye over the Conduct of all those who are entrusted with publick Affairs. Such Attention is the Peoples great Security. But there is Decency & Respect due to Constitutional Authority, and those Men, who under any Pretence or by any Means whatever, would lessen the Weight of Government lawfully exercised, must be Enemies to our happy Revolution & the Common Liberty."[81]

As we have seen, historians too contributed to these efforts. By stressing Americans' long-standing independence, they sought to disavow radical responses to state and federal authority, particularly those drawing on revolutionary rhetoric. They also sought to minimize Americans' expectations that the Revolution would bring about further popular innovations. Of course, Americans on the ground forged such innovations themselves, in part by electing non-elites to local and state offices and passing state-level legislation benefiting debtors at the expense of creditors. The theme of unity and union sought to bind together not only Americans from different states but also Americans of different classes, especially in the wake of popular innovations that were decidedly unpopular among the post-revolutionary ruling elite.

That these historical cultural productions and their themes simultaneously attempted such progressive goals as forging a more broadly shared national identity while conservatively quelling dissent and proto-class conflict is not a contradiction or a reflection of hypocrisy or disingenuousness. Rather, they reflect the complex interrelationship between history and politics and between politics and culture in the uncertain moment of the early republic. Ultimately, historical cultural production, like the politics and culture of the period itself, sought to reconcile those two impulses in a time of political instability exacerbated by groups who wanted primarily to create something new and other groups who wanted primarily to preserve something old. Resolving those two shared though conflicting impulses has ever since been one of the fundamental challenges of American politics and culture.

Put simply, contemporary politics shaped the cultural nationalists' historical memory of the colonial past, while, in turn, they hoped that memory would help shape contemporary politics. They excluded slavery from national histories hoping that would exclude it from the national political debate, partly because it contradicted the fundamental character of the story they were telling about themselves. Ultimately, reimagining the colonial past to look like the present in the decades following the war reframed both the causes and consequences of the Revolution by minimizing the degree of fundamental change it had wrought and highlighting continuities between the colonial past and post-revolutionary present. These new perspectives on the use of history and the relationship between the past and present were definitive features of the history culture of the early republic. The impulse to read the past through the lens of the present served the interrelated cultural and political goals of cultural nationalists, namely establishing cultural independence from Britain by creating a national culture for the new nation and buttressing the legitimacy of the new government and its political authority and institutions.

This historical memory of the colonial past and its place in the national historical narrative is perhaps most clearly crystallized and explicated in Ramsay's *A Map, Historical and Biographical Chart of the United States,* published in 1810, and its accompanying pamphlet, *A Chronological Table of the Principal Events which have taken place in the English Colonies Now United States, from 1607, till 1810* (1811). Building on recent developments in historical and biographical chart making, the chart offered a geographical map, a chronological timeline, a biographical timeline, and, at the bottom, a succinct summary of the nation's history to that point. Both the map and the historical timeline were strikingly color coded, the painting done by Ramsay's daughters, though Ramsay did sell a number of uncolored copies. The pamphlet included a chronology intended to give details about the timelines, even though Ramsay claimed the chart "scarcely needs any other explanation than is given on its face."

Drawing on the shared colonial past developed during the imperial crisis, the timeline shows colonies enjoying "free government" throughout the seventeenth century until the Glorious Revolution, which established parliamentary supremacy. This remnant of colonists' reconsideration of the British past during the imperial crisis remained crucial to the narrative of the new national history. After the colonies declared independence, Ramsay wrote, "Men from the plough, the shop, and the counter, animated with the inspiration of liberty, became soldiers, and led on by Washington under the smiles of heaven, successfully contended with the veteran armies of Britain till her rulers acknowledged the Colonies to be Independent States." The chart and its accompanying text tell the story of a Revolution that had restored the first principles of "free government." That is, the independence and unity that the colonial settlers had supposedly enjoyed before the Glorious Revolution and parliamentary supremacy had been restored by independence. Intended for "popular use," particularly in schools, Ramsay's chart codified the historical memory of the colonial past as fashioned and propagated over the previous decades by Ramsay and his fellow cultural nationalists in a variety of political writings and historical cultural productions. Moreover, it served as a visual representation of how that historical memory of the colonial past fit into cultural nationalists' broader national historical narrative.

The challenges faced by the historians and other characters in this chapter were not theirs alone. Rather, they reflected the challenges that faced citizens of the new republic more broadly. American identities had been cast into flux during the imperial crisis. Changing understandings of both the colonial and British pasts called into question the historical foundation of those identities. Following the end of the war, developing a national identity to replace their previous colonial and imperial identities became increasingly necessary for Americans, for both political and cultural reasons. As Americans themselves tried to figure out who they were as citizens of a new nation created seemingly out of thin air, historians and other intellectuals were engaged in the same process. Their major contribution to that process was the creation of a national history. For them, the new Americans were to be defined by their entire past, not just the revolutionary past of the previous eight years. During the imperial crisis, colonists began to see themselves as different, both culturally and politically, from their fellow native-born subjects. That sense continued to develop after the Revolution, turning Britain into a political and cultural Other against whom these new Americans could define themselves.

Ultimately, this new historical memory of the colonial past revealed a number of cultural fissures in the postwar decades beyond the issue of national identity. Political independence had not dissolved completely the cultural bands that had connected America with Britain. In the tenuous cultural moment of postwar America, those remaining bands proved problematic. Americans had not completely lost their Britishness over the course of the war, and the new nation could not live in political, economic, or cultural isolation from the former mother country. Britishness remained visible in parts of the culture of the early republic and parts of the structure of its politics. These bands could not be cut completely right away, but they could be loosened a bit. The creation of a historical memory of the colonial past that minimized the role and impact of Britain tried to do just that. In part, it was an attempt to mediate the uncomfortable continuity of Britishness in the early republic and to negotiate the terms of the relationship going forward, a relationship between equally independent nations rather than that of a parent and a child who had recently reached maturity. Cultural nationalists also understood that developing a sense of cultural independence from Britain would help foster a national identity, which, in turn, could also help Americans negotiate their conflicted relationships with each other. To that end, they constructed a shared past that they hoped citizens of the new nation could recognize and hold in kind, one that stressed their historical independence from Britain and their internal unity. Finally, this new historical memory of the colonial past is significant because it reveals one of the ways in which Americans sought to reconcile the paradox of a progressive Revolution produced by a decidedly conservative impulse. By getting Americans to accept the conservative narrative of the relationship between the colonial past and the Revolution defined by independence, unity, and minimal change, cultural nationalists hoped to promote a more conservative impulse in contemporary politics after the war. In the 1780s and 1790s, Americans came to view their colonial past through the lens of the present, and, rather than reject it, they sought to use that colonial past to shape an independent though uncertain present. But a new colonial past alone was not enough; they would also need an even deeper past.

CHAPTER SIX

CREATING A DEEP PAST FOR A NEW NATION

Establishing a sense of historical and cultural independence from Britain after the war required more than reimagining the colonial past through the lens of the politics of the 1780s and 1790s. Cultural nationalists in the decades following the war also began creating a shared "deep national past," one that went beyond the new nation's primarily British colonial origins.[1] The historian Benedict Anderson has argued, "If nation-states are widely conceded to be 'new' and 'historical,' the nations to which they give political expression always loom out of an immemorial past."[2] The new United States, however, had no time immemorial. More recently, Don Doyle and Mario Pamplona have explained this distinguishing feature of New World nationalism: "The pluralism as well as the newness of American nations undermined any attempt to envision the nation along the lines of the European paradigm as a people bound and distinguished by common descent, a deep collective past, or homogenous cultural traditions." "As former colonial settler societies," they argued, "the new American nation-states had to stake their claim to independence on grievances and interests rather than on ethno-nationalist ideas of primordial differences with the mother country or myths of some previous common history as a nation."[3] Anderson, too, had previously noted this distinction in the American context, pointing out that the "Declaration of Independence of 1776" was not "in any way 'historical,' in the sense of highlighting the antiquity of the American people."[4] The loyalist lawyer George Chalmers noted the same at the very start of his history of colonial British America published in 1779, arguing, "Of these colonies it cannot be asserted, as it is of European nations, that their origin is uncertain or unknown [or] that their ancient history is fabulous and dark."[5]

Yet, when one looks at the cultural production in this period, we find that, at the same time that the colonial past was being reimagined, historians, poets, dramatists, essayists, and institutions were also effectively creating a sense of a "deep past" for the new nation, an American "time immemorial," both primordial and mythic. This American antiquity, or deep national past, was both a product of and contribution to the new nation's need to define itself culturally in non-British terms. In early national history culture, that process of definition included the creation of a deep national past that transcended the nation's British imperial origins altogether.[6]

Through exploring a few seemingly disparate efforts that contributed to the creation of a deep national past, we can develop a sense of the scope of the variety of cultural contexts in which it was created. First, Columbus's tercentenary in 1792—celebrated through public festivities, the erection of monuments, poems, orations, pamphlets, and newspaper coverage throughout the nation—marked a pivotal moment through which Columbus became accepted as the "discoverer of America" and, therefore, the beginning of the new republic's national historical narrative. Second, historical cultural productions of all kinds adopted the symbolism of "Columbia" as an allegorical and gendered personification of the new nation that simultaneously referenced the national past as well as the national future. Historical and epic poetry and renderings of the national past in a biblical style helped contribute a mythical and epic character to the new republic's deep national past. Finally, the nationalization of the continent's natural history and the indigenous past after the Revolution gave Americans a tangible connection to a past deep enough to be wholly independent of Britain. While those engaged in these efforts were not coordinating explicitly with one another to specifically manufacture individual parts of a deep national past, they were all driven by the same nationalist, historical, political, and cultural impulses and contexts. So while many of these efforts have been studied by scholars on their own, considering them together within the context of early national history culture reveals their contributions to a historical memory of a deep national past that could provide a crucial additional context for the new nation's origins.

These contributions to the creation of a sense of a deep national past were unavoidably influenced by the unique circumstances in which the nation found itself following the war. The postcolonial society of the early republic produced a historical memory of the deep national past that incorporated both anti-colonial and settler colonial perspectives and practices. At the same time that Americans sought to distance themselves from the history of British imperialism, they employed distinctly colonial practices in crafting their new national history as well as in their political and diplomatic relationships with Native Americans. We can see this in cultural nationalists' attempts not to "erase" the histories of Native Americans (as many historians in the nineteenth century would do) so much as appropriate their indigenous pasts into serving as an important part of the foundation for a new national identity that would distinguish Americans from the British. Looking at this deep national past constructed within the history culture of the early republic reveals the unreconciled tension between the anti-colonial rhetoric that defined the recent revolution and this decidedly colonial approach to the process of creating a new national history. Generations of subsequent Americans have tried to reconcile the nation's anti-colonial, revolutionary origins with the settler colonial expansionism and slavery that followed. In many ways, this tension between rhetoric and reality, whether acknowledged or dismissed, has shaped how Americans have thought about national identity and "American history" ever since.

At the time of independence, Christopher Columbus was not yet canonized as the discoverer of America. Though historians often quote Samuel Sewall's insistence in 1697 on calling America "Columbina, from the magnanimous heroe Christopher Columbus," it was only in the 1770s and 1780s that the Italian explorer began to figure prominently in the American historical imagination. Before the Revolution, another Italian, John Cabot, held a higher pride of place among early explorers in the colonies, primarily because he had sailed under commission from England, unlike Columbus who had sailed for the Castilian monarchs. A popular educational text published the year before the tercentenary, Noah Webster's *The Little Reader's Assistant* (1791), began with "The Story of Columbus." The story stressed his mistreatment at the hands of a European monarchy and analogized that experience with the revolutionary generation of Americans. It concluded the tale by saying, "Let every child in America learn to speak the praises of the great Columbus."[7] Columbus's lack of connections to England made him a much more useful discoverer of America for those trying to express historical independence from Britain, even though he never actually set foot on the North American continent.[8] Celebrating the Columbian tercentenary less than a decade after the end of the war contributed to the creation of a deep national past by codifying an origins story for the new American republic that transcended British (though not European) imperialism.[9]

The fall of 1792 witnessed loosely coordinated celebrations marking Columbus's tercentenary from Boston to South Carolina. The commemorations began on August 3 when the Chevalier d'Anemours erected "the Corner-stone of an *Obelisk*" at his "Country Seat" outside Baltimore, as reported in the *Columbian Centinel.*[10] He followed that up on October 12 by affixing "suitable inscriptions, on Metal Tables" to the monument. In New York City, the recently formed Tammany Society, or Columbian Order (a name that combined Columbus with that of a native Delaware chief), also erected a monument in the shape of an obelisk as part of a broader slate of festivities.[11] The fourteen-foot obelisk depicted the landing of Columbus on one side "in a state of adoration; his followers prostrate as supplicants around him, and a group of American natives at a distance." The second side showed his triumphant reception in Spain upon his return. A third side, drawn from Joel Barlow's epic poem, *The Vision of Columbus* (1787), showed Columbus in his prison cell in chains with "The Ingratitude of Kings" scrawled on the wall. The fourth side simply read: "Sacred to the Memory of Christopher Columbus, the Discoverer of a New World, October 12, 1492." The *New-York Journal* assured its readers that the depictions on the monument represented "historical truth."[12]

In Boston, the recently established Massachusetts Historical Society organized a day of festivities to mark the event on October 23. Advertised weeks in advance, the civic events—attended by John Hancock, Samuel Adams, and other prominent political figures—included a procession, a dinner, and the society's first sponsored public lecture. The speaker was Jeremy Belknap, a driving force behind the establishment of the institution and early national history culture generally. Soon after, he published his oration in pamphlet form. In it, he focused on a passage from Daniel 12:4 AV: "Many shall run to and fro and knowledge shall be increased." Belknap saw this prophecy fulfilled not only in the apostles' spreading knowledge of the gospel but also in the westward movement of science, commerce, and knowledge. In his masterwork about the rise of the arts and sciences, *The Great Instauration* (1620), Francis Bacon had famously included the passage on the frontispiece underneath an image of ships sailing off into the Atlantic Ocean. The idea of progress moving westward across the Atlantic was an article of faith among cultural nationalists. Belknap celebrated both Columbus and the United States for playing a pivotal role in this westward march of enlightenment. In doing so, he effectively intertwined the historical identity of the new nation with this broader world-historical process.[13] These public festivities celebrating Columbus gave a historical dimension to popular participation in shaping the politics of nationalism by offering citizens the chance to participate in the construction and celebration of a past that went beyond the more common festivities commemorating the recent revolution.[14]

In addition to being a valuable subject of educational texts and popular festivities, Columbus was also used as a nationalist symbol in historical fiction. *Reuben and Rachel; or Tales of Old Times* (1798) was the final novel by Susannah Rowson, "the first bestselling novelist in America" and one of the most widely read authors of the 1790s and 1800s.[15] Especially popular with young women, her novel told the tale of the fictionalized familial descendants of Christopher Columbus, recounting his voyages to the New World in the process. In her preface she wrote, "When I first started the idea of writing '*Tales of Old Times,*' it was with a fervent wish to awaken in the minds of my young readers, a curiosity that might lead them to the attentive perusal of history in general, but more especially the history of their native country." The novel concludes with the main character offering a paean to the "young country, where the only distinction between man and man should be made by virtue, genius and education." "Our sons are true-born Americans, and while they strive to make that title respectable, we wish them to possess no other." Similarly, later on, though rooted in "historic research" in Spanish archives, Washington Irving's three-volume *A History of the Life and Voyages of Christopher Columbus* (1828) was effectively a work of historical fiction.[16] Although he began the research with the intent of merely translating into English an edited collection of primary sources, Irving, the first great satirist of the American past, quickly realized that "the subject was of so interesting and national a kind" that writing his own version of the history of Columbus would be "a more acceptable work to my country, than the translation I had contemplated."[17] Works such as these reinforced the relationship between Columbus and national identity established by the tercentenary commemorations.

During the quincentenary, historian Thomas J. Schelereth argued that Columbus's legacy through the nineteenth century had gone through three phases between the late eighteenth and late nineteenth centuries: from the feminine "Columbia," idyll of republican motherhood; to the masculine Columbus, patron saint of westward expansion and Manifest Destiny; and, finally, Columbianism, which incorporated recent immigrants into accepted American forms of patriotism.[18] These usages tied present developments to future glory. Yet, an important part of the symbolism of Columbus in the decades immediately following the war lay in its historical connotation and the way it linked the present to the past. His symbolic utility ran deeper than symbolizing republican motherhood or a justification for westward expansion. In the decades following the War for Independence, Columbus became a highly meaningful national cultural symbol of the new republic's origins, one that not only transcended British imperialism but also placed the establishment of the nation within a larger historical process that understood the progress of mankind as inexorably moving westward, thereby also affirming Americans' notions of the importance of the new republic to the world.

This historical memory of the deep national past included mythical and epic elements in which Columbus also figured, primarily in the feminine personification of America as "Columbia."[19] In the 1780s and 1790s, the term became more commonplace, and its rhetorical power grew, providing a symbolic counterpart to Britain's own ancient personifications, Britannia (the Greco-Roman name for the British Isles) and Albion (the Greek name for England specifically). With its ancient pretensions, "Columbia" provided cultural nationalists with a powerful symbolic tool to help foster a sense of national identity distinct from that of Britain.

The use of that personification by Americans began during the imperial crisis, most notably in the poem "To His Excellency George Washington" (1775) written by Phillis Wheatley.[20] Enslaved by a family of the same name in Boston, she had achieved an unusual degree of notoriety in the British Empire due to the publication of her *Poems on Various Subjects, Religious and Moral* (1773). After she sent her poem to George Washington, the southern slaveholding general replied in a letter in which he thanked her for the poem, invited her to visit with him at Cambridge, and signed himself as "your Obed[ien]t and Humble Servant." Wheatley was subsequently emancipated but died a few years later at the age of thirty-one in 1784. Her poem provided one of the first and most high profile uses of "Columbia" as a mythical personification of both America and the Goddess of Liberty; it was the writing of a former slave more than anything else that contributed to and helped define its subsequent usage and prominence in American poetry. Wheatley's role in the adoption of "Columbia" as a national symbol is an early example of the tension between the rhetoric of political anti-colonialism and the reality of cultural colonialism at the heart of the early national project of establishing a new national identity.

"Columbia" quickly became a pervasive and effective device in the literary cultural production of this period, particularly in poetry and drama. Many of the most famous prospect poems predicting inevitable future national glory used it. David Humphreys mentioned "Columbia" in the first few lines of a number of his most popular prospect poems from the 1780s.[21] Through his work and that of others, the use of "Columbia" in the opening lines of a poem became a definitive marker in the poetry of this period. It was intended to set a tone from the beginning and speak to both the independent present and the glorious future where America would serve as a light to the world. In a common usage, Humphreys's "A Poem, on the Happiness of America" (1786) contained the couplet: "Then wake, Columbia! daughter of the skies, / Awake to glory and to greatness rise!" Yet, it also implied an important connection between the past and that glorious future. Although Humphreys and others used "Columbia" to look to that future, her figure was simultaneously rooted in the deep national past through its inherent and inseparable connection with the Columbian origin story. Therefore, the connotations of "Columbia" as both a symbol of the past and the sign of a glorious future were inherently bound. In this way, the use of "Columbia" served as a secularized and nationalized form of the "city on a hill" allegory.

In addition to the past and the future, "Columbia" also carried symbolic value in the present. While a number of Americans rued that "Columbia" should have been the rightful name of the new nation, it nevertheless came to mark the landscape through place-naming. During the imperial crisis and the war, King's College in New York City had served as the educational home of many New York loyalists. Within a few months of the end of British occupation in November 1783, the city and state undertook the reorganization of the college. On February 19, 1784, James Duane brought a bill to the state assembly "for establishing a University within this State." As a member of the college's board, he also submitted a petition from the board to the assembly asking permission to alter the original charter. Because the college had been originally chartered by the king as a de facto Anglican seminary, an "Alteration of th[e] Charter" was necessary. After extended debate, on April 16, 1784, the assembly declared "King's College, be forever hereafter called and known by the Name of Columbia College."[22] In so doing, New York literally removed the king from the city's landscape and replaced him with a feminine symbol of the deep national past.

Just over seven years later, the new nation established its first permanent capital. President Washington tasked a committee of three commissioners—Daniel Carroll, Thomas Johnson, and David Stuart—with naming the ten-square-mile federal district in which the new national capital sat. While naming the new city after Washington was a fait accompli, it was almost as widely assumed that "Columbia" would figure in some way. The committee suggested the name "Columbia" at a meeting with Pierre L'Enfant, the designer of the city, and Secretary of State Thomas Jefferson on September 8, 1791. The following day, the commissioners wrote to L'Enfant saying, "We have agreed that the federal District shall be called 'The Territory of Columbia.'"[23] The discussion within the committee for choosing the name took less than a day, forever embedding in the new republic's capital the developing mythos of its deep past.

The use of "Columbia" and "Columbus," as well as local Native American–derived terms, as place names for towns, counties, and rivers throughout the country further inscribed the deep past on the landscape of the new nation. In many cases, the appropriation of indigenous words for place-naming represented a form of rhetorical violence that reflected in the history culture the actual violence the new nation was bringing to bear in its efforts to physically displace Native Americans. The deep past was also alluded to in the development of international trade, as the *Columbia* was the first American ship to circumnavigate the globe, thereby opening trade between Boston, the Northwest coast, and Canton.[24] Additionally, it was inscribed on the cultural landscape of the new nation through its use in naming a variety of cultural expressions, including voluntary associations, such as the "Tammany Society or Columbian Order," and periodical publications, such as the *Columbian Centinel, Columbian Magazine,* and the *Columbian Kalendar.*

In November 1791, one thousand Native Americans dealt a crushing defeat to a larger contingent of the new United States Army in the Northwest Territory near Fort Washington. The defeat of Major General Arthur St. Clair's forces by a confederated contingent of Miami, Shawnee, and other tribes shocked the country as news of it circulated quickly.[25] It was soon followed by a broadside that named the defeat "the Columbian Tragedy." The broadside, complete with a description of the events and "a funeral elegy," described the battle as "perhaps the most shocking that has happened in America since its first discovery."[26] The elegy concludes by telling readers that ultimately God will help shield the Americans ("*Columbia's Sons*") and "destroy" the Indians "tho' thousands against us rise." The Columbian symbolism here not only defined the defeat as a tragedy for the new nation personified but also contextualized it within the broader perspective of the deep national past and divinely justified the righteousness of the continuing westward march, begun by Columbus himself, that marked that new nation's origins.

We can see how Columbia symbolically bound the past, present, and future visually in *America Guided by Wisdom* (1815), a drawing by John Barralett. The left side of the allegorical scene depicts a rural home outside which a woman works a spinning wheel. In the middle of the scene, the ocean is filled with ships, recalling settlement. On the right side of the scene, a large equestrian statue of George Washington stands before a neoclassical building reminiscent of the Capitol. In the foreground, Columbia, a feminine personification of America, holds a shield engraved with the words "union and independence." At her feet lies a cornucopia symbolizing the plenty and prosperity that lies in the nation's future. In addition to symbolizing the nation's past, present, and future, the drawing also visually combines the historical memories of the deep past and the colonial past by highlighting the themes of independence and unity on Columbia's shield.

Ultimately, inscribing Columbus and "Columbia" on both the cultural and physical landscapes—particularly in reorganizing a prominent college in an important city, both with checkered ideological pasts, and in defining the new federal seat of authority—show not only its symbolic power but also the impact of the deep past in shaping and defining both the present and future in the early republic. It also shows the increasingly malleable interrelationship between the past, present, and future in early national history culture. Put simply, the name of "Columbia" lent the historical weight of antiquity to a new nation, symbolically binding the present and the future with the deep past.

This bond between the past, present, and future in Columbian symbolism is perhaps most evident in the epic poetry of Joel Barlow. Born in Connecticut in 1754, Barlow graduated from Yale during the war and went on to various professions, including publishing, the law, politics, and diplomatic service. Despite his various adventures (and misadventures) both at home and abroad, he is best remembered for his epic poem *The Vision of Columbus* (1787) and its later, more secularized revision, *The Columbiad* (1807). The poem began with the scene depicted on the Tammany Society's monument in which Columbus, the new American hero, is visited by an angel while languishing in a Spanish prison cell. The visitor's purpose was to present the downtrodden Columbus a vision "in order to satisfy his benevolent mind, by unfolding to him the importance of his discoveries, in their extensive influence upon the interest and happiness of mankind, in the progress of society."[27] That vision was a history of Europe and the New World that began with the mythical origins of natives, covered the discovery and settlement of America, and, ultimately, culminated with the Revolution.

In book V of the poem, Columbus is shown a vision of the future imperial struggles over the world he discovered, including a disturbed darkness overtaking the land of "my brave children" at the end of the Seven Years' War. But he is assured that his children—the Americans—will rise "to change the source of power."[28] Subsequently, the figures of Washington, Adams, Franklin, and other political and military leaders are revealed, and Columbus is shown scenes from the Revolution beginning with Bunker Hill. The rest of books V and VI narrated the war, and books VII and VIII addressed the cultural progress of the new nation and the obstacles yet standing in its way. The poem ends with book IX, wherein the vision concludes with a "general council of all nations assembled to establish the political harmony of mankind." Barlow's *Vision of Columbus* was half historical poem and half prospect poem. It wove together a progressive, linear narrative in which the independent present and glorious future could hardly be understood without the historical context of the deep national past that helped to create that present and future. That is, America in the 1780s and 1790s was presented as the result of historical forces deeper than that of British imperialism alone (though still not deeper than *European* imperialism).

Of course, the most familiar epic with which Americans were familiar was the Bible, and cultural nationalists used that familiarity to their advantage. Timothy Dwight, along with Joel Barlow, David Humphreys, and John Trumbull, was part of a group of cultural nationalist poets and writers known as the "Connecticut Wits."[29] Dwight served as a chaplain in the Continental Army and, later, as president of Yale College, but he is also remembered for his poetic works. His most important was the epic poem, *The Conquest of Canäan* (1785).[30] This first American epic recounts the biblical tale of Joshua and the Israelites. And though Dwight claimed in the preface that he had "chose[n] a subject, in which his countrymen had no national interest," the dedication of the poem on the previous page to "George Washington, Esquire" meant that the poem was read as a biblical allegory of the Revolution, with Joshua playing the role of George Washington.

The history of the Revolution itself was explicitly "biblicized," that is, rendered in a style that directly imitated the Bible. The historian Perry Miller once aptly described the Bible in early America as "the air that people breathed." It was, for early Americans, "as familiar as their own backyards."[31] Works that adopted the biblical form and style were, according to a recent historian, published "at such a rate that attempts to assess them all are futile and pointless."[32] The first notable biblicization of the Revolution was published serially before independence. John Leacock, a Philadelphia silversmith and merchant, wrote and published six chapters of *The First Book of the American Chronicles of the Times* (1775) as individual pamphlets in serial format with sequential pagination so they could be collected and bound.[33] His narrative began in 1773 with the Boston Tea Party and concluded with the "Olive Branch Petition" sent to the king in the summer of 1775. Leacock's *American Chronicles of the Times* was unusually popular. It was published in dozens of imprints in every major city in the colonies and advertised regularly in newspapers by booksellers throughout the colonies.[34] It was also excerpted in newspapers, with the *Virginia Gazette* serializing the entirety of the work between January and June of 1775.[35] Indeed, the first two installments were published on the front page of consecutive issues. Leacock subsequently published a play on the eve of independence, entitled *The Fall of British Tyranny, or, American Liberty Triumphant* (1776).[36]

Perhaps the most popular work in this genre after the war was Richard Snowden's two-volume *The American Revolution; Written in the Style of Ancient History* (1793). Snowden's work, according to Eran Shalev, represents "the pinnacle in the history of the tradition of writing in biblical style."[37] His biblicized narrative of the Revolution—beginning with the Tea Act—mimicked the style and form of the Old Testament, replete with chapter and verse numbers. Moreover, Snowden wrote as though he was addressing an ancient audience, using King James–style language and offering vague and purposefully ignorant descriptions of modern inventions and ideas. He referred to individuals by their first name (as though they had no surname) and used biblical-sounding names for places and things, referring to London as "Lud," and Parliament as "the Sanhedrin." Snowden adopted the biblical style, he wrote, "for its conciseness and simplicity" and because it was "the most suitable to the capacities of young people."[38] Historical biblicist writings, particularly those rendering the American past, were "a distinctly novel American cultural production" dedicated to translating the past into a style with which many Americans were intimately familiar while also imparting to that past a sense of awe similar to that inherent in readers' perceptions of the biblical past.[39]

These works are noteworthy for being emblematic of the liminal historiographical moment in which early national history culture developed. Toward the end of the eighteenth century, historical writing was neither fully secularized nor wholly devoid of providence.[40] Works like Snowden's biblicized history of the Revolution, his poem entitled *The Columbiad, or, a Poem on the American War, in Thirteen Cantoes* (1795), Dwight's *Conquest of Canäan* and his *America, or, a Poem on the Settlement of the British Colonies*, as well as works by numerous others translated American history into the language and context of an epic past deeper even than that of Columbus yet still instantly recognizable to many Americans.[41] The epic and ancient qualities embodied within these historical cultural productions were not just recognizable, they were inherently appealing to citizens of a new republic attempting something often identified with the ancient republics, particularly Rome.

The symbolic use of Columbus, "Columbia," and epic and biblical allegories of the historical past served two primary functions within the history culture of the early republic. First, like the historical memory of the colonial past, they fostered a sense of historical distance from the former mother country by contributing to a deep national past that transcended the British Empire. Second, the deep national past to which they contributed offered the new nation a culturally manufactured past that could be shared by the nation in kind, much like the shared colonial past created during the imperial crisis had done. Commemorative festivities that took place and were reported throughout the colonies, the nationwide use of "Columbia" in place-naming, and the allegorical nationalization of literary forms only recently produced by Americans all contributed to the creation of a sense of a deep national past with which citizens of a new republic could identify. Yet, the deep national past consisted of more than the abstractions of origins, myths, and epics. It also encompassed the land itself.

Perhaps the most important aspect of the creation of a historical memory of a deep national past was the nationalization of the natural history of the continent.[42] Alexis de Tocqueville drew on these historical memories of the colonial past and deep past when he concluded that the nature of the "origin of the American settlements" and the "boundless continent" were the "principal circumstances" that contributed to the establishment of the United States as a democratic republic.[43] The importance of natural history and the continent itself was embedded in the origins of American national identity by the cultural nationalists of the 1780s and 1790s. But they were contesting some long-held ideas about the natural history of the continent. In 1766, the French naturalist Georges-Louis Leclerc, Comte de Buffon published the fifth volume of his *Histoire naturelle, générale et particu-*

lière, in which he described the landscape of North America and its animal inhabitants as "degenerated" compared to their European counterparts. Because of the colder, wetter, and more humid climate of North America, Buffon reasoned, animals in the New World were smaller and weaker than those found in the Old World.[44]

Buffon's theory was not merely biological but historical. The continent, he argued, was immature, having risen above the ocean much later than that of the Old World. This immaturity was reflected, in Buffon's mind, in the historical behavior of its human inhabitants that resulted in the lack of development of civilization and culture. Native Americans had "neither stopped the torrents, nor directed the rivers, nor drained the marshes." Buffon's historical argument about the effects of the continent's environment on its native inhabitants was extended polemically to the present and its current inhabitants by other European writers. Abbé de Raynal and Corneille de Pauw tied environmental and cultural inferiority together. They argued that the degenerated landscape produced natives (including those of European descent) with "no vivacity, no activity of mind."[45] In 1770, Raynal argued that this explained why "America has not yet produced one good poet, one able mathematician, one man of genius in a single art or a single science."[46]

The debate gained wider attention when it was featured in William Robertson's highly popular *History of America* (1777), which was reprinted in the United States, excerpted in many newspapers and magazines, and serialized *in its entirety* in Isaiah Thomas's newspaper, the *Massachusetts Spy,* in eighty-two consecutive installments over seventeen months in 1784–45.[47] The degeneracy theory, which had become quite popular in Europe, denied the possibility of cultural nationalists' ultimate goal of creating a substantive American culture and threatened to render the Revolution—as a giant leap forward in the westward progress of mankind—moot.

In the decades following the war, natural history became an increasingly important part of American cultural production. Essays on innumerable topics related to natural history appeared in newspapers and magazines in the 1780s and 1790s, with many devoting regular columns to the topic. Prospect and pastoral poems were a literary rebuttal of the degeneracy argument, turning the New World environment from a natural hindrance to a cultural benefit. Poems such as Dwight's *Greenfield Hill* served as a defiant celebration of the gentility of the American environment brought about by the triumphal conquering of Native Americans during the Pequot Wars. Joel Barlow's epic poem, *The Vision of Columbus,* began with a 450-line stanza devoted to a lyrical evocation of the natural history of the continent. In terms of historical writing, colonial histories had described the immediate environment in no small part to stress the value of the colonies' natural resources to the empire. After the Revolution, however, natural history took on greater visibility and significance in nationalist historical writing and cultural production, more generally.[48]

To directly refute the degeneracy theory, most general histories of the United States devoted significant portions of their work to detailing the natural history of the new nation, including its original inhabitants.[49] State histories did so at length and with particularity. For example, Jeremy Belknap devoted the entire third and final volume of his *History of New-Hampshire* (1794) to essays on the natural history of the state, including one that directly rebutted Buffon's claims about the New World environment.[50] Thomas Jefferson devoted a chapter of his *Notes on the State of Virginia* to detailing the state's animal life, also refuting Buffon by name.[51] Samuel Williams, in *The Natural and Civil History of Vermont* (1794), devoted the first eight chapters of his work to detailing the natural history of his state, also responding to Buffon, Mably, and De Pauw directly.[52] Historical works from this period that did not address natural history at some length were the exception not the rule. The degree to which American newspapers regularly excerpted the parts of these works dealing directly with Buffon, Raynal, and De Pauw suggests a corresponding degree of public interest in the debate.

Nationalist sentiment fueled this desire to prove Buffon wrong (and, on the part of readers, to see him proven wrong). This context helped to politicize and nationalize natural history, giving it a greater cultural urgency in the context of a new republic attempting to define itself in opposition to Britain and Europe.[53] After the Revolution, the former connection between natural history and "civil history" became a more inseparable connection between natural and national history. The new historical memory of the colonial past had served as a way of trying to bind together the North and South. Likewise, focusing on the natural history of the continent incorporated the frontier into the national historical memory, thereby fostering attempts to bind together the East and West, a relationship that was in many ways driven by similar degrees of ignorance, suspicion, and animus as that of North and South.[54] This new interrelationship between the natural history of the continent and the historical past of the nation can be seen, in part, by looking at the rise of the nation's first natural history museum and the growing importance of the continent's original inhabitants in historical cultural productions.

The nation's first natural history museums, like the establishment of historical societies, contributed to the institutionalization of history culture in the early republic.[55] These early museums were efforts to preserve the natural history of the new nation, thereby contributing to Americans' sense of a deep national past and the interrelationship between natural history and national history. Drawing on the Enlightenment form of the "curio cabinet," they turned that deep past into a form of enlightened, though albeit commercialized, entertainment. The Charleston Museum in South Carolina, founded in 1773, is generally considered the first American museum. Originally part of the Charleston Library Society, it collected items relative to the natural history of the Lowcountry. In Philadelphia, beginning in the late 1770s, the Swedish emigré and antiquarian extraordinaire Pierre Eugène du Simitière created the American Museum in his home on Fourth Street. There he displayed various natural specimens, his unprecedented collection of print ephemera dating back to the 1760s, and artifacts from the recent revolution.[56] But the nation's first truly successful museum was founded in postwar Philadelphia by the famed portrait painter (and network participant) Charles Willson Peale.

Between his service in the Continental Army, his travels, and his residence in Philadelphia, Peale made the acquaintance of many prominent military leaders and future politicians, for whom he painted many portraits, especially miniatures. Like many eighteenth-century artists, Peale kept a gallery in his home as a résumé of his work. In the fall of 1782, he opened his home gallery, featuring his many portraits of revolutionary heroes and a few nonextant historical-themed paintings, to the public.[57] In 1784, Peale was commissioned to do some naturalist drawings of some very large bones found in the Ohio Territory. A surprising degree of public interest in those drawings gave him the idea of establishing a natural history museum.[58]

In July 1786, Peale announced the opening of his museum in a newly built wing of his home.[59] The Peale Museum commercialized natural history as a form of entertainment, while serving as a model for future institutions. The museum developed methods of preservation and presentation that still inform modern practices. It also contained a noncirculating research library and sponsored lectures and other events aimed at the general public, with admission discounts for students and teachers. Peale sought to make his museum useful "to every class in our country" and able "to instruct the adult of each sex and age."[60] The museum was so successful that by 1791 he no longer needed to paint portraits for income and devoted himself to it full time. Moving the national capital temporarily to Philadelphia the following year further stoked the museum's growth, and in 1802 it was moved to the upper floor of the State House (now Independence Hall).

Peale's museum was most famous for its turn-of-the-century exhibit of an eleven-foot-tall skeleton of the long-rumored mastodon. Scattered bones and teeth had been found throughout the eighteenth century, particularly in the Ohio and Hudson valleys, but the search for "the vast Mahmot" intensified in the 1780s and 1790s becoming an obsession for naturalists and nationalists alike.[61] Peale, like his fellow naturalists, longed desperately to find a full skeleton. In 1799, John Masten, a farmer outside Newburgh, New York, found some bones on his property. After the news reached Philadelphia, Peale visited the Masten farm. By the time he got there, a good number of bones had been excavated, and others had been ruined when the local, amateur excavation turned into an alcohol-fueled party.

After eating lunch with Masten and his family, Peale offered two hundred dollars for the bones that had already been excavated. Masten slept on the offer. When Peale returned in the morning, Masten proposed a counteroffer: two hundred dollars *plus* a rifle for his son and an expensive gown from New York City for each of his daughters. Peale agreed. He then offered another hundred dollars for the right to excavate the property for more remains. Upon returning to Philadelphia, Peale secured an extra five-hundred-dollar loan from the American Philosophical Society to assemble and furnish a team to undertake the excavation in 1801. Peale hit pay dirt, literally, when he found an almost complete skeleton. The remains were excavated and transported to Philadelphia where, with great fanfare, the skeleton went on display at the Peale Museum.

Beyond its scientific import, the skeleton carried great nationalist significance.[62] The mastodon proved that the American continent had produced at least one species larger and more powerful than any ever found in Europe. A few years earlier, in 1796, the first elephant was brought from Asia to tour the United States. The broadside that publicized the events began by noting, "The Elephant, according to the account of the celebrated BUFFON, is the most respectable Animal in the world. In size he surpasses all other terrestrial creatures."[63] It also claimed that the four-year-old elephant "drinks all kinds of spiritous liquors; some days he has drank 30 bottles of porter, drawing the corks with his trunk." People in cities and towns throughout the country paid a quarter to see "the greatest natural curiosity ever presented to the curious" up close and in person. The elephant, however, paled in comparison to the discovery of the eleven-foot American mastodon by Masten and Peale. Americans had been rhetorically refuting Buffon for decades. By finally finding an animal larger than the one Buffon claimed to be the largest in the Old World, the discovery scientifically refuted the degeneracy argument. Its subsequent display in the museum, Peale's painting of the event, "Exhuming the First American Mastodon," and reporting by newspapers and magazines made sure that this tangible refutation of American degeneracy was known to the nation and to the rest of the world.

The Peale Museum's primary focus was natural history, but its collection of about three dozen portraits of revolutionary heroes and a number of busts was also an important part of the permanent exhibit. In "the Long Room," two horizontal rows of the portraits in ornate gold frames occupied the entire upper part of the left wall, with specimen cases underneath (figure 5). At the end of the hall, larger framed portraits formed a single row across the upper wall. On the right side stood numerous cabinets holding smaller specimens with busts of historical figures lined on top of them. Accompanying the portraits were short biographies. As the *Guide to the Philadelphia Museum* (1805) noted: "Their several names are in frames over each Portrait, yet there is a number which refers to a concise account of each person in small frames on the opposite cases."[64] Peale published two catalogues of the paintings (in 1795 and 1813) that included detailed biographical information on all of the subjects in the Long Room portraits, as well as those in other rooms of the museum.

The most common reading of the museum's exhibition design has seen it as a product of the Enlightenment.[65] The rise of natural philosophy and

FIG. 5. Charles Willson Peale, *The Artist in His Museum* (1822). Behind the curtain are gold-framed portraits of revolutionary figures, along the wall on the left, and the skeleton of the mastodon, on the right. Courtesy of the Pennsylvania Academy of the Fine Arts, Philadelphia. Gift of Mrs. Sarah Harrison (The Joseph Harrison, Jr. Collection).

natural history were fundamental components in the development of enlightened thought in the seventeenth and eighteenth centuries. One of the principal developments of Enlightenment natural philosophy was the development of taxonomy, particularly the system for classifying species created by the Swedish botanist Carl Linnaeus. First published in the Netherlands, his *Systema Naturae* (1735) laid out his classification scheme, which grew over the following decades as readers from all over the world sent him specimens. The Linnaean system reflected the Enlightenment ethos of discovering and ordering the natural world with humans at the top of the natural order. In this reading, the portraits, perched atop cabinets of animal specimens, served as examples of the human species and its place in the natural order, with the Revolution's heroes representing the most exemplary specimens of humankind.

Yet, the role of the portraits in the museum also speaks to the new interrelationship between natural and civic history, which became constituent parts of the new national history. In the museum's catalog, Peale wrote of "the tendency which a knowledge of Natural History has to promote National and Individual Happiness."[66] For visitors to the museum, the prominent placement of the revolutionary portraits and busts within the "Long Room" provided an immediate and meaningful visual connection between the revolutionary past, which established the nation, and its deep past through natural history. Peale often described himself as a "memorialist," someone who "painted the dead in the service of a future memory." As Charles Sellers, a Peale biographer, wrote, "He loved construction, the balancing of cause and effect, bringing together of elements into a harmonious whole." We can see the layout of the Long Room as making an argument about the relationship between the new nation's natural history and the recent revolution that created it. The Long Room provided both a tangible and aesthetic refutation of the degeneracy theory itself not just by showing individual animal specimens but by juxtaposing them with the portraits of exemplary individuals from the recent revolutionary past. In doing so, Peale visually integrated the new republic's natural and civic histories into a national history for a public audience.

Over the next two decades, museums that combined natural and civic history for nationalist purposes were established in multiple cities, including New York, Baltimore, Charleston, and Boston. For example, in 1791,

Daniel Bowen established the Columbian Museum in Boston, to which he directed the public with his somewhat complicated description of its location: "near the new court-house, and Stone Chapel, Tremont Street, and which is accessible from Court Street, through the New Avenue, and also from School Street, Boston."[67] Bowen's Columbian Museum held not only specimens of "A large White POLAR BEAR" and "the Great OX" but also a collection of paintings, prints, Native American artifacts, and "Large War-Figures," including "WASHINGTON, with a cherub," Benjamin Franklin, and the "GENIUS of AMERICA, weeping over a Bust of Washington."

The nation's first historical societies were also committed to the nationalization of natural history. Jeremy Belknap's original proposal for Massachusetts Historical Society stated its goal of collecting and preserving anything "which may elucidate the natural and political history of America from the earliest times to the present day."[68] Similarly, John Pintard devoted his New-York Historical Society to collecting objects "relate[d] to the natural, civil, literary and ecclesiastical history of the United States in general, and of this state in particular."[69] Isaiah Thomas, in describing the "intended objects" of the American Antiquarian Society, quoted William Jones of the Asiatic Society: "Man and Nature—whatever is, or has been performed by the one, or produced by the other."[70] As we saw in chapter 1, natural and "civil" history had been linked before the Revolution in colonial historical works, but the meaning of that connection took on both new and added significance in the context of a young nation engaged in creating its own national history. The museums that followed Peale, like the nation's first historical societies, further manifested the new nature of this interrelationship between natural and national history. In doing so, they made a significant contribution to both the historical memory of a deep national past and the institutionalization of history culture itself.

The presence of numerous Native American artifacts among Peale's exhibits, and in the ever-growing collections of antiquarians and societies, reflected a growing interest in this period in the history of the continent's original inhabitants. Recent postcolonial scholarship on the relationship between European Americans and Native Americans has focused on the process of "Othering," through which Americans defined themselves in opposition to Native Americans (as well as African Americans).[71] Recently, historians have asserted an "unusual cultural and political consensus among American intellectuals" that the Native American "represented a completely foreign culture" and "stood for savagery, the antithesis of civilization."[72] These intellectuals, it is argued, "constructed a naturalized savage Other, devoid of cultural complexity, integrity, and history, in order to define their own very different identity."[73] While these types of portrayals do indeed abound in the early republic, the historical cultural production of the 1780s and 1790s offers a more complicated picture.

Beginning with the "Act to regulate trade and intercourse with the Indian tribes" in 1790, the federal government initially adopted a diplomatic posture, seeking out and securing treaties with Native Americans that would ostensibly benefit both parties by managing trade and the disposition of lands between them.[74] Such policies gave the federal government oversight of those who sought to trade with Native Americans or purchase their land. In George Washington's third annual message in 1791, he declared, "It is sincerely to be desired that all need of coercion in future may cease and that an intimate intercourse may succeed, calculated to advance the happiness of the Indians and to attach them firmly to the United States." To achieve that, he went on, required an "impartial dispensation of justice" relating to "the mode of alienating their lands," which was "the main source of discontent and war," and to securing "equitable deportment" by those engaged in commerce with Native Americans. Subsequent acts throughout the 1790s and first decade of the nineteenth century continued these policies, including establishing government trading houses to regulate and monitor Americans' trade with Native Americans.[75] These policies, however, failed to achieve their oversight goals. Americans poured westward into Native territories, making it ever more difficult for the federal government to enforce these policies. Illicit commerce and shady land deals by Americans seeking to steal Native lands abounded. These actions violated treaties between Native tribes and the federal government, leading to increasing political and military hostilities. In his third annual message, Washington stated clearly that the goal of these policies was not just to mediate Native Americans' interactions with settlers but to "impart to them the blessings of civilization." That is, federal policy—both official and unofficial—sought to impose acculturation upon the indigenous population by forcing them to give up not only their land but also their culture and traditions, which for Native Americans provided a deep connection to their ancestors and their historical past.

Disrupting Native Americans' relationship to their own past was an important part of the federal government's endgame of securing their lands for white settlers. In a letter to William Henry Harrison in 1804, President Thomas Jefferson described the unofficial policy of seeing "good and influential individuals among them run in debt, because we observe that when these debts get beyond what the individuals can pay, they become willing to lop them off by a cession of lands." Jefferson went on, "In this way our settlements will gradually circumscribe and approach the Indians, and they will in time either incorporate with us as citizens of the United States, or remove beyond the Mississippi. The former is certainly the termination of their history most happy for themselves." In closing, Jefferson suggested that it was "improper for the Indians to understand" this policy because "for their interests and their tranquility, it is best they should see only the present age of their history."[76] In other words, Jefferson and others knew that the surest way of disrupting Native American communities and cultures was by separating them from their past. At the same time that Jefferson was encouraging Joel Barlow to write a new Republican history of the United States, he was also seeking "the termination of [Native Americans'] history." He preferred that Native Americans "see only the present age of their history" because he understood the inherent and political power of a historical narrative, whether for the new United States or the historical traditions of Indigenous Peoples.[77] By trying to deny Native Americans their own shared past, Jefferson and the federal government sought to make it harder for them to reproduce their group identities, thereby making it harder for them to resist assimilation, acculturation, and annihilation.

Rather than ignoring the Native American past, American writers, especially historians, appropriated it to serve as a crucial part of the deep national past. As a result, these writers often appeared to be defending the abstract or idyllic Native American from the literary attacks of Europeans. As one French natural history writer noted in 1804, "[Americans] make it their favorite business to combat European writers. They act as if they were the advocates and avengers of their predecessors, the Indians."[78] Yet, their interest was fundamentally utilitarian, driven, in part, by the nationalist goals of refuting the degeneracy theory and providing cultural cover for federal policies. Ultimately, early nationalist historical cultural productions did not deny Native Americans' "cultural complexity, integrity, and history" so much as they tried to appropriate them for their own political, cultural, and historical purposes.[79] In the process, these writers employed a decidedly colonial approach in trying to work out their own postcolonial political and cultural circumstances.

Many histories, both state and general, provided highly detailed portraits of Native Americans, some delving into Native customs and traditions in great detail and many offering forthright defenses of the Native American. In *A General History of the United States* (1810), Benjamin Trumbull noted: "The Indians have been represented by some writers, as the most sordid and contemptible part of the human species; as the very ruins and dregs of mankind. However, in justice to their character, it ought to be observed, that on the first arrival of the English, both in Virginia and New-England, they treated them with great kindness."[80] Similarly, in his *History of New-Hampshire*, Jeremy Belknap reflected on the negative impact settlement had on Native Americans and imagined that they could have lived together peacefully if only the European settlers had treated them better. He wrote, "However fond we may have been of accusing the Indians of treachery and infidelity, it must be confessed that the example was first set them by the Europeans. Had we always treated them with that justice and humanity which our religion inculcates, and our true interest at all times required, we might have lived in as much harmony with them, as with any other people on the globe."[81]

These types of treatments of Native Americans were common in most histories, state and general, from this period, so much so that those without them are aberrations. Yet, they tended to focus on either the Native American in the abstract or those who lived before and at the time of European settlement. Much as early national Peruvian historians used the Incas to create "an antiquity for Creole America," American historical writers used an abstract idyll of the original inhabitants for the nationalist ends of connecting the new nation to the deeper history of the continent on which it stood.[82] As for the descendants of the original indigenous inhabitants, such accounts often ended with calls to "communicate to them, the blessings of civilization, liberty, and Christianity," which served as the official language of the federal government's policies of removal.[83]

The history of Native Americans appeared in other forms of historical cultural production, for example, as small or excerpted histories in newspapers and magazines, often under the heading, "Natural History."[84] In a letter to Ezra Stiles published in the *American Magazine,* Noah Webster wrote of "the striking Analogy between certain Customs of the Indians and ancient Britons" to minimize the differences and accentuate similarities between white Americans and historical Native Americans. Other works made similar seemingly favorable comparisons between Indigenous and various ancient peoples.[85] In 1792, Jeremy Belknap arranged for the publication of the *Historical Collections of the Indians in New England,* an unpublished account written by Daniel Gookin in the 1670s of "their several nations, numbers, customs, manners, religion, and government, before the English planted there." In addition, Native Americans were a regular topic in the earliest volumes of the published *Collections* of the historical societies of Massachusetts and New York. When Belknap was compiling his *American Biography,* Ebenezer Hazard suggested, "Could any thing certain be collected respecting any of the Indians, it will be worth inserting," though he acknowledged that it "w[ould] be difficult to get such anecdotes of them as may be depended on."[86]

A lack of primary sources however did not keep writers of fiction and drama from using the indigenous past. In spring 1808, James Barker's play *The Indian Princess* premiered at the Chestnut Street Theatre in Philadelphia. Based on the life of Pocahontas, Barker's play was the first dramatic attempt to culturally incorporate her into the national historical narrative. It was also perhaps the first play about Native Americans written by an American. Barker's play told the tale of the founding of Jamestown, the relationship between Pocahontas and John Rolfe, his capture, and her rescuing of him from Powhatan, concluding with a very grand, very ahistorical speech by Rolfe predicting the greatness of the future nation. Interestingly, Barker divided his characters into two categories with the settlers called "Europeans" and the Native Americans called "Virginians."

The play's premiere was ignominious and its fate ironic considering it depicted the story of a strong female heroine; the audience's outrage at the effeminacy of one of the male actors forced the curtain to close early. Nevertheless, the play went on to be performed throughout the country, including in New York, Baltimore, and Alexandria. It was also one of the first plays by an American staged in London, though it was heavily adapted for the British audience. In subsequent decades, more dramas and literary works featuring Native Americans followed, including James Fenimore Cooper's *The Last of the Mohicans* (1826). The inclusion of Native Americans in historical cultural productions, particularly the first national biographical dictionary and popular plays, reflects some of the ways in which cultural nationalists sought to use Native Americans as cultural symbols in the new national historical narrative, at a time when the federal government, which their work sought to support, was engaged in the politics of removing Native Americans from that land.

This effort to incorporate contact-era Native Americans in the deep national past derived, in part, from the cultural need to defend the continent against the degeneracy theory. Arguing against their own degeneration required white Americans to "defend" Native Americans, who inhabited the same land, from those charges. At the same time, some historians continued to portray Native Americans as part of the wild American environment that was tamed by colonists. And, of course, colonial wars with Native American enemies figured prominently in regional and state histories, particularly those of New England. Beginning with the end of the period covered by this work, American historians would increasingly erase Native Americans from national and regional histories.[87] Yet, in the unique political, cultural, and intellectual contexts of the postwar period, the historical nationalism of the first generation of American historians gave them reasons to appropriate and incorporate contact-era Native Americans and their history into the deep national past.[88] Rather than being "blinded" to the history of Native Americans, early national historians saw it, took it, and crafted it into a usable past for their own nationalist purposes.

The interest in recovering the early history of Native Americans (and, hence, the continent) can be seen in the efforts of Thomas Jefferson and the American Philosophical Society. In *Notes on the State of Virginia,* Jefferson discussed the need to research, catalogue, and preserve Native American languages.[89] Around this time, he printed a blank form for collecting vocabularies of Native dialects containing approximately 282 English words with space for their Native equivalents.[90] Others took up his call, and Jefferson engaged in much correspondence with natural history enthusiasts who sent him vocabularies they had collected.[91] Like many others, he believed comparative studies of Native dialects with those spoken in Asia would allow him "to discover what resemblances actually do subsist between the American languages and those of Northern-Asia."[92] This, Jefferson hoped, would lead to proof of the long-standing theory that Native Americans had migrated to the New World from the Far East over the Bering Straits. Along with many others throughout the country, he tried to use language as a key to unlocking the deepest past of Native Americans and, by extension, the continent.[93] Proof of the Bering Strait theory would contradict indigenous historical traditions that claimed that Native peoples inhabited the continent since the beginning of time. Moreover, in cataloguing information about the Native American past, they were simultaneously attempting to preserve a part of the natural history of the new nation, not least because their own policies were designed to destroy the peoples who spoke those languages.

As was clear in his revolutionary pamphlet, *A Summary View of the Rights of British America,* Jefferson had long subscribed to the Anglo-Saxon myth that claimed that the inhabitants of England had enjoyed liberty and representative government until the Norman Invasion of 1066. Although the myth had no basis in historical truth, it was a powerful historical memory in England and for American colonists in the eighteenth century. This myth of purity corrupted was used to bolster the authority of Parliament (which it claimed existed in a different form before 1066) over the Crown (which was analogized to the invaders who brought monarchy to England). In the postcolonial moment of the 1780s and 1790s, however, an American version of this prelapsarian myth was developed. The interest of Jefferson and many others in the abstract Native Americans of the distant past was very much about using them as the basis of an Anglo-Saxon-like historical narrative stressing the deep historical origins of the new nation's republicanism and liberty. Cultural nationalists' efforts to humanize and, in a sense, deracialize the abstract historical Native Americans so they could be included in the national history had the implicit result of hyper-racializing contemporary African American slaves and further justified the latter's exclusion from the first national historical narratives. As a result, in the early nineteenth century slaves would replace Native Americans as the primary domestic enemies in state and regional narratives as slave revolts became more feared in the present than attacks from Native Americans.

The historical interest in Native American dialects culminated in 1815 when the American Philosophical Society, which until then had been a primarily scientific institution, established a Historical and Literary Committee for the express purpose of studying Native American languages and history. One of the main published products of the committee was John Heckewelder's *An Account of the History, Manners, and Customs of the Indian Nations* (1819). Heckewelder, a German Moravian missionary, emigrated as a young boy with his father in 1734 to Bethlehem, Pennsylvania. He subsequently spent decades as a missionary among Native Americans in the Ohio Country before and during the war. In the 1790s, he aided the federal government in negotiating treaties with those Native tribes with which he was familiar. In 1810, he moved back to Bethlehem permanently and dedicated the remainder of his life to assisting the American Philosophical Society's Historical and Literary Committee.

Heckewelder drew on the large amount of knowledge he gained while living among the Native Americans. During that time, in addition to creating "a dictionary of the Mohawk language in MSS," he actively collected oral histories from the Native Americans, including stories of their ancestors' first encounters with Europeans.[94] The first four chapters of Heckewelder's work recounted these stories, forming what he called the "historical tradition of the Indians."[95] He wrote, "There are men among them, who have by heart the whole history of what took place between the whites and the Indians, since the former first came into their country; and relate the whole with ease and with an eloquence not to be imitated. On the tablets of their memories they preserve this record for posterity."[96] Heckewelder recounted those histories as best he could in extended form. Despite the inherent problems of perspective and translation, he approached the task sympathetically, detailing Indigenous Peoples' oral traditions of European contact and their subsequent forced removal by the settlers.

Tocqueville must have been unaware of Heckewelder's efforts when, two decades later, he wrote, "The Indians of our day cannot give any information about the history of that unknown people. Nor did those who lived three hundred years ago, at the discovery of America, say anything from which one can even infer an hypothesis. Traditions, those perishable and constantly re-emergent monuments of a primitive world, furnish no light."[97] This is clearly an assumption from ignorance on his part, but it is an ignorance Jefferson and the federal government tried to create. It seems likely that many Americans less educated than Tocqueville would have held a similar idea. Such a belief reinforced a sense by white Americans that Native Americans lacked the ability or interest to preserve their own past. Early settlers had justified taking the Native Americans' land by the "use theory"—that is, because they were not "improving" the land (according to European standards) they had no claim to it and could be legally dispossessed. Likewise, the early national generation appears to have used similar reasoning regarding the past, implicitly if not explicitly. As with Native land, white Americans believed that because Native Americans did not preserve their own pasts, it meant those pasts could be claimed and Indigenous Peoples dispossessed of them. Because one of the defining features of civilization was a relationship to the past, this notion was yet another marker of the impossibility of "civilizing" and incorporating Native Americans into the national polity. Such a perception likely allowed many Americans to justify to themselves their own support for federal policies of removal and confiscation.

Unsurprisingly, the memories that Heckewelder recorded were anything but flattering to the Europeans, whom Native Americans generally remembered as dishonest and wantonly violent. "Long and dismal," Heckewelder began, "are the complaints which the Indians make of European ingratitude and injustice." Like the accounts from historians in the 1780s and 1790s above, Native American memories—described by Heckewelder as "bitter, but too just reflections"—stressed the initial kindness and generous disposition of their ancestors toward the European visitors who repaid them by forcing them off their land and setting tribes against one another.[98] Incorporating contact-era Native Americans into the deep national past required confronting these stubborn historical facts and the connections between them and the present.

Cultural nationalists did this by stressing that the settlers who perpetrated the original offenses against the Native Americans were not "Americans" (as they understood that term after the Revolution) but transplanted Europeans, who were corrupted like the Old World from which they had come. American historians and other writers created critical renderings of the initial settlers' treatment of the native inhabitants and, more generally, of the initial imperial ventures of European powers in the New World, without implicating the contemporary Americans who made up their target audience. Such intellectual dissonance was initially made possible temporarily by a combination of faith in the morality of the federal policy of "civilizing" Native Americans and creative historical interpretation.

For example, David Ramsay's *History of the American Revolution* began with a highly critical account of the origins of European settlement. In it he argued, "No European prince could derive a title to the soil from discovery, because that can give a right only to lands and things which either have never been owned or possessed." Going even further, Ramsay wrote, "The right of the Indian nations to the soil in their possession was founded in nature. It was the free and liberal gift of Heaven to them, and such as no foreigner could rightfully annul."[99] To dispossess them, he argued, European sovereigns created "a new law of nations," which resulted in them having "sported with the rights of unoffending nations."[100] With such language, Ramsay and others were drawing historical analogies between the experiences of both the Native Americans of the early seventeenth century and the Americans of the eighteenth century. Both were "unoffending nations" whose societies had been impinged upon and had their "rights" threatened by imperial European powers. Clearly, there were times when early national Americans' connections to the original settlers were celebrated and other times when they were denied based largely on political and cultural utility as they sought to find ways to reconcile their past with the present.

Analogies between contact-era Native Americans and the Americans of the 1780s and 1790s extended to the earliest forms of Native American governance and society. For example, in his *Natural and Civil History of Vermont* (1794), Samuel Williams spent nearly 100 pages detailing the customs and history of the "original inhabitants" of the state. When Williams wrote of "the *tendency* and *effect*" of a certain government being "equality, freedom, and independence," he was speaking of the "savage government" of the original inhabitants. That is, Williams drew a clear analogy (using a shared terminology) between pre-contact Native American governance and the new federal government.[101] Similarly, John Lendrum used the first 120 pages of his compiled work, *A Concise and Impartial History of the American*

Revolution, to detail Native culture, explicitly refuting specific arguments made by Buffon and De Pauw. Lendrum wrote, "Liberty, therefore, is the prevailing passion of the [Native] Americans; and their government under the influence of this sentiment" puts them "pretty much upon an equality."[102]

Both the depth of treatment and analogous renderings of contact-era Native Americans in Ramsay, Williams, Lendrum, Trumbull, Belknap, and others were a common feature of the treatment of natural history in both state and general histories in this period. Like the historical move of arts and science westward, these works implied that the displacement and contemporary treatment of Native Americans was the result of broader, long-term historical forces. By implicitly historicizing displacement in this way, these writers avoided directly implicating either the federal government or the large portion of their audience that supported its policies of removal and confiscation. Moreover, these analogies mutually reinforced the growing propensity in this period to use Indigenous women as visual personifications of America, in addition to that of Columbia. Such depictions symbolically emasculated Native Americans and reduced their past to the mere prologue of the nation.

These analogies were also found in historical discourse, generally. In 1812, John Pintard invited Gouverneur Morris to deliver a discourse before the recently established New-York Historical Society on "our history from the year 1763 to the year 1783." Despite being asked to talk about the American Revolution specifically, Morris began his discourse like many historical works of the period, that is, by describing the natural history of New York, including its original inhabitants. Also, as with most historical works, such description served as the foundation of his subsequent argument. "We, gentlemen, grew out of this same ground with our Indian predecessors," he said. "Have we not some traits to mark our common origin?" "Let us see then," he continued, "whether some other characteristic of the aborigines may not open us to a view of ourselves, and the perspective of our country." Morris continued on drawing parallels between Native cultural development and that of the new nation: "The Mohawks had not, like the Romans, naturalized those whom they subdued. It was a federal nation, a federal government, a people as free as the air they breathed; acute, dextrous, eloquent, subtle, brave." "The most strongly marked, perhaps, of their moral features," he continued, "was a high sense of personal independence." "The soul of this nation cannot be subdued," he intoned. Morris made the connection plain: "Neither will those who tread the soil in which the Mohawks are entombed submit to be slaves." Of course, the colonial settlers had been the ones who had "entombed" the Mohawks, but inconvenient facts, like the absence of slavery in the historical memory of the colonial past, were—and often continue to be—suppressed in the service of creating a past usable in fostering group identity.

The impetus behind the intertwining of the character of the nation with that of both its original inhabitants and the continent was noted in the conclusion of his discourse: "It is by the lights of history and geography that we discern the interest of a country, and the means by which they can best be pursued and secured."[103] This linking of "history and geography" had its roots in the historical writing of the colonial period but took on a new, decidedly nationalistic purpose in the early republic. The existence of supposed similarities in such fundamental ideas about governance, society, and character embedded first principles in the land, thereby detaching them from their British origins much as the turn to natural law rhetoric during the imperial crisis detached patriot ideas from the British constitution. This perspective was echoed over a decade later when Daniel Webster, in commemorating the anniversary of the Battle of Bunker Hill, intoned, "The *Principle* of Free Governments adheres to the American soil. It is bedded in it, immovable as its mountains."[104]

For the purposes of cultural nationalists intent on appropriating Native Americans into the deep national past, these seemingly historical parallels were highly useful. They drew analogies between contemporary Americans and the contact-era Native Americans, who, in these renderings, shared similar ideals of governance and saw imperial Europe as a common enemy. In his *Discourse,* Morris noted that "our Dutch ancestors" had defeated the Spanish Empire before coming to the New World where "they entered into treaty with the natives; in whom they found patience, fortitude, and a love of liberty like their own."[105] In doing so, cultural nationalists like Morris argued that the first principles of independence, self-government, and unity through federalism were such fundamentally American ideas that they were embedded in the nation's landscape and the land's pre-imperial past. Such a narrative shows the interrelationship between the deep national past and the new historical memory of the colonial past and how ideas from one reinforced the other.

But these efforts to incorporate historical Native Americans into the national past while absolving contemporary Americans of their own treatment of Indigenous Peoples did not go uncontested. In a piece from the *National Gazette* reprinted in local newspapers in the early 1790s, a writer recounted a dream in which he was standing on a dock when "the fine Indian Head of the ship Delaware . . . assumed the mien and attitude of an orator."[106] "With a menacing frown," the carved Indian Head spoke to the white men gathered there. He began by noting the traits the new Americans had appropriated through its image. "I have every reason to believe, gentlemen, that I was placed here as the emblem of valour, activity, perseverance, industry and cunning." Yet he immediately pointed out the contradiction between these abstract renderings of the Native American and their actual treatment by white Americans: "Alas, it is too evident from their actions, that they place us upon a footing with the beasts of the wilderness."

After rehearsing a history of Natives' treatment at the time of settlement, the "Indian Head" then turned to the more recent revolutionary past, pointing out the contradictions between the Americans' revolutionary rhetoric and their treatment of Native Americans: "You detest us for having the feelings of men; you despise, in us, the virtue of patriotism, so natural to all mankind, and so extolled by yourselves. But what were your feelings when, only a few years ago, the great king on the other side of the water intruded upon your rights? You filled the world with your clamors—heaven and earth were called to witness, that you were determined to defend those rights which had been bestowed upon you by the Great Man above. . . . You yourselves are now, in your turn, become the oppressors. Do not blame us then for possessing the same feelings with yourselves on the same occasion. Your desperation carried all before it, and why would not ours do the same, when we are obliged to act against you from the same motives." He concluded by calling out the Americans for "propagat[ing] a principle as disgraceful to your pretended age of philosophy, as it is repugnant to truth and reason, that the rights of an Indian, are not the rights of a man!"

In offering a historical perspective on Native Americans' situation in early national America, this piece used a number of conventions common in early national history culture. First, it truncated the historical distance between past and present by referring to and tying together the distant past of early settlement with that of the more recent revolution. It did so to point out both the devastating effects of settlement and the contradictory nature of the American Revolution and the interrelationship between the two (and, hence, between the past and the present). These pasts, according to the Head, could only culminate in the inevitable result of "an end to the children of the forest" and their "probable extirpation from the continent of America." The piece used a long historical perspective to chastise Americans for attempting to absolve themselves of the historical treatment of Native Americans by pointing out that their own treatment was merely a continuation of such. Finally, by saying that Americans had now "become the oppressors," the piece offers its own analogy from an indigenous perspective to counter the appropriative analogies made by cultural nationalists.

When we consider the common treatment of Native Americans in colonial histories of New England solely as enemies-at-war and their erasure from regional histories in the nineteenth century, the appropriation of their past for incorporation into the national history detailed here in the years between the end of the war and the 1810s appears to be an aberration. Anthropological literature on "settler colonialism," however, has described a phenomenon known as "imperialist nostalgia," in which "colonizing agencies often celebrate native society as it was before they came and destroyed it." Indeed, as one scholar has argued, "Colonialism does not appropriate a historical indigeneity; it replaces it with a conveniently mythical one of its own construction."[107] Such a description fits the context of the treatment of Native Americans in the historical cultural production of the early republic. Cultural nationalists constructed an indigenous past for the new nation that absolved its citizens of the historical actions of their ancestors while, at the same time, it justified the continuance, in the new national context, of the settler colonialism that would continue to define the nation's imperial continental ambitions throughout the nineteenth century. Much as the new United States fought an anti-colonial rebellion only to begin forging its own empire across the rest of the continent, these cultural nationalists adopted common colonial cultural practices in trying to navigate postcolonial circumstances, just as the state and federal governments did in the spheres of politics and policy.

In the specific context of the early republic, the abstract Native Americans of the past proved useful to cultural nationalists in constructing a deep national past for a number of reasons, particularly to defend themselves against Buffon's degeneracy theory and to draw analogies between the experiences of contact-era Natives and eighteenth-century Americans. Hence, they intertwined Americans' historical and national connections to the land and bolstered their own non-British past. Taken together, American writers found interest in and stressed real and imagined commonalities with the abstract Native Americans of the past as part of their efforts to effectively turn Britain into a cultural Other, thereby contributing to a sense of cultural independence from the former mother country.[108] Of course, they did this while actual living contemporary Native Americans were the targets of both land-hungry Americans moving westward and a new federal government seeking to "civilize" and displace Native tribes. Such a situation reflected one of the fundamental contradictions in the emergence of the idea of "American history": the coexistence of the anti-colonial rhetoric of the Revolution and the political and cultural settler colonialism of the early republic. The tension between rhetoric and reality created by that contradiction would remain a permanent feature of the republic's national history and identity.

The degeneracy theory required Americans to consider, defend, and nationalize their deep past, and they did so vigorously through literary, scientific, and institutional means. The goal of the museums and the refutations of Buffon were part of a broader effort to increase knowledge of and pride in the nation's natural history among its citizens. This historical memory of the deep past made the history of the land itself part of the national history. Ultimately, the adoption and symbolic use of Columbus, "Columbia," biblicism, natural history, and Native Americans in historical and literary works, as well as the establishment of such institutions as museums and philosophical societies, buttressed the independence theme of the reimagined colonial past by providing the young republic with a deep national past that transcended Britain and Europe entirely. To do so, however, required treating the history of Native Americans as colonially as the early settlers had treated their ancestors and much as the state and federal governments were treating them contemporaneously. Much as the expansion and growth of the United States rested in part on the appropriation of indigenous lands, so too did the idea of "American history" and development of American national identity rest in part on the appropriation of indigenous pasts. Through celebrating the discovery of the continent, writing of it in mythical and epic terms, and nationalizing its natural history, Americans created their own time immemorial by appropriating the pasts of others and crafting their own, with both endeavors divorced from historical reality but nonetheless useful in the project of forging national identity in the new republic.

EPILOGUE

America's pre-revolutionary past did not pass into obscurity after the Revolution. Rather, it became even more important, developing a significant salience and resonance in American culture long after independence and the war. As unique as their situation was in the decades after the war, Americans understood there were things to be learned from their shared colonial past. More importantly, they understood that their colonial past could actually aid in helping to shape their republican present. Not only did the colonial past matter but they went even further by creating a deep national past that was instructive as well as entertaining, running through the very first examples of American fiction, poetry, drama, and cultural institutions. As the beginnings of American nationalism developed in these decades, the collective memory of Americans was shaped by their construction of the colonial past. Long after the Revolution there remained deep, abiding cultural continuities between the colonial period and the early republic, of which the past was one. Close study of history culture and these historical memories of the pre-revolutionary past in particular reveal those continuities and show some of the ways in which they were negotiated. Such study offers new insights into how early national America perceived and managed its cultural relationship with the past, and how that relationship affected the politics of the period.

The Revolution opened up a future of seemingly limitless possibility to white Americans, but navigating the transition from subject to citizen significantly increased the importance of the past as it took on new cultural and political meaning in the early republic. During the colonial period, colonists knew who they were. They were British subjects, with all the historical and cultural baggage attached to that civic identity. But beginning with the imperial crisis, as that identity first came under question and then was ultimately discarded, the past became a critical part of the process of forging a new civic identity. Ultimately, the Revolution, and the uncertainty it wrought in its wake, reoriented the cultural relationship between the past and the present.

The past acquired a greater cultural importance in the early republic due to the political and cultural circumstances created by the Revolution. Indeed, Americans' relationship to the past in this period changed significantly. Before the Revolution colonists had used the British past to understand their colonial present. That is, they generally looked at the present through the lens of the past. British history, tradition, and custom had shaped their imperial identities. The relatively recent British past of the seventeenth century also shaped their political cultures. But the imperial crisis began a reconsideration of their relationship to the British past and the construction of a newly shared colonial past, which became even more important after independence had been secured. In the early republic, Americans increasingly began looking at the past through the lens of the present. They used the present to shape the past and used the past to shape the present, each informing and shaping the other. This complex reciprocity, lacking in colonial history culture, defined the new cultural relationship between the past and present in the early republic.

Because of its cultural and political nature, however, inclusion and incorporation into the national history was limited to those with access to the cultural and political spheres of American life in these decades. Unsurprisingly, African Americans—and slavery for that matter—were largely nonexistent in the national historical narratives of the 1780s and 1790s. Northern historians generally did not see either African Americans or slavery as having played a major part in the new nation's history. Meanwhile, southern historians sought to actively minimize the role of slavery in both regional and national historical narratives. The differently biased perspectives of both northerners and southerners gave each a reason to exclude slavery from the national history. In the decades that followed, African Americans would begin to construct their own narratives, but this minimization contributed to a historical sense organized more around their own communities and families than the nation itself. In contrast, Native Americans saw their pre-contact indigenous pasts appropriated and incorporated into the national history. Yet, from the point of settlement on in the historical narrative, their primary role remained that of the enemy Other in various colonial wars. In the subsequent antebellum period, Native Americans would be actively erased from the developing regional historical memories, particularly in New England.

Meanwhile, from the 1780s onward, women increasingly began to figure in history culture as producers and consumers of historical cultural productions. They would not feature as characters in the national history itself, however, until the work of Elizabeth Ellet in the late 1840s. The women who wrote histories and participated in the informal historical network clearly understood the decidedly masculine nature of both early national history culture and the national histories it produced, and they often wrote their histories to conform to contemporary masculine ideas and conventions of history and historical writing. In doing so, female historians such as Mercy Otis Warren and Hannah Adams had among the strongest authorial voices of any writers in this period and were held up as role models to young women studying in the many new female academies established after the Revolution. But as historical societies and museums were created to preserve the past and present, the voices of women who did not produce textual artifacts (or material artifacts deemed to be worthy of interest, as Native Americans did) were largely excluded from the archive. The constructed nature of and choices made by the institutions and archives that historians have relied on for generations down to the present day to tell the story of American history has had long-term consequences in obscuring the histories of groups not represented in those archives. Inevitably, these historical memories created in the early republic reflected the iniquities of the society that produced them, but their effects continued to be felt long after that society changed.

Because of the unique historical context of the 1780s through the 1800s, there may be no period when a national historical narrative mattered more. Immediately following the Revolution, there was a distinct void in terms of national history. The urgency surrounding the need to create a national history that distinguished Americans from Britons can be seen partly in the fact that in constructing a historical memory of the deep national past cultural nationalists identified Americans with a Catholic discoverer and Native Americans, two groups that were long-standing political and cultural enemies of Anglophone America. Cultural nationalists identified and discussed that void within the public sphere as a cultural and political problem requiring a solution. The absence of and need for a coherent national history was acutely felt throughout American culture, thereby contributing to the development of a national history culture in the early republic and of historical memories that lived well beyond the time in which they were created.

Ultimately, it is not too much of a stretch to say that the revolutionary generation—and the cultural nationalists of the early republic, in particular—created the idea of "American history," partly by being the first to define it. As a result, they set the temporal and spatial terms on which Americans for many generations to come would understand American history. It is easy to assume that perceiving American history as consisting of the combined colonial histories of the thirteen mainland colonies that eventually became the first states was a fait accompli, something so obvious it could have been no other way. But that was not the case. In the 1780s and 1790s, what American history would be and what it would mean was a completely open question. Through their works, the cultural nationalists of the revolutionary era created a historical grammar for the new nation, and the ways in which they defined American history both chronologically and geographically formed a foundation that succeeding generations have both inherited and taken for granted. Moreover, the narrative they created would have a much longer cultural life than their actual works.

The narrative of George Bancroft—the most widely read and respected American historian of the nineteenth century—is not fundamentally different than that created by the cultural nationalists decades earlier. A pious man, he introduced an ecumenical providence into his narrative. Bancroft saw God as a primary, intervening force in the linear progress from Old

World monarchy to New World constitutional democracy that defined American history. In doing so, he turned the narrative from one of declension and redemption into a linear story of progress and triumph. But while his framing may have been different, he adhered to the chronology and geography established in the first national historical narrative created during the early republic. The temporal and spatial boundaries erected around "American history" to define it in the first place are still in place in the way many schoolchildren are introduced to American history. Moreover, as late as just a decade ago, historian Pauline Maier wrote about the continuing challenge for current academic historians of addressing the "disjunction" between colonial and early national history. Indeed, it is only in the last few decades that historians developed Atlantic, transnational, and, most recently, continental perspectives on the United States' pre-revolutionary past to challenge those boundaries. As times continue to change, so do historical perspectives, with historians now viewing the narrative created specifically to help de-Anglicize the new nation in the 1780s and 1790s as requiring revision for being too Anglo-centric.

Nevertheless, much that went into crafting the nation's first historical narrative and memories remains, for better and worse. Historians, antiquarians, and, ultimately, institutions engaged in a large-scale project of collecting, preserving, and publishing historical documents and artifacts relating to the nation's revolutionary, colonial, and deep pasts. Contemporary historians continue to draw on those sources and benefit from the work and support of those institutions, while also trying to address the iniquities and silences embedded in their archives. Also, the practice and ideology of historical writing in the early republic became recognizably more modern than that of the colonial era, and thereby set a foundation for subsequent American historical writing and practice. Indeed, modern academic historians are the direct descendants and beneficiaries, for better and worse, of the historians and antiquarians of the revolutionary generation.

In writing this book I set out to achieve three goals. First, and most broadly, to make a case for the importance of history culture as an analytical concept, particularly regarding early American history, in which the importance of the past has not always been fully appreciated. Second, to foreground the cultural origins and causes of the American Revolution by focusing on the role of history culture in the imperial crisis. Doing so does not obviate the need for the previous constitutional, ideological, and economic interpretations. Rather, in this book I offer an additional cultural dimension to our understanding of the nation's founding, of which history culture is just one part. Finally, in these chapters I have made the case for the importance of the past in the culture of the early republic and in the origins of American nationalism. In doing so, I have sought to show the continued relevance and impact of the pre-revolutionary period in the early republic, rather than seeing 1776 or 1787 as a clear dividing line for early Americans between the past and the future.

Most fundamentally, this book is the story of how Americans came to create the very idea of "American history" and how that idea was not a nineteenth-century result of the Revolution but a driving force behind it throughout the long revolutionary era. When the centenary of the landing of William III at Torbay came on November 5, 1788, it was widely commemorated in Britain, but in the United States it passed with relatively little notice. Most of that notice consisted of brief mentions in newspapers of how, in each of the preceding three centuries, the years ending "'88" were "remarkable for giving birth to the most important events: Spanish armada defeated in 1588. English revolution, 1688, Federal constitution ratified, 1788." Americans now not only had their own '88 but also referred to their recent revolution as "the glorious revolution." The British past they had once held as their own had come to be replaced by their revolutionary, colonial, and deep pasts, all of which formed the basis of the young republic's new national history. Indeed, while some contemporary political commentators decry the prevalence of "revisionist history" that challenges older understandings of American history, this book shows that the act of revising and reimagining the past was a key part of the founding of the nation.

History is fundamental to national identity. The United States and its history culture, however, are unusual because both were created not by the forces of "time immemorial" but, in part, by each other in response to specific events and developments due to documented cultural and political forces. In the early republic, cultural nationalists—including the new nation's foremost political and military leaders—understood from the start that a national history would be fundamental to the creation of an American national identity. That is, a national history would contribute to the process by which "the United States" would go from being a plural to a singular noun. American history since has, to some extent, corroborated their understanding. How the founding of the nation and its colonial past has been remembered has always played a fundamental role in American political life, helping define what it means to be an American at any given time. From the beginning, American national identity has been constantly developing, always changing, always being debated and contested, right down to the present. That process—so recognizable in our contemporary political culture of the early twenty-first century—began in the history culture of the pre-revolutionary period and helped shape the earliest decades of the new republic. In the end, the relationship between history culture and the American Revolution—between politics and memory in the revolutionary era—is simultaneously the story of the creation of the idea of "American history" itself, the origins of American national identity, and the debates over defining each, all of which redound to the present as part of all Americans' political and cultural inheritance, for better and worse.

NOTES

Prologue

1. Michael Kammen, *Mystic Chords of Memory: The Transformation of Tradition in American Culture* (New York, 1993), 5.

2. Jack P. Greene, *The Intellectual Construction of America: Exceptionalism and Identity from 1492 to 1800* (Chapel Hill, 1997), 163; Benedict Anderson, *Imagined Communities: Reflections on the Origin and Spread of Nationalism* (New York, 1991), 192.

3. Antonello Gerbi, *The Dispute of the New World: The History of a Polemic, 1750–1900* (Pittsburgh, 1973), 247.

4. Thomas Jefferson to John Adams, August 1, 1816, in *The Adams-Jefferson Letters: The Complete Correspondence between Thomas Jefferson and Abigail and John Adams* (Chapel Hill, 1988), 483–85.

5. See Matthew Shaw, *Time and the French Revolution: The Republican Calendar, 1789–Year XIV* (Woodbridge, 2011).

6. Ronald Grigor Suny, "Constructing Primordialism: Old Histories for New Nations," *Journal of Modern History* 73, no. 4 (2001): 863.

7. Anthony Kemp, *The Estrangement of the Past: A Study in the Origins of Modern Historical Consciousness* (New York, 1991), 106.

8. Joyce Appleby, Margaret C. Jacob, and Lynn Hunt, *Telling the Truth about History* (New York, 1995), 94.

9. Keya Ganguly, "Migrant Identities: Personal Memory and the Construction of Selfhood," *Cultural Studies* 6, no. 1 (1992): 29–30.

10. R. G. Collingwood, *The Idea of History* (1946; repr. New York, 1993), 247; Raphael Samuel, *Theatres of Memory* (London, 1996), 175–76.

11. Anderson, *Imagined Communities,* 11.

12. Don H. Doyle and Marco Antonio Pamplona, "Americanizing the Conversation on Nationalism," in *Nationalism in the New World,* ed. Don H. Doyle and Marco Antonio Pamplona (Athens, 2006), 5, 3.

13. David Waldstreicher, *In the Midst of Perpetual Fetes: The Making of American Nationalism, 1776–1820* (Chapel Hill, 1997), 51.

14. Jörn Rüsen, "Was ist Geschichtskultur? Überlegungen zu einer neuen Art, über Geschichte nachzudenken," in *Historische Faszination. Geschichtskultur heute* (Cologne, 1994), 5.

15. Fernando Sánchez Marcos, "Historical Culture," *Cultura Historica,* accessed July 10, 2016, http://www.culturahistorica.es/historical_culture.html.

16. For some of the theoretical works that have informed my thinking about collective memory, see Alon Confino, "Memory and the History of Mentalities," in *Cultural Memory Studies: An International and Interdisciplinary Handbook* (Berlin, 2008), 77–84; Confino, "Collective Memory and Cultural History: Problems of Method," *American Historical Review* 102, no. 5 (1997): 1386–1403; Jan Assmann and John Czaplicka, "Collective Memory and Cultural Identity," *New German Critique* 65 (1995): 125–33; Peter Burke, "History as Social Memory," in *Memory: History, Culture and the Mind* (New York, 1989), 97–114; *The Collective Memory Reader,* ed. Jeffrey K. Olick, Vered Vinitzky-Seroussi, and Daniel Levy (New York, 2011); Maurice Halbwachs, *On Collective Memory* (Chicago, 1992).

17. Assmann and Czaplicka, "Collective Memory and Cultural Identity," 128.

18. Confino, "Collective Memory and Cultural History," 1386–1403.

19. Ibid., 1387, 1388.

20. Confino, "Memory and the History of Mentalities," 81.

21. Alexis de Tocqueville, *Democracy in America,* ed. and trans. Harvey C. Mansfield and Delba Winthrop (Chicago, 2012), 267.

22. On the "attempt to create a national history that would justify the Revolution and develop a sense of nationhood," see Arthur H. Shaffer, *The Politics of History: Writing the History of the American Revolution, 1783–1815* (Chicago, 1975); Shaffer, *To Be an American: David Ramsay and the Making of the American Consciousness* (Charleston, 1991). On the "historical revolution" from providential to secular historical writing in this period, see Lester H. Cohen, *The Revolutionary Histories: Contemporary Narratives of the American Revolution* (Ithaca, 1980). On the transitions from local to national (and back to local) historical perspectives from settlement to the Civil War, see David Van Tassell, *Recording America's Past: An Interpretation of the Development of Historical Studies in America, 1607–1884* (Chicago, 1960).

23. Trevor H. Colbourn, *The Lamp of Experience: Whig History and the Intellectual Origins of the American Revolution* (Chapel Hill, 1965); Catherine L. Albanese, *Sons of the Fathers: The Civil Religion of the American Revolution* (Philadelphia, 1976); Brendan McConville, *The King's Three*

Faces: The Rise and Fall of Royal America, 1688–1776 (Chapel Hill, 2006), esp. chs. 3, 7, 9; Eric Nelson, *The Royalist Revolution: Monarchy and the American Founding* (Cambridge, 2014); Peter C. Messer, *Stories of Independence: Identity, Ideology, and History in Eighteenth-Century America* (DeKalb, 2005).

24. For the definitive works on republicanism in early America, see Bernard Bailyn, *The Ideological Origins of the American Revolution* (Cambridge, 1967); Gordon S. Wood, *The Creation of the American Republic, 1776–1787* (Chapel Hill, 1969); J. G. A. Pocock, *The Machiavellian Moment: Florentine Political Thought and the Atlantic Republican Tradition* (Princeton, 1975). Also, see Caroline Robbins, *The Eighteenth-Century Commonwealthman* (Cambridge, 1959). For historiographical analysis of this interpretation, see Daniel T. Rodgers, "Republicanism: The Career of a Concept," *Journal of American History* 79, no. 1 (1992): 11–38.

25. For the competing ideological interpretation that favored the importance of liberalism over republicanism, see Joyce Appleby, *Liberalism and Republicanism in the Historical Imagination* (Cambridge, 1992); Steven Dworetz, *The Unvarnished Doctrine: Locke, Liberalism, and the American Revolution* (Durham. 1990); Isaac Kramnick, *Republicanism and Bourgeois Radicalism: Political Ideology in Late Eighteenth-Century England and America* (Ithaca, 1990). Richard Ashcraft, *Revolutionary Politics and Locke's Two Treatises of Government* (Princeton, 1986). For influential earlier works that argued for the importance of Locke, see Louis Hartz, *The Liberal Tradition in America: An Interpretation of American Political Thought since the Revolution* (New York, 1955); Carl L. Becker, *The Declaration of Independence: A Study in the History of Political Ideas* (New York, 1942).

26. Jack P. Greene, *The Constitutional Origins of the American Revolution* (New York, 2011); Greene, *Peripheries and Center: Constitutional Development in the Extended Polities of the British Empire and the United States, 1607–1788* (Athens, 1986); John Phillip Reid, *Constitutional History of the American Revolution*, 4 vols. (Madison, 1986–93); Reid, *The Ancient Constitution and the Origins of Anglo-American Liberty* (DeKalb, 2005); Mary Sarah Bilder, *The Transatlantic Constitution: Colonial Legal Culture and the Empire* (Cambridge, 2004); Daniel J. Hulsebosch, *Constituting Empire: New York and the Transformation of Constitutionalism in the Atlantic World, 1664–1830* (Chapel Hill, 2005); Hulsebosch, "Imperia in Imperio: The Multiple Constitutions of Empire in New York, 1750–1777," *Law and History Review* 16, no. 2 (1998): 319–79; Barbara Black, "The Constitution of Empire: The Case for the Colonists," *University of Pennsylvania Law Review*, 124 (1976): 1157–211; Craig W. Yirush, *Settlers, Liberty, and Empire: The Roots of Early American Political Theory, 1675–1775* (New York, 2011).

27. Greene, *Constitutional Origins*, ix.

28. John Phillip Reid, *Constitutional History of the American Revolution*, abr. ed. (Madison, 1995), 4–5. For a similar reading, see H. T. Dickinson, "Britain's Imperial Sovereignty: The Ideological Case against the American Colonies," in *Britain and the American Revolution*, ed. H. T. Dickinson (London, 1988), 81.

29. For example, see Steven Pincus, *The Heart of the Declaration: The Founders' Case for an Activist Government* (New Haven, 2016); Allan J. Keuthe and Kenneth J. Andrien, *The Spanish Atlantic World in the Eighteenth Century: War and the Bourbon Reforms, 1713–1796* (Cambridge,

2014), 231–304; Justin du Rivage, *Revolution against Empire: Taxes, Politics, and the Origins of American Independence* (New Haven, 2017), 36–44; 147–77; James M. Vaughn, *The Politics of Empire at the Accession of George III: The East India Company and the Crisis and Transformation of Britain's Imperial State* (New Haven, 2019); Stanley J. Stein and Barbara H. Stein, *Apogee of Empire: Spain and New Spain in the Age of Charles III* (Baltimore, 2003); 37–41, 58–50; Manuel Lucena-Giraldo, "The Limits of Reform in Spanish America," in *Enlightened Reform in Southern Europe and Its Atlantic Colonies,* ed. Gabriel Paquette (Burlington, 2009), 312–18; Jeremy Adelman, *Sovereignty and Revolution in the Iberian Atlantic* (Princeton, 2006), 22–31.

30. Edmund S. Morgan, "The American Revolution: Revisions in Need of Revising," *William and Mary Quarterly,* 3rd ser., 14, no. 1 (1957): 3–15; T. H. Breen, "Ideology and Nationalism on the Eve of the American Revolution: Revisions Once More in Need of Revising," *Journal of American History* 84, no. 1 (1997): 13–39.

31. For a small sampling of recent works on early American nationalism focused on the early republic, see Waldstreicher, *In the Midst of Perpetual Fetes;* Benjamin H. Park, *American Nationalisms: Imagining Union in an Age of Revolutions* (Cambridge: Cambridge University Press, 2018); Carroll Smith-Rosenberg, *This Violent Empire: The Birth of an American National Identity* (Chapel Hill, 2010); Len Travers, *Celebrating the Fourth: Independence Day and the Rites of Nationalism in the Early Republic* (Amherst, 1997); Susan-Mary Grant, "A Nation before Nationalism: The Civic and Ethnic Construction of America," in *The SAGE Handbook of Nations and Nationalism,* ed. Gerard Delanty and Krishnan Kumar (London, 2006), 527–51. For a few comparative works that do the same, see Liah Greenfeld, *Nationalism: Five Roads to Modernity* (Cambridge, 1995), 397–484; Lloyd S. Kramer, *Nationalism in Europe and America: Politics, Cultures, and Identities since 1775* (Chapel Hill, 2011).

32. Michael Zuckerman, "Beyond the Rebirth of the Revolution: Coming to Terms with Coming of Age," in *The American Revolution Reborn,* ed. Patrick Spero and Michael Zuckerman (Philadelphia, 2016), 304.

33. For an exception, see Jon Butler, *Becoming America: The Revolution before 1776* (Cambridge, 2000). For a recent and thorough rendering of this long-running debate, see Jasper M. Trautsch, "The Origins and Nature of American Nationalism," *National Identities* 18, no. 3 (2016): 289–96.

34. For brief summaries of the cultural nationalist project, see Jack P. Greene, "Revolution and Redefinition," in *The Intellectual Construction of America: Exceptionalism and Identity from 1492 to 1800* (Chapel Hill, 1993), 162–99; Merrill Jensen, *The New Nation: A History of the United States during the Confederation, 1781–1789* (New York, 1950), 88–110. On the creation of a national literature in this period, see Herbert W. Spencer, *The Quest for Nationality: An American Literary Campaign* (Syracuse, 1957), 22–72. For more recent works, see Jill Lepore, *A Is for American: Letters and Other Characters in the Newly United States* (New York, 2002); Joseph J. Ellis, *After the Revolution: Profiles in Early American Culture* (1979; repr. New York, 2002), 3–41; For an anthology of cultural nationalist writings, see Eve Kornfeld, *Creating an American Culture, 1775–1800: A Brief History with Documents* (Boston, 2001).

35. For thinking of America as a postcolonial society, see Kariann Akemi Yokota, *Unbecoming British: How Revolutionary America Became a Postcolonial Nation* (New York, 2011); Sam W. Haynes, *Unfinished Revolution: The Early American Republic in a British World* (Charlottesville, 2010). For a work that challenges the Anglophobia of Haynes, see Elisa Tamarkin, *Anglophilia: Deference, Devotion, and Antebellum America* (Chicago, 2008). On the challenges of defining "postcolonial" in an American context, see David Armitage, "From Colonial History to Postcolonial History: A Turn Too Far?," *William and Mary Quarterly*, 3rd ser., 64, no. 2 (2007): 1–4; Jack P. Greene, "Colonial History and National History: Reflections on a Continuing Problem," *William and Mary Quarterly*, 3rd ser., 64, no. 2 (2007): 235–50; Michael Zuckerman, "Exceptionalism after All; or, The Perils of Postcolonialism," *William and Mary Quarterly*, 3rd ser., 64, no. 2 (2007): 259–62.

36. Haynes, *Unfinished Revolution*, 2.

37. Yokota, *Unbecoming British*, 9, 11.

Chapter 1. History Culture in Pre-Revolutionary British America

1. Stow Persons, "The Cyclical Theory of History in Eighteenth-Century America," *American Quarterly* 6, no. 2 (1954): 147–63.

2. Polybius, *The Histories of Polybius* (Cambridge, 1922–27), 3:273–93. For the classic eighteenth-century explication of the cyclical theory, see M. De Secondat, Baron de Montesquieu, *The Spirit of Laws* (London, 1750), 1:11–41, 159–82.

3. John Adams, "An Essay on Man's Lust for Power, with the Author's Comment in 1807," in *The Papers of John Adams*, ed. Robert J. Taylor, et al. (Cambridge, 1977–2016), 1:81–84.

4. David Hume, "Of the Study of History," in *Essays, Moral and Political. The Third Edition* (London, 1748), 56.

5. Henry St. John Bolingbroke, *Letters on the Spirit of Patriotism* (London, 1749), 136.

6. For the interrelationship between classical republicanism and the cyclical theory, see Bailyn, *Ideological Origins of the American Revolution*, 46, 83, 90, 135, 370–72; Pocock, *Machiavellian Moment*, 462–552; Robbins, *Eighteenth-Century Commonwealthman*, 293.

7. For the most recent synthesis of chronographic representation, see Daniel Rosenberg and Anthony Grafton, *Cartographies of Time* (Princeton, 2010), esp. chs. 1–2.

8. Joseph Priestley, *A Description of a New Chart of History* (London, 1769), 7, 8, 11–12.

9. Joseph Priestley, *A Description of a Chart of Biography* (Warrington, 1764); Priestley, *Description of a New Chart of History*.

10. Bolingbroke, *Letters on the Spirit of Patriotism*, 136. On "first principles" in eighteenth-century America, see Gerald Stourzh, *Alexander Hamilton and the Idea of Republican Government* (Stanford, 1970), 9–37.

11. Algernon Sidney, *Discourses Concerning Government* (Edinburgh, 1750), 1:210.

12. For a fuller account of this idea, see John Phillip Reid, "The Jurisprudence of Liberty:

The Ancient Constitution in the Legal Historiography of the Seventeenth and Eighteenth Centuries," in *The Roots of Liberty: Magna Carta, Ancient Constitution, and the Anglo-American Tradition of Rule of Law,* ed. Ellis Sandoz (Indianapolis, 1993), 283–95.

13. J. G. A. Pocock, *The Ancient Constitution and the Feudal Law: A Study of English Historical Thought in the Seventeenth Century* (Cambridge, 1957).

14. John Demos, *Circles and Lines: The Shape of Life in Early America* (Cambridge, 2005), 45–47; Hannah Arendt, *On Revolution* (New York, 1962), ch. 1; Christopher Hill, "The Word 'Revolution' in Seventeenth-Century England," in *For Veronica Wedgwood These: Studies in Seventeenth-Century History,* ed. R. Ollard and P. Tudor-Craig (London, 1986), 135–49; Reinhart Koselleck, *Futures Past: On the Semantics of Historical Time,* trans. Keith Tribe (Cambridge, 1988), 41–45; Raymond Williams, *Keywords: A Vocabulary of Culture and Society* (1976; repr. New York, 2015), 209–13.

15. Samuel Johnson, *A Dictionary of the English Language* (London, 1755), 2:1702.

16. Isaac Watts, *The Improvement of the Mind* (London, 1743), 221.

17. Isaac Kramnick, "Augustan Politics and English Historiography: The Debate on the English Past, 1730–35," *History and Theory* 6, no. 1 (1967): 33–56; Kathleen Wilson, "A Dissident Legacy: Eighteenth Century Popular Politics and the Glorious Revolution," in *Liberty Secured? Britain before and after 1688* (Stanford, 1992), 299–366; Wilson, "Inventing Revolution: 1688 and Eighteenth-Century Popular Politics," *Journal of British Studies* 28, no. 4 (1989): 349–86; H. T. Dickinson, "The Eighteenth-Century Debate on the 'Glorious Revolution,'" *History* 61, no. 201 (1976): 28–45.

18. Isaac Kramnick, *Bolingbroke and His Circle: The Politics of Nostalgia in the Age of Walpole* (Ithaca, 1968), 127–36, 177–81.

19. For an early eighteenth-century example of how elite colonists made the new fiscal-military state and standing army work for them, see Douglas Bradburn, "The Visible Fist: The Chesapeake Tobacco Trade in War and the Purpose of Empire, 1690–1715," *William and Mary Quarterly,* 3rd ser., 68, no. 3 (2011): 361–86.

20. On these themes and British national identity in the eighteenth century, see Linda Colley, *Britons: Forging the Nation, 1707–1837* (New Haven, 1992); David Armitage, *The Ideological Origins of the British Empire* (Cambridge, 2000), 8.

21. Rutherford Delmage, "The American Idea of Progress, 1750–1800," *Proceedings of the APS* 91, no. 4 (1947): 307–14; David Spadafora, *The Idea of Progress in Eighteenth-Century Britain* (New Haven, 1990).

22. Marquis de Condorcet, *Outlines of an Historical View of the Progress of the Human Mind* (Philadelphia, 1796), 11, 206.

23. Spadafora, *Idea of Progress in Eighteenth-Century Britain,* 211–12.

24. John Millar, *The Origin of the Distinction of Ranks* (London, 1779), 5.

25. Adam Smith, *The Glasgow Edition of the Works and Correspondence of Adam Smith* (New York, 1976–83), 5:26–27.

26. On the influence of the Scottish Enlightenment on America, see Henry F. May, *The*

Enlightenment in America (New York, 1976), 307–62; Garry F. Wills, *Inventing America: Jefferson's Declaration of Independence* (Boston, 1978), 167–258.

27. *Maryland Gazette*, June 7, 1745.

28. Jonathan Belcher to Jonathan Belcher, Jr., October 20, 1732, Jonathan Belcher letter-books, 1682–1757, Massachusetts Historical Society (hereafter MHS).

29. *Weekly Rehearsal*, March 12, 1732.

30. Richard Rawlinson, *A New Method of Studying History, Geography, and Chronology* (London, 1730), 1:25.

31. *Monthly Review; or, Literary Journal*, 41 (July 1769): 533.

32. John Adams, "February 1, 1763," in *The Diary and Autobiography of John Adams*, ed. L. H. Butterfield (Cambridge, 1961–66), 1:233–37.

33. *Virginia Gazette*, November 29, 1739; *New-York Weekly Journal*, July 23, 1739. On the phrase "secret history," see Steven C. Bullock, *Tea Sets and Tyranny: The Politics of Politeness in Early America* (Philadelphia, 2017), 104–5.

34. John Oldmixon, *The British Empire in America*, 2 vols. (London, 1708); William Douglass, *A Summary, Historical and Political, of the First Planting, Progressive Improvements, and Present State of the British Settlements in North-America* (Boston, 1747).

35. For recent scholarship on early modern British historiography and historical culture, see Daniel Woolf, *The Social Circulation of the Past: English Historical Culture, 1500–1730* (Oxford, 2003); Philip S. Hicks, *Neoclassical History and English Culture: From Clarendon to Hume* (Basingstoke, 1996); Mark Phillips, *Society and Sentiment: Genres of Historical Writing in Britain, 1740–1820* (Princeton, 2000); Daniel R. Woolf, *Reading History in Early Modern England* (Cambridge, 2001); Woolf, *The Idea of History in Early Stuart England: Erudition, Ideology, and the "Light of Truth" from the Accession of James I to the Civil War* (Toronto, 1990); Joseph M. Levine, *The Battle of the Books: History and Literature in the Augustan Age* (Ithaca, 1991); Laird Okie, *Augustan Historical Writing: Histories of England in the English Enlightenment* (Lanham, 1991); Paulina Kewes, ed., *The Uses of History in Early Modern England* (San Marino, 2006).

36. Hicks, *Neoclassical History and English Culture*, 1–3, 136–37.

37. Kramnick, "Augustan Politics and English Historiography"; Okie, *Augustan Historical Writing*, 115–94.

38. Paul de Rapin de Thoyras, *The History of England*, 14 vols. (London, 1726–31).

39. M. de Voltaire, *The Age of Lewis XIV* (London, 1752), 2:64.

40. For more on this debate in the colonial context, see Colbourn, *Lamp of Experience*, 25–47.

41. "On the Use of History, particularly Rapin's," *American Magazine & Historical Chronicle* (August 1746), 368–69.

42. See Donald Lundberg and Henry F. May, "The Enlightened Reader in America," *American Quarterly* 28, no. 2 (1976): 267, 278.

43. *New-York Gazette*, January 7, 1734.

44. *South-Carolina Gazette*, October 29, 1737.

45. *Boston Evening-Post,* November 19, 1744.

46. Richard Beale Davis, *A Colonial Southern Bookshelf: Reading in the Eighteenth Century* (Athens, 1979), 24.

47. Income information from Peter H. Lindert and Jeffrey G. Williamson, "American Incomes before and after the Revolution," *Journal of Economic History* 73, no. 3 (2013): 725–65.

48. For example, see *New-York Weekly Journal,* April 29, 1734; *Pennsylvania Gazette,* November 21, 1737; *New-York Gazette,* February 16, 1747; *Boston Evening-Post,* January 11, 1762.

49. David Hume, *The History of England,* 6 vols. (London, 1759–62).

50. *Maryland Gazette,* April 8, 1773; John Adams to Thomas Jefferson, July 15, 1813, in *The Papers of Thomas Jefferson, Retirement Series,* ed. J. Jefferson Looney (Princeton, 2009), 6:296–98; Thomas Jefferson to Horatio G. Spafford, March 17, 1814 in ibid., 7:248–49.

51. Thomas Jefferson to John Norvell, June 11, 1807, in Thomas Jefferson Papers, Series 1: General Correspondence, 1651 to 1827, Library of Congress.

52. Colbourn, *Lamp of Experience,* 23.

53. Mark G. Spencer, *David Hume and Eighteenth-Century America* (Rochester, 2005), 25–28.

54. Lundberg and May, "Enlightened Reader in America," 268.

55. The first full printing of a major historical work in the colonies was Robert Bell's edition of William Robertson's *History of the Reign of the Emperor Charles V* at Philadelphia in 1771.

56. For eighteenth-century British American reading habits, see Davis, *Colonial Southern Bookshelf;* Edwin Wolf, 2nd, *The Book Culture of a Colonial American City: Philadelphia Books, Bookmen, and Booksellers* (New York, 1988); Kevin J. Hayes, *A Colonial Woman's Bookshelf* (Knoxville, 1996); Lawrence C. Wroth, *An American Bookshelf, 1755* (1934; repr. New York, 1969). For examples of elite personal libraries, see *The Library of James Logan of Philadelphia* (Philadelphia, 1974); *The Library of William Byrd of Westover* (Lanham, 1997); *The Library of Benjamin Franklin* (Philadelphia, 2006).

57. *A Catalogue of Mein's Circulating Library* (Boston, 1765).

58. Thomas E. Keys, "The Colonial Library and the Development of Sectional Differences in the American Colonies," *Library Quarterly* 8 (1938): 377–83.

59. Davis, *Colonial Southern Bookshelf,* 24.

60. Mark Boonshoft, "Creating a 'Civilized Nation': Religion, Social Capital, and the Cultural Foundations of Early American State Formation" (PhD diss., Ohio State University, 2015), 38–98.

61. Joe W. Kraus, "The Development of a Curriculum in the Early American Colleges," *History of Education Quarterly* 1, no. 2 (1961): 64–76.

62. "An Account of the Fire at Harvard-College, in Cambridge; with the Loss sustained thereby," February 2, 1764, broadside, Harvard University Archives (HUY 129).

63. David R. Whitesell, "The Harvard College Library and Its Users, 1762–1764: Reassessing the Relevance of Colonial American College Libraries," *Proceedings of the AAS* 118, no. 2 (2008): 399, 394, 390.

64. *Catalogus Librorum in Bibliotheca Cantabrigiensi selectus* (Boston, 1773).

65. See table 3 in Jesse H. Shera, *Foundations of the Public Library: The Origins of the Public Library Movement in New England, 1629–1855* (Chicago, 1949), 55.

66. *The Charter, Laws, Catalogue of Books, List of Philosophical Instruments, &C. of the Juliana Library-Company, in Lancaster* (Philadelphia, 1766), ix.

67. *Massachusetts Gazette,* March 31, 1774.

68. The summations in this paragraph are drawn from an examination of eighteen library catalogues published between 1741 and 1770 in Philadelphia, New London, New Haven, Newport, New York, Providence, and Charleston. For full list, see Michael D. Hattem, "Past and Prologue: History Culture and the American Revolution" (PhD diss., Yale University, 2017), 68–69.

69. See *A Catalogue of Books belonging to the Library Company of Philadelphia;* Director's Minutes, 1731–1768, The Library Company of Philadelphia (hereafter LCP). This tabulation is drawn from my own examination of the catalogue and is also corroborated in Edwin Wolf II, "Franklin and His Friends Choose Their Books," *Pennsylvania Magazine of History and Biography* 80, no. 1 (1956): 15.

70. *Catalogue of Mein's Circulating Library,* cover.

71. *New-York Weekly Journal,* February 4, 1733.

72. *Maryland Gazette,* June 7, 1745.

73. Nathanael Low, *An Astronomical Diary; or, Almanack for the Year of Christian Æra, 1774* (Boston, 1774). A Hartford edition of the almanac (which misspells Low's first name) does not include the woodcut on its cover.

74. Jonathan Mayhew, *A Discourse concerning Unlimited Submission and Non-Resistance to the Higher Powers* (Boston, 1750).

75. John Locke, *Two Treatises of Government* (London, 1728), 289, 243–47, 291–95.

76. Ibid., 41.

77. Ibid., 43, 47.

78. Pocock, *Ancient Constitution and the Feudal Law,* xi.

79. On the establishment of "The Sodality," a legal club in Massachusetts, see *Diary and Autobiography of John Adams,* 1:2–25, 251–55. For New York's version called "The Moot Club," see Moot Club Minute Books, 1770–1775, New-York Historical Society. John Adams's "A Dissertation on the Canon and Feudal Law" was largely the product of these types of conversations. It was published anonymously and untitled in the *Boston Gazette,* August 12, 19; September 30; October 21, 1765. Its title was christened by Thomas Hollis, a British radical, who reprinted the essay in the *London Chronicle,* November 23, 28; December 3, 26, 1765.

80. *New-York Weekly Journal,* February 4, 1733.

81. *Pennsylvania Journal,* January 7, 1746; *Boston Evening-Post,* January 13, 1746.

82. *New-York Gazette,* September 10, 1750; *Boston Gazette,* May 17, 1748; *Pennsylvania Gazette,* December 27, 1753.

83. *Pennsylvania Journal,* January 21, 1746; *Boston Evening-Post,* August 4, 1746.

84. Wilson, "Inventing Revolution," 353.

85. Greene, "Glorious Revolution and the British Empire," 87. Also, see Greene, *Periph-*

eries and Center, 55, 58, 72; Greene, "Empire and Identity from the Glorious Revolution to the American Revolution," in *The Oxford History of the British Empire* (New York, 1998), 2:208–30.

86. *Boston Gazette,* February 1, 1773; *Papers of John Adams,* 1:277–80.

87. Jack P. Greene, "'By Their Laws Shall Ye Know Them': Law and Identity in Colonial British America," in Greene, *Creating the British Atlantic: Essays on Transplantation, Adaptation, and Continuity* (Charlottesville, 2013), 268.

88. Bailyn, *Ideological Origins of the American Revolution,* 31.

89. Charles Carroll to Charles Carroll, Sr., September 16, 1760, in "Extracts from the Carroll Papers," *Maryland Historical Magazine* 10 (1915): 328. Also, see "The Letters and Papers of Cadwallader Colden, IX, Additional Letters and Papers, 1749–1775, and Some of Colden's Writings," *Collections of the N-YHS* 68 (New York, 1937), 251.

90. Demos, *Circles and Lines,* 40. Similarly, in the British context, Julia Rudolph recently argued, "Common law thought and common law culture were, after all, a form of historical thought and culture: common law spoke in the language of custom, precedent, and prescription, and valued tradition as it evolved through human and social experience." See Julia Rudolph, *Common Law and Enlightenment in England, 1689–1750* (Rochester, 2013), 28.

91. François Weil, *Family Trees: A History of Genealogy in America* (Cambridge, 2013), chs. 1–2.

92. Karin Wulf, "Bible, King, and Common Law: Genealogical Literacies and Family History Practices in British America," *Early American Studies* 10, no. 3 (2012): 467–502.

93. Ibid., 502.

94. See Thomas Jefferson to Thomas Adams, February 20, 1771, in *The Papers of Thomas Jefferson* (Princeton, 1950–2016), 1:61–62; "Notes on the Franklin Family, with a genealogical chart," Historical Society of Pennsylvania collection of Benjamin Franklin papers (Collection 215), Historical Society of Pennsylvania.

95. John Walrond to Rev. William Waldron, March 8, 1725/6, in "Letter from Rev. John Walrond of Ottery, Eng., to Rev. William Waldron, Minister of Boston, and Brother of Secretary Waldron," *New England Historical and Genealogical Register* 1 (1847): 66. Also, see Weil, *Family Trees,* 8–10.

96. Ibid., 10.

97. Ibid.; Wulf, "Bible, King, and Common Law," 500.

Chapter 2. The Colonial Past in the Imperial Crisis

1. "The Records of the Old Colony Club," in *Proceedings of the Massachusetts Historical Society, Vol. III—Second Series, 1886–1887* (Boston: Published by the Society, 1888), 381–444. For quotes, including the previous paragraph, see 389, 400–405. In the early 1770s, such Boston luminaries as John Adams, James Otis, James Warren, and Daniel Leonard were among the invited attendees of Old Colony Day in Plymouth.

2. Michael Zuckerman expressed the standard interpretation of the non-role of identity in the coming of the Revolution when he wrote, "The American break with Britain was essentially if not entirely political and sprang from administrative and diplomatic sources

rather than from any deeper disconnection between the antagonists." See Michael Zuckerman, "Identity in British America: Unease in Eden," in *Colonial Identity in the Atlantic World, 1500–1800,* ed. Nicholas Canny and Anthony Pagden (Princeton, 1989), 115. On Britons' developing sense of cultural difference with American colonists, see Stephen Conway, "From Fellow-Nationals to Foreigners: British Perceptions of the Americans, circa 1739–1783," *William and Mary Quarterly,* 3rd ser., 59, no. 1 (2002): 65–100.

3. See Pincus, *Heart of the Declaration,* 51–88; Keuthe and Andrien, *Spanish Atlantic World in the Eighteenth Century,* 231–304; du Rivage, "Taxing Empire," 42–57; 221–50; Vaughn, *Politics of Empire at the Accession of George III;* Stein and Stein, *Apogee of Empire,* 37–41, 58–50; Lucena-Giraldo, "Limits of Reform in Spanish America," 312–18; Adelman, *Sovereignty and Revolution,* 22–31.

4. See John M. Murrin, "Anglicizing an American Colony: The Transformation of Provincial Massachusetts" (PhD diss., Yale University, 1966). For an excellent synthesis of this idea in Murrin's work, see Andrew Shankman, "Introduction—The Revolutionary Republic of a Radical, Imperial Whig: The Historical and Historiographical Imagination of John M. Murrin," in John M. Murrin, *Rethinking America: From Empire to Republic,* ed. Andrew Shankman (New York, 2018), 1–30.

5. *A Letter to the Right Honourable the Earl of Hillsborough, on the Present Situation of Affairs in America* (Boston, 1769), 2; *Providence Gazette,* January 20, 1770.

6. On these earlier debates, see Greene, *Peripheries and Center,* 19–78; Yirush, *Settlers, Liberty, and Empire,* 83–182.

7. For the various versions of the Virginia Resolves, see *Prologue to Revolution: Sources and Documents on the Stamp Act Crisis, 1764–1766,* ed. Edmund S. Morgan (Chapel Hill, 1959), 47–50; *Newport Mercury,* June 24, 1765; *Maryland Gazette,* July 4, 1765.

8. *Prologue to Revolution,* ed. Morgan, 50–52, 58.

9. For example, see the resolves of Providence, Rhode Island, *Boston Evening-Post,* August 19, 1765; "Gloucester Resolves of Mar. 27, 1770," *Boston Evening-Post,* April 16, 1770.

10. *Prologue to Revolution,* ed. Morgan, 51–52, 54–57, 60–62.

11. *New-York Mercury,* April 23, 1764; *Pennsylvania Journal,* April 26, 1764; *Boston-Gazette,* April 30, 1764; *Newport Mercury,* April 30, 1764; *Providence Gazette,* May 5, 1764. For similar constructions in use later in the crisis, see Samuel Webster, *The Misery and Duty of an Oppress'd and Enslav'd People* (Boston, 1774); "The Examiner, No. III," *Pennsylvania Gazette,* May 11, 1774; *Boston Post-Boy,* June 13, 1774.

12. James Otis, *The Rights of the British Colonies asserted and proved* (Boston, 1764), 37.

13. [Thomas Jefferson], *A Summary View of the Rights of British America* (Williamsburg, 1774), 8.

14. *Pennsylvania Gazette,* July 7, 1768; *Pennsylvania Journal,* July 7, 1768; *Boston-Gazette,* July 18, 1768; *Connecticut Journal,* July 22, 1768. "Heart of Oak" is the official march of the Royal Navy.

15. James Lovell, *An Oration delivered April 2d, 1771 . . . to commemorate the bloody tragedy of the fifth of March, 1770* (Boston, 1771), 7.

16. "Gloucester Resolves of Mar. 27, 1770," *Boston Evening-Post,* April 16, 1770.

17. *Authentic Account of the Proceedings of the Congress held at New-York* (London, 1767), 11–2; *Proceedings of the Congress at New-York* (Annapolis, 1766), 18.

18. *Pennsylvania Journal,* August 23, 1764. For more on this theme, see Albanese, *Sons of the Fathers,* 19–45; Michael Kammen, "The Meaning of Colonization in American Revolutionary Thought," *Journal of the History of Ideas* 31, no. 3 (1970): 337–58.

19. *The Journal of the House of Burgesses* (Williamsburg, 1765), 90; *Boston News-Letter,* March 21, 1765; *Boston Post-Boy,* March 25, 1765; *Providence Gazette,* March 30, 1765; *Newport Mercury,* April 1, 1765. For a similar interpretation, see Jeremiah Dummer, *A Defence of the New-England Charters* (1721; repr. Boston, 1765), 4; Richard Bland, *The Colonel Dismounted: or the Rector Vindicated* (Williamsburg, 1764); Andrew Eliot, *A Sermon Preached Before His Excellency Francis Bernard, Esq.* (Boston, 1765), 53.

20. *Journal of the House of Burgesses,* 92; [Thomas Fitch], *Reasons why the British Colonies in America, should not be charged with Internal Taxes* (New-Haven, 1764); 7; *Boston News-Letter,* March 21, 1765; *Boston Post-Boy,* March 25, 1765; *Providence Gazette,* April 6, 1765.

21. *The Power and Grandeur of Great-Britain* (Philadelphia, 1768), 5. Also, see "Petition to the King, tracing the history of the colony and its charters, and affirming the loyalty of the people," February 11, 1768, box 1, folder 26, Samuel Adams Papers, 1760–1803, Manuscripts and Archives Division, New York Public Library (hereafter NYPL); *The True Sentiments of America* (London: J. Almon, 1768).

22. Also, see Jonathan Mayhew, *Observations on the Charter and Conduct of the Society for the Propagation of the Gospel in Foreign Parts* (Boston, 1763), 157, 175; Thacher, *Sentiments of a British American; Public Advertiser,* January 23, 1766; Hicks, *Nature and Extent of Parliamentary Power Considered,* 15–16, 37–38.

23. "John Hampden to Wm. Pym," *Boston-Gazette,* December 9, 1765.

24. John Adams to Hezekiah Niles, February 13, 1818, MS 1814, Maryland Historical Society.

25. Supplement, *Boston Evening-Post,* December 30, 1765.

26. *Power and Grandeur of Great-Britain,* 4.

27. Alexander Hamilton, *The Farmer Refuted* (New-York, 1775), 31.

28. *Proceedings of the Congress at New-York,* 18. Alternatively, the settlers were referred to as "free" or "individual" adventurers. See *Considerations upon the Rights of the Colonists to the Privileges of British Subjects* (New-York, 1766), 4; Jefferson, *Summary View,* 7–8.

29. Jefferson, *Summary View,* 6.

30. William Pym, "To the Printer of the *Public Ledger,*" *Public Ledger,* August 13, 1765.

31. *London Chronicle,* July 31, 1764. For the longevity of this argument, see *Morning Chronicle,* March 27, April 4, 1775.

32. *Colonising, or a Plain Investigation of that Subject* (London, 1774), 7.

33. *Some Hints to People in Power, on the Present Melancholy Situation of Our Colonies in North America* (London, 1763), 42. For more on the meaning of the familial metaphor in the imperial debate as an expression of the colonies' "comparative weakness and inferiority," see

Edwin G. Burrows and Michael Wallace, "The American Revolution: The Ideology and Psychology of National Liberation," *Perspectives in American History* 6 (1972): 226–67.

34. For the same argument later in the crisis by a loyalist writer, see [Daniel Leonard], "To the Inhabitants of the Province of Massachusetts-Bay," *New-Hampshire Gazette,* December 30, 1774.

35. Jared Ingersoll to Thomas Fitch, February 11, 1765, in *Proceedings and Debates of the British Parliaments Respecting North America, 1754–1783,* 5 vols. (Millwood, 1982), 2:16.

36. Ibid., 2:16–17.

37. *Boston Post-Boy,* April 29, 1765; *Providence Gazette,* April 13, 1765.

38. See "Petition to the King," Samuel Adams Papers, 1760–1803, NYPL; *True Sentiments of America,* 3–4, 20. On the legal debate over rights and migration, see Reid, *Constitutional History of the American Revolution,* 1:114–38; Yirush, *Settlers, Liberty, and Empire,* 34–50; Greene, *Constitutional Origins of the American Revolution,* 15–16; Greene, *Peripheries and Center,* 23–28.

39. [Stephen Hopkins], *The Rights of Colonies Examined* (Providence, 1765), 8. Also, see Webster, *Misery and Duty of an Oppress'd and Enslav'd People,* 22–23.

40. *Pennsylvania Journal,* April 26, 1764.

41. Dummer, *Defence of the New-England Charters,* 21.

42. Bland, *Colonel Dismounted,* 20–21.

43. Eliot, *Sermon Preached before His Excellency Francis Bernard,* 52; *London Evening-Post,* November 23, 1765. This sentiment is clear in the majority of the colonial assemblies' resolves against the Stamp Act, including Virginia, Rhode Island, Maryland, Connecticut, South Carolina, and New York. For the colonial resolves, see *Prologue to Revolution,* ed. Morgan, 50–62.

44. "At a large Meeting of the respectable Populace held at the Town of *Pomfret* in the County of Windham, on the 25th Day of *December,* 1765," *Boston Post-Boy,* January 6, 1766; *Boston News-Letter,* January 9, 1766; *Newport Mercury,* January 13, 1766.

45. "The Freeholders of Botetourt, Virginia to Col. Andrew Lewis and Mr. John Boyer, 1775," MSS, Thomas Jefferson Papers, 1775–1825, American Philosophical Society (hereafter APS).

46. *Extracts from the votes and proceedings of the American Continental Congress, held at Philadelphia, 5th September, 1774* (New-York, 1774), 6.

47. On Fergusson and her poem, see Caroline Wigginton, "Letters from a Woman in Pennsylvania, or Elizabeth Graeme Fergusson Dreams of John Dickinson," in *Community without Consent: New Perspectives on the Stamp Act,* ed. Zachary McLeod Hutchins (Hanover, 2016), 89–112; For the poem, see Elizabeth Graeme Fergusson, "The Dream," in *Poemata Juvenilia,* Papers, 1752–1799, LCP; Caroline Wigginton and William J. Crosby, "The Dream" (1768, 1790) by Elizabeth Graeme Fergusson," *Commonplace: The Journal of Early American Life* 16, no. 4.5 (2016), http://commonplace.online/article/dream-1768-1790-elizabeth-graeme-fergusson.

48. For an argument against understanding these debates as "history," see Reid, *Constitutional History of the American Revolution,* 1:129.

49. *Authentic Account of the Proceedings of the Congress held at New-York,* 5.

50. *Providence Gazette,* May 11, 1765; *Boston Post-Boy,* July 15, 1765.

51. For examples, see the second and third resolutions of the "Declarations and Resolves of the First Continental Congress," in *Journals of the Continental Congress, 1774–1789* (Washington, D.C., 1904–37), 1:68; *New-Hampshire Gazette,* November 18, 1774.

52. Reid, *Constitutional History of the American Revolution,* 2:97. As a legal historian, and like those who came before him, Reid was primarily concerned with the legal standing (or validity) of the colonists' arguments and not their broader cultural connotations.

53. "To the Honourable the Knights, Citizens and Burgesses, representing the Commons of Great-Britain, in Parliament assembled," in *Journal of the Votes and Proceedings of the General Assembly of the Colony of New York. Began the 8th Day of November, 1743; and Ended the 23d of December, 1765. Vol. II* (New-York, 1766), 776.

54. Hamilton, *Farmer Refuted,* 38.

55. "The British American. Number VI," *New-York Journal,* August 25, 1774.

56. Otis, *Rights of the British Colonies,* 51.

57. *Boston News-Letter,* January 9, 1766. For a similar religious rendering of the charter as "a solemn covenant between [the King] and our *fathers,*" see Webster, *Misery and Duty of an Oppress'd and Enslav'd People,* 22. For some other uses of the phraseology, see *Providence Gazette,* March 9, 1765; *New-York Mercury,* January 20, 1766; *Boston-Gazette,* August 31, 1772; *Dunlap's Pennsylvania Packet,* June 19, 1775.

58. *Boston Evening-Post,* October 21, 1765.

59. On these previous conflicts over colonial charters, see Yirush, *Settlers, Liberty, and Empire,* 83–112.

60. Richard Bland, *An Inquiry into the Rights of the British Colonies* (Williamsburg, 1766), 14–15. Also, see *Boston Evening-Post,* December 30, 1765.

61. Moses Mather, *America's Appeal to the Impartial World* (Hartford, 1775), 24–25. Also, see *Boston-Gazette,* May 4, 1767; *Pennsylvania Gazette,* May 14, 1767; *New-York Gazette,* May 21, 1767; *Virginia Gazette,* May 28, 1767.

62. William Pym, "To the Printer of the *Public Ledger,*" *Public Ledger,* August 19, 1765; *Boston Evening-Post,* November 25, 1765.

63. Israel Maduit, *A Short View of the History of the New England Colonies, with respect to their Charters and Constitution,* 4th ed. (London, 1776), 16, 20–21.

64. Ibid., 30.

65. For the rhetorical role of Magna Carta in the conflict, see H. T. Dickinson, "Magna Carta in the Age of Revolution," *Enlightenment and Dissent,* no. 30 (2015): 35–59.

66. *Public Ledger,* August 13, 1765.

67. Suny, "Constructing Primordialism," 863.

68. For example, see Greene, *Pursuits of Happiness;* Butler, *Becoming America.*

69. Bailyn, *Ideological Origins of the American Revolution,* 33–34.

70. Fischer, *Albion's Seed,* 6–7; David Grayson Allen, *In English Ways: The Movement of Societies and the Transferral of English Local Law and Custom to Massachusetts Bay in the Seventeenth Century*

(Chapel Hill, 1981); James Horn, *Adapting to a New World: English Society in the Seventeenth-Century Chesapeake* (Chapel Hill, 1994).

71. Woolf, *Social Circulation of the Past in Early Modern England,* 45.

72. Ibid., 44.

73. Bernard Bailyn, *To Begin the World Anew: The Genius and Ambiguities of the American Founders* (New York, 2003), 3–36.

74. Zuckerman, "Identity in British America," 117.

75. Kammen, *People of Paradox,* 30, 14–30.

76. On the "quest for legitimacy in colonial America," see ibid., 31–56.

77. John Oldmixon, *A Critical History of England, Ecclesiastical and Civil,* 2 vols. (London, 1724–26), 1:2.

78. [John Adams], "The Earl of Clarendon to Wm. Pym," *Boston-Gazette,* December 23, 1765.

79. [Fitch], *Reasons why the British Colonies,* 23.

80. *Boston Evening-Post,* October 21, 1765.

81. McConville, *King's Three Faces,* 193.

82. Woolf, *Social Circulation of the Past in Early Modern England,* 392.

83. [Fitch], *Reasons why the British Colonies,* 13, 14.

84. "Copy of the Instructions, given by the Town of Providence, on the 13th of August 1765, to their Deputies in the General Assembly," *Boston Post-Boy,* August 19, 1765.

85. "The New York Petition to the House of Commons," October 18, 1764, in *Prologue to Revolution,* ed. Morgan, 9.

86. *Boston Chronicle,* February 13, 1769.

87. Richard Henry Lee to Lord Shelburne, May 31, 1769, in *The Letters of Richard Henry Lee,* ed. James Curtis Ballagh (New York, 1911), 1:37.

88. "Virginia House of Burgesses draft petition to the House of Lords, December 18, 1764," Pennsylvania Stamp Act and Non-Importation Resolutions Collection, APS.

89. *Journals of the House of Burgesses of Virginia, 1761–1765,* ed. John Pendleton Kennedy (Richmond, 1907), 360, 302.

90. Jonathan Mayhew, *A Thanksgiving-Discourse . . . Occasioned by the Repeal of the Stamp-Act* (Boston, 1766), 2–3.

91. "A Letter to the Right Honourable the Earl of Hillsborough, on the present Situation of Affairs in America," *Providence Gazette,* January 20, 1770; Jefferson, *Summary View,* 18; *Gazetteer and New Daily Advertiser,* January 3, 1766.

92. *New-York Mercury,* December 31, 1764; *Pennsylvania Gazette,* January 10, 1765; *Pennsylvania Journal,* January 10, 1765; *Boston-Gazette,* January 14, 1765; *Newport Mercury,* January 14, 1765; *Boston Post-Boy,* January 21, 1765; *New-Hampshire Gazette,* January 25, 1765.

93. *Boston Evening-Post,* August 19, 1765; *New-Hampshire Gazette,* August 30, 1765; *Maryland Gazette,* September 5, 1765.

94. For just a few examples covering the time and geography of the imperial crisis, see *Boston Evening-Post,* October 21, 1765; *Boston Evening-Post,* November 4, 1765; "Meeting of the

Inhabitants of the County of Dinwiddie, in Virginia," in *American Archives, Fourth Series* (Washington, D.C., 1837), 1:552; "Meeting of a majority of the Committees," in ibid., 1:610; "Meeting of the Inhabitants of Westmoreland, Pennsylvania, May 16, 1775," in ibid., 2:615.

95. [John Dickinson], "Letter from a Farmer, no. II," *Pennsylvania Gazette,* December 10, 1767.

96. *Rights of Parliament Vindicated,* 4.

97. *The Justice and Necessity of Taxing the American Colonies* (London, 1766), 6.

98. Francis Bernard to Lord Barrington, November 23, 1765, in *The Barrington-Bernard Correspondence and Illustrative Matter, 1760–1770,* ed. Edward Channing and Archibald Cary Coolidge (Cambridge, 1912), 94. Very similar language was used in opposing the proposed religious innovations that brought about the Bishop Crisis a few years later. See William Livingston's sixty-four essays as "The American Whig" in the *New-York Gazette* from March 14, 1768 to July 24, 1769.

99. Reid, *Constitutional History of the American Revolution,* 2:40–41.

100. *Boston Evening-Post,* October 21, 1765.

101. *Pennsylvania Gazette,* March 6, 1767.

102. "Extract of a Letter from London, dated March 24," *Boston Post-Boy,* June 11, 1764.

103. [John Dickinson], "Letter from a Farmer in Pennsylvania, no. I," *Pennsylvania Gazette,* December 3, 1767.

104. *Considerations upon the Rights of the Colonists to the Privileges of British Subjects* (New-York, 1766), 23.

105. Bailyn, *Ideological Origins of the American Revolution,* 144–59; Gordon S. Wood, "Conspiracy and the Paranoid Style: Causality and Deceit in the Eighteenth Century," *William and Mary Quarterly,* 3rd ser., 39, no. 3 (1982): 401–41.

106. [Dickinson], "Letter from a Farmer, no. I," *Pennsylvania Gazette,* December 3, 1767.

107. Josiah Tucker, "The respective Pleas of the Parent-State and of the Colonies examined and compared together; and the Impossibility of their making any mutual Concessions, consistently with their respective Claims, proved and demonstrated," *Hibernian Magazine* (March 1775): 137.

108. They received this treatment in both the poetry and literature of the period. See Rosemary Sweet, *Antiquaries: The Discovery of the Past in Eighteenth-Century Britain* (New York, 2004), xiii, 4–5, 9, 18, 132, 247, 382.

Chapter 3. The British Past in the Imperial Crisis

1. John Adams to William Tudor, Sr., June 1, 1818, John Adams Letters, Columbia University Library.

2. "The Association of the Sons of Liberty of New-York," *Pennsylvania Gazette,* December 22, 1773.

3. Otis, *Rights of the British Colonies,* 90.

4. *London Chronicle,* November 2, 1765.

5. *Boston Evening-Post,* October 28, 1765.

6. Andrew Eliot to Thomas Hollis, September 27, 1768, in *Collections of the Massachusetts Historical Society* (hereafter *CMHS*), *5th Ser.* (Boston, 1876–1879), 4:429.

7. On this topic more generally, see Michelle Orihel, "'All Those Truly Acquainted with the History of Those Times': John Adams and the Opposition Politics of Revolutionary England, ca. 1640–41," *New England Quarterly* 86, no. 3 (2013): 433–66.

8. *Public Ledger,* August 13, 1765. For other letters, see *Public Ledger,* August 19, 1765; *Public Ledger,* August 26, 1765; *Public Ledger,* August 30, 1765; *Boston Evening-Post,* November 25, 1765.

9. See John Adams to Elbridge Gerry, May 2, 1785, Adams Papers, MHS; John Adams to Charles Adams, December 16, 1793, in *The Adams Family Correspondence* (Cambridge, 1963–2017), 9:473–74.

10. John Adams, "1765. December. 23d.," in *Diary and Autobiography of John Adams,* 1:273n; Orihel, "'All Those Truly Acquainted with the History of Those Times,'" 444.

11. Colin Nicolson, "The Revolutionary Politics of John Adams, 1760–1775," in *A Companion to John Adams and John Quincy Adams* (Malden, 2013), 69.

12. See [John Adams], "Governor Winthrop to Governor Bradford," in *Boston Gazette,* January 26, February 9, 16, 1767. Also, see *Papers of John Adams,* 1:174–211.

13. See G. Coade, Jun. Merchant at Exeter, *A Letter to a Clergyman, relating to his Sermon on the 30th of January . . . giving, also, a very particular History of that unfortunate Prince, Charles I* (New-York, 1773). For an important colonial version of such a pamphlet, see Mayhew, *Discourse concerning Unlimited Submission.*

14. For the shifting legacies of the Stuarts in the eighteenth-century colonies, see McConville, *King's Three Faces,* 81–104, 161–219.

15. On Cromwell as folk hero, see Alfred F. Young, "Tar and Feathers and the Ghost of Oliver Cromwell: English Plebeian Culture and American Radicalism," in *Liberty Tree: Ordinary People and the American Revolution* (New York, 2006), 144–79.

16. On Cromwell's memory, see Peter Karsten, "Cromwell in America," in *Images of Oliver Cromwell: Essays for and by Roger Howell* (Manchester, 1993), 207–21; Jim Piecuch, "Washington and Specter of Cromwell," in *George Washington: Foundation of Presidential Leadership and Character* (Westport, 2001), 193–208.

17. Samuel Peters, *A General History of Connecticut* (London, 1781), 231–32.

18. *Boston Gazette,* February 25, 1771; November 29, 1769. Also, see [John Leacock], *The First Book of the American Chronicles of the Times* (Boston, 1775), esp. ch. 4.

19. For example, see Virginian Arthur Lee's pamphlet, *An Essay in Vindication of the Continental Colonies of America,* in which he proudly noted the influx of "a considerable reinforcement in the depressed royalists" fleeing the Civil Wars and the rule of Cromwell. He also recalled proudly that Virginia was "said to have been the first which threw off the yoke, and proclaimed King Charles II." See Arthur Lee, *An Essay in Vindication of the Continental Colonies of America* (London, 1764), 21.

20. "Sentiments of the Sons of Liberty February 1769," folio 10, no. 18, Jared Sparks Collection, III, Harvard University, quoted in Young, "Tar and Feathers," 163. Also, see McConville, *King's Three Faces,* 270–72.

21. *Consideration on the American Stamp Act, and on the Conduct of the Minister Who planned it* (London, 1766), 33.

22. See Galloway, *Historical and Political Reflections,* 23–33.

23. [Martin Howard], *A Letter from a Gentleman at Halifax* (Newport, 1765), 4.

24. Thomas Bradbury Chandler, *A Friendly Address to all Reasonable Americans* (Boston, 1774), 33, 29–30.

25. *Gazetteer and New Daily Advertiser,* September 7, 1772.

26. Samuel Adams Drake, *Old Landmarks and Historic Personages of Boston* (Boston, 1873), 61–62.

27. Carl F. Kaestle, "The Public Reaction to John Dickinson's *Farmer's Letters,*" *Proceedings of the American Antiquarian Society* 78 (1968): 323–59.

28. "Letter from a Farmer in Pennsylvania, no. I," *Pennsylvania Chronicle,* December 2, 1767. For a list of reprints, see the appendices of Kaestle, "Public Reaction to Dickinson's *Farmer's Letters,*" 350–59.

29. "Letter from a Farmer in Pennsylvania, no. II," *Pennsylvania Chronicle,* December 7, 1767.

30. Ibid.

31. "Letter from a Farmer in Pennsylvania, no. IV," *Pennsylvania Chronicle,* December 21, 1767.

32. "Letter from a Farmer in Pennsylvania, no. III," *Pennsylvania Chronicle,* December 14, 1767.

33. Maier, *From Resistance to Revolution,* 234.

34. H. T. Dickinson, "The Eighteenth-Century Debate on the Sovereignty of Parliament," *Transactions of the Royal Society* 26 (1976): 189.

35. Hopkins, *Rights of the Colonies Examined,* 4

36. [James Otis, Jr.], "John Hampden to Wm. Pym," *Boston-Gazette,* December 16, 1765.

37. Otis, *Rights of the British Colonies,* 61, 48, 56.

38. Ibid., 47; *New-York Gazette,* April 4, 1768; Jefferson, *Summary View,* 18. For the British context, see Dickinson, "Eighteenth-Century Debate on the 'Glorious Revolution,'" 36–40; Kramnick, *Bolingbroke and His Circle,* 177–81.

39. Gerald M. Straka, "Sixteen Eighty-Eight as the Year One: Eighteenth-Century Attitudes towards the Glorious Revolution," in *Studies in Eighteenth-Century Culture* (Cleveland, 1971), 143–67; Kramnick, "Augustan Politics and English Historiography," 33–56.

40. [Lord Hervey], *Ancient and Modern Liberty Stated and Compar'd* (London, 1734), 40.

41. William Blackstone, *Commentaries on the Laws of England* (Oxford, 1765–69), 1:156–57. For an early historical-based refutation of this idea, see [Benjamin Franklin], "To the Printer of the London Chronicle," *London Chronicle,* October 20, 29, 1768.

42. Otis, *Rights of the British Colonies,* 59.

43. James Otis, Jr., *Considerations on Behalf of the Colonists* (London, 1765), 36. Despite this, Otis anticipated the common reasoning behind colonists' later position regarding the arbitrary nature of parliamentary authority when he claimed "the arbitrary commands of a minister, are no more obligatory, than the bulls of the pope." Ibid., 37.

44. On the Revolution Settlement, see Jennifer Carter, "The Revolution and the Constitution," in *Britain after the Glorious Revolution, 1689–1714* (London, 1969), 39–58; Dickinson, *Liberty and Property;* Dickinson, "Eighteenth-Century Debate on the 'Glorious Revolution'"; Dickinson, "Eighteenth-Century Debate on the Sovereignty of Parliament"; J. P. Kenyon, *Revolution Principles: The Politics of Party, 1689–1720* (Cambridge, 1977); Jack P. Greene, "The Glorious Revolution and the British Empire, 1688–1763," in *The Revolution of 1688–89: Changing Perspectives* (Cambridge, 1992), 260–71.

45. Silas Downer, *A Discourse delivered in Providence . . . at the Dedication of the Tree of Liberty* (Providence, 1768), 13–14.

46. George Washington to George Mason, April 5, 1769, in *Papers of George Washington, Colonial Series,* 8:177–78.

47. *The Votes and Proceedings of the Freeholders and other Inhabitants of the Town of Boston* (Boston, 1772), 12. Also, see Marblehead Resolves, December 12, 1772, box 1, folder 1, pp. 9–10, Boston Committee of Correspondence records, 1772–1784, NYPL.

48. "House of Commons. Monday, May 15, 1775," in *American Archives, Fourth Series,* 1:1819.

49. [James Otis, Jr.], "John Hampden to Wm. Pym," *Boston-Gazette,* December 16, 1765.

50. Mather, *America's Appeal,* 25.

51. The sources of this debate are so well laid out in the work of Eric Nelson that only a brief rehearsal is necessary. See Eric Nelson, "Patriot Royalism: The Stuart Monarchy in American Political Thought, 1769–75," *William and Mary Quarterly,* 3rd ser., 68, no. 4 (2011): 533–72; Nelson, *Royalist Revolution,* ch. 1.

52. [Edward Bancroft], *Remarks on the Review of the Controversy between Great Britain and her Colonies* (London, 1769), 10.

53. Ibid., 15.

54. *Considerations upon the Rights of the Colonists to the Privileges of British Subjects, Introduc'd by a brief Review of the Rise and Progress of English Liberty* (New-York, 1766), 21.

55. Benjamin Franklin, "Marginalia in Protests of the Lords against Repeal of the Stamp Act, [March 1766]," in *Papers of Benjamin Franklin,* 13:207–32.

56. Downer, *Discourse delivered in Providence,* 3.

57. "A Letter to the Right Honourable the Earl of Hillsborough, on the present Situation of Affairs in America," *Providence Gazette,* January 20, 1770.

58. Lovell, *Oration delivered April 2d, 1771,* 13–14.

59. Ibid., 11.

60. Ibid., 12.

61. "The British American. Number VI," *Virginia Gazette,* July 7, 1774; *New-York Journal,* August 25, September 1, 1774.

62. Ibid.

63. "The British American. Number IV," *Virginia Gazette,* June 16, 1774, Colonial Williamsburg Foundation.

64. *Pennsylvania Chronicle,* August 31, 1767.

65. [John Dalyrmple], *The Address of the People of Great Britain to the Inhabitants of America* (London, 1775), 14. For a similar expression, see William Laight to John Vardill, March 27, 1775, AO 13/105, [n.f.], National Archives, Kew.

66. "Letter to the Right Honourable the Earl of Hillsborough," *Providence Gazette,* January 20, 1770.

67. Hamilton, *Farmer refuted,* 31.

68. [William Knox], *The Controversy between Great Britain and her Colonies reviewed . . . and the Nature of their Connection with, and Dependence on, Great Britain, shewn upon the evidence of Historical Facts and Authentic Records* (London, 1769), 201.

69. Ibid., 138.

70. *The Parliamentary Register* (London, 1776), 3:43; *Parliamentary History of England,* 18:771; *American Archives, Fourth Series,* 6:45, 3:43.

71. P. D. G. Thomas, *The Townshend Duties Crisis* (New York, 1987), 2.

72. William Samuel Johnson to William Pitkin, October 20, 1768, in *CMHS, 5th Ser.,* 9:296. Johnson, Connecticut's agent in London, reported Hillsborough's remarks to Pitkin, the colony's governor.

73. *Virginia Gazette,* June 14, 1770.

74. *Essex Gazette,* January 14, 1772; *New-Hampshire Gazette,* January 10, 1772. For similar coverage in Caribbean newspapers, see *Dominica Mercury,* September 3, 1768; *Saint Jago Intelligencer,* April 16, 1768.

75. *New-York Journal,* April 4, 1771.

76. *Virginia Gazette,* June 20, 1771.

77. *New-York Gazette,* February 29, 1768.

78. Maier, *From Resistance to Revolution,* 161–63. Also, see Michael Roberts, *The Age of Liberty in Sweden,* 1719–1772 (Cambridge, 1986), 176–217; John Lind, *Letters Concerning the Present State of Poland* (London, 1773); *A Parallel between the English Constitution and the Former Government of Sweden* (London, 1772).

79. *Maryland Journal,* December 20, 1773; *Pennsylvania Gazette,* December 29, 1773; *Connecticut Gazette,* January 7, 1774.

80. *Pennsylvania Journal,* May 25, 1774.

81. *New-Hampshire Gazette,* November 4, 1774; *Essex Journal,* November 2, 1774.

82. *The Speeches of His Excellency Governor Hutchinson* (Boston, 1773), 59, 6, 4, 10.

83. Similar arguments would later be made by loyalists about the Continental Congress itself. For example, see [Samuel Seabury], *Congress Canvassed* (New-York, 1774).

84. *Speeches of His Excellency Governor Hutchinson,* 59, 124, 4, 80, 11, 82.

85. Ibid., 36, 37, 39, 49, 33, 56, 57. For a popular defense of the House's position and critique of Hutchinson's arguments, see *Massachusetts Spy,* July 22, 1772.

86. John Barker, *The British in Boston: Being the Diary of Lieutenant John Barker* . . . (Cambridge, 1920), 40; *New-York Gazette,* July 24, 1775; *Pennsylvania Evening-Post,* March 11, 1775.

87. *Connecticut Journal,* November 18, 1774.

88. Hamilton, *A Full Vindication of the Measures of the Congress,* 26.

89. [William Henry Drayton], "Judge Drayton's Charge to the Grand Jury of Charlestown, South-Carolina," in *American Archives, Fourth Series,* 5:1025–32.

90. The turn toward the king, referred to by some historians as the "dominion theory" has recently enjoyed renewed scholarly interest. See Nelson, "Patriot Royalism," 573–96; Greene, *Constitutional Origins of the American Revolution,* 117–21, 134–39; McConville, *King's Three Faces,* 193–219.

91. [Drayton], "Judge Drayton's Charge to the Grand Jury," in *American Archives, Fourth Series,* 5:1032.

92. Ezra Stiles to Catherine Macaulay, December 6, 1773, Ezra Stiles Papers, General Collection, Beinecke Rare Book and Manuscript Library, Yale University.

93. Timothy Dwight, *A Valedictory Address to the Young Gentlemen, who commenced Bachelors of Arts, at Yale-College, July 25th. 1776* (New-Haven, 1776), 12.

94. My argument in this book is that there are clear shifts in patriot rhetoric from equality with native Britons between 1764 and 1767 toward focusing on parliamentary supremacy and arbitrary power after 1768, followed by a turn toward natural law around 1773. Keyword searches for the term "arbitrary" in Readex's Early American Newspapers, Series 1, 2, 4, 6, 7, and 10 revealed 495 uses of the term "arbitrary" in colonial newspapers between 1764 and 1767 for an average of 124 per year. Between 1768 and 1772, there were 1,644 uses for an average of 329 per year. Finally, between 1773 and 1776, there were 2,626 uses for an average of 657 per year, an increase of five times more than in the early years of the crisis. When including imprints (e.g., books, pamphlets, and broadsides), the numbers grow largely in accordance with the growth in newspapers, with the exception that the rate of growth of the use of "arbitrary" in imprints from the period 1768–1772 (averaging 41 per year) to 1773–1776 (averaging 128 per year) is just over 100 percent more than in newspapers, likely driven by its prominence in resistance pamphlets and broadsides. If the search is made more specific by using a Boolean search string to look for instances of "arbitrary power," the rate of relative increase between the three periods is even larger, with 92 uses in imprints and newspapers between 1764 and 1767 (for an average of 23 per year), 285 uses between 1768 and 1772 (for an average of 57 per year), and 659 uses between 1773 and 1776 (for an average of 165 per year). The same searches were run on Google's N-Gram Viewer and produced similar results. This is clearly not a scientific inquiry, but it does show that the idea of arbitrariness generally became more prominent in colonial media over this time, and the term "arbitrary power" became relatively even more prominent, quantitatively suggesting support for the qualitative assertion the idea became more important in patriot rhetoric in the corresponding periods.

95. *Journals of the Continental Congress,* 1:68, 67. In the "Declaration and Resolves," members of the Congress refer to their "ancestors" three times.

96. "Why Captain Levi Preston Fought: An Interview with One of the Survivors of the Revolution by Hon. Mellen Chamberlain of Chelsea," *Danvers Historical Collections* 8 (1920): 68–70.

97. On arbitrary rule as "the antithesis of liberty," see John Phillip Reid, *The Concept of Liberty in the Age of the American Revolution* (Chicago, 1988), 55–59.

98. "Records of the Old Colony Club," 404.

99. *By the King. A Proclamation for Suppressing Rebellion and Sedition,* broadside, London, 1775.

Interlude. Natural Law, Independence, and Revolutionary History Culture, 1772–1776

1. Yirush, *Settlers, Liberty, and Empire,* 215–59.

2. Tucker, "The respective Pleas of the Parent-State and the Colonies," 137.

3. Keyword searches for the phrases "natural rights" and "natural law" in all of Readex's online databases covering this period—including *Early American Imprints, Series I: Evans, 1639–1800; Early American Imprints, Series I & II: Supplements from the Library Company of Philadelphia; Early American Imprints, Series I & II: Supplements from the American Antiquarian Society, 1652–1819; American Broadsides and Ephemera, 1749–1800;* and *Early American Newspapers,* series 1, 2, 4, 6, 7, and 10—revealed mentions in 279 imprints and newspaper issues (or, an average of 35 per year) throughout the colonies in the first eight years of the crisis (1765–72) and 328 (for an average of 82 per year) in the last four years of the crisis (1773–76). That is a 133 percent increase in the years between 1773 and independence. Similar searches with Google's N-Gram Viewer revealed similar results. The problems of making hard claims based on such an unscientific analysis of incomplete databases notwithstanding, it does appear that the degree to which patriots referred to natural rights and natural law increased rapidly after 1772.

4. *Votes and Proceedings of the Freeholders and other Inhabitants of the Town of Boston,* 2, 3, 6.

5. Ibid., 8–9.

6. Alexander Hamilton, *A Full Vindication of the Measures of the Congress* (New-York, 1774), 39, 5. At the start of the pamphlet, he used the same order having written, "The pretensions of Parliament are contradictory to the law of nature, subversive of the British constitution, and destructive of the faith of the most solemn compacts."

7. *Votes and Proceedings of the Freeholders and other Inhabitants of the Town of Boston,* 8.

8. For other examples of the same language in substance and order, see resolutions from a variety of local towns, including Tewksbury, Pelham, Storr, Shrewsbury, and Stoughton, box 1, folder 3, pp. 237–66, Boston Committee of Correspondence records, 1772–1784, NYPL.

9. "At a Town Meeting Held at Providence, on the 17th Day of May 1774, Called by Warrant," *Newport Mercury,* June 13 1774; *Providence Gazette,* May 21, 1774.

10. "At a meeting of the Freeholders and other respectable Inhabitants of the County of Salem in New-Jersey," *Pennsylvania Journal,* July 20, 1774; *Pennsylvania Packet,* July 25, 1774.

11. "At a legal town meeting of the Inhabitants of the town of Goshen, convened on the 20th of Sept. A. D. 1774," *Connecticut Journal,* October 21, 1774.

12. "At a very full meeting of the respectable inhabitants of the town of Hartford," June 20, 1774, reprinted in *A Historical Collection, from official records, files, &c.* . . . (Hartford, 1842), 64; "At a meeting of the Freeholders, Merchants, and other Inhabitants of the country of Prince William . . . ," *Pennsylvania Journal,* June 22, 1774; "Queen Anne County, Maryland, Resolutions," May 30, 1774, in *American Archives, Fourth Series,* 1:366.

13. *Boston Evening-Post,* May 2, 1765.

14. *Connecticut Gazette,* November 18, 1774.

15. Jefferson, *Summary View,* 5, 6, 6, 11, 15, 7, 15.

16. [Thomas Paine], *Common Sense; addressed to the inhabitants of America* (Philadelphia, 1776), 87.

17. Thomas Paine, *Rights of Man part the second* (Philadelphia, 1792), 28. Here, Paine was speaking about the moment in the wake of the new federal constitution, but it is an eloquent exposition of the same argument he made when the colonies were on the eve of independence.

18. [Paine], *Common Sense,* 58.

19. For examples of all three aspects, see McConville, *King's Three Faces;* Breen, *Marketplace of Revolution;* Bailyn, *Ordeal of Thomas Hutchinson.*

20. See Ray Raphael, *A People's History of the American Revolution* (New York, 2001), esp. ch. 2.

21. Fred Junkin Hinkhouse, *The Preliminaries of the American Revolution as Seen in the English Press, 1763–1775* (New York, 1926), 100.

22. *Public Advertiser,* January 25, 1775; *London Packet,* January 4, 1775.

23. See Pauline Maier, *American Scripture* (New York, 1998), 47–96.

24. William Meredith, *Historical Remarks on the Taxation of Free States, in a Series of Letters to a Friend* (London, 1778), 7.

25. William Pym, "To the Printer of the *Public Ledger,*" *Public Ledger,* August 13, 1765.

Chapter 4. The Expansion of Early National History Culture

1. Timothy Dwight, "An Essay on American Genius," *New-Haven Gazette,* February 1, 1787.

2. John Adams, *A Defence of the Constitutions of Government of the United States of America* (Philadelphia, 1787), xii; excerpt reprinted in *Monthly Review* (1795): 551.

3. *Massachusetts Centinel,* January 12, 1785.

4. Kenneth Silverman, *A Cultural History of the American Revolution* (New York, 1976), xv.

5. The overall number of printers (for whom there are extant imprints) more than doubled from 1764 to 1783. For statistics through 1783, see Thomas G. Tanselle, "Some Statistics on American Printing, 1764–1783," in *The Press and the American Revolution* (Worcester, 1980), 315–63. No tabulations seem to exist for the subsequent period, but the enormous growth

in the number and locations of printers can be seen at a glance in Frances P. Newton, *American Bibliography, A Preliminary Checklist, 1801 to 1819* (Metuchen, 1983).

6. For a contemporary complaint, see Thomas Paine, *A Letter Addressed to the Abbe Raynal: On the Affairs of North-America* (Philadelphia, 1782), vn.

7. The "first" "history" of the Revolution was actually written by an exiled French Jesuit before the war was over. See Abbé Raynal, *The Revolution of America* (London, 1781). Because of Raynal's distance and unfamiliarity with America, his account contained numerous inaccuracies and misinterpretations for which he was criticized in print, not least by Thomas Paine and John Adams.

8. John Lendrum, *A Concise and Impartial History of the American Revolution,* 2 vols. (Boston, 1795); Thomas Pemberton, *An Historical Journal of the American War* (Boston, 1795); Charles Smith, *The American War from 1775 to 1783* (New York, 1797); *The History of the British Empire, from the year 1765, to the end of 1783,* 2 vols. (Philadelphia, 1798); Bernard Hubley, *The History of the American Revolution* (Northumberland, 1805); *The History of the American Revolution* (Charleston, 1808).

9. Alexander Hewat, *An Historical Account of the Rise and Progress of the Colonies of South Carolina and Georgia,* 2 vols. (London, 1779); Samuel Peters, *A General History of Connecticut* (London, 1782); Jeremy Belknap, *The History of New-Hampshire,* 3 vols. (Philadelphia, 1784; Boston, 1791; Boston, 1792); Thomas Jefferson, *Notes on the State of Virginia* (London, 1787); John Filson, *The Discovery, Settlement, and Present State of Kentucky* (London, 1793); Samuel Williams, *The Natural and Civil History of Vermont* (Walpole, N.H., 1794); James Sullivan, *The History of the District of Maine* (Boston, 1795); Robert Proud, *The History of Pennsylvania,* 2 vols. (Philadelphia, 1797–98); Benjamin Trumbull, *A Complete History of Connecticut* (Hartford, 1797); George Richards Minot, *A Continuation of the History of the Province of Massachusetts Bay* (Boston, 1798); John Daly Burk, *The History of Virginia,* 3 vols. (Petersburg, 1804–5); David Ramsay, *The History of South-Carolina, from Its Settlement in 1670 to the Year 1808* (Charleston, 1809); Hugh McCall, *The History of Georgia* (Savannah, 1811).

10. Isaac Backus, *A History of New-England,* 2 vols. (Boston, 1777–84); Hannah Adams, *A Summary History of New-England* (Dedham, 1799); Jedidiah Morse, *A Compendious History of New England Designed for Schools and Private Families* (Charlestown, 1804).

11. Van Tassell, *Recording America's Past,* 30.

12. *Courier, Boston Evening Gazette and Universal Advertiser,* November 28, 1795; *United States Chronicle,* December 17, 1795.

13. David Ramsay to John Eliot, August 11, 1792, in Brunhouse, "David Ramsay, 1749–1815," 133. This idea was widely expressed in the 1780s and 1790s.

14. David Ramsay to Jeremy Belknap, August 11, 1792, in Brunhouse, "David Ramsay, 1749–1815," 133.

15. For general histories, see Richard Johnson, *The History of North America* (London, 1789); John McCulloch, *A Concise History of the United States* (Philadelphia, 1795); [John Lendrum], *The History of America* (Philadelphia, 1795); James Thomson Callender, *Sketches of the History of America* (Philadelphia, 1798); Abiel Holmes, *American Annals: or, a Chronological History of*

America, from Its Discovery, 2 vols. (Cambridge, 1805); Richard Snowden, *A History of North and South America,* 2 vols. (Philadelphia, 1805); Benjamin Trumbull, *A General History of the United States of America* (Boston, 1810); David Ramsay, *History of the United States, from their First Settlement As English Colonies, in 1607, to the Year 1808,* 3 vols. (Philadelphia, 1816).

16. Lendrum, *Concise and Impartial History of the American Revolution,* preface.

17. Trumbull, *General History of the United States,* 1:xii.

18. Lendrum, *Concise and Impartial History of the American Revolution,* preface.

19. Morgan Edwards, *Materials Towards a History of the Baptists in Jersey* (Philadelphia, 1792).

20. John Winthrop, *A Journal of the Transactions and Occurrences in the Settlement of Massachusetts and the Other New-England Colonies, from the Year 1630 to 1644* (Hartford, 1790); Daniel Gookin, *Historical Collections of the Indians in New England* (Boston, 1792).

21. The second edition of Ramsay's biography, published in 1811, was sold at Philadelphia, New York, Albany, New Haven, Hartford, Boston, Portland, Maine, and Middlebury, Vermont.

22. Scott Casper, "Constructing American Lives: The Cultural History of Biography in Nineteenth-Century America," (PhD diss., Yale University, 1992), 27–29; Casper, "Biographies," in *An Extensive Republic: Print, Culture, and Society in the New Nation, 1790–1840,* ed. Robert A. Gross and Mary Kelley (Chapel Hill, 2010), 458–66.

23. See *History of the Book in America,* vol. 2: *An Extensive Republic,* 75–174. For the role of books and literature in early national culture, see Richard Bushman, *The Refinement of America: Persons, Houses, Cities* (New York, 1992), 280–312.

24. Catherine O'Donnell, "Print Culture after the Revolution," in *The Oxford Handbook of the American Revolution* (New York, 2013), 522.

25. Eighty-five libraries were established in Connecticut alone between 1786 and 1795. See Jesse H. Shera, "The Beginnings of Systematic Bibliography in America, 1642–1799," in *Essays Honoring Lawrence C. Wroth* (Portland, 1951), 274.

26. Ibid., 274, 151. The numbers suggest roughly that historical and biographical works comprised 30 to 35 percent of titles in social libraries in the 1790s. Because many historical works were multivolume, the percentage of volumes in these libraries dedicated to historical and biographical works was even higher.

27. Clarence S. Brigham, *History and Bibliography of American Newspapers, 1690–1820,* 2 vols. (Worcester, 1947).

28. *Massachusetts Spy,* January 1, 1784, to June 16, 1785 (except March, 31, 1785).

29. *Continental Journal,* January 22, 1784, to August 11, 1785.

30. *Vermont Gazette,* January 8, 1784.

31. *City Gazette,* January 17 to September 10, 1788. I have not been able to find any mention by Ramsay regarding this serialization. It may be that what was being serialized were excerpts from the *Annual Register,* from which Ramsay had copied liberally. Even in that case, it seems that Ramsay may have had some influence in the serialization since a vast majority of the passages turn up verbatim in his *History,* which was already mostly written by this time.

32. For example, between 1791 and 1792, Ramsay's histories were excerpted in *General*

Advertiser, February 1, 1792; *Independent Gazetteer,* February 4, 1792; *Vermont Gazette,* February 13, 1792; *Norwich Packet,* February 16, 1792; *Connecticut Journal,* February 22, 1792; *Daily Advertiser,* March 2, 1792; *American Mercury,* March 19, 1792; *Boston Gazette,* October 1, 1792; *The Diary, or Loudon's Register,* October 6, 1792. State histories excerpted in this period included, among others, Samuel Peters' *General History of Connecticut* (in *Massachusetts Spy,* April 28, 1791; *New Hampshire Gazetteer,* May 13, 1791; *General Advertiser,* May 18, 1791; *Salem Gazette,* May 24, 1791; *The Mail, or Claypoole's Daily Advertiser,* July 1791; *Frothingham's Long Island Herald,* August 9, 1791; *Weekly Museum,* August 20, 1791) and Jeremy Belknap's *History of New-Hampshire* (in *Herald of Vermont, or, Rutland Courier,* September 10, 1792; *Morning Ray,* September 25, 1792; *General Advertiser,* December 12, 1792). For a few examples of widely reprinted essays on the topic of history generally from this period, see [Philalogus], "Observations on History," *New-Haven Gazette,* June 29, 1791; *General Advertiser,* July 4, 1791; *The Mail, or Claypoole's Daily Advertiser,* July 5, 1791; *New-York Packet,* July 7, 1791; *Vermont Gazette,* July 18, 1791; *Massachusetts Spy,* July 21, 1791; "Genius, History, and Experience," *General Advertiser,* July 18, 1792; *Daily Advertiser,* July 24, 1792; *The Diary, or Loudon's Register,* July 25, 1792; *Columbian Centinel,* August 1, 1792; *Massachusetts Spy,* August 23, 1792; "From Dr. Priestley's Lectures on History," *New Hampshire Gazetteer,* February 12, 1790; *Daily Advertiser,* October 29, 1790; *Pennsylvania Packet,* November 3, 1790; *American Mercury,* November 8, 1790; *New York Daily Gazette,* November 8, 1790; *Connecticut Courant,* November 8, 1790; *New-York Packet,* November 8, 1790; *Middlesex Gazette,* July 8, 1791; *Boston Gazette,* September 12, 1791; *General Advertiser,* September 20, 1791. The preceding lists do not contain every excerpting or serialization of the respective works; rather, they are intended to be illustrative.

33. *New-York Morning Post,* March 3, 1789. The selling point here seems to be: "Why buy 4 books when you can buy 507 issues of my newspaper?"

34. *Massachusetts Spy,* June 16, 1785.

35. *Connecticut Journal,* August 18, 1784; *Massachusetts Centinel,* August 25, 1784; *Boston Gazette,* August 30, 1784; *Connecticut Courant,* August 31, 1784; *South-Carolina Gazette,* September 29, 1784.

36. See *Connecticut Journal,* August 18, 1784; *Massachusetts Centinel,* August 25, 1784; *Boston Gazette,* August 30, 1784; *Connecticut Courant,* August 31, 1784; *South-Carolina Gazette,* September 29, 1784; *Pennsylvania Gazette,* March 29, 1786; *Massachusetts Centinel,* October 18, 1786; *Fowle's New-Hampshire Gazette,* October 26, 1786; *Independent Gazetteer,* October 30 1786; *Charleston Morning Post,* November 9, 1786.

37. Subsequent coverage of his publishing problems in England delighted some newspaper readers. See. *Massachusetts Centinel,* October 18, 1786; *Independent Gazetteer,* October 30, 1786; *Charleston Morning Post,* November 9, 1786; *Fowle's New-Hampshire Gazette,* October 26, 1786; *Massachusetts Centinel,* December 23, 1786.

38. *American Herald,* February 26, 1786.

39. *Massachusetts Centinel,* March 1, 1786.

40. *Independent Chronicle,* February 9, 1786; *Massachusetts Spy,* February 26, 1786; *American Herald,* March 20, 1786; *Daily Advertiser; Political, Historical and Commercial,* April 26, 1786;

Massachusetts Centinel, December 23, 1786. For a revival in the press of the debate over Gordon's history thirty-six years later, see *Columbian Centinel,* January 5, 9, 16, 1822; *Massachusetts Spy,* January 30, February 20, 1822; *Essex Register,* March 16, 1822.

41. William Gordon, *The History of the Rise, Progress, and Establishment, of the Independence of the United States of America,* 4 vols. (London, 1788), preface, John Adams Library, Boston Public Library.

42. *Massachusetts Centinel,* December 23, 1786.

43. On magazines in the early republic, see Jared Gardner, *The Rise and Fall of Early American Magazine Culture* (Urbana, 2012), 91–5; Frank Luther Mott, *A History of American Magazines,* vol. 1 (Cambridge, 1957).

44. *American Monitor* 1, no. 1 (October 1785): 1.

45. For an example of the interrelationship between poetry and history in early republic magazines, see [Phillip Freneau], "On prohibiting the sale of dr. David Ramsay's history of the revolution of South Carolina, in London," in *American Museum; or, Repository of Ancient and Modern Fugitive Pieces* 1, no. 2 (February 1787): 167. Freneau's poem was a lyrical critique of those in England who were actively attempting to keep Ramsay's *History of the Revolution of South-Carolina* from being published and circulated there.

46. This brief summary analysis is derived from an examination of the complete runs of ten of the most popular and longest running magazines published between 1779 and 1800, including the *American Magazine,* the *American Monthly Review,* the *American Museum,* the *Boston Magazine,* the *Columbian Magazine,* the *Massachusetts Magazine,* the *New-York Magazine,* the *United States Magazine,* the *Universal Asylum,* and the *Worcester Magazine.*

47. This summary analysis is derived from an examination of seventy-eight almanacs published between 1783 and 1795 (six per year) spread geographically from New England to South Carolina. I did not detect any significant differences in the number or type of historical events related in almanac calendars in this period that could conceivably be attributed to regional distinctions. Exploring the form with that question foregrounded would require a far larger sample than mine and a deeper engagement with the individuals producing the almanacs. Such a query is worthy of further inquiry.

48. *American Poems, Selected and Original,* vol. 1 (Litchfield, 1793), iv.

49. On nationalist poetry, see Christopher Grasso, *A Speaking Aristocracy: Transforming Public Discourse in Eighteenth-Century Connecticut* (Chapel Hill, 1999), ch. 6.

50. Some examples include John Trumbull's "Prospect of the Future Glory of America" (1770), Brackenridge's "A Poem, on the Rising Glory of America" (1772), Barlow's "The Prospect of Peace" (1778), and Humphreys' "A Poem on the Happiness of America" (1786). A few popular examples of more historically contextualized prospect poems include Timothy Dwight, *America: or, a Poem on the Settlement of the British Colonies* (New-Haven, 1780?); Dwight, *The Conquest of Canaan* (Hartford, 1785); Joel Barlow, *The Vision of Columbus* (Hartford, 1787); *America Invincible: An Heroic Poem; in two books* (Danvers, 1779).

51. *American Poems,* iv; *The Columbian Muse* (New-York, 1794).

52. Patricia M. Burnham and Lucretia Hoover Giese, eds., *Redefining American History Paint-*

ing (New York, 1995); Jochen Wierich, *Grand Themes: Emanuel Leutze,* Washington Crossing the Delaware, *and American History Painting* (University Park, 2012), 1–48; *Picturing History: American Painting, 1770–1930* (New York, 1993); William H. Gerdts and Mark Thistlethwaite, *Grand Illusions: History Painting in America* (Fort Worth, 1988); Lloyd Goodrich, "The Painting of American History: 1775 to 1900," *American Quarterly* 3, no. 4 (1951): 283–94.

53. See Trumbull's account books, which tracked sales of his prints in Series II, box 4, folders 55, 56, 59, 61, John Trumbull Papers, 1792–1826, Yale University Library.

54. Abigail Adams to Elizabeth Smith Shaw, March 4, 1786, in *Adams Family Correspondence,* 7:82; *Proposals by John Trumbull, for Publishing by Subscription, Two Prints, from Original Pictures Painted by Himself* (New-York, 1790), portfolio 112, folder 1, Printed Ephemera Collection, Library of Congress. Also, see *Gazette of the United States,* April 21, 1790.

55. John Trumbull, "*Battle of Bunker's Hill/Death of General Montgomery in the Attack on Quebec,*" Series II, box 4, folder 58, John Trumbull Papers, 1792–1826, Yale University Library. On the subsequent meaning of the painting, see Elisa Tamarkin, *Anglophilia: Deference, Devotion, and Antebellum America* (Chicago, 2007), 133–34. Also, see Patricia Burnham, "John Trumbull, Historian: The Case of the Battle of Bunker's Hill," in *Redefining American History Painting,* ed. Burnham and Giese (New York, 1995), 44–50; Minardi, *Making Slavery History,* 49–56.

56. Abigail Adams to Elizabeth Smith Shaw, March 4, 1786, in *Adams Family Correspondence,* 7:82.

57. John Trumbull, "Description of the four pictures . . . now placed in the rotunda of the capitol," Series II, box 4, folder 62, John Trumbull Papers, 1792–1826, Yale University Library.

58. John Trumbull to Thomas Jefferson, June 11, 1789, in *Papers of Thomas Jefferson,* 15: 176–78. On iconography, see Michael Kammen, "From Liberty to Prosperity: Reflections upon the Role of Revolutionary Iconography in National Tradition," *Proceedings of the American Antiquarian Society* 86, part 2 (October 1976): 237–72.

59. Andrew M. Schocket, *Fighting over the Founders: How We Remember the American Revolution* (New York, 2015), 49–84.

60. Michael Kammen, *Meadows of Memory: Images of Time and Tradition in American Art and Culture* (Austin, 1992), 135–38.

61. On drama in this period, see Jeffrey H. Richards, *Drama, Theatre, and Identity in the American New Republic* (New York, 2005);); Jared Brown, *The Theatre in America during the Revolution* (New York, 2007); Heather S. Nathans, *Early American Theatre from the Revolution to Thomas Jefferson* (New York, 2003).

62. *Columbian Centinel,* February 22, 1797.

63. Ibid.

64. *Boston Price-Current,* February 16, 1797; *Massachusetts Mercury,* February 17, 1797.

65. *Massachusetts Mercury,* February 21, 1797. The author of one reminiscence on Burk's life described the play: "The tragedy had not a particle of merit, except its brevity. . . . It was as destitute of plot and distinctness of character, as it was of all claim to poetry."

66. *Boston Price-Current,* February 23, 27, 1797; *Aurora General Advertiser,* March 2, 1797; *Columbian Centinel,* May 10, 1797.

67. To drum up attendance, many of them were advertised as "positively the last night." *New-York Gazette,* September 6, 1797; *Diary or Loudon's Register,* September 6, 7, 1797, October 16, 1797.

68. *Petersburg Republican,* April 23, 1808.

69. *Polar-Star, and Boston Daily Advertiser,* January 6, 1797. This issue contains notice of Burk's copyright registration dated November 21, 1796.

70. For a survey organized chronologically by topic rather than production, see Ernest Erwin Leisy, *The American Historical Novel* (Norman, 1950). On the rise of fiction, see Cathy N. Davidson, *Revolution and the Word: The Rise of the Novel in America* (New York, 1986); Jane Tompkins, *Sensational Designs: The Cultural Work of American Fiction, 1790–1860* (New York, 1986); Elliott, *Revolutionary Writers.*

71. See John Davis, *The First Settlers of Virginia, An Historical Novel* (New-York, 1806); Unca Eliza Winkfield, *The Female American; or, The Extraordinary Adventures of Unca Eliza Winkfield* (Vergennes, 1814); Ezra Sampson, *The Youth's Companion, or, An historical dictionary* (New York, 1807); John Smith, *The True Travels, adventures and observations of Captaine John Smith,* 2 vols. (Richmond, 1819); *The Life and adventures of Capt. John Smith* (Philadelphia, 1813); Noah Webster, *The Little Reader's Assistant* (Hartford, 1790). For a few examples of their appearance in magazines, see *American Magazine* for December 1787 and February 1788, *Columbian Magazine* (July 1787): 548–51; *Massachusetts Magazine* (July 1791): 423–25. For newspapers, see *Washington Federalist,* September 12, 1804.

72. On education, see Mark Boonshoft, *Aristocratic Education and the Making of the American Republic* (Chapel Hill, 2020); Lawrence A. Cremin, *American Education: The National Experience, 1783–1876* (New York, 1980).

73. Ramsay, *Oration on the Advantages of American Independence,* 7.

74. Noah Webster, "On the Education of Youth in America," in *American Museum* (December 1792): 312. This essay was first printed in the *American Magazine* during 1787–88 and widely reprinted in magazines and excerpted in newspapers.

75. "An act to incorporate and establish a society for the cultivation and promotion of arts and sciences," May 4, 1780, broadsheet, MHS.

76. Benjamin Rush, *A Plan for the Establishment of Public Schools and the Diffusion of Knowledge in Pennsylvania . . .* (Philadelphia, 1786); Robert Coram, *Political Inquiries To Which Is Added, a Plan for the General Establishment of Schools Throughout the United States* (Wilmington, 1791); Samuel Harrison Smith, *Remarks on Education Illustrating the Close Connection between Virtue and Wisdom* (Philadelphia, 1798); Samuel Knox, *An Essay on the Best System of Liberal Education Adapted to the Genius of the Government of the United States* (Baltimore, 1799).

77. [Noah Webster], "Education," in *American Magazine* (March 1788): 216.

78. See *Columbian Gazetteer,* August 26, 1793. This essay was reprinted in *Massachusetts Mercury,* October 18, 1793; *United States Chronicle,* October 31, 1793; and *Boston Gazette,* March 16, 1795.

79. Webster also included "A Federal Catechism, being a short and easy explanation of the Constitution of the United States." Noah Webster, *The Little Reader's Assistant* (Hartford, 1790). Expanded stories of the same type were included in Webster's *An American Selection of Lessons in Reading and Speaking.*

80. E. Jennifer Monaghan, *A Common Heritage: Noah Webster's Blue-Black Speller* (Hamden, 1983), 219.

81. The abridgment of *American Geography,* entitled *Geography Made Easy,* went through twenty editions (and many more illicit reprints in both the US and Britain) between 1790 and 1819.

82. Mary Beth Norton, *Liberty's Daughters: The Revolutionary Experience of American Women, 1750–1800* (New York, 1980), 256–94; Linda K. Kerber, *Women of the Republic: Intellect and Ideology in Revolutionary America* (Chapel Hill, 1980), 185–232.

83. Benjamin Rush, *Thoughts upon Female Education* (Boston, 1787), 6.

84. Ibid., 11.

85. Hannah More, *Strictures on the Modern System of Female Education,* 2 vols. (Philadelphia, 1800), 146. More, a Briton, was a prolific author of moral literature and her works were reprinted often throughout the United States, including in Boston, Charleston, Salem, New Haven, Hartford, New York, Philadelphia, and Virginia.

86. As Mary Kelley has uncovered, by the middle of the nineteenth century, "More than 150 women were writing history during these decades. Together they published 350 narratives." See Mary Kelley, *Learning to Stand and Speak: Women, Education, and Public Life in America's Republic* (Chapel Hill, 2006), 57, 193, 191–244.

87. John Bennett, *Letters to a Young Lady, on a Variety of Useful and Interesting Subjects,* 2 vols. (Hartford, 1791), 1:100–120, quote on 100. For a few reprints, see *American Museum* (September 1791): 146; *Eastern Herald,* April 25, 1793. Other works by Bennett on this topic were also published throughout the United States—including in Worcester, Newburyport, Brattleboro, Hartford, Norwich, New York, Philadelphia, and Baltimore—in the decades after the war.

88. See Rosemarie Zagarri, *A Woman's Dilemma: Mercy Otis Warren and the American Revolution,* 2d ed. (Malden, 2015); Kate Davies, *Catherine Macaulay and Mercy Otis Warren: The Revolutionary Atlantic and the Politics of Gender* (New York, 2006); Gary D. Schmidt, *A Passionate Usefulness: The Life and Literary Labors of Hannah Adams* (Charlottesville, 2004).

89. Timothy Alden, *Quarterly Catalogue of the Names of the Young Ladies, who belong to the Newark Academy* (Newark, 1810).

90. Jeremy Belknap to Ebenezer Hazard, January 13, 1784, Jeremy Belknap Papers, 1637–1891, MHS.

91. Jeremy Belknap to Ebenezer Hazard, August 3, 1788, in *CMHS, 5th Ser.,* 3:56. For Hazard's acknowledgment of receipt of "the Roxbury Records," see Hazard to Belknap, September 9, 1788, in ibid., 62.

92. On Hazard, see George Pilcher, "Ebenezer Hazard and the Promotion of Historical Scholarship in the Early Republic," *Pennsylvania History* 56, no. 1 (1989): 3–14; Fred Shelley,

"Ebenezer Hazard: America's First Historical Editor," *William and Mary Quarterly*, 3rd ser., 12, no. 1 (1955): 44–73.

93. The two traded many hundreds of letters spanning three decades. On the correspondence as a whole, see Russell M. Lawson, *Ebenezer Hazard, Jeremy Belknap, and the American Revolution* (London, 2011).

94. Ebenezer Hazard to Jeremy Belknap, January 29, 1779, Belknap Papers, MHS.

95. Jeremy Belknap to Ebenezer Hazard, February 2, 1779, ibid.

96. Ebenezer Hazard to Jeremy Belknap, April 17, 1781, ibid. For Hazard's two volumes of transcripts, see Peter Force Papers and Collection, 1492–1977, Series VIII, box 8 B: 8, reel 10, Manuscript Division, Library of Congress, Washington, D.C.

97. Ebenezer Hazard to Jeremy Belknap, April 17, 1781, Belknap Papers, MHS.

98. Ebenezer Hazard to Jeremy Belknap, August 7, 1790, in *CMHS, 5th Ser.,* 3:226.

99. Ebenezer Hazard, *Historical Collections; consisting of State Papers, and other authentic Documents; intended as Materials for an History of the United States of America,* vol. 2 (Philadelphia, 1794).

100. John Adams to Abbé de Mably, January 15, 1783, in *Papers of John Adams,* 14:172–80.

101. Ibid.

102. See Thomas Jefferson to David Ramsay, August 31, 1785, in *Papers of Thomas Jefferson,* 8:457–58; George Washington to David Ramsay, April 5, 1786, in *Papers of George Washington, Confederation Series,* 4:5–6; *Papers of John Adams,* 14:165–85; "Warren-Adams Letters, Vol. II, 1778–1814," in *CMHS,* vol. 73 (Boston, 1925); Hannah Adams to Abigail Adams, May 12, 1788; Abigail Adams to Hannah Adams, June 18, 1798, Adams Papers, MHS.

103. Ebenezer Hazard to Ezra Stiles, August 23, 1774, Ezra Stiles Papers, General Collection, Beinecke Rare Book and Manuscript Library, Yale University. For "Proposals for Printing by Subscription a Collection of State Papers, intended as materials for an History of the United States of America," see Ebenezer Hazard to Thomas Jefferson, August 23, 1774, in *Papers of Thomas Jefferson,* 1:144–49; Ebenezer Hazard, "Proposal to Form a Collection of American States Papers," broadsheet, in *Letters and Papers of Ezra Stiles, President of Yale College, 1778–1795* (New Haven, 1933), 40.

104. Thomas Jefferson to Ebenezer Hazard, April 30, 1775, Ebenezer Hazard Papers, 1766–1813, APS. Jefferson's *Notes* mentioned Hazard's project in Query XXIII. See Jefferson, *Notes on the State of Virginia,* 296.

105. *Journals of the Continental Congress* (Washington, 1904–1937), 11:682, 704–5.

106. David Ramsay to Benjamin Rush, April 13, 1786, Rush MSS, vol. 45, LCP. Ebenezer Hazard, who was not a member of Congress had much more trouble gaining access to the Congress's archives. In August 1779, he complained to Belknap that "though Congress have recommended it to me to furnish me with copies of such parts of their records as I may want, they have not yet done it in any one instance." See Ebenezer Hazard to Jeremy Belknap, August 31, 1779, Belknap Papers, MHS.

107. David Ramsay to Elias Boudinot, April 13, 1786, Rush MSS, vol. 45, LCP.

108. "Drafts of rough minutes delivered to Doctor Ramsey for his book on the history of

the late war," May 1786, Henry Knox Papers, January–August 1786, Gilder Lehrman Institute of American History (hereafter GLI), New York; "Notes and explanations of Doctor Ramsay's history respecting the Campaigns of 1777—the affairs of Trenton 1776," ca. 1788–1789, Henry Knox Papers, Undated: Revolutionary War, GLI. Also, see David Ramsay to Benjamin Rush, April 13, May 3, August 6, September 26, 1786; August 18, 1787; February 17, September 29, 1788, Rush MSS, vol. 45, LCP; David Ramsay to Thomas Jefferson, November 8, 1786, in Brunhouse, "David Ramsay, 1749–1815," 108; David Ramsay to John Adams, September 20, 1787, in ibid., 114.

109. David Ramsay to Benjamin Rush, May 3, 1786, Rush MSS, vol. 45, LCP.

110. Gordon and Washington traded ninety letters between May 1776 and January 1798, of which Gordon authored sixty-six.

111. William Gordon to George Washington, December 19, 1776, in *The Papers of George Washington: Revolutionary War Series* (Charlottesville, 1985–2013), 7:374–76.

112. George Washington to William Gordon, October 23, 1782, George Washington Papers, Series 3, Varick Transcripts, 1775–1785, Subseries 3H, Personal Correspondence, 1775–1783, Letterbook 2: January 2, 1780–December 18, 1782, Library of Congress.

113. George Washington to William Gordon, July 8, 1783, in *The Writings of George Washington* (New York and London, 1889–1891), 10:274. For an additional instance of a budding historian prevailing upon Washington, see John O'Connor to George Washington, October 5, 1789, in *Papers of George Washington, Presidential Series* (Charlottesville, 1993–2017), 4:138–39.

114. Washington's offer of access to his official military correspondence was predicated upon Gordon first receiving permission from Congress to access its archives. For Gordon's petition to Congress, see "Extracts from the Journal of Congress, May 25," *Political Intelligencer and New-Jersey Advertiser,* August 3, 1784. The original copy is in the Papers of the Continental Congress, No. 19, II, folio 427, U.S. National Archives and Records Administration. For the Congress's approval, see *Journals of the Continental Congress,* 27:427–48. Gordon's visit to the Congress in August 1785 is noted in ibid., 29:626. For Gordon's access to Washington's personal papers, see William Gordon to George Washington, March 8, 1784; William Gordon to Nathanael Greene, April 5, 1784, in John T. Morse, Jr., "Letters of the Reverend William Gordon, Historian of the American Revolution, 1770–1799," *Proceedings of the Massachusetts Historical Society* 63 (1929–30): 502–3. For Washington's initial offer, see George Washington to William Gordon, June 18, 1783, in ibid., 493.

115. Ramsay, *History of the American Revolution,* 1:iii.

116. William Gordon to Catherine Macaulay, March 25, 1777, in Catherine Graham Macaulay Papers, GLI.

117. *Pennsylvania Journal,* February 1, 1786. Not only historians sought to leverage the implicit or explicit approval of such figures. Judith Sargent Murray, in circulating a subscription proposal for *The Gleaner* assumed that "the knowledge that I have received the sanction of the Presidents Washington and Adams may facilitate the filling up my subscription." See Judith Sargent Murray to Noah Webster, April 8, 1797, Series I.B., box 2, folio 11, Noah

Webster Papers, 1764–1843, NYPL; *The Gleaner: A Miscellaneous Production,* 3 vols. (Boston: I. Thomas and E. T. Andrews, 1798).

118. David Ramsay to Benjamin Rush, September 26, 1786, Rush MSS, vol. 45, LCP. Ramsay appears to have sent out a number of manuscripts of his first six chapters. I have found an unidentified copy at the New-York Historical Society that is likely the only extant copy. Thomson appears to have forwarded it to William Livingston. See [David Ramsay], "History of American Revolution commencing with the settlement of the American Colonies coming down to Novr. 8. 1775. Found among the papers of Govr. Wm Livingston," folder 1, John Jay Papers, New-York Historical Society (hereafter N-YHS).

119. See Charles Thomson to David Ramsay, November 4, 1786, in *Collections of the New-York Historical Society for the Year 1878* (New York, 1879), 215–29. See David Ramsay to Charles Thomson, September 20, 1809, in ibid., 261. The copied passages can be found on pp. 115–19 in the first volume of the original 1790 edition.

120. [Ramsay], "History of American Revolution commencing with the settlement of the American Colonies coming down to Novr. 8. 1775," folder 1, John Jay Papers, N-YHS. Until I identified this manuscript, it had sat unidentified in the Jay Papers since it was donated by William Jay on October 26, 1847. See *Proceedings of the New-York Historical Society* (New York, 1847), 135.

121. For the beginning of their relationship, see Jeremy Belknap to Jedidiah Morse, July 28, 1784, Belknap Papers, MHS.

122. Jedidiah Morse to Jeremy Belknap, January 18, 1788, in *CMHS, 6th Ser.* (Boston, 1886–1899), 4:381–84.

123. Jedidiah Morse to Jeremy Belknap, March 3, 1788, in ibid., 399–400.

124. Jeremy Belknap to Ebenezer Hazard, February 12, 1789; Ebenezer Hazard to Jeremy Belknap, March 14, 1789, Belknap Papers, MHS.

125. Jeremy Belknap to Ebenezer Hazard, August 19, 1789, Belknap Papers, MHS.

126. Ebenezer Hazard to Jeremy Belknap, June 21, 1789, Belknap Papers, MHS. Hazard was forthright in noting that Gordon's researches that would be "useful to some future writer who will hold a better pen." He also recalled, "Dr. Ramsay, who is now in this city (whose History of the Revolution is now in the press at Philadelphia), told me the other day that Gordon's History contains a very valuable collection of authentic materials." See Ebenezer Hazard to Jeremy Belknap, August 27, 1789, Belknap Papers, MHS.

127. Jeremy Belknap to Ebenezer Hazard, July 18, 1789, Belknap Papers, MHS.

128. David Ramsay to Benjamin Rush, August 16, 1784, Rush MSS, vol. 45, LCP.

129. David Ramsay to Jedidiah Morse, November 30, 1787, in Brunhouse, "David Ramsay, 1749–1815," 117.

130. Jeremy Belknap to Ebenezer Hazard, March 20, 1782, in *CMHS, 5th Ser.,* 2:122. Belknap is referring to Israel Evans, *A Discourse Delivered Near York in Virginia On the Memorable Occasion of the Surrender of the British Army* (Philadelphia, 1782); [Gouverneur Morris], *Observations on the American Revolution* (Philadelphia: Styner and Cist, 1779).

131. Ebenezer Hazard to Jeremy Belknap, April 10, 1782, Belknap Papers, MHS. Ramsay eventually went with Aitken and was highly unsatisfied describing his work as error-ridden. "The printing the spelling the ink the form of the lines are in many cases execrable," he wrote, "I am sure he is no printer." David Ramsay to Ashbel Green, October 4, 1791, in Brunhouse, "David Ramsay, 1749–1815," 130.

132. For example, on negotiating terms with a printer to publish Belknap's *The Foresters,* see Ebenezer Hazard to Jeremy Belknap, June 12, 1789; Jeremy Belknap to Ebenezer Hazard, June 20, 1789, in *CMHS, 5th Ser.,* 3:137–18, 141–13. For an example of a printing contract from this period, see Ebenezer Hazard's contract with Thomas Dobson for publishing his *Historical Collections.* "Contract for printing of 'State Papers,'" August 9, 1791, folder 1971, Gilder Lehrman Collection, GLI.

133. For the ups, see David Ramsay to Jonathan Elmer, July 15, 1779, in Brunhouse, "David Ramsay, 1749–1815," 61–62. For the downs, see David Ramsay to John Eliot, June 18, 1796, in ibid., 144.

134. David Ramsay to Joel Barlow, April 10, 1787, in ibid., 111. Also, see David Ramsay to William Gordon, January 18, 1786, Theodorus Bailey Myers Collection, 1542–1879, Series III, NYPL; David Ramsay to John Eliot, April 20, 1787; David Ramsay to Joel Barlow, April 25, 1788, in Brunhouse, "David Ramsay, 1749–1815," 111, 121.

135. In June of 1789, Belknap, describing to Hazard William Spotswood's offer to publish a new edition of *The Foresters,* wrote, "Before I finally close with his proposal, I wish to know whether there is any prospect of an Act of Congress respecting literary property." Jeremy Belknap to Ebenezer Hazard, June 6, 1789, in *CMHS, 5th Ser.,* 3:135–36.

136. William Gordon to David Ramsay, January 18, 1786, in Brunhouse, "David Ramsay, 1749–1815," 96.

137. Ebenezer Hazard to Jeremy Belknap, March 14, 1789, in *CMHS, 5th Ser.,* 3:111.

138. Noah Webster Papers, 1764–1843, Series I.A. and I.B., NYPL.

139. *Pennsylvania Journal,* February 4, 1786; *Hough's Concord Herald,* January 19, 1791; David Ramsay to John Eliot, April 20, 1787, in Brunhouse, "David Ramsay, 1749–1815," 111; David Ramsay to Thomas Jefferson, June 15, 1785, in ibid., 88.

140. David Ramsay to Joel Barlow, April 25, 1788, in ibid., 121.

141. *Pennsylvania Journal,* February 1, 1786.

142. Hugh Gaine to Ebenezer Hazard, May 2, 1791, Gilder Lehrman Collection, GLI.

143. Ebenezer Hazard to Jeremy Belknap, January 17, 1783, Belknap Papers, MHS.

144. Benjamin Rush to Noah Webster, February 13, 1788, Series I.B., box 2, folio 3, Noah Webster Papers, 1764–1843, NYPL.

145. Mathew Carey to Ebenezer Hazard, January 11, 1787; William Spotswood to Jeremy Belknap, February 3, 1787; Jeremy Belknap to William Spotswood, February 27, 1787, Belknap Papers, MHS.

146. Jeremy Belknap to John Adams, September 19, 1789, Adams Papers, MHS.

147. Jeremy Belknap to Mathew Carey, May 18, 1787, Belknap Papers, MHS. Two years

later, Carey was still attempting to persuade Belknap to contribute. See Mathew Carey to Jeremy Belknap, October 16, 1789, in *CMHS, 6th Ser.*, 4:450.

148. Noah Webster to Jeremy Belknap, February 9, 1788, in ibid., 4:385–87. A few months later, William Spotswood asked Belknap to provide him with an introduction to Ramsay in the hopes of securing content from him. See William Spotswood to Jeremy Belknap, June 19, 1788, in ibid., 4:410.

149. Jeremy Belknap to John Eliot, June 18, 1774, Belknap letterbook, Belknap Papers, MHS.

150. Ebenezer Hazard to New-York Committee of Safety, December 16, 1776, in Force, *American Archives, Fifth Series* (Washington, D.C., 1848–53), 3:1248–49.

151. Jeremy Belknap to John Adams, July 18, 1789, Adams Papers, MHS.

152. John Pintard to Thomas Jefferson, August 26, 1790, in *Papers of Thomas Jefferson*, 17:352–53n. For a transcript, see Papers of the Continental Congress, U.S. National Archives and Records Administration, 4:151.

153. Belknap. *History of New-Hampshire*, 1:vii.

154. Belknap to Adams, July 18, 1789, Adams Papers, MHS.

155. John Adams to Jeremy Belknap, July 24, 1789, Adams Papers, MHS. Adams famously wrote: "My experience has very much diminished my Faith in the veracity of History.—it has convinced me that many of the most important facts are concealed.—some of the most important characters but imperfectly known—many false facts imposed on historians and the world—and many empty characters displayed in great pomp—All this, I am sure, will happen in our American history."

156. Jeremy Belknap to Ebenezer Hazard, August 21, 1795, in *CMHS, 5th Ser.*, 3:356–57.

157. For the specifics of some of these efforts, see Tucker, *Clio's Consort*, 110–22.

158. *An Account of the American Antiquarian Society, incorporated, October 24th, 1812* (Boston, 1813), 10.

159. Thomas Jefferson to Ebenezer Hazard, February 18, 1791, in *Papers of Thomas Jefferson*, 19:287–89.

160. Ibid.

161. "Introductory Address from the Historical Society. To the Public," *American Apollo*, January 6, 1792.

162. Jeremy Belknap to John Adams, July 18, 1789, Adams Papers, MHS.

163. Ibid.

164. *New-York Herald*, February 13, 1805.

165. "Petition to the Legislature of Massachusetts, October 1812," in *The Origin of the American Antiquarian Society* (Worcester, 1820), 17–20.

166. *New-York Herald*, February 13, 1805.

167. "Circular Letter of the Historical Society, In Massachusetts," *City Gazette and Daily Advertiser*, July 22, 1793.

168. *New-York Herald*, February 13, 1805

169. *Account of the American Antiquarian Society*, 7.

Chapter 5. The Colonial Past in the Early Republic

1. Gordon S. Wood, *Empire of Liberty: A History of the Early Republic, 1789–1815* (New York, 2009), 1–4.

2. David Ramsay to Benjamin Rush, August 17, 1787, Rush MSS, vol. 45, LCP.

3. [Ramsay], "History of American Revolution commencing with the settlement of the American Colonies coming down to Novr. 8. 1775. Found among the papers of Govr. Wm Livingston," folder 1, John Jay Papers, N-YHS.

4. Thomas P. Slaughter, *Independence: The Tangled Roots of the American Revolution* (New York, 2014), xvi.

5. Arthur H. Shaffer, "Between Two Worlds: David Ramsay and the Politics of Slavery," *Journal of Southern History* 50, no. 2 (1984): 175–76. I have chosen to use David Ramsay's work in particular when explicating many of the fundamental interpretations and narrative of this historical memory, primarily because he was, by far, the most popular, widely known, and well-respected American historian of the period. His works, particularly his *History of the American Revolution,* played a prominent role in establishing both this historical memory of the colonial past and the first national historical narrative. References to his works, arguments, and ideas can be found throughout most of the subsequent general histories of the United States in this period. Indeed, an obituary for Ramsay following his assassination in 1815 noted: "As a *historian,* particularly, it may be truly observed, that no one has ever met with more undivided and unqualified approbation." See *Niles' Weekly Register,* February 24, 1816. Also, on Ramsay's reputation, see *Monthly Review* (June 1791): 177–80; *American Republican Gazette,* November 16, 1802.

6. *Weekly Visiter,* June 24, 1815. See Joyce Appleby, *Inheriting the Revolution: The First Generation of Americans* (Cambridge, 2000), 240–41.

7. Gordon, *History of the Rise, Progress, and Establishment, of Independence,* 1:32.

8. Ramsay, *History of the American Revolution,* 1:34.

9. Ibid., 1:29, 28–29; Lendrum, *Concise and Impartial History of the American Revolution,* 236–37. These arguments were also used word-for-word in a number of other historical works covering settlement.

10. Ramsay, *History of the American Revolution,* 1:34.

11. Ramsay, *History of the United States,* 1:47

12. David Ramsay, *A Chronological Table of the Principal Events which have taken place in the English Colonies. Now United States, from 1607, till 1810* (Charleston, 1811), 10. This interpretation was common in the historical writing of the period, even in loyalist histories such as George Chalmers, *An Introduction to the History of the Revolt of the Colonies* (London, 1782), 8–9.

13. Ibid., 11.

14. In his *Chronological Table,* Ramsay made a point of including the first legislative assembly in each colony under the pretense that the colonial assemblies were popular bodies representing popular participation, as he perceived state legislatures as doing in the 1780s and 1790s. For 1683, he noted the first assemblies in Pennsylvania and in New York, saying

of the latter, "The province for the preceding nine years had been governed in an arbitrary manner without any participation of the people." Ibid., 17, 10.

15. Ramsay, *History of the American Revolution,* 1:31.

16. Sullivan, *History of the District of Maine,* 290.

17. For a few examples, see Trumbull, *General History of the United States,* 1:108; Adams, *Summary History of New-England,* 22; Williams, *History of Vermont,* 2:426–31; Lendrum, *Concise and Impartial History of the American Revolution,* 221.

18. Ramsay, *History of the American Revolution,* 1:28–29.

19. Hewat, *Historical Account,* 2:309–10. Ramsay was certainly aware of Hewat's work, having used it in preparation for writing his own history of South Carolina in the years immediately following publication of Hewat's history.

20. Ramsay, *History of the American Revolution,* 1:28–29.

21. Gordon, *History of the Rise, Progress, and Establishment, of the Independence,* 1:95.

22. Jonathan Boucher, *A View of the Causes and Consequences of the American Revolution* (London, 1797), 475–76.

23. Williams, *History of Vermont,* 1:6.

24. Ibid., 2:427.

25. *America Invincible,* 9.

26. Ramsay, *History of the American Revolution,* 1:18.

27. Ebenezer Hazard to Jeremy Belknap, August 4, 1779, in *CMHS, 5th Ser.,* 2:7.

28. Ebenezer Hazard to Jeremy Belknap, August 7, 23, 1790, September 9, 1792, in ibid., 3:226, 229, 309.

29. Jeremy Belknap, *The Foresters: An American Tale* (Boston, 1792), 59–60.

30. Lendrum, *Concise and Impartial History of the American Revolution,* 158–59; McCulloch, *Concise History of the United States,* 29–30; William Winterbotham, *A Geographical, Commercial, and Philosophical View of the Present Situation of the United States of America,* 4 vols. (New-York, 1795), 2:36; Trumbull, *General History of the United States,* preface, 117; Webster, *Elements of Useful Knowledge,* 101–3; Morse, *Geography Made Easy,* 72; *Carey's American Pocket Atlas* (Philadelphia: Mathew Carey, 1796), 16; *Gaine's Universal Register, or, Columbian Kalendar, for the year 1786* (New-York, 1786), 140; *Fleet's Pocket Almanack for the year of our Lord 1788* (Boston, 1787), 2.

31. Ebenezer Hazard to Jeremy Belknap, April 17, 1781, in *CMHS, 5th Ser.,* 2:92.

32. Morse, *Geography Made Easy,* 72. This passage was also copied in Winterbotham, *Geographical, Commercial, and Philosophical View,* 2:36; Morse, *American Universal Geography,* 1:348; *Carey's American Pocket Atlas,* 16; *Gaine's Universal Register,* 140; *Fleet's Pocket Almanack,* 2.

33. Trumbull, *Complete History of Connecticut,* 126; Trumbull, *General History of the United States,* 116–19.

34. On the United Colonies and the origins of "federalism," see LaCroix, *Ideological Origins of American Federalism,* 20–22.

35. For the siege in just a few historical works, see Belknap, *History of New-Hampshire,* 2:188–214 (repr. *The Massachusetts Magazine, or Monthly Museum* 3, no. 11 [November 1791], 698–99); Backus, *History of New-England,* 1:173; Thomas Hutchinson, *The History of Massachu-*

setts (Boston, 1795), 2:366–95; McCulloch, *Concise History of the United States,* 27; *American Remembrancer, and Universal Tablet of Memory* (Philadelphia, 1795), 135, 145; Adams, *Summary History of New-England,* 205–10; Morse, *Compendious History of New-England,* 188–90. For the use of the event in framing contemporary events, see *Connecticut Magazine* 2, no. 35 (October 18, 1787): 277. This piece was reprinted in more than a dozen newspapers throughout the states. For the social historical importance, see the obituary of the Hon. Thomas Wesbrook Waldron, Esq., *Fowle's New-Hampshire Gazette,* April 15, 1787. At the head of his accomplishments, it notes, "He was the first volunteer in New-Hampshire who enlisted in the memorable expedition to Cape-Breton, in 1745, where he bore a Captain's commission."

36. "Letters relating to the Expedition against Cape Breton," in *CMHS, for the year 1792, Vol. 1* (1792; repr. Boston, 1806), 5–60.

37. Ibid., 4.

38. Beyond the poem and dramatic verse cited here, the siege was also a topic for popular songs. For example, see "On the Taking of Louisbourg," *Vocal Magazine,* no. 4 (April 1781): 124.

39. *America Invincible,* 14–15.

40. Jabez Peck, *Columbia and Britannia: A dramatic piece* (New-London, 1787), 10. In Peck's drama, this is a crucial early moment just before Britannia is seen "on an elevated seat with her nobles around her, concerting measures for the ruin of Columbia."

41. Ramsay, *History of the American Revolution,* 1:33.

42. Adams, *Summary History of New-England,* 209.

43. Backus, *History of New-England,* 1:173.

44. David Ramsay to Jeremy Belknap, August 11, 1792, in Brunhouse, "David Ramsay, 1749–1815," 133. In an 1810 letter, Ramsay told Eliot, "New England sets a good example to the other states by perpetuating the names & histories of their deceased benefactors." See David Ramsay to John Eliot, April 7, 1810, in ibid., 166.

45. Tocqueville, *Democracy in America,* 267.

46. Peters, *General History of Connecticut,* iii.

47. John Daly Burk, *The History of Virginia, from its First Settlement to the Present Day,* 3 vols. (Petersburg, 1804–1805), 1:i.

48. Friedman and Shaffer, "Ramsay and the Quest for an American Historical Identity," 352.

49. Burk, *History of Virginia,* 2:233.

50. This period was deemed crucial for early national historians of Virginia. In his then-unpublished history of Virginia, Edmund Randolph devoted sixty-two pages to the period "from the establishment of a legislative assembly to the dissolution of the Virginia Company," by far the largest chapter of the manuscript. Following that, the entire period of 1651 to 1774 was accounted for in a chapter of only twenty-seven pages. See Edmund Randolph, *History of Virginia* (Charlottesville, 1969).

51. Burk, *History of Virginia,* 1:295.

52. Ibid., 1:303.

53. Ibid., 2:91. This argument was echoed in Randolph's unpublished manuscript history of Virginia. He argued that "these articles argue a strong, awakened sense of right" and "the spirit which they display is the native spirit of Virginia." See Randolph, *History of Virginia*, 153.

54. Jeremy Belknap—like Ebenezer Hazard, David Ramsay, Benjamin Rush, and many other network participants—was decidedly antislavery. In 1795, responding to a query from St. George Tucker of Virginia, Belknap wrote a history of slavery and its eradication in Massachusetts. See Jeremy Belknap, "Queries respecting the Slavery and Emancipation of Negroes in Massachusetts, proposed by the Hon. Judge Tucker of Virginia, and answered by the Rev. Dr. Belknap," *CMHS, 1st Ser.* (Boston, 1792–1808), 4:191–211.

55. Shaffer, "Between Two Worlds," 175. On Belknap's antislavery sentiments and writings, see Minardi, *Making Slavery History*, 13–23.

56. Ramsay's awkwardness allowed these specific passages of Ramsay's *History* to be used to argue against emancipation almost as soon as the book was published. See "Ramsay's *History of the American Revolution*," *Monthly Review* (June 1791): 177–80. Other magazines excerpted the same passages (among others) including the *Analytical Review* (June 1791): 149–55.

57. Ramsay, *History of the United States*, 1:25.

58. On the creation of African American historical memory itself, see Stephen G. Hall, *A Faithful Account of the Race: African American Historical Writing in Nineteenth-Century America* (Chapel Hill, 2009); John Ernest, *Liberation Historiography: African American Writers and the Challenge of History, 1794–1861* (Chapel Hill, 2004); Elizabeth Rauh Bethel, *The Roots of African-American Identity: Memory and History in Free Antebellum Communities* (New York, 1997); *History and Memory in African-American Culture* (New York, 1994).

59. Burk, *History of Virginia*, 1:211.

60. David Ramsay, *History of the United States, from their first settlement as English colonies, in 1607, to the year 1808*, 3 vols. (Philadelphia, 1816–1817), 3:xxxii–iii.

61. Robert Gross, "From Citizens to Subjects: The Formalization of Authority in Post-Revolutionary Massachusetts," in *People and Power: Rights, Citizenship, and Violence* (Milan, 1992), 27.

62. Ebenezer Hazard to Jeremy Belknap, April 10, 1782, in *CMHS, 5th Ser.*, 2:124. For an exemplary statement of this argument from this time, see *Pennsylvania Mercury*, February 4, 1785.

63. Jeremy Belknap to John Adams, July 18, 1789, Adams Papers, MHS; Shaffer, *Politics of History*, 103–8.

64. Robert A. Gross, "White Hats and Hemlocks: Daniel Shays and the Legacy of the Revolution," in *The Transforming Hand of the Revolution: Reconsidering the American Revolution as a Social Movement*, ed. Ronald Hoffman and Peter J. Albert (Charlottesville, 1995), 287.

65. On loyalist histories, see *The Colonial Legacy, vol. 1: Loyalist Historians* (New York, 1971); Eileen Ka-May Cheng, "American Historical Writers and the Loyalists, 1788–1856: Dissent, Consensus, and American Nationality," *Journal of the Early Republic* 23, no. 4 (2003): 491–519; Cheng, "Plagiarism in Pursuit of Historical Truth: George Chalmers and the Pa-

triotic Legacy of Loyalist History," in *Remembering the Revolution: Memory, History, and Nation,* ed. Michael McDonnell, Clare Corbould, Francis Clarke, and W. Fitzhugh Brundage (Amherst, 2013), 144–61.

66. Boucher, *View of the Causes and Consequences of the American Revolution,* ix.

67. Jonathan Boucher to Rev. Mr. James, December 23, 1777, in *Maryland Historical Magazine* 10 (1915): 27; Boucher, *View of the Causes and Consequences of the American Revolution,* 6; Galloway, *Historical and Political Reflections,* 86–93; Thomas Hutchinson, *The History of the Province of Massachusetts Bay, from 1749 to 1774* (London, 1828), 120–28; Peter Oliver, *Peter Oliver's Origin and Progress of the American Rebellion: A Tory View* (Stanford, 1961), 39–45, 83–99; Hewat, *Historical Account,* 2:314–15.

68. Galloway, *Historical and Political Reflections,* 23–33; Hewat, *Historical Account,* 2:308–9.

69. Boucher, *View of the Causes and Consequences of the American Revolution,* 475.

70. Chalmers, *Political Annals of the Present United Colonies, from their Settlement to the Peace of 1763* (London, 1780), 686.

71. Ramsay, *History of the American Revolution,* 1:27.

72. David Ramsay to John Eliot, January 19, 1788, in Brunhouse, "David Ramsay, 1749–1815," 118.

73. David Ramsay to Benjamin Rush, April 21, 1788, Rush MSS, vol. 45, LCP.

74. Ramsay, *History of the American Revolution,* 2:354. The entire, lengthy passage was reprinted in newspapers and magazines throughout the country in the early 1790s.

75. For a similar dynamic in France following the July Monarchy, see Pim Den Boer, "Historical Writing in France, 1800–1914," in *Oxford History of Historical Writing,* vol. 4, 188–89.

76. Linda K. Kerber, *Federalists in Dissent: Imagery and Ideology in Jeffersonian America* (Ithaca, 1970), 212.

77. *Massachusetts Gazette,* November 27, 1787.

78. *Newport Mercury,* March 17, 1788; "Letters from the Federal Farmer, no. VII," December 31, 1787, in *An Additional number of letters from the Federal farmer to the Republican* (New-York, 1788).

79. *Newport Mercury,* March 17, 1788.

80. See especially *Additional number of letters from the Federal farmer to the Republican.*

81. Samuel Adams to Noah Webster, April 30, 1784, box 6, folder 13, Samuel Adams Papers, 1760–1803, NYPL.

Chapter 6. Creating a Deep Past for a New Nation

1. On "time immemorial" in England, see Woolf, *Social Circulation of the Past in Early Modern England,* 275–80.

2. Anderson, *Imagined Communities,* 11.

3. Doyle and Pamplona, "Americanizing the Conversation on Nationalism," 5, 3.

4. Anderson, *Imagined Communities,* 197.

5. Chalmers, *Political Annals of the Present United Colonies,* 1.

6. See Gordon M. Sayre, "The Mound Builders and the Imagination of American Antiquity in Jefferson, Bartram, and Chateaubriand," *Early American Literature* 33, no. 3 (1998): 225–49; Caroline Winterer, *American Enlightenments: Pursuing Happiness in the Age of Reason* (New Haven, 2016), 73–109.

7. Noah Webster, *The Little Reader's Assistant* (Hartford, 1791), 3–5. Indeed, as previously noted, the first of five chapters was devoted to "A number of Stories, mostly taken from the history of America."

8. Claudia L. Bushman, *America Discovers Columbus: How an Italian Explorer Became an American Hero* (Hanover, 1992); John Noble Wilford, *The Mysterious History of Columbus: An Exploration of the Man, the Myth, and the Legacy* (New York, 1991); Kirkpatrick Sale, *The Conquest of Paradise: Christopher Columbus and the Columbian Legacy* (New York, 1990).

9. Bushman, *America Discovers Columbus,* 41. Also, see John P. Larner, "North American Hero? Christopher Columbus 1702–2002," *Proceedings of the American Philosophical Society* 137, no. 1 (1993): 46–63.

10. *Columbian Centinel,* September 1, 1792. The monument—located near the current intersection of Harford Road and Walther Avenue—was defaced in August 2017 in reaction to the "Unite the Right" rally in Charlottesville, Virginia. The plate containing the inscriptions that was mounted on October 12, 1792, was destroyed. See *Baltimore Sun,* August 21, 2017.

11. For the list of toasts prepared for the event by the Tammany Society, see Society of Tammany, or Columbian Order Records, vol. 1, 16–18, NYPL. In 1809, the New-York Historical Society held a similar public commemoration—minus the obelisk—to mark the two-hundredth anniversary of Henry Hudson.

12. *New-York Journal,* October 17, 1792. For one of the songs sung "at the Great Wigwam of the Tammany Society," see *Federal Gazette,* October 19, 1792.

13. Jeremy Belknap, *A Discourse intended to commemorate the Discovery of America by Christopher Columbus* (Boston, 1792).

14. On festivities, nationalism, and popular politics, see Waldstreicher, *In the Midst of Perpetual Fetes;* Simon Newman, *Parades and the Politics of the Street: Festive Culture in the Early American Republic* (Philadelphia, 1997).

15. Davidson, *Revolution and the Word,* 8. Despite Davidson's deep analysis of novels in the early republic, she largely ignored *Reuben and Rachel.*

16. Susannah Rowson, *Reuben and Rachel; or, Tales of Old Times* (Boston, 1798), iii, 363; Washington Irving, *A History of the Life and Voyages of Christopher Columbus,* 4 vols. (London, 1828), 1:vi. The myth that most of Europe believed the earth was flat and Columbus's voyages proved them wrong, which remains in the American popular imagination, had its origin in Irving's work.

17. Ibid., 1:iv.

18. Thomas J. Schlereth, "Columbia, Columbus, and Columbianism," *Journal of American History* 79, no. 3 (1992): 937.

19. Delno C. West and August King, "Columbus and Columbia: A Brief Survey of the Early Creation of the Columbus Symbol in American History," *Studies in Popular Culture* 12, no. 2 (1989): 45–60; E. McClung Fleming, "From Indian Princess to Greek Goddess: The American Image, 1783–1815," *Winterthur Portfolio* 3 (1967): 37–66.

20. Phillis Wheatley to George Washington, October 26, 1775, in *Papers of George Washington, Revolutionary War Series,* 2:242. She enclosed the poem with the letter. For Washington's reply, see George Washington to Phillis Wheatley, February 28, 1776, in ibid., 3:387.

21. David Humphreys, *A Poem, addressed to the Armies of the United States of America* (New-Haven, 1780), 7; Humphreys, *The Glory of America; or, Peace Triumphant over War: A Poem* (Philadelphia, 1783), 3; Humphreys, *A Poem, on the Happiness of America; addressed to the Citizens of the United States* (Hartford, 1786), 5.

22. University of the State of New York, *Eighty-Ninth Annual Report of the Regents of the University* (Albany, 1876), 673, 683.

23. William Tindall, *Standard History of The City of Washington* (Knoxville, 1914), 121.

24. Robert Haswell, *Voyages of the "Columbia" to the Northwest Coast, 1787–1790 and 1790–1793* (1941; repr. Portland, 1990).

25. Susan Sleeper-Smith, *Indigenous Prosperity and American Conquest: Indian Women of the Ohio River Valley, 1690–1792* (Chapel Hill, 2018), 275–79.

26. *The Columbian Tragedy,* Boston, 1791, broadside, Connecticut Historical Society.

27. Joel Barlow, *The Vision of Columbus: A Poem in Nine Books* (Hartford, 1787), xx.

28. Ibid., 162.

29. For a rare recent work that addresses the Wits, focusing on the religious foundation to their nationalist literary productions, see Sam Haselby, *The Origins of American Religious Nationalism* (New York, 2015), 51–116. Haselby notes, "It is in the writings of the Connecticut Wits where one finds the first fully articulated vision of American nationality." Ibid., 6.

30. Timothy Dwight, *The Conquest of Canäan* (Hartford, 1785).

31. Perry Miller, "The Garden of Eden and the Deacon's Meadow," *American Heritage* 7, no. 1 (1955).

32. Eran Shalev, *American Zion: The Old Testament as a Political Text from the Revolution to the Civil War* (New Haven, 2013), 94.

33. The chapters were recently reprinted in an edited and fully annotated version as *John Leacock's The First Book of the American Chronicles of the Times, 1774–1775* (Cranbury, 1987).

34. Imprints of individual chapters are extant from Philadelphia, Boston, Providence and Newport, Norwich (CT), New Bern (NC), and New York. Advertisements appeared in the *Providence Gazette,* October 29, November 5, 1774, January 14, February 4, 11, 1775; *Pennsylvania Journal,* December 28, 1774; *New-York Journal,* January 12, March 2, 1775; *Boston Evening-Post,* January 23, 1775; *Pennsylvania Gazette,* February 8, 1775; *Pennsylvania Ledger,* February 18, March 4, 1775; *Pennsylvania Evening-Post,* February 28, 1775; *Boston Gazette,* March 13, April 3, 10, 1775.

35. See *Virginia Gazette,* January 12, January 19, March 30, April 6, June 29, 1775. The

work was also serialized in English in the German-language newspaper, *Der Wöchentliche Pennsylvanische Staatsbote.*

36. For an advertisement of the play before independence, see *Constitutional Gazette,* July 3, 1776.

37. Shalev, *American Zion,* 93–100.

38. [Richard Snowden], *The American Revolution; Written in the Style of Ancient History* (Philadelphia, 1793), 1:1–2.

39. Shalev, *American Zion,* 95.

40. Cohen, *Revolutionary Histories,* 57–113; Shaffer, *Politics of History,* 59–63; Messer, *Stories of Independence,* 110–17; Cheng, *Plain and Noble Garb of Truth,* 303n.

41. [Richard Snowden], *The Columbiad, or, a Poem on the American War, in thirteen cantoes* (Philadelphia, 1795); [Dwight], *America: or, a Poem on the Settlement of the British Colonies.*

42. On the growth of interest in natural history in the early republic (and the democratization of its practice), see Andrew J. Lewis, *A Democracy of Facts: Natural History in the Early Republic* (Philadelphia, 2011); Lee Alan Dugatkin, *Mr. Jefferson and the Giant Moose: Natural History in Early America* (Chicago, 2009); Pamela Regis, *Describing Early America: Bartram, Jefferson, Crèvecoeur, and the Rhetoric of Natural History* (DeKalb, 1992).

43. Tocqueville, *Democracy in America,* 267.

44. George Louis LeClerc, Comte de Buffon, *Natural history, general and particular,* 8 vols. (London: William Smellie, 1781), 5:124–52, esp. 136–38.

45. James W. Ceaser, *Reconstructing America: The Symbol of America in Modern Thought* (New Haven, 1997), 19–42; Henry Ward Church, "Corneille de Pauw and the Controversy over His *Recherches philosophiques sur les Américains,*" *Publications of the Modern Language Associations* 51 (1936): 178–206.

46. Abbé Guillaume Thomas François Raynal, *Histoire Philosophique et Politique des Établisement et du Commerce des Européens dans le deux Indes* (Amsterdam, 1770), 92; Corneille de Pauw, *Recherches Philosophiques sur les Americains, ou Mémoires intéressants pour servir à l'Histoire de l'Espèce humaine* (Berlin, 1768).

47. Gerbi, *Dispute of the New World,* 158n.

48. For rare direct inquiries into the nationalization of natural history in this period, see James David Drake, *The Nation's Nature: How Continental Presumptions Gave Rise to the United States of America* (Charlottesville, 2011); Joyce Chaplin, "Nature and Nation: Natural History in Context," in *Stuffing Birds, Pressing Plants, Shaping Knowledge: Natural History in North America, 1730–1860,* ed. Sue Ann Prince (Philadelphia, 2003), 75–95; Cohen, *Revolutionary Histories,* 122–27, 193.

49. Trumbull, *General History of the United States,* 1:9–51, 112; Lendrum, *Concise and Impartial History of the American Revolution,* 9–85; [Cooper], *History of North America,* 13–31.

50. Belknap, *History of New-Hampshire,* 3:171–76.

51. Jefferson, *Notes on the State of Virginia,* 64–112; Thomas Jefferson to Marquis de Chastellux, June 7, 1785, in *Papers of Thomas Jefferson,* 8:185–86. Also, see Dugatkin, *Mr. Jefferson and*

the Giant Moose, ix–xii; Keith S. Thomson, *A Passion for Nature: Thomas Jefferson and Natural History* (Chapel Hill, 2008).

52. Williams, *Natural and Civil History of Vermont,* 1:97, 129–59.

53. The most in-depth exploration of this dynamic remains Ralph N. Miller, "The Historians Discover America: A Study of American Historical Writing in the Eighteenth Century" (PhD diss., Northwestern University, 1946).

54. Smith-Rosenberg, *This Violent Empire,* 207–17.

55. On museum culture in the early republic, see David R. Brigham, *Public Culture in the Early Republic: Peale's Museum and Its Audience* (Washington, D.C., 1995); William Thomas Alderson, *Mermaids, Mummies, and Mastodons: The Emergence of the American Museum* (Washington, D.C., 1991).

56. He was said to have had Major John André's sword on display. Hans Huth, "Pierre Eugène du Simitière and the Beginnings of the American Historical Museum," *Pennsylvania Magazine of History and Biography* 69, no. 4 (1945): 317. For biographical information on du Simitière, including his stunning antiquarian activities of the 1760s and 1770s, see Paul G. Sifton, "Pierre Eugène du Simitière, 1737–1784: Collector in Revolutionary America" (PhD diss., University of Pennsylvania, 1960).

57. *Independent Gazetteer,* November 16, 1782. The nonextant historical paintings included those entitled, "The Temple of Independence," "The Genius of America Trampling Discord," and "Dependence." *Pennsylvania Packet,* December 4, 1781; *Freemen's Journal,* December 12, 1781.

58. Charles Coleman Sellers, *Mr. Peale's Museum: Charles Willson Peale and the First Popular Museum of Natural Science and Art* (New York, 1980); Ellis L. Yochelson, "Mr. Peale and His Mammoth Museum," *Proceedings of the American Philosophical Society* 136, no. 4 (1992): 487–506.

59. *Pennsylvania Packet,* July 18, 1786.

60. "The Autobiography of Charles Willson Peale," in *The Selected Papers of Charles Willson Peale and His Family,* ed. Lillian B. Miller, Sidney Hart, and David C. Ward (New Haven, 1983–2000), 5:xxx.

61. See Filson, *The Discovery, Settlement, and Present State of Kentucky,* 26–27; John M. Clarke, "Mastodons of New York: A List of Discoveries of their Remains, 1705–1902," *Report of the State Paleontologist: N. Y. State Museum Bulletin* 69 (1902): 921–33.

62. Paul Semonin, *American Monster: How the Nation's First Prehistoric Creature Became a Symbol of National Identity* (New York, 2000), 341–61.

63. "The Elephant," broadside, September 19, 1797, Newburyport, Mass., New-York Historical Society.

64. *Guide to the Philadelphia Museum* (Philadelphia, 1805), 4–5.

65. Susan Stewart, "Death and Life, in that Order, in the Works of Charles Willson Peale," in *The Cultures of Collecting* (Cambridge, 1994), 205–6.

66. *A Scientific and Descriptive Catalogue of Peale's Museum* (Philadelphia, 1796), viii.

67. "The Columbian Museum at the head of the Mall, Boston," broadside, 1811, microform, Early American Imprints, Readex.

68. See facsimile of proposal on facing page in *CMHS, 5th Ser.,* 3:231.

69. "Constitution of the New-York Historical Society," *New-York Herald,* February 13, 1805.

70. *An Account of the American Antiquarian Society, Incorporated Oct. 24, 1812* (Boston: Published by Isaiah Thomas, Jun., November 1813), 7.

71. Smith-Rosenberg, *This Violent Empire,* ch. 4; Eve Kornfeld, "Encountering the Other: American Intellectuals and Indians in the 1790s," *William and Mary Quarterly,* 3rd ser., 52, no. 2 (1995): 285–314; Regis, *Describing Early America,* xii, 142–45. On "Othering" African Americans, see Mechal Sobel, *Teach Me Dreams: The Search for Self in the Revolutionary Era* (Princeton, 2000), 55–134.

72. Bernard W. Sheehan, *Seeds of Extinction: Jeffersonian Philanthropy and the American Indian* (Chapel Hill, 1973), 86.

73. Kornfeld, "Encountering 'the Other,'" 291.

74. Leonard J. Sadosky, *Revolutionary Negotiations: Indians, Empires, and Diplomats in the Founding of America* (Charlottesville, 2009).

75. *Documents of United States Indian Policy,* 3rd ed., ed. Fancis Paul Prucha (Lincoln, 2000), 14–21.

76. Thomas Jefferson to William Henry Harrison, February 27, 1803, in *Papers of Thomas Jefferson,* 39:589–93.

77. Thomas Jefferson to Joel Barlow, May 3, 1802, in ibid., 37:399–402.

78. Comte de Volney, *A View of the Soil and Climate of the United States* (Philadelphia, 1804), xix–xx.

79. Kornfeld, *Creating an American Culture,* 68.

80. Trumbull, *General History,* 29, 16–51; Burk, *History of Virginia,* 1:308–9.

81. Belknap, *History of New-Hampshire,* 1:3–4.

82. Mark Thurner, "Peruvian Genealogies of History and Nation," in *After Spanish Rule,* 143. For another aspect of this dynamic, see R. Tripp Evans, *Romancing the Maya: Mexican Antiquity in the American Imagination, 1820–1915* (Austin, 2004). For earlier context, see Jorge Cañizares-Esguerra, *How to Write the History of the New World: Histories, Epistemologies, and Identities in the Eighteenth-Century Atlantic World* (Stanford, 2004).

83. Trumbull, *General History,* 29

84. For example, see "History of the original Inhabitants of AMERICA," *Vermont Gazette,* April 28, 1788.

85. [Noah Webster], "Letter III to Dr. Stiles," *American Magazine,* February 1788, 146–55.

86. Ebenezer Hazard to Jeremy Belknap, August 31, 1779, in *CMHS, 5th Ser.,* 2:13.

87. On the historical treatment of Native Americans in the nineteenth century, see Jean M. O'Brien, *Firsting and Lasting: Writing Indians out of Existence in New England* (Minneapolis, 2010); Daniel R. Mandell, *Tribe, Race, History: Native Americans in Southern New England, 1780–1880* (Baltimore, 2008); Steven Conn, *History's Shadow: Native Americans and Historical Consciousness in the Nineteenth Century* (Chicago, 2006); Amy E. Den Ouden, *Beyond Conquest: Native Peoples and the Struggle for History in New England* (Lincoln, 2005).

88. Pamela Regis has argued that "natural historical discourse did not differentiate between vegetable and human," which led natural historians to "depict human beings as if they were just another type of natural production." See Regis, *Describing Early America,* xii. In her work, Regis has argued that natural historical writing "cast the American Indians it depicted into the timeless 'now' of the historical present, [and] blinded its practitioners to the history of the people they were depicting." Ibid., 37.

89. Jefferson, *Notes on the State of Virginia,* 163–65. Historical accounts of Native Americans and their language abound in the earliest volumes of the Massachusetts Historical Society's published *Collections.* On Native languages in the society's earliest collections, see "Roger Williams's Key into the Language of the Indians of New England, 1643," in *CMHS, for the year 1794. Vol. III* (Boston, 1794), 203–38. Also, see *Grammar of the language of the Lenni Lenape or Delaware Indians* (Philadelphia, 1816).

90. For a surviving example of the earliest form, see Thomas Jefferson, "Vocabulary form: List of Words, in English, with space for listing the Indian equivalent, ca. 1792," broadside, American Indian Vocabulary Collection, APS. For a completed example of the form see the enclosure to William Vans Murray to Thomas Jefferson, September 18, 1792, American Indian Vocabulary Collection, APS. Also, see Thomas Jefferson, "Comparative vocabularies of several Indian languages, 1802–1808," American Indian Vocabulary Collection, APS.

91. For example, see Thomas Jefferson to Thomas Hutchins, December 29, 1783, in *Papers of Thomas Jefferson,* 6:427; Thomas Jefferson to Bernard Moore, December 29, 1783, in ibid., 6:431; Benjamin Hawkins to Thomas Jefferson, June 14, 1786, in ibid., 9:640–42; Thomas Jefferson to Benjamin Hawkins, August 4, 1787, in ibid., 11:683–84; "Jefferson's Vocabulary of the Unquachog Indians," June 14, 1791, in ibid., 20:467–70.

92. Benjamin Smith Barton to Thomas Jefferson, October 25, 1796, in ibid., 29:200–202. Barton ultimately published a work on the topic, which he dedicated to Jefferson. See Benjamin Smith Barton, *New Views of the Origin of the Tribes and Nations of America* (Philadelphia, 1797).

93. Anthony F. C. Wallace, *Jefferson and the Indians: The Tragic Fate of the First Americans* (Cambridge, 2001), 91–92, 130–61; John Kane, *Between Virtue and Power: The Persistent Moral Dilemma of U.S. Foreign Policy* (New Haven, 2008), 123–44; Gordon M. Sayre, "Jefferson and Native Americans: Policy and Archive," in *The Cambridge Companion to Thomas Jefferson,* ed. Frank Shuffleton (Cambridge, 2008), 61–72.

94. This reference to Heckewelder's Mohawk dictionary is found in "List of books in Iroquois language," box 8, folder 127, Pierre Eugène du Simitière collection, LCP.

95. John Heckewelder, *An Account of the History, Manners, and Customs of the Indian Nations, who once inhabited Pennsylvania and the Neighbouring States* (Philadelphia, 1819), 47–70. His original manuscript can be found in "Communications to the Historical and Literary Committee of the American Philosophical Society, 1816–1821," APS. Also, see John Gottlieb Ernestus Heckewelder letters, 1816–1822, to Peter Stephen Du Ponceau, APS; John Heckewelder,

"Indian tradition of the first arrival of the Dutch at Manhattan Island, now New-York," in *Collections of the New-York Historical Society,* 2nd Ser. (New York, 1841), 1:69–74.

96. Heckewelder, *Account of the History, Manners, and Customs of the Indian Nations,* 80. The concluding turn of phrase refers to a popular early eighteenth-century history manual, *The Tablet of Memory; or, the Historian's Assistant.*

97. Tocqueville, *Democracy in America,* 26.

98. Heckewelder, *Account of the History, Manners, and Customs of the Indian Nations,* 76–77, 78.

99. Ramsay, *History of the American Revolution,* 1:2.

100. Ibid., 1:3. This argument was reflected in numerous subsequent general histories over the following decades. For example, see Callender, *Sketches of the History of America,* 35–36; Ramsay, *History of the United States,* 1:9.

101. Williams, *Natural and Civil History of Vermont,* 1:169–70.

102. Lendrum, *Concise and Impartial History of the American Revolution,* 1:26.

103. Gouverneur Morris, *Discourse Delivered before the New-York Historical Society, at their anniversary meeting, 6th December 1812* (New-York, 1813), 5, 20, 23, 24, 40.

104. Daniel Webster, *An address delivered at the laying of the corner stone of the Bunker Hill Monument, June 17, 1825* (Boston, 1843), 70.

105. Ibid., 12.

106. Reprinted in *New-Jersey Journal,* February 1, 1792.

107. Patrick Wolfe, *Settler Colonialism and the Transformation of Anthropology: The Politics and Poetics of an Ethnographic Event* (New York, 1999), 208; Renato Ronaldo, *Culture and Truth: The Remaking of Social Analysis* (Boston, 1989), 68–88; Denise Cuthbert and Michele Grossman, "Trading Places: Locating the Indigenous in the New Age," *Thamyris* 3, no. 1 (1996): 18–36.

108. Pamela Regis has noted how some natural history writers, in applying "the natural historical method and rhetoric to European settlers, turn[ed] them into Others in the process." See Regis, *Describing Early America,* xiii, 126.

INDEX